MADRASA EDUCATION IN MODERN INDIA

Madrasa Education in Modern India

A Study

SARAL JHINGRAN

MANOHAR

2010

First published 2010

© Saral Jhingran, 2010

ISBN 978-81-7304-856-2

Published by
Ajay Kumar Jain *for*
Manohar Publishers & Distributors
4753/23 Ansari Road, Daryaganj
New Delhi 110 002

Typeset by
Kohli Print
Delhi 110 051

Printed at
Salasar Imaging Systems
Delhi 110 035

To
the children
and youth of India

Contents

FOREWORD   9

PREFACE   15

1. Society, Religion, Education, and Modernity   27

2. Reasons for Some Muslims' Preference for Madrasa
   Education: Trying to Understand the Issues Involved   69

3. Historical Background of Madrasa Education   125

4. Madrasa *Nisabs*: An Effort to Understand Them
   and a Critique   169

5. Islam, *Shari'a*, Women and Their Education   226

6. Madrasa 'Reforms' (I): Reforms from Within   278

7. Madrasa 'Reforms' (II): Schemes for 'Modernization
   of Madrasas'   331

8. Concluding Remarks   372

BIBLIOGRAPHY   405

INDEX   417

Foreword

Madrasa education has become an entangled subject with opinions sharply divided between two lines of argument. One sees them as the bastion of religious conservatism and fundamentalism. The other sees them as a vital instrument for the preservation of Muslim religion and cultural identity. It is daring of Dr Saral Jingran to have undertaken to write a book on madrasa education.

Dr Jhingran's book is certain to evoke a sharp reaction. Muslim clerics and a good number of traditional Muslims, who espouse the belief that the community is their exclusive concern and non-Muslims have no legitimate right to meddle with its religious and cultural traditions and practices, are likely to dismiss the book as yet another attempt by a non-Muslim (more explicitly Hindu) author who knows next to nothing about Muslim life ways and has not experienced it at any time of her life.

Dr Jhingran anticipated this kind of adverse reaction. She had experience of such snide remarks being made to her by some Muslim clerics and traditional Muslims when she went about seeking some initial guidance on how to go about her research. This must have been extremely discouraging and may have dampened her spirits. It has to be appreciated that despite such initial setbacks she persisted in her effort. She has succeeded in producing a book covering many dimensions of madrasa education from the perspective of an outsider, but with the empathy and understanding that looking at another culture or society necessarily always entails.

There is no need for me to try to defend Dr Jhingran. She is eminently capable of defending herself as any author who has worked on a subject for many years should. Let me deal instead with the more substantive question raised by such adverse and negative reactions as she encountered in her work. It is true that community perceptions are highly strung and each community thinks that what it knows about its own community is beyond the reach of the outsider. While this may truly be the case in society, it cannot be made into a dictum that only a member of a community has the right to write about his or her community. Such a division of labour, were it actually to exist in reality, would be most disastrous for the growth of understanding and knowledge. For only through different, and often opposite, views and formulations coming face to face does understanding really grow. From this perspective Dr Jhingran's effort should be welcomed.

One does not necessarily always write to inform and teach others. One also sometimes writes for self-education and self-reflection. This is the spirit with which Dr Jhingran undertook this study. One can be reasonably certain that the entire process of writing this book was also a self-enlightening experience for her as much as an opportunity to put across to others her own understanding and criticism of madrasa education as it is imparted and the negative consequences this has for the education of Muslim children in what she sees, and to some extent correctly, as an exclusivist environment. She feels that for healthy citizenship to grow and thrive in a country like India, children should as far as possible go to common schools and learn what is likely to be relevant for them to imbibe a multicultural and open perspective about one's self as well as about others. There is a long tradition of scholarship in educational studies which has always emphasized the virtues of acceptance of cultural diversity, knowing the limits of attachment to the community and country, and displaying empathy for the struggles for equality. This may not have been the perspective from which Dr Jhingran started to look at madrasa education and its limitations. She may have approached it from a more limited and narrow perspective of nation-building in a diverse society such as India has been and is. Even so, her point that a more healthy state of affairs would be a situation where all children are exposed to education in general schools and the curriculum should consist of modern subjects is worth serious consideration.

Of course, in making such an assertion Dr Jhingran is not entirely unaware of the importance of religious education. However, she is of the view that religious education should either be taken care of in the family or carried out in the maktabs whose timings do not clash with the classes for general education. Only those children who intend to become religious functionaries should go to the madrasa. Others should combine education in the maktabs and general schools. There is much variation across the communities in the way they have taken care of the problem of teaching religion to children. Christians use Sunday schools to impart religious education to their children. The Jews and Sikhs follow a similar model. Hindus like to let the family take care of religious education for their children. This is not the position that Muslims have as yet been willing to take. They think that all children should be exposed to religious education up to a point, and thereafter those who are training to be religious functionaries should continue their pursuit of madrasa education. Others should enter the modern school structure. This is the broad pattern that exists across communities and holds equally for the large majority of Muslim parents who prefer to send their children to general schools rather than madrasas. It is only in those areas where Muslims are unduly preoccupied with their cultural identity do they fear to send their children to general education as they feel that school ambience and the general tenor of textbooks is weighted against their culture and community.

Dr Jhingran has chosen a wide canvas on which to paint. She looks at why Muslim children go to the madrasas in considerable numbers, whether the explanation for this is poverty or religious commitment, what is the curriculum and pedagogy followed in schools and whether modernization of madrasa education, a strategy recommended both by the government and well-meaning educated Muslims, can do the trick in transforming madrasa education. Dr Jhingran does not have settled answers to these dimensions and what she has to say or suggest is likely to be deeply contested. Nonetheless, she has raised questions in the process which Muslims as much as others ought to think deeply about.

One of the points that Dr Jhingran repeatedly makes is that the pedagogy and teaching methodologies followed in the madrasas lays a great deal of emphasis upon memorization rather than on reflection, and to that extent they can be said to produce a conservative or backward looking outlook and orientation. Is this a problem particular to madrasa education? Or is it a problem which plagues our educational system and processes more generally. For reasons that may be deeply rooted in history and culture, educational processes in this country do not as a rule contribute towards a heightened critical outlook on the part of the students. Therefore, the substantial point made by Dr Jhingran that madrasa education cultivates a conservative and backward-looking outlook has to be tempered with the understanding that what she says about madrasa education is a problem common to all traditional and religion-based systems of education.

There are many reasons for this. Most traditional and religion-based educational systems are designed and oriented to preserve a cultural tradition rather than to bring about social change and transformation. This makes it necessary for them to lay a greater emphasis on the tradition as it is believed to have existed since the early times and to reinforce traditional ways of practising religion. Whether it is the case of Christian theological seminaries or the Sanskrit pathshala at Wai in Maharashtra, where priests are trained, or Muslim madrasas, the situation is somewhat similar. Madrasa education may be a somewhat more exaggerated example of this, but it is not unique. If this was not the case, there would have been no enlightened *alims* (Islamic scholars). Neither would theological debates have been possible. Even within the madrasa graduates outlook varies greatly and indicates that despite the ideal of promoting a uniform outlook and orientation, sharp differences do arise. Social science studies comparing the cognitive levels and outlook of madrasa and other school children do not show that there are very marked differences setting them apart on any of these counts.

I should like to conclude with a passage from William Dalrymple's book, *The Last Mughal*, describing the state of madrasa education in imperial Delhi:

Before long the older boys would be heading off down the lanes to arrive at the madrasas in time for the beginning of the study: to work on memorising the Koran by heart, or to hear an explication of its mysteries by the maulvi: or maybe it would be [a] day for studying the arts of philosophy, theology or rhetoric. Far from being a tedious chore, this was for many a thrilling business: one eager pupil who came to Delhi from a small town on the Grand Trunk Road used to go to the lectures at the Madrasa i-Rahimiya even in the pouring monsoon rain, carrying his books in a pot in order to protect them from getting wet. The elderly Zakaullah remembered running at breakneck speed through the *galis* of Shahajahanbad, such was his excitement at the new learning—and especially the mathematics— he was being taught at the Delhi College. Even Colonel Sleeman . . . had to admit that the madrasa education given in Delhi was something quite remarkable. 'Perhaps there are few communities of the world among whom education is more generally diffused than among Muhammadans in India,' he wrote on a visit to the Mughal capital. 'He who holds an office worth twenty rupees a month commonly gives his sons an education equal to that of the prime minister. They learn through the medium of Arabic and Persian languages, what young men in our colleges learn through those of Latin and Greek— that is grammar, rhetoric and logic. After his seven years of study, the young Muhammadan binds his turban upon a head almost as well filled with the things which appertain to these branches of knowledge as the young man raw from Oxford—he will talk as fluently about Socrates and Artistotle, Plato and Hippocrates, Galen and Avicenna (alias Sokrat, Aristotalis, Alfalatun, Bokrat, Jalinus and Bu Ali Sena); and, what is much to his advantage in India, the languages in which he has learnt what he knows are those which he most requires through life.

The crucial question is why the madrasas became a closed shop after the establishment of colonial rule. So long as this question is not satisfactorily and properly understood and answered, madrasa education would remain an enigma.

19 August 2008   Imtiaz Ahmad

Preface

Recently madrasas have been in the focus of media attention, the alleged reason being the terrorist activities around the world, which led the populist journalists in the West to zero in on Islamic seminaries or madrasas. Very few Indian writers have taken this route, but somehow the attention on madrasas has caught on.

However, the idea of the book had germinated in me long before that, in the late 1980s to be precise. I was trying to write on the conception and practice of secularism in India when I read some books by various Islamic scholars who either recommended madrasa education for Muslim children, or proposed that there should be separate schools and colleges for them with their own syllabus giving equal weightage to two kinds of educational disciplines, modern and Islamic. The idea of a separate syllabus, and naturally separate educational institutions and accordingly a separate Board of Higher Secondary Education, even universities for Muslims, an integral part of Indian nation, did not appeal to me.

It was so because I had argued in the above-mentioned work (*Secularism in India*) that a sharp division of the Indian populace into the categories of 'majority' and 'minorities' on the exclusive basis of religion falsifies the ground realities. From my point of view, religion alone does not determine the identity of a person or a people, even though it may be a very important factor in the lives of some persons or a group; there are other factors, such as region, language, education, urban or rural habitat and above all economic status, which go to mould their identity. A human being is a very complex and multidimensional entity: s/he follows a religion, lives in a certain region of the country, speaks a certain language, shares with his/her neighbours local customs, even norms, as well as the local needs. His/ her personality is also determined by the family to which s/he belongs, whether it is highly conservative or liberal, elite or deprived, as also the neighbourhood, *biradari* and caste (peculiar to India alone) to which s/he belongs. These different dimensions of human life together make the human personality. It is quite possible that in some persons or groups one aspect predominates, in others another aspect. Equally important, someone aspect or the other may become predominant according to the needs of circumstances, or some external influences, such as a family crisis or some socio-political upheaval.

The purpose of this study is not to undermine the importance of religion in the life of the Indian people and of Muslims in particular. It is often said that man cannot live by bread alone; but he needs bread also, and many other things. For all those things a person or a family has to live in and constantly interact with the wider society. According to my thinking, if Indian children start their early life and education in separate institutions, their identities as belonging to separate 'communities' are firmly established from the start, so that throughout their lives they are likely to remain as Hindus, Muslims, Christians or Sikhs, and not become Indians.

This led me to madrasas which are bringing forth a large number of Muslim children who, as adults, are virtually cut-off from wider society and the practical matters of modern life, both techno-scientific and socio-political. I did not know then, and I do not know now, either the number of madrasas or that of children and youth passing out of them.

At first I was hesitant to take up a study of the Madrasa system in India which was from my point of view a sociological issue, and I am trained in the discipline of philosophy. In a way mine is not a sociological study, as most such studies limit their scope both in time and place; and I was interested in the whole of India which is just impossible for an individual to even attempt in field study; I have not even attempted any extended field study. At the same time, as a philosopher I am trained to understand any subject comprehensively in a wider context and also to analyse various interrelated issues, their causes and possible consequences, as well as the conceptual framework in which any line of thinking has developed. Perhaps my attempt to understand all concerned matters in the wider perspective of the larger nation-society, and the needs and demands of modern times may have some worth, different than that of a sociological study.

My second doubt as to the advisability of any such study of madrasas by me was concerned with the fact that I am an 'outsider' in every sense of the term, not being Muslim and above all not knowing the Arabic language, I am not expected to understand either Islam, its religious texts, or Muslims' need for religious education. And as pointed out by a *maulvi* in a prestigious multidisciplinary Seminar, 'why should "outsiders" try to interfere with or impose their ideas upon madrasas, when they themselves know nothing about them?' He added 'do we tell engineering or medical colleges what and how they should teach?' I agreed with him, and hence my doubts about taking up the study. I was also hesitant in taking up this study on the Madrasa system of education for fear of offending religious sensitivities, as I was painfully conscious that my views and suggestions would not find approval with a large section of Muslims, both the *ulama* and perhaps the general middle class. But then I was encouraged to take up the study by late Professor Ravinder Kumar and Professor Bipan Chandra. I was also spurred into doing a study of madrasa system of education by the repeated claims of Muslim intellectuals—first, that madrasas have made a laudable contribution towards the national goal of universal education; and second, that 'poor' Muslim children have no other alternative but to study in madrasas. I now wanted to verify these assertions, as by themselves they did not sound convincing to me.

However, let me clarify in the beginning: First, the reference to terrorism in the context of madrasas never occurred to me. (There may be exceptions now but they prove nothing. Significantly, recent terrorist attacks were carried out by those young men who had a high level of Western education, and not by madrasa educated youth.) I find it strange that most writers on Madrasa system of education labour the point that madrasas are in no way connected with terrorist activities. Madrasa *maulvis* have become acutely conscious of this allegation of some connection between madrasas and terrorism, based on the fact that once in a while the government and others have suspected some particular madrasa of harbouring militants. As a result they have become even more hostile to the government, and withdrawn further into their shells. This is an unfortunate outcome of the media focus on madrasas and terrorist activities. Also, it should be remembered that all this hype about Islam and terrorism is West-based. As far as I think, in spite of occasional references to this supposed connection between Islam and terrorism, it has not been taken seriously by most people in India.

Second, even though I am theoretically not in favour of separate educational institutions for different 'communities', I have now realized the relatively greater hold of religion on Muslims which necessitates the training of experts in Islam and *shari'a* in madrasas. At the same time, I find no justification for the process of establishing more and more madrasas all over India, especially in the North. I was told by a learned professor that the ever-increasing number of madrasas is needed in order to fill the posts of clerics who are required to satisfy the religious needs of Muslims. I do not think that the Muslim population is increasing at the speed with which new madrasas are being set up! I have, however, always kept in mind the Muslims' need for a certain amount of religious education. I also fully recognize that 'minorities' have the constitutional right to establish their own religious and educational institutions.

Third, my interest here is mostly in the primary and secondary, and at most high school level education of Indian children, and not in higher education, whether modern or that of religious specialization (madrasas). This does not mean that higher studies are less important, but only that I am interested more in basic education. This is so because first, earlier education is foundational to higher education; and second and more importantly, education up to the secondary level is meant to be universal, that is, meant for *all* children, irrespective of their religious or other differences, and this is most important in a democracy.

Fourth, I am also an enthusiastic advocate of modern education, suited to modern times, and have a problem with the advocacy of madrasa education for most Muslim children, as is done by *ulama* and even by certain Muslim intellectuals. However, I accept the Muslims' need for religious education, which acknowledgement, along with my prior ideological commitments stated above, defines the task of my study: How to reconcile the two demands, one that of national integration and progress in modern life; and second that of the need for religious education for Muslim children. In other words, if we accept that Muslim children need formal religious education, does it imply that they all study in madrasas and forego modern, secular education? Alternatively, if they opt for modern education, how can their need for religious education be met?

My aim in this study, therefore, has been to achieve an objective understanding and evaluation of the madrasa system of education with a view to understanding how far it contributes to the goal of universal education at the primary and secondary levels, so that it makes its students not only better Muslims, the avowed goal of Islamic education, but also more rational and knowledgeable persons, better adjusted to and conscious of their duties and rights in the wider society around them. It was also to know why it is argued by several Muslim intellectuals that Muslim children do not have any opportunity of receiving modern education which is, in spite of its very poor quality, at least available to all the rest.

Now after some study and visits to many nearby madrasas, I feel that the teachings and ambience of most madrasas are very conservative, and if I may say so, regressive. They take their pupils to the middle ages and want to keep them there, cut-off from the realities of the modern world. Therefore, I have also tried to understand the curriculum and syllabuses of madrasas. Not knowing Arabic, which is almost an unpardonable drawback in any attempt to understand madrasa *nisabs*, and the prescribed texts being so numerous and voluminous, I did not even attempt to understand the detailed contents of the books taught but have relied on secondary sources, both English and Urdu. Still I have very seriously tried to understand various sects of Islam and their differing syllabuses (which I procured mostly directly from the concerned institutes) with the help of an Arabic scholar Farid Ahmad, an ex-student of Nadwat-al-Ulama who during the early days of my study read out to me several Urdu books and *nisabs* (syllabuses) of various madrasas, as also explained to me the correct meaning and connotations of various Arabic terms, Islamic concepts and rituals, and introduced me to various *hadiths* (*ahadis*) and schools of Islamic *fiqh* (jurisprudence).

Having understood some aspects of madrasa *nisabs* and the general ambience of madrasas, mostly from those writers who have themselves studied in madrasas, and my own personal observations, I have realized that largely the backwardness of Muslims is due to either having studied in madrasas alone, or being too much emotionally and socially dependent on the *fatwas* and general attitudes and ways of madrasa graduates. The latter have a tendency to look backward to the early centuries of Islam, not only in religious matters but also in all aspects of life. Their approach, ways and rhetoric, in turn, influence and condition the minds of common Muslim folk, and make them reluctant to accept modern thought, knowledge and values. My intention is not to downgrade Islamic value system; but we still need to question whether the contemporary Muslims should live by the norms and customs of the Arab society during the period between seventh to tenth centuries when the *hadiths* were written down, or try to move ahead with the times. My concern thus is not terrorism at all but this backward looking stance and approach of the religious leaders of Islam which are strengthened by the madrasa system of education with its books which are often those written centuries ago. Their attitudes directly influence and condition the entire Muslim community.

Some madrasas/maktabs in big cities are trying to introduce modern subjects, though often half-heartedly, while a few have accomplished this successfully. I have therefore also tried to understand the controversial issue of 'Modernization of Madrasas'. The entire issue has to be studied in the context of the syllabuses and approach of the madrasas on the one hand and the needs of modern times on the other. I have tried to study the various aspects of the issue involved instead of repeating the well-known semi-apologetic arguments in favour of such a modernization. The issues which I found to be most relevant in this context are: the impossibility of any student successfully understanding and mastering two such different and heavy courses; radical differences in the course content, pedagogy and *mahaul* (ambience) of madrasas and those of modern schools and a similar difference in their values and approaches. We must also remember that if modern subjects are to be included in madrasa curriculum, the educationists would have to opt for a drastic reduction of traditional syllabus of madrasas which reduction, if undertaken, would defeat the very purpose of *dini madaris* (specialized institutions of religious education). The facts that the number of madrasas and still greater number of maktabs in India is not known, while some madrasas which exist on paper are untraceable, and the autonomy of madrasas which makes them resist any outside interference are also to be taken into consideration.

I have also discussed various half-hearted suggestions of Muslim writers, as also two government schemes of modernization of madrasas, as well as the evaluation of the first scheme by Hamdard Education Society. The first scheme is too casually conceived and carried out to be considered seriously; the second, like most government schemes, is both half-baked and has several shortcomings in its very conception and plan, which may finally result in its failure. However, there are some State Madrasa Boards that have taken into consideration all the factors and developed a balanced syllabus. It is my serious advice that those boards and others which are floundering but trying to include both kinds of subjects, though with reduced content, must be encouraged and helped by the government. But as I envisage, even the successful modernization of madrasas affiliated to Madrasa Boards, which can offer education equivalent to modern schools along with religious education, is going to take decades, if it happens at all. Dealing with individual autonomous madrasas on the part of the government is a near impossible task.

It is important that existing madrasas should be left as they are to continue producing experts in Islamic jurisprudence (*fiqh*) and *shari'a*. And, this again is important, those madrasas that want to introduce some modern subjects must be helped in their efforts; but excessive resources and energies need not be spent in trying to modernize more and more madrasas. Also, it would be better if the modern subjects that are proposed to be taught in madrasas are introductory and not of the level of modern schools. In the final analysis, I still feel that it would be best that Muslim children go to common modern schools, so that they become an integral part of Indian society, achieving the same goals and discharging their responsibilities to the society as others. And only those few Muslim children should go to madrasas for detailed Islamic studies who want to become specialists in Islamic jurisprudence and become *muftis* and *maulanas*.

For those whose parents want religious education for their children in addition to the modern one, morning and evening maktabs must be organized on the so-called Kerala model. Finally and most importantly, excepting a few Muslim children opting for specialized studies in the madrasas, all others must study in common schools. Urdu medium sections in common schools must be arranged for those whose parents want them to study in that medium. Other objections regarding the objectionable contents of the school books, etc., must be dealt with promptness and sensitivity. Equally important is the duty of the wider society to own up to its responsibility to see that Muslim children get equal opportunities for receiving education. Educational or any other deprivation of any section of the society must not be perceived in isolation as concerning this or that community, but as a matter of concern for the entire nation-society, because in the end it is the entire society that suffers if a certain section thereof lags behind.

What is more difficult and at the same time most urgent is to radically improve the conditions and standard of education in all government and government-aided schools. In spite of the tall claims by the government, especially by its flagship project Sarva Shiksha Abhiyan the fact remains that the condition of most government and aided schools remains extremely poor and much more needs to be done. I strongly feel that the first priority of the government and other agencies must be to make arrangements so that these schools could provide good quality education up to High School, and if that is not possible at present, then up to the secondary stage at least, to all those majority of Indian children whose parents cannot afford the high fee of private English medium schools. A sound foundation in primary and secondary education is the first requirement of any person's development, or conduct as a responsible citizen of a democracy. And that is where all our resources and efforts should be directed.

If the above seems to be too unsympathetic a point of view regarding Muslims' special need to preserve their religion and Islamic culture, let me add that I fully recognize and respect the Muslims' emotional need for preserving their Islamic culture, and the related need for religious education for their children. However, it does not mean that most Muslim children should study in madrasas. In the detailed study that follows I have tried to consider all the relevant issues in a sympathetic manner and a holistic perspective.

Moreover, my critique of the madrasa system of education does not mean that I am unaware of, or am trying to downplay, the similar lacunae in the Hindu institutions of religious education. Actually, my original plan was to include a chapter on such institutions in this study before the concluding remarks, which would then have applied to all systems of education which zealously assert that the golden age of humanity was left behind one, two or even three millenniums ago. But this study itself became so lengthy that I had to give up this idea. I hope to take up a study of the system of religious education in the relatively fewer number of Hindu institutions or gurukuls, and the curriculum of various Saraswati Vidya Mandirs established by Hindu organizations, immediately after this study.

I am most grateful to all those academics, both liberal and orthodox, who helped me to understand Islam and the madrasa system of education. First of all, I am grateful to Dr Saiyyid Hamid, the most well-known advocate of 'modernization of madrasas', whom I met in the beginning of the research of this study, and who kindly explained to me the Islamic need of religious education, which perhaps leads a large number of Muslim children to seek their education in madrasas, along with their need for modern education which, in turn, points to the need of the 'modernization of madrasas'. I am equally grateful to the two *maulanas*—Mufti Dr M. Mukkarram Ahmed, the Shahi Imam of Fatehpuri Masjid, and Maulana Wahiduddin Khan. They accepted me, a total stranger, and explained certain aspects of Islam to me, very kindly answering my queries in detail with patience. They are quite orthodox in their views regarding the Islamic *shari'a* and related issues, but are equally liberal and insist that Muslim children must go in for modern education.

Though I do not agree with all the views of the above three learned men, I am very thankful to them for their kindness and help.

I want to thank Professor Mushirul Hasan for arranging exclusively for me a 'get-together' of various professors from different departments of Jamia Millia Islamia and a few *maulanas* who discussed the various dimensions of madrasa education and the desirability or otherwise of 'madrasa modernization'. This meeting helped me considerably in understanding the various issues involved in a holistic socio-religious perspective.

Above all, I am most grateful to Professor Imtiaz Ahmad. Although he is a very busy person, constantly engaged in his academic work, talks and interviews but he read through two drafts of my entire work, suggested changes and guided me at every stage. More than that, he even chided me whenever due to lack of confidence I slackened in completing this study! Very few academics can do that. This study would not have seen the light of the day but for his, and even his wife's, encouragement. He has also very kindly written the Foreword to this study; I thank him warmly for his help and guidance.

I am equally thankful to my old friend Dr Asghar Ali Engineer who is both an academic and social activist of renown. In spite of being extremely busy, he went through my manuscript, made constructive suggestions, and gave his opinion. I also thank Professor Yogendra Singh who gave his time first for discussions and then for going through my manuscript, in order to give me his 'opinion'.

I am also thankful to the unknown 'reviewer' of my typescript who read through the entire work and gave me excellent critical suggestions on some important points, which I have accepted. I also appreciate the help of Farid Ahmad, the Arabic scholar, during the early stage of my study.

Last, but not the least, I appreciate the help of my son, Dhir Jhingran who has gone through and literally corrected several drafts of each chapter at every stage of the development of the study. I owe to him my becoming aware of the need for basic education as the first step for realizing our goal of becoming a successful democratic welfare state. I also thank the Publisher and Editor of Manohar, especially the latter for taking a keen interest in the entire project and its publication.

In the end, I can only say that I have tried to be both sympathetic and objective in this study; however, I accept my modernist and nationalist biases. So I leave the study for discerning readers to judge its worth for themselves.

January 2009 SARAL JHINGRAN

1

Society, Religion, Education, and Modernity

During the course of our study, we would be continuously using the terms—'society', 'religion', 'education' and 'modern/modernization'. It would be better, therefore, to make clear what is meant by these terms to avoid unnecessary confusion.

1. SOCIETY

1.1. THE CONCEPT OF SOCIETY

The term 'society', like so many others used in everyday language, has various connotations. If it is to be used in sociological discourse one has to formulate its meaning in more definite terms. At the level of ordinary language, society may mean wider or larger social formations, though smaller groups coming together sharing the same ideology or some common interest are also called societies. Thus, in English usage there are such smaller societies as Society for the Prevention of Cruelty to Animals, etc. That is why Western sociologists are reluctant to use the term 'society' in understanding social relationships. According to them, there are a large number of social relationships—economic, political, personal—each of which involves a sense of community or 'a sense of belonging together'. In other words, it involves both mutual recognition of belonging to the same community and 'a sense of something held in common'.[1] This also means a sense of likeness, because 'without this consciousness of resembling one another in some degree, there can be no mutual recognition of "belonging together", and therefore no society'.[2] Western sociologists have rightly noted the very general nature of the word society. Sociologists and postmodernist writers often prefer the term 'community' when trying to understand some social phenomenon or individual psyche. The modern Western emphasis on community, rather than on society, is due to the fact that they are talking of a social relationship which is not only intimate but to a certain extent formative of an individual's personality. Such a group can be either a family or a close-knit community. A community is a relatively smaller formation of people who share some basic similarities of interest and feel a bond which binds them together. In the West, generally it is the locality that is regarded as the most important bond uniting a group of people who share various common interests, though some writers admit that this bond is gradually becoming weaker with the mobility of people. Postmodernists, however, use the term community as an existential category which defines and determines the individual's attitudes, views, and even perceptions. Strangely enough, they do not give any specific criterion to define the community. And, of course, religion is almost never referred to in Western discussions on society or community as a possible constitutive factor or basis for the feeling of community bonds.[3]

However, it is clear that the word 'community' applies to quite small groups with some specific distinguishing characteristics. It cannot therefore be applied to very large sections of the populace spread throughout the length and breadth of a country, as is done in India. Significantly, the terms 'community' and 'communal' have a very positive connotation in the West.

In Hindustani (Hindi and Urdu) the term *samaj* is the exact equivalent of the English word society, and its meaning is similarly vague and wide. Thus we have Hindu *samaj* or Muslim *samaj*, as well as Arya Samaj, Brahmo Samaj, Agrawal Samaj and Brahmana Samaj.

Another Hindustani term that has created havoc in Indian social thinking and discourse is *kaum*. Like the term *samaj*, the term *kaum* is nebulous in its meaning and usage, and is often used in the twin languages very loosely. It was, however, used in the nineteenth and early twentieth centuries to denote Hindus and Muslims as separate communities. Things worsened when *kaum* was translated as 'nation' in English, and political leaders, both Hindu and Muslim, started talking of the two religious communities as forming two nations. Religion was arbitrarily accepted as the basis of determining the boundaries of *samaj* or *kaum*, though the use of the term *kaum* for nation was definitely politically motivated. The terms *samaj* and *kaum* have a much wider connotation and varied usage than the above brief discussion would indicate. But when translated into 'nation' they create literal havoc.

In view of the problems related with the above terms, one can also understand society as a 'social structure' or a nation-society which includes all other institutions and groupings. Or, it can be conceived as an organization or dynamic whole whose constitutent parts, such as the individual, family, group or community and socio-political institutions, have both a relatively independent existence of their own and are interdependent to form an integral whole.[4] Rule of law, a definite social and economic structure, and also a network of communications are the prerequisites of a nation-society. Political independence is important, but not a precondition of a society. A definite geographical location is more important. It is not necessary that all people forming a society follow the same religion or speak the same language or practise the same customs, though such similarities do strengthen the sense of belonging together. There can be successfully cohesive but plural nation-societies such as those of the USA and India. According to Jawaharlal Nehru, 'Probably the essential characteristic of national consciousness is a sense of belonging together and of together facing the rest of mankind.'[5]

When confronted with the Two Nation theory solely on the basis of religious distinctions, Indian national leaders made special efforts to challenge and reject the thesis that religion alone could be the basis of nationhood. Mahatma Gandhi strongly opposed the Two Nation theory and asserted that one's nation is one which is one's *watan* (land of birth and habitat). He declared that,

India cannot cease to be one nation because people belonging to different religions live in it. [. . .] The Hindus, the Mahomadens, the Parsis and the Christians who have made India their country are fellow countryman. In no part of the world are one nationality and one religion synonymous terms; nor has it ever been so in India.[6]

Jawaharlal Nehru was even more emphatic in his rejection of the Two Nation theory.[7] It may be objected here that I am talking of nation here and not of society as such. Since the terms *samaj* (society) and *kaum* have been too loosely construed in India, I found the idea of a nation-society as the most comprehensive and appropriate for our purpose. In case of any objections, let it be a stipulated definition of *samaj* or society, and there does not seem to be any particular reason why others also should not agree with this.

Given the above understanding of society, the conception of *umma* or *millat* as a universal Muslim society transcending all national boundaries cannot be sustained. From the point of view of this study, it is very difficult indeed to conceive peoples of South-East Asia, those of Saudi Arabia, and those of African countries forming one universal society along with those of Turkey and other countries (e.g., Kazakhstan) which have a European culture and way of life.

Maulana Azad, once a strong advocate of universal Muslim *umma*, became a staunch supporter of the idea of India as one nation-state, perhaps under the influence of Gandhi. He repeatedly declared:

Providence brought us—Hindus and Muslims—together over a thousand years ago. We have fought, but so do blood brothers fight [. . . .] No, it is no use trying to emphasize the differences. For that matter no two human beings are alike. Every lover of peace must emphasize the similarities.[8]

Maulana Hussain Ahmad Madni contended as far back as 1938 that, *qaums* (nations) are determined by their homelands (*watans*). Race or religion does not make a *quam*. Madni, clearly and emphatically, contradicted Iqbal who had recently got converted to Pan-Islamism. As Maulana asserted, there is a difference between the two words—*qaum* and *millat*—because '*millat* implies a *shar* (way) or *din* (religion)', while the word *quam* means 'a group of men and women living together.'[9] Therefore, 'The Hindustani *qaum* comprises every inhabitant of India whether he speaks Urdu or Bengali, whether his colour is dark or fair, whether he is a Muslim or a Hindu, a Parsi or a Sikh, every Hindustani, regardless of these differences, is an Indian.'[10]

He asserted his conviction repeatedly. To quote him again:

We, the inhabitants of India, in so far as we are Indians, have one thing in common and that is our Indianness (*Hindustani*) which remains unchanged in spite of our religious or cultural differences. [. . .] Our religious and cultural differences do not affect our association with our homeland.[11]

I think that even cultural differences are not as prominent in India as they are sometimes made out to be by the country's communalist leaders. Indians do share a common culture which may not be the whole of the culture of a particular religious community, but which can still be described as Indian culture, or the essence of Indianness.

It is more significant and sad when contemporary Muslim writers talk about the *umma* and 'our culture' and the need to preserve it. They seem to imply that the 'nation' and its culture do not have much meaning for Indian Muslims, as their society (*umma*) and culture are unique and different from the rest. To quote one such writer, Manzoor Ahmad:

The need of the times is an integrated and unified system of education [. . .] to ensure the preservation of *our* civilization and culture. [. . .] It is to educate people about our religion and value system, as well as modern physical sciences. [. . .] It has also to educate the young people about the dangers of fragmentation of the *Ummah*, the world over. That the unity of the *Ummah*, in the face of challenges both from the West and the East, is a pre-requisite for *our survival as a free people* should be a cardinal point in the political and social consciousness of our young generation.

The new education shall also have to inculcate a sense of self-confidence and justified pride in *our* value system as well as in *our* historical achievements.[12] (Emphasis added)

He goes on to argue for the existence of an international Muslim community, and advocates that Indian Muslims should maintain their fraternal ties with the other components of Muslim *umma*, and so on. It is not that Manzoor Ahmad alone is talking of a Muslim *umma* with a unified religion and culture; there are many such writers, writing in Urdu, and some even writing in English, who talk in this way. No sense of nationhood or mutual belonging to one integrated nation-society can ever be developed without a sense of shared history. Even if that sense of shared history is missing—which is very unfortunate—at least

there should be an awareness of sharing a full millennium together with other sections of the populace. The 'us' and 'our'
should refer to Indian people and the composite culture that
Indians have built together. When a person or a group identifies
herself/itself with the culture and history of other countries, she/
it at the same time rejects sharing a nationhood and culture with
the rest of the population of the country.

As against the above, the present study advocates a conception of the society with definite national boundaries, a common
system of government, common laws (which may or may not include personal laws), as well as customary practices which are
often shared by different sections of the populace, somewhat
wrongly called 'communities'. This sharing of a common space and
a relatively common culture facilitate the integration of various
religious, regional and linguistic groups, without overwhelming
the rich mosaic of their plurality, in short, a pluralist nation-state.[13]

1.2. RELIGION AS THE CRITERION

In sharp contrast to the Western conceptions of society and community in which religion finds no place, in India religion is
understood as the sole criterion for defining a community or
society. The entire populace is divided into a majority community, meaning Hindus, and several minority communities, this
division being exclusively based on the criterion of their affiliation to different religions. There is no definite vernacular term
that can be regarded as the equivalent of the term 'community'.
The word *samaj* is mostly used for both society and community,
thus creating quite a bit of confused thinking. As a result,
Muslim *samaj* is declared to have an independent, separate existence, with its own religion and culture, as if the Muslims form
a separate society within Indian society. The terms community
and communal have become negatively loaded ones in India,
suggesting a social phenomenon which divides people of a society and may even create conflicts between them.[14] Jawaharlal
Nehru's explanation of this unique phenomena called 'communalism' is worth considering. According to him, communalism[15]
is a unique phenomena in the Indian subcontinent which is
supposedly caused by religious differences but which actually

has nothing to do with religion, or is simply the use of religion for political purposes.

This understanding of religious 'communities' as separate societies or communities within one nation-society depends upon two uncritical assumptions—First, that religion is the only and sufficient criterion to identify a large segment of the population, spread over an equally large space and time. And second, that because of that one identifying factor, all those millions of people form one homogeneous 'community' with identical needs and interests.[16] It is this strange 'communal' mindset of the Indian people that causes the Hindus, a numerical majority, claim that their religion and culture are threatened by the very presence of other religious groups which are numerical minorities. It is the same mindset that makes Muslims feel insecure and, in turn, makes them cling to their religious identity and emphasize the peripheral matters of their religion even more, and, what is worse, live together in ghettos almost separated from the rest of society.

There is no denying that religion is very important in the lives of Indian people following different faiths. Generally it is believed and practised not as a personal affair but as something to be shared with one's co-religionists. This sharing of religion with others naturally leads to a communitarian fellow feeling. Further, religion is regarded in India, as against the West, as determining the rest of the beliefs, norms, values and way of life of its followers. (This is somewhat more true of Islam than Hinduism.)

I am not suggesting here that religion is, or should be, less important for Muslims, but only that there are so many other factors that have an equally determinative influence on both one's personality and life. Apart from religion, perhaps the most important difference between man and man is based on economic status. There are hardly any meeting points between the really poor sections of the population and the richer class of any so-called community. Of course, Islam puts great emphasis on equality of all human beings, but it would be futile to say that divisions between the rich and poor are not equally marked in Muslim societies. The differences based on educational status, urban or rural habitat, etc., are no less important in everyday life and determine the identity and role of a person or group.[17]

Tremendous differences exist between the cultures of north and south India. There are many factors which influence and qualify the sense of identity among the followers of a religion. An important difference here is that south Indian Muslims are the descendants of Arab traders who reached Indian coasts as traders and not as aggressors. They were welcomed by the locals (Hindus) and gradually amalgamated with the local culture without losing their religious rooting. Also, the kingdoms of Muslim rulers of the North did not always stretch to far South; and when they did these kingdoms were often short-lived. As a result, there is generally no animosity or even the feeling of the 'other' among south Indian Muslims and Hindus. In contrast, the Afghans and Turks, who happened to be Muslims, came to north India as aggressors, and some of them even looted and destroyed temples, etc. This made amalgamation of the conquerors and the vanquished difficult. And yet, even though there is a difference in the degree of cultural amalgamation between the North and the South, gradually a beautiful synthesis of Hindu and Muslim cultures did emerge both in the North and in the South.

Mushirul Hasan has argued again and again that the conception of the Muslim community as a 'monolithic *umma*' which is normally expected to 'remain the same across divisions in space and time, is misleading'.[18] This view, according to Hasan, just glosses over the internal differences between various Muslim communities.[19] He adds that ordinary Muslims have never been a monolithic community, but have been active participants in regional cultures whose perspective they have shared; and that at the regional level the Indian people followig various religions have behaved as an integrated society, building together a shared culture with almost common values and responses. Together the two peoples of India have developed their composite culture.[20]

Mushirul Hasan, Imtiaz Ahmad and many others have documented in detail the intra-community differences among Muslims—differences of sects, such as Shi'a, Sunni, and various sub-sects of the two, and castes, generally called *beradaris*. Even differences between 'high' and 'low'—the *ashrafs* and the *ajlafs* exist among Muslims, based on their supposedly being descendents of foreign Muslims or Indian converts respectively and also their hereditary professions.[21] It is also not to be forgotten that at the regional level Muslims mostly speak the regional language. Even Bangladeshi Muslims speak and write in chaste Bengali. In Lucknow, the centre of nawabi culture and Urdu literature, Muslim masses still speak in a sweet dialect of Hindustani—Avadhi. Moreover, language is not a lifeless instrument of human use; rather it comes loaded with concepts and meanings particular to that regional, linguistic, and cultural milieu. The family structure, social customs, as also socio–moral values, are mostly shared by all segments of the local population.

If one can find so many internal differences among Muslims, a numerical minority, it would be ridiculous to talk of the numerically greater Hindu majority as representing one 'monolithic community'. The Hinduism and Hindutva or Hindu *rashtra*, whose hegemony the Hindu communalists so much desire, are constructs and not an actuality. The protagonists of Hindutva were faced in the very beginning with the dilemma that the 'majority' whose cause they were advocating did not exist in the sense of a unified Hindu community. Hindus mostly understand themselves on the basis of hierarchically arranged and highly stratified castes and sub-castes; they worship different deities and belong to different sects; and there exist significant differences of regional cultures and customary laws. These differences go back to, and are recorded by Hindu scriptures and the two Epics.[22]

On the other hand, there has been constant interaction between Hindus and Muslims which gradually resulted in the emergence of a common composite culture. Of course, some Muslims, and religious leaders in particular, would not agree with this understanding of communal (or communitarian) identity, To reiterate, I am not undermining Islam's claim to uniqueness, or its claim to be the final guide in all matters to Muslims; but only that adherence to a religion should not be taken as the only and exclusive basis of a person's or group's identity.

That neither Hindus nor Muslims nor Christians are homogeneous communities is enforced by a recent research project undertaken by the Anthropological Survey of India. Its results were published in 1994 in the form of a book by K.S. Singh, entitled *People of India: An Introduction*. This survey used 'indicators' or cultural traits which characterize a certain cohesive group or community. Though their criteria are too complex, and not necessarily right, the conclusions of the survey are interesting. It identifies 4,634 'communities' within India, out of which more than 300 are supposedly among Muslims.[23] Obviously, by 'communities' the survey and Singh mean what the term *beradari* in common parlance means. *Beradaris*, whether Muslim or Hindu, are much more cohesive. There is far closer contact between the members of *beradaris*; and unfortunately far stronger control of *beradari* panchayats on their members. Indian masses often perceive themselves and act more as members of this or that *beradari*, rather than as Muslim, Hindu, or Sikh, and far less as Indians (though they are aware of their wider identity).

The idea here is simply to point out that to tag Hindus, Muslims, Christians, spread throughout the entire subcontinent as separate communities, each with a separate common culture and identity, in spite of their innumerable differences at different levels due to the permutations and combinations of so many other equally relevant factors, falsifies the reality of everyday life. Probably all of the country's socio-economic and communal problems arise from this approach of creating artificial communities.

2. RELIGON: ITS MEANING AND NATURE

2.1. THE MEANING OF RELIGION

Religion is the most profound dimension of human personality. Even to propose to discuss it in a few pages seems in some sense blasphemous. In spite of realizing the near impossibility of the task of understanding religion/s we have still to try to answer two related questions because of the nature of our study. First, what do we mean by religion? And second, can detailed religious instructions take priority in the education of Indian children, and can they be reconciled with modern, secular education?

'Religion' is understood very differently in Semitic religions and those of Indian origin. The semitic conception of religion, echoed by its philosophers, such as R.C. Zaehner, Ninian Smart, and Margaret Chatterjee, emphasizes the uniqueness of each religion, its being integrally related to its cultural and linguistic roots. It is further considered as a whole consisting of various integrally related dimensions, such as creed, rituals, and socio-moral norms (in Islam law or *shari'a*). According to this point of view, there are several dimensions of religions:[24]

(a) *Revelation*: Each religion is centred around a unique 'revelation'. For Christianity, it is Jesus, the Christ, himself (though it also has a Book, the New Testament); for Islam it is the Holy Book of Quran, every word of which is claimed to have been directly revealed to Prophet Mohammad. The 'revelation', as well as its expression, is more or less definite and determinate, and the task of the following generations is confined to the comprehension, elaboration and rationalization of the 'revelation'.

(b) *Doctrine or Creed*: During the process of explanation and elaboration of the primal 'revelation' new problems arise which, in turn, necessitate a new interpretation of some aspects of 'revelation'. This doctrinal dimension or creed may include the basic creed as well as the later doctrines developed to explain and elaborate this creed, what can be called the theology. The understanding and interpretation of 'revelation' are now based on the theological formulations.

(c) *The Ritual Dimension*: Even the simplest form of religious service or prayer has a ritual dimension, consisting of some prescribed acts and behaviour. In Islam this ritualistic dimension is very important. Namaz is not only the recital of a definite creedal belief, every stage of this recital is accompanied by definite prescribed postures. The latter are performed in unison in the mosque, but even individual performance of namaz must include these postures. Catholic Christianity's rituals are equally elaborate.

(d) *The Ethical Dimension*: It consists of values and virtues the specific religion extols, and socio-religious norms that its followers are expected to follow. Every religion has an ethical code; it may or may not be clearly spelt out. Also, this ethical code is closely related to the basic creed or doctrinal dimension of that religion.

(e) *The Social Dimension*: This dimension is perhaps more important in Semitic religions. Most religions are institutionalized. As put by Ninian Smart, 'Religion is not a personal matter here, it is part of the life of the community. It is built into the institutions of daily life.'[25] It is expected to influence and direct the personal conduct of its followers. In Christianity and Islam, religion is mostly a community affair. Islam emphasizes the brotherhood of all Muslims who together form the *umma*. Social and ethical dimensions of a religion are influenced by its doctrinal dimension, but often enough they are also influenced by the society and age in which the religion happens to operate.

(f) *The Experiential Dimension*: While it is given prime importance in religions of Indian origin, the experiential dimension is not that important in Semitic religions. Sometimes it is even discouraged as reliance on experience is feared to undermine the centrality and supreme authority of 'revelation'. However, a minimum of religious experience is required even in the performance of everyday rituals to give it a religious meaning. True prayer is an effort to relate oneself to God, the profoundest form of which is mystical experience.[26]

(g) *Concrete and Unique Nature of Religion*: Margaret Chatterjee has argued (though I do not fully agree with her) that not only is each religion unique, it is also rooted in its culture and is necessarily embodied in the conceptual framework of its own culture, without constant reference to which it cannot be fully understood.[27] According to this view, shared by Ninian Smart and other Western thinkers, in each religion there is a different or unique pattern in which its various dimensions are organized. Therefore, according to Ninian Smart, 'We are confronted with religions. And each religion has its own style, its own inner dynamic, its own special meanings, and has to be understood in its own terms.'[28]

Emphasizing the total conceptual framework and the pattern in which various dimensions of religion are organized, which in turn are conditioned by the culture of their origin, the above approach seems to imply some form of cultural relativism. It suggests that even the original 'revelation', at least some aspects of it, are conditioned by the culture and times in which the 'revelation' occurs. For example, Jesus believed himself to be, and was accepted by his followers, as the Messiah because the Jews of that time were expecting one.

Similarly, the 'revelation' in the Quran can be properly under-stood and appreciated best if it is read in the context of the seventh-century Arabic world. The same is even more true for the *hadiths* and *shari'a*; the contribution of the later writers who interpreted and codified the *shari'a* cannot be taken lightly. Other-wise the existence of six to eight schools of Islamic law (*fiqh*), including both the major sects of Islam, could not be explained.

The position of Hinduism is rather different from that of Semitic religions. First, Hinduism is too varied and multidimen-sional to have a concrete, clearly defined creed. It also does not have either a Book, or a Prophet. As a result Hindus cannot honestly define their religion in definite, determinate terms.

2.2. INTERNAL DIFFERENCES WITHIN RELIGIONS

An unbiased study of world religions would show first, that though there are different religions there are as many differences within a particular religion as between one religion and another. Second, it would show that these different strands of religion find an affinity in similar strands in other religions.[29] For ex-ample, the Sufi tradition in Islam would find a greater concor-dance with the Hindu Bhakti tradition than with the orthodox creed of Islam. This suggests that no religion should be under-stood as monolithic or closed. Each religion is a complex whole, and its various dimensions are not necessarily harmonious with each other. Third, it would show that every religion has been changing with the times due to its own inner dialectics and also under the influence of other religions and cultures. Hinduism, of course, has changed beyond recognition due to the influence of Buddhism, Jainism, and Islam. Both Christianity and Islam, in spite of their insistence on one 'revelation' and one creed, have become diversified and got transformed through the centuries due to the influence of the cultures of countries where they expanded, as also with the changing times.

Ancient Hindu philosophy (Vedanta of Shankara) and a few modern Western philosophers, such as Arnold Toynbee and W.T. Stace, make a distinction between the 'higher' and 'peripheral' (lower or ritualistic) dimensions of a religion.[30] However, most Western philosophers belonging to the Semitic traditions believe that every religion is an integrated whole, rejecting any such distinction. Especially the Muslim clergy would resist any suggestion of such a distinction between the essentials and non-essentials of Islam. Interestingly, Maulana Abul Kalam Azad subscribed to the above thesis. In his famous *Tarjuman al Quran*, Azad has argued that one should make a distinction between the universal message or the 'essence' of a religion (its roots), and its secondary or derivative matters (its branches). He further argues that differences in various religions are not in their *din* (faith) but *shari'a* (path). He also argues that this *din* is similar in all religions, and all religions and religious teachers deserve equal respect.[31]

Similarly, there is the problem of reconciling the claims to finality and absoluteness asserted by all world religions. Hinduism generally does not make any such claim; but such a claim is very basic to Semitic religions. Here also, Toynbee counts seven world religions, and points out that all of them make this claim to finality and that their claims cancel out each other.[32] This is a very crucial issue. No sincere commitment to one's religion can be felt without this faith in its being the final truth. Both major Semitic religions—Christianity and Islam—emphatically affirm their absoluteness and finality. But when this claim is made before others of different faiths, conflict arises, as they too believe in the absolute truth of their respective religions. Such a claim can only be sustained by denouncing the claims of other religions. Without undermining the emotional commitment to the finality and truth of one's own religion, one can at least acknowledge at the intellectual or rational level the possibility of the truth of other religions also, as Mahatma Gandhi used to assert.[33] I am fully aware that the followers of Semitic religions, especially of Islam, do not agree with the above suggestion. They assert that one can 'tolerate' other religions—and Indian Muslims excel in their attitude of religious toleration—but they add that one cannot 'respect' other religions as having equal worth because that is tantamount to confessing that they are as 'true and final' as one's own religion, which would mean being unfaithful to one's religion.[34] This question is open for further discussion. Here we would 'respect' the orthodox Muslims' dilemma and would not question their faith in the finality of their 'revelation'.

2.3. RELIGIONS' NEED FOR RELIGIOUS INSTRUCTION

Every religious tradition, like any other dimension of human culture, seeks to preserve itself. It seeks to pass on the tradition to coming generations by both word of mouth and formal instructions in some institutions. Before the stage of formal instruction starts, the religious tradition remains oral for some time. The Vedas were thus handed down from generation to generation through the oral tradition before they were written down. In the Christian religion, the Gospels were written down long after the four apostles' lifetime. The same is true for the Quran and *hadiths*. The nature of formal instruction to the young depends upon the corpus of religious texts and their internal configuration, or their relative importance.

Christianity has developed a regular mechanism of passing on its religious heritage through sermons which are an integral part of the Sunday church service and Sunday church schools. Children and the youth, generally between the ages of 6 and 17–18, are expected to and do attend Sunday school where they are taught general morality, as well as the fundamentals of Christianity in a very systematic manner. The young are divided into classes and are given regular examinations and promoted to the next class. Thereafter also, the youth are expected to join Christian youth organizations with special emphasis on their religion. There are separate regular colleges or seminaries to train clerics.

Buddhism too had regular schools and colleges for those who wanted to specialize in the higher doctrines of their Dharma. The children and youth of the two upper castes of Hindus were sent to gurus who taught them in their forest *ashrams*. As Hinduism gave freedom to its followers to understand and believe according to their mental capacities and needs, it made regular religious instruction almost irrelevant. The responsibility for religious training and minimum instruction for the masses was therefore met by the family, as well as regular *satsangs* (religious sermons in the open).

The case of Islam is entirely different. Since it spread to the entire Middle East and Central Asia, it was confronted by very different religious and cultural traditions and its *ulama* felt a compelling need to standardize not only the basic creed and rituals but also the Islamic way of life (*shari‘a*). Very early two things were realized—first, the Quran cannot be fully understood without the help of *hadiths* which were the reports of the sayings and approvals and disapprovals of others' conduct by Prophet Muhammad; and second, Islam being the total guide to the lives of Muslims, the Quran alone does not provide that guidance in every eventuality of life and therefore the help of *sunna* consisting of *hadiths* has to be taken. In the third and fourth centuries *hijri*, a concerted effort was made to select and standardize them by discarding the fake ones and saving the authenticated ones by writing them down. That is how about the tenth century of the Christian era there developed a well-defined corpus of Islamic religious books so that the next generations could be taught Islam in a generally agreed written format.

Gradually *shari'a* developed out of these two sources, the Quran and the *sunna*. Actually in the formation of *shari'a, sunna* or *hadiths* (*ahadis*) were even more important than the Quran. Later on even that *shari'a* was elaborated on and added to, thus developing a very detailed corpus of laws (*fiqh*) which was to be followed blindly (*taqalid*) by the coming generations. Hence arose the need for detailed religious instruction which could be mastered by only a few who then became Islamic experts (*ulama, muftis* or *qazis*). At the same time, prayer or worship in Islam, as in Christianity, is a community affair; and as such certain rituals are prescribed which are to be strictly followed in community prayers (*namaz* or *salat*). Also, since Islam has a definite prescribed text, reading it is considered meritorious. Therefore, a certain amount of minimum education was considered essential for the masses also, consisting of learning certain rituals and elementary reading of the Holy Quran. Since then the maktabs have been the most popular educational institutions for Muslim children, which are attached to the neighbourhood mosques and which teach the necessary rituals and impart minimum knowledge of Arabic, as also some verses of the Quran. There are regular madrasas which teach very detailed religious and other traditional subjects. While the *ulama* and the majority of Muslims think that the religious instruction provided in the maktabs is sufficient for most Muslim children, some thinkers believe that Muslim children must also know the *sunna* or *hadiths*.

Maulana Abul Kalam Azad believed that knowledge of religion is essential for a person to develop a moral personality.[35] Azad's views are in concurrence with the general Islamic point of view that the development of the moral character of the student is the primary aim of education, and that it can only be realized through Islamic education. To quote Syed Hamid Hasan,

[The aim of Islamic education] is to provide for the most harmonious development of body, mind and soul in a way that an individual is not only able to achieve what is best in the present life but what is beneficial for his soul when it leaves the body.[36]

According to S.S. Hussain and S.S. Ashraf,

The true aim of education is to produce men who have faith as well as knowledge, the one sustaining the other. Islam does not think that the pursuit of knowledge by itself without reference to the spiritual goal that man must try to attain can do humanity much good.[37]

3. EDUCATION: ITS NATURE AND AIMS

3.1. THE RECIPIENTS OF EDUCATION

Before trying to assess any system of education, in this case the madrasa system of education as it is prevalent in modern India, it is necessary to first have a clear idea as to what we mean by 'education'. It must be made clear that the main interest of the present study in education is limited to elementary and secondary education, that is, education up to at the most high school level. It does not mean that higher education is not important, but only that basic or elementary education, being foundational, is more so. Various questions or issues arise when one discusses education: First, what is education and what should its aims be? Second, who are the right recipients of education? Here let us take up the second question first.

In ancient and medieval times, education was meant for the elites of the society. In India it was meant for the upper two *varnas* of the priestly class (brahmans) and warrior class (kshatriyas), and was aimed at teaching them the perfected skills of their specific professions. In the Muslim world, education was mostly meant to teach and train the sons of elite classes for high state posts, such as magistrates (*qazis*), etc. The strong contention made by many Muslim scholars, that while India had an education system which was limited to the two upper classes, Islam provided education for all, is only partially true. Though there was no distinction in Islam on the basis of rich or poor, it was mostly the children of the upper classes who were motivated to go in for higher education which opened the doors of high profile careers for them, as the children of the poor masses could not afford to spend so much time in seeking knowledge alone.

Similarly, Western society was firmly based on the distinction between citizens and serfs. Education was meant for citizens only. In the Middle Ages in Europe even the most ardent followers and protagonists of Christianity accepted the institution of slavery, so that education again was meant for the upper classes only.

Up to the Renaissance and to some extent the Enlightenment, education remained confined to the sons of the upper classes. Rousseau, the great protagonist of egalitarianism and freedom, chalked out the system of education by private tutors at home for Emile, obviously the son of a nobleman. For Rousseau even the girls of upper classes were to be given a different kind of education. Such an education was meant for the lucky few and not for the masses.

The idea of universal education is a relatively new one. It can be traced to Immanuel Kant (eighteenth century), perhaps the greatest philosopher of the West. He proclaimed that all humans are essentially rational and autonomous beings; that is, there is no basis to differentiate between them, and hence no basis to educate a few, leaving out all the others.[38]

The outright rejection of all social distinctions and the declarations of equality of all human beings, in the sense that they all have right to equality, freedom, justice and happiness, was the pivotal slogan of nineteenth-century liberalism. J.S. Mill was the greatest champion of equality and above all the individual's freedom. Mill's most important and at that time radical proposal was for universal education. He regarded it a 'moral crime' for the state to fail to provide for 'the training of a child's mind'. However, Mill at the same time deprecated any state control over children's education. A similarly radical proposal of his was a demand for equal access of women to education at all levels. A third contentious proposal by Mill was that on 'disputed sub-jects', notably religion, children must not be taught or examined on the truth or falsity of certain propositions, as they cannot be proved by reliable evidence.[39]

From the nineteenth century onwards, the equal right of all individuals to education, including children of all classes, boys and girls, became unquestionable. Thus, the second question above as to who is to be educated is answered once for all. Universal education is the duty of every state and the right of every child. The Indian constitution recognized this right of every child for free education, but unfortunately it kept the duty of the state to provide this free education among the non-enforceable Directive Principles. However, the Government Policy of Education, 1986 declares the right of every child to free education up to fourteen years of age irrespective of all other distinctions. Ever since it has been the central government's effort, especially under the auspices of its Sarva Shiksha Abhiyan (drive for universal education), to make this goal possible. This limit of 'up to the age of 14 years' is a result of past history. In 1937 the Congress party had passed a resolution to this effect. It would, however, be better if this limit is removed and the right to free education is extended to high school at least. Now the Right of Children to Free and Compulsory Education Bill, 2008 has been finally passed by the Parliament and got the President's approval, let us hope that it would speed up the goverment's efforts to provide universal education to every child.

3.2. MUSLIM VIEWS ON EDUCATION AND REASON

Once the question as to who is to be educated is decided in everybody's favour, the next question naturally would be what should be the aims of such an education, and what type of education should it be.

Not only a consideration of the Muslims' views on education is relevant to this study, they are also valuable in themselves. The Quran and the *hadiths* put the greatest stress on education or knowledge (*ilm*). These will be discussed later. Here quoting one such *Sura* from the Quran which is regarded as its very first verse will suffice:

Read (*iqra*) in the name of thy Lord who createth. [. . .] Read. And thy Lord is the most bounteous, who teacheth by the pen, teacheth man that which he knew not.[40]

Both the Quran and the *hadiths* continuously assert that the merit of a man of learning is far greater than that of a man who performs all his religious duties.[41] While Christianity has distinguished the sacred from the profane from the beginning, Islam makes no such distinction. And it is noteworthy that when the early Muslim traditions and scholars extolled knowledge, they made no distinction between religious or secular knowledge. This single affirmation resulted in an unprecedented boost to the search for knowledge by the Arabs.

In the very first century of Prophet Muhammad's declaration of Islam, it started expanding, sometimes by the sword, at other times by the appeal of its simple creed. It reached Iran and other Middle East countries; it was so open and liberal in its first centuries that it started absorbing the cultures, lifestyles, and even social norms of the countries it conquered. Sometimes these influences offered a welcome corrective to its earlier austere culture, at other times they undermined some of its basic values.[42]

However, the greatest positive result of this pliable and knowledge-seeking attitude of the early protagonists of Islam was that Muslim academics became like magnets who attracted and collected all knowledge available globally. They learnt astronomy, numbers, the concept of zero, and algebra from India;[43] later on Europe learnt all these things from the Arabs. They interested themselves in Greek logic and philosophy and translated the works of Aristotle and other Greek philosophers into Arabic, Armenian, and other languages of the then Muslims. Having studied these and other works the Muslims then set about further developing those sciences or disciplines such as mathematics, astronomy and logic.

Knowledge and science were given full encouragement during the time of the first four Khalifas and the Abbasid period. Especially under Khalifa Mamu'n, Muslims became the centre of world knowledge and intellectual activity. According to Humboldt, 'Their unexampled intellectual activity marks a distinct epoch in the history of the world.'[44] The University of Kahira became the renowned centre for scientific learning and was called *Dar-ul-Hikmat*.

The social and intellectual milieu of the then Arab society (seventh to eleventh centuries) was somewhat similar to that of Renaissance Europe (fifteenth–sixteenth centuries)! A man of letters was one who was an expert in all known fields of knowledge—from philosophy to mathematics, astronomy and medicine.[45] The Arabs particularly excelled in deductive reasoning going from effect to cause, which method was later adopted by modern science. Starting from the astronomy of Ptolemy they tried to correct its anomalies. They contributed to trigonometry, invented the pendulum for the measurement of time, studied and explained natural phenomena such as the refraction of light, and even developed optics. They were particularly interested in chemistry, and also made advances in medicine and even surgery.[46]

On the one hand, the aggressive assertions of a few Christians of the time regarding the superiority of their creed and doctrines and their rationalistic polemics over the Muslim views gave a spurt to the Muslims' interest in logic and polemics; and on other, Muslims, Christians, and Jews engaged together in the pursuit of knowledge.[47] As a result of this mutual communication, as well as the widespread study of Greek works on logic and philosophy, the Arabs accepted them as their own. Gradually they were included in the curriculum of madrasas as an integral part of Islamic tradition. Moreover, interest in logic and polemics gave early Muslims a rationalistic thrust.

Interestingly, early Muslims used reasoning not only in secular matters but also in religious controversies. The Quran speaks of God as an absolute Unity (*Tawhid*), but at the same time speaks of His various qualities, sometimes even in anthropomorphic terms. On this issue two schools of philosophy—the Mutazilites and the A'sharites—argued long and passionately. The Mutazilites were rationalists and they argued that the Absolute or God cannot be said to have those qualities as it would create duality. Instead, God *is* will, kindness, etc. They declared that the Essence and Attributes of God are identical. The A'sharites tried to save both the Unity of God and the distinction between the Essence of God and His Attributes, as this approach was closer to the Quranic conception of God.[48]

Asma Afsaruddin has created a word picture of an extremely volatile people who were active both intellectually and physically. They created science and literature, and did not much bother about religious do's and don'ts.[49] Against them there were a large number of *ulama* who subscribed to the traditional education with its elaborate content and goals, and who ultimately won the controversy, which we would have opportuity to discuss in the third chapter.

These days many Muslim scholars try to argue that the inclusion of Greek logic and philosophy in the curriculum was meant only to tell the students of the opponents' point of view against which they had to defend their religion and culture. If Ameer Ali and Asma Afsaruddin are to be believed, there was an atmosphere of mutual cooperation in the pursuit of knowledge and not antagonism.[50] Muslims started with the earlier works of Greeks and developed those disciplines further.

These very works were lost to Europe during the Dark Middle Ages. Later, when Arabs translated them back into European languages, Aristotelian logic, natural philosophy (science), and stress on reasoning are said to have triggered the Western Renaissance.

Medieval Muslim scholars not only valued knowledge (*ilm*) above all, they also tried to develop a philosophy of education. Muhammad Ibn Ahmad al Ghazali (eleventh century) was not only the foremost philosopher, theologian, and mystic of his time, his views on education were also equally valuable. He distinguished two realms of knowledge: one consisting of the inner eye or mystic vision which, with the help of original 'revelation', gives a glimpse of the Ultimate Reality; and the second, that of the sensory world which is open to sensory perception and reason. He valued reason and logic very highly. He emphasized the role of rational thinking in education. However, ultimately it was obedience to Islamic *shari'a* (Islamic law) that was considered the key to a meaningful life, and education was expected to prepare the student to perform his duties towards the society. Education, for him, was a total process which should take care of every aspect of human beings—intellectual, psychological, social, physical, and spiritual.[51]

The most important part of Islamic education was and is the emphasis on the goal of education. Though individual Arabs might have pursued knowledge for its own sake, it was firmly asserted that all education or knowledge should aim first, at man's appreciation of the Glory of Allah, and second, at the transformation of man into a pious Muslim (*momin*). Al-Ghazali declared that this goal could best be achieved by following the Islamic *shari'a*.

3.3. DEVELOPMENT OF WESTERN VIEWS ON EDUCATION

Both Plato and Aristotle understood education to be a means for preparing the future citizens of the Greek state. For both human perfection (eudemonia in Aristotelian terminology) consisted of a combination of wisdom and virtue, and education should lead to it. The education of male citizens, as envisaged by Aristotle, was to be very comprehensive, consisting of practice in virtue (discipline), and later in mature age, the study of mathematics, logic, metaphysics, ethics, politics, aesthetic, music, poetry, rhetoric, physics, and biology. This later and most important phase of education was understood by Aristotle to have intrinsic value.

Education so far imparted in the West has been more or less on the same pattern, and is known as classical education. The British grammar schools are the prototype of such an education. This view favours the imparting of knowledge so far achieved by humanity to the next generation. It includes science, humanities, and to a lesser extent the arts. It is still the pattern of education, with minor innovations, in most countries, including India. This view contends that education or imparting of knowledge should aim at the development of a child's mind and intellect. That is, it should relate to intellectual pursuits such as mathematics, science, literature, and history, and it need not include such practical training as crafts, etc. Philosophers belonging to this school assert that all children, irrespective of their backgrounds or even perceived faculties and interests, should be provided with 'culture' or mental refinement.[52]

John Dewey leads a majority of modern philosophers who oppose the traditional type of modern education which largely consists in filling the pupils' minds with intellectual, often unrelated information. He points out that miscellaneous knowledge stored in a passive mind is useless. It not only does not help in the growth of the powers of mind, but also hampers thinking. Pupils who have been recipients of such knowledge have no training in thinking for themselves. Rather, 'the attitudes which spring from getting used to and accepting half-understood and ill-digested material weaken vigor and efficacy of thought'.[53]

A.N. Whitehead is similarly a strong critic of the present system of education. He warns us against 'inert ideas', that is, ideas that are received passively without testing or utilizing them in life. He points out that even the study of literature, such as Shakespeare, is imparted in an artificial manner, with detailed explanatory notes which the student is expected to learn by rote; all of which does not lead to the real appreciation of the literary piece.[54]

R.S. Peter has rightly asserted that the word 'education' has 'normative implications'. It has 'the criterion built into it that something worthwhile should be achieved'. To quote him,

It implies that something worthwhile is being or has been intentionally transmitted in a clearly acceptable manner. It would be a logical contradiction to say that a man had been educated but that he had in no way changed for the better. Such a connection between 'education' and what is valuable does not imply any particular commitment to content. . . . All that is implied is a commitment to what is thought valuable.[55]

Here three assertions are being made: first, worthwhile things alone are to be transmitted; second, they should be transmitted in a clearly acceptable manner; and third, they should in some way transform the learner into a better, not only more knowledgeable but also wiser, more moral and noble person. This seems to be a tall order. Does the present-day education at all make children and youth better human beings? Knowing the laws of mathematics or physics, or even history or geography does not transform a person. Experience tells us that the present system of education has hardly any impact on the person and character of the individual.

3.4. MODERN INDIAN VIEWS ON EDUCATION

Dewey strongly recommends practical orientation of the entire education system. However, the way he visualizes that orientation cannot be actuated in a poor country such as India.

Mahatma Gandhi recommended the same practical orientation a long time ago. He advocated universal education up to the age of fourteen years. It was meant for the masses, and was rooted in Indian conditions. His ideas were developed and systematized by Dr Zakir Husain, the future President of India, in the form of Nayee Taleem based on the initial Wardha Scheme. According to it, education should involve the training of both body and mind. It should also prepare the child for some future profession by teaching him agriculture or a craft. This education would have an important intellectual content also. As envisaged by Gandhi and Zakir Husain, it would contain all subjects that are taught in the usual modern schools. But there would be two differences: all knowledge would be imparted through the medium of the mother tongue; and all care would be taken to relate the intellectual content to the practical skills that were being taught. Science and mathematics were to be imparted as explaining principles of their crafts or other activities. In addition, children were to be encouraged to read and think on their own.[56]

Of course, Gandhi's conception of productive activities was ultra-conservative, and cannot be accepted in the present-day world. But the central message of the Nayee Taleem pattern is that education should develop and nurture the whole personality, and not merely the intellect. Also, by relating and utilizing knowledge to everyday activities children would be far better equipped to understand and appropriate that intellectual knowledge than in the usual system of education in which they are just expected to passively receive it and memorize it.

The latest National Curriculum Framework, 2005, developed by the National Council of Educational Research and Training (NCERT) says much the same thing. It emphasizes that the curriculum load on children must be reduced; knowledge should not be equated with filling the children's minds with more or less irrelevant information; education should be child-centred and not book centred; it should be connected to life outside schools; it must aim at the overall development of the child and not merely his or her mind; and education, at least in the early period, should be through the medium of the mother tongue; and so on.[57]

One thing is clear, however, and that is that education must not consist of mere imparting of information by the teacher and passive receiving by the pupils. Apart from theory, one can learn from experience of schools in India that such an education does not inspire any interest in the pupils and their entire aim in sitting in the class is to be able to memorize the matter being taught so that they can answer the questions in the examinations and pass them. Such an education cannot influence the personality of the student; it does not inspire him/her to understand and draw the implications of what is being taught, far less apply it in real life. For example, we see science graduates around us behaving in a very dogmatic way in real life, believing and acting according to astrology, numerology, and so on. The lessons of history rarely change our approach towards the society around us. Moral sense and the consciousness of social responsibility are very weak in us in spite of the relatively good education that Indian children receive, both in modern schools and madrasas. On the other hand, the more passive a learner is in the classroom, the greater are the chances that some of the negative aspects of the school curriculum will be interiorized without any critical thought. It is because it is easier to absorb others' (teacher's) attitudes than to develop a critical approach to the subject matter oneself.

Immanuel Kant, the most important thinker of the Western Enlightenment, conceived humans as rational beings. If we accept the Kantian conception of a human being, and it seems quite a reasonable one, it follows that the aim of education should be to help our children and youth realize their rational nature, or become fully rational persons. A rational person is one who thinks, speaks, and acts on the basis of sound reasons. It also means that he/she does not do what others—society or religious authority—tell him/her to do, but what his/her rational will (call it conscience) tells him/her to do. If this view sounds like extreme individualism, it is not so as this rational nature is shared by all human beings.[58]

This view implicitly accepts that reason is the most important dimension of a person. It may sound like narrow rationalism, long out of fashion. Here, the only reason in asserting that human beings are rational is to contend that education should train and strengthen the reasoning powers of children and the youth.

An educated youth must not be one who is ruled by prejudices, dogmas, or raw passions. He or she should be able to critically select the reasons of his/her conduct and must not give in to either the verdict of authority or to popular opinion. To enable the young minds to understand one's subject matter, to put it in the proper context or perspective, to appreciate it with a critical attitude, and then to make it one's own, so that the principles or information learnt so far will be at hand in future life, should be the aim of education. Education must transform a youth into a rational person, changing the way he/she thinks, understands, and reacts to the phenomena around him/her.

Education also imparts information. It is perhaps the most important task of the educator to select the material to be taught to the children out of the very vast storehouse of human knowledge and experience so far collected. Such an educational curriculum would definitely include mathematics, elementary logic, science, the social sciences like history and geography of one's own country and the world, as well as elementary civics or political science and economics. Of course, it is most important that what is taught should be in the correct perspective, without any historical or cultural bias.

This means that the development not only of rational personality but also the building of moral character of the future citizens of any society must be the concern of education. We agree with R.S. Peter that education means nothing if it does not consist in imparting or learning something thought to be worthwhile. The conception of what is worthwhile may differ from society to society and time to time. Or, we can enter into dialogue with different cultures, or at least with different sections of our populace, and reach some agreement as to what our children ought to be taught. Personally, I do not believe in the cultural relativism of the extreme kind, expounded by the postmodernists in the West. I rather think that there are certain sociomoral values, such as truthfulness, not hurting others (Gandhi's ahimsa), equality, fraternity and justice; and certain fields of worthwhile information, such as mathematics and the sciences, including medical science, which cannot be relative to cultures (the level of knowledge is often relative to time, but not to culture), and are the common heritage of entire humankind. If that is so, then all humans deserve to know them, or rather all children ought to be taught these subjects.

We also agree with our Muslim scholars that education must make the children-youth more upright morally, honest, and dutiful towards others; that is, the moral uplift of the individual should be the main goal of education. As to moral education, it should never be imparted separately because then it simply becomes one more set of opinions to be learnt in order to pass the examination, and not something to be made one's own. Moral norms and values should not be like Whitehead's 'inert ideas'; rather they should be integrated with what is being taught. But whereas religion finds no place in the thesis of 'worthwhile' knowledge in Western thought, for Muslims it is the most important truth to be taught to the youngsters.[59] This latter view goes against the autonomy of ethics as asserted by Kant and almost all modern Western moral philosophers. However, we must admit that all world religions have understood ethics as integral to religion.

Of course, the characteristic features of every culture are its precious heritage which must also be taught. We do not envisage any conflict between the two, that is, the specific cultural heritage and the common human heritage, as it is not expected that any culture would be opposed to some universal moral values, as suggested above, and the knowledge of science and mathematics. Teaching of the social sciences presents greater difficulty as cultural and social biases often tend to distort the facts. But a way out will have to be worked out by social scientists themselves. There could be differences according to historical and cultural specificities of different societies, but not mutual conflicts.

There would be some conflict between what is called here the common heritage of humanity and those cultures that are based on religions, specifically those religions that claim to determine the entire life of the individual and society, as Islam. It would be pertinent to say here that the religion-centric nature of a given culture need not create any hurdles in the modern educational curriculum, as no religion would be opposed to the universal moral values, and almost all religions at their inception were not opposed to the level of scientific knowledge that was available at that time. The problem arises when the understanding of nature (science) as understood in the earliest version of that religion is taken to be the ultimate truth and whatever knowledge has been gained by humankind ever since is discarded.[60] Today even the conservative protagonists of religions mostly agree that science and its assertions have to be acknowledged and there is no necessary conflict between religion and science.

3.5. CAN MODERN EDUCATION BE COMBINED WITH RELIGIOUS EDUCATION?

We have seen earlier that imparting religious education to their future generations is valued by various religions, but the need for such an education in a detailed form is emphasized by Muslims more than others for various reasons. However, such a detailed religious education cannot be imparted in common secular schools. The very definition of the term 'secular' implies not the rejection of religion but the distancing of the government and other secular institutions from religion. The problem of providing religious knowledge in secular schools is further compounded by the fact that India is a multi-religious society, and if religious instruction is to be imparted at all, it would have to be about so many different religions. Perhaps it was due to these difficulties that Mahatma Gandhi, though an intensely religious person himself, was not in favour of including religious instruction in his scheme of education:

We have left out the teaching of religions from the Wardha scheme of education because we are afraid that religions as they are taught and practiced today lead to conflict rather than unity. But on the other hand, I hold that teachings that are common to all religions can and should be taught to all children.[61]

And,

I do not believe that the state can concern itself or cope with religious education. I believe that religious education must be the sole concern of religious associations.[62]

It seems that though Gandhi asserted that religion should be basic to all walks of life and even talked of the marriage between religion and politics, he did not want young minds to be encumbered with the details of different religious creeds. Here it can be noted that Indian thinkers have mostly asserted the commonalities between different religions, while the followers of Semitic religions have insisted on the uniqueness of various religions. Therefore, the values common to all religions and cultures that he wanted to be imparted to children would have to be mostly moral values.

Maulana Abul Kalam Azad, however, did not agree with the exclusion of religious education from the proposed scheme of universal education. He regarded religious education as imperative for the development of a child's personality. According to him, 'If national education was devoid of this element there would be no appreciation of moral values, of moulding of character on humane lines'.[63]

For Gandhi and Azad, character building of children and youth was of primary importance. The difference between the two lies only in the fact that while Gandhi believed that the truths and values common to all world religions alone should be taught, Azad wanted specific religious instruction also to be included. Interestingly, the latter opined that religious education imparted in private institutions (e.g., madrasas) makes people narrow-minded. Therefore, the government itself should take up the responsibility of imparting religious instructions. Here obviously he meant religious education of different specific religions. This is an impractical suggestion. It is not clear as to what Azad meant by compulsory religious education in secular schools. He could not have meant the detailed knowledge of religions, as such a detailed knowledge would involve the entire time and energy of the students. He was also aware of the religious plurality of Indian society. Imparting detailed religious knowledge of all these religions to different groups of students in thousands of public schools spread in every nook and corner of India would have been an impossible task. If Azad had meant only a general type of religious education, even that might not have been possible in a secular framework. But it seems he was suggesting a detailed knowledge of all those religions followed by the myriads of Indians, which is a very naïve idea.

4. 'MODERN', 'MODERNITY' AND 'MODERNIZATION'

4.1. THE CONCEPTS OF 'MODERN' AND 'MODERNITY'

The modern period began with the Renaissance in the West. It was characterized by a revolt against medieval scholasticism (though not against Christianity) and an assertion of humanism. Francis Bacon (sixteenth century) heralded the scientific spirit of free inquiry, and Rene Descartes (seventeenth century) reintroduced rationalism or the method of deductive reasoning as the surest means of indubitable knowledge. However, the real beginning of the modern period started with the Enlightenment (eighteenth century). John Locke, Voltaire, Pierre Bayle, Jaques Rousseau, etc., became the pioneers of the Enlightenment culminating in the philosophy of Immanuel Kant (eighteenth century).

Locke (seventeenth century), David Hume (eighteenth century) and Immanuel Kant (eighteenth century) made epistemology the basis of philosophy. Before asserting anything about the world or oneself with certainty, one must know how one reached that knowledge and whether one can defend and justify it rationally.

The modern spirit ever since the Renaissance has been chiefly a spirit of revolt against all authority and the medieval mindset, its conceptions, social structure, and institutions. It has been one of self-assertion of the human mind and the right of humans to live their own life without interference either from the Church or from old prejudices. It expresses full confidence in the human capacity to understand life and nature, and solve their problems on their own. In addition to the intellectual problems of knowledge, the Enlightenment thinkers were further interested in liberty, especially liberty of conscience, and equal opportunity for and equality of all human beings before the law. Without going into the details of the philosophical thought and *Weltanschauung* of modernity as represented by the Enlightenment, the following can be stated as the characteristics of modernity:

1. It represents the quest for indubitable certainty and objectivity of knowledge (of this world). There were two schools of thought: the empiricists such as Bacon, Locke, and Hume men-

tioned above, and the rationalists such as Descartes, Leibniz, and Hegel. At the same time the two agreed on several points. For example, if by rationalism one means the attitude that makes reason instead of revelation or authority the standard of knowledge, all modern systems of thought are rationalistic; indeed it is this characteristic that makes them qualify as modern. Or, if one understands rationalism as the view that genuine knowledge consists of universal and to some extent necessary judgements, even then most modern thinkers would agree with the contention.

Similarly, if by empiricism one means that one's world of experience is the object of philosophy, then all modern philosophy is empirical, barring perhaps the metaphysical systems of a Leibniz or a Hegel. If one means by empiricism that one cannot know unless one's knowledge is grounded in experience, that pure thought or thought absolutely independent of experience is impossible, then again modern thought is largely empirical. These two schools of thought differ only in their assertions as to the origins of knowledge, whether it is experience or reason. Here we need not bother about the intricacies of these schools of thought. Kant sought to synthesize the two, and gradually it came to be accepted that a combination of the two—experience (observation and experimentation) and reason—is the source and basis of valid knowledge.

2. The Enlightenment rationalists, and later modern thinkers, are further convinced about the universality of reason, that is, reason is universally shared by humankind. Kant declared that all humans are essentially rational beings, and that 'rational nature exists as an end in itself'. Also, the truths arrived at through rational methods are true for every time and place. That means what is true for one would be true for others also, and vice versa.

3. It is important to note that for almost all modern thinkers it is this world (phenomena in Kantian terminology) which alone is the real object of knowledge, and not the other world (*noumena* or things in themselves for Kant). Interestingly, all world religions would agree with this contention, as God and other related subjects are a matter of 'revelation' (or inner experience in Indian religions) and not of empirical knowledge.

4. Modern thought, as inspired by the Enlightenment, is con-

vinced of the rule of law in nature and stresses their (laws') knowledge through scientific approach so that nature can be harnessed for the welfare of humankind. Semitic religions should have no problem with this approach, as nature, including the animal world, is created by God, according to them, for the use of human beings. (Religions of Indian origin have a different view on the matter.)

5. Enlightenment-inspired modern approach further expresses a revolt against tradition and traditional authority. Moreover, it stresses that the individual, and not the community, is the locus of both reason and human rights. That is, the criterion for judging what is true or false comes not from traditional thinking and norms but from universal reason which is exercised by every rational human being. Also, human rights do not belong to the community as citizens and serfs, or brahmans and shudras in the past, but to the individuals as rational beings.[64] Human rights, like human reason, are universal and distinctions of culture, community, or even religion are irrelevant to the assigning of human rights.

The chief values of the Enlightenment are freedom and equality of all humans. Though equality was declared rather conditionally by Locke, Hobbes, and Rousseau, it was given a rational grounding in Kant's philosophy. Adam Smith (eighteenth century) declared that each man is to count for one and no one is to count for more then one. J.S. Mill (nineteenth century) emphasized the freedom of the individual as almost an absolute value. By freedom or liberty Mill mostly meant freedom of thought which could challenge both the authority of tradition and the tyranny of majority opinion.[65] There is a certain conflict between the values of equality and liberty which conflict is almost central to the modern Western societies, but it is not possible to enter into its details here.

The above approach seems to be raw individualism, but it is not so. Its main contention is that the locus of human rights is the individual and not the community, and the latter is also the judge of what is wrong or right. Modern thought never denies the responsibility of the individual to the society. According to Kant, the fact that every individual is an end in his/her self also means that every individual must respect all others as ends in themselves; and that together they constitute a kingdom of ends. That is to say, the values of equality and freedom (autonomy in Kantian language) do not come in the way; rather they provide a firmer foundation for a more harmonious society.

5. SOME CONCLUDING REMARKS

The above discussion has put forward certain ideas. First, the term society must mean the entire nation-society, at least in the Indian context. The differences of religion and region, sub-cultures, languages, etc., do not make us a group of nationalities. Rather these differences make up the mosaic of a multi-religious, multilingual plural nation-society.

Second, religion is a very complex phenomenon, which is impossible to understand in a few pages. Inasmuch as our main interest here is in Islam, we can generally say that it regards itself as possessing God's final 'revelation', as well as being a comprehensive whole which includes not only the Holy Quran but also the *sunna* as recorded in the *hadiths*. As such, religious education is more important and detailed for Muslims, especially the orthodox ones.

Third, education is imparting knowledge to the students in such a way that they can relate it to everyday life and use it in their future life. Education also aims at developing the rational powers of the youth and making them capable of independently taking their decisions in future life. Modern education only deals with this world, and seems not to have any place for religion.

The Islamic conception of education is different. It emphasizes the need to follow the precepts of Islam, and learn through education to be a true Muslim. Building of moral character is very important in Islam. Of course, there can be no doubt about the need to build the moral character of students, as also the fact that somehow modern education has failed to produce morally upright citizens. The crucial issue is whether detailed religious education is needed for providing a motivation for practising moral values, as Islam thinks, or can moral values be imparted to children and youth without recourse to religious beliefs, as Western thinkers believe. Alternatively, can they be introduced to certain common ideas of all faiths and thereby be inspired to be morally upright citizens? In present times we are witnessing a total decline in moral values in the subcontinent, while at the same time there is a great upsurge of outward religiosity everywhere in all religious communities. This dilemma is left for the discerning reader to understand and find a solution.

Fourth, as regards the conception of modernity, which needs to be understood in the context of the projects for the 'modernization' of madrasas, we have here taken the Western approach, as modernity is all about the values of the Renaissance and Enlightenment periods, as well as the liberalism of the nineteenth century. These values are rationality, freedom, and autonomy of the individual, as well as the values of justice, and an unconditional equality of all human beings.

The essence of education is to impart worthwhile things to the young minds. Two questions arise. First, how does one decide what is worthwhile to be included in the curriculum of education? Second, can religion be included in the education system of a secular state, even if one accepts that religion is the most worthwhile thing to impart?

In spite of the assertion by the postmodernists to the contrary, we firmly believe in the common humanity of all human beings belonging to different races, cultures and religions. We also believe that dialogue between different cultures is possible, that it has been carried out throughout the history of humanity. If dialogue could exist between people of such diverse cultures and languages as Sanskrit–Pali and Chinese in the context of the spread of Buddhism to eastern countries; if Arab intellectuals could achieve a unique synthesis of Greek and Islamic philosophy during the days when distant travel was so rare, how can there not be successful dialogue between modern cultures and cultures based on religion as that of Islam, when the world has shrunk to a village due to mass means of communication? And once dialogue is established, there are good possibilities of arriving at a certain consensus regarding scientific truths, and even common human values. This is truer of subcultures within one nation-society, such as India's. We believe that we can arrive at consensus of what our children, the future citizens of India, should be taught.

But the most crucial issue of the study remains—the Muslims' special need for religious education, and the related question of whether detailed religious education is necessary for all Muslim children. The final and a very important question would be that if a certain amount of religious education is required for every Muslim child, how should it be arranged so that he/she gets it without foregoing his or her normal, i.e. modern, education?

In view of the above, we have to acknowledge that here is a genuine problem in the national goal of achieving universal education. Since government schools and even private modern schools in a secular socio-political set-up cannot impart religious education, does it mean that Muslim children must go to madrasas only, and they cannot learn modern knowledge? Alternatively, can all madrasas be modernized to the extent that they can teach modern subjects to the level of common schools? Above all, since we do not believe in our children studying in separate educational institutions from the beginning to the end, we seem to have reached an impasse. We hope that it is not so. The above spells out the real issues of this study. We expect to find some working solution to this problem in the course of our study.

NOTES

1. R.M. MacIver and Charles H. Page, *Society: An Introductory Analysis*, London: Macmillan, 1961, p. 6.
2. Ibid., p. 7.
3. See Daniel Bell, *Communitarianism and its Critics*, Oxford: Clarendon Press, 1996, chapter V: 'A Discussion about the Value of Language-Based Communities, Gay Community, and the Family', pp. 156 ff.
4. There is a large number of theories regarding what society means. A comprehensive and balanced definition is found in a lesser known work, *Chamber's Encyclopaedia*, New Edition, London: Newnes Ltd., 1963, vol. XII, pp. 670–1. According to it 'A society is a system of interconnected actions, distributed over a determinate territory and maintaining an approximate identity of its main components through time.'
5. Jawaharlal Nehru, *The Discovery of India*, New Delhi: Oxford University Press, 1989, p. 392.

6. M.K. Gandhi, *Hind Swaraj or Indian Home Rule*, Ahmedabad: Navjivan Publishing House, 2001, pp. 42–3.

7. 'Why only two I do not know, for if nationality was based on religion, then there were many nations in India. Out of two brothers one may be a Hindu, another a Muslim; they would belong to two different nations. These two nations existed in varying proportions in most of the villages in India. They were nations which had no boundaries; they overlapped.' *The Discovery of India*, p. 392.

8. Quoted in Rajmohan Gandhi, *Understanding the Muslim Mind*, New Delhi: Penguin Books, rept. 1990, p. 238.

9. *Composite Nationalism and Islam* (*Muttahida Qaumiyat aur Islam*), tr. Muhammad Anwar Hussain and Hasan *Imam*, New Delhi: Manohar, 2005, pp. 47, 55, 103, etc. (These quotes are not found as such in the above translation, but the meaning is the same.)

10. Ibid., pp. 55, 58, 59, etc.

11. Ibid., p. 118.

12. Manzoor Ahmad, *Islamic Education: Redefinition of Aims and Methodology*, New Delhi: Qazi Publishers and Distributors, 1990, pp. 17–18. This view seems to separate out Indian Muslims from the rest of the nation. The further contention that Muslims face threat not only from the West but also from the East (obviously meaning non-Muslim Indians) is both sad and provocative.

13. If our secular historians are to be believed, then a sense of belonging together and sharing a common cultural space existed in medieval India, at least among the masses and those sections of the populace who were not directly under the influence of orthodoxy. See S.A.A. Rizvi, *The Wonder That Was India*, vol. 2, London: Sidgwick & Jackson, 1987, chapter 6. Volume 2 of his monumental work *The History of Sufism in India*, New Delhi: Munshiram Manoharlal, 1997 gives a detailed account of how Muslim and Hindu saints mingled together. See chapters 8 and 9 of the same work. Also see M. Mujeeb, *The Indian Muslims*, New Delhi: Munshiram Manoharlal, 1967, chapters 6, 7, 8.

14. [We use the term communalism] 'when some one demonstrates behaviourally an excessive commitment to his/her religious community [. . .] Second, we also use it to condemn what we take to be illegitimate use of the community, its resources, its symbol and its identity.' Raghavendra Rao, 'Secularism, Communalism and Democracy in India', in Bidyut Chakrabarty (ed.), *Secularism and Indian Polity*, New Delhi: Segment Book Distributors, 1990, p. 44.

15. 'Minorities in India, it must be remembered, are not racial or national minorities, as in Europe; they are religious minorities. Latterly religion in any real sense of the word has played little part in Indian political conflicts. [. . .] Religious differences as such do not come in the way, for there is a great deal of mutual tolerance for them. In political matters, religion has been displaced by what is called communalism, a narrow group mentality basing itself on a religious community.' *The Discovery of India*, p. 382.

16. The classical definition of communalism comes from Bipan Chandra: 'Simply put, communalism is the belief that because a group of people follow a particular religion they have, as a result, common social, political and economic interests.' He goes on to explain that such a mindset believes first, that all the secular interests of a large group are alike because of their common religious identity; and second, that these interests are 'naturally antagonistic, exclusive and incompatible' with those of other groups. Bipan Chandra, *Communalism in Modern India*, New Delhi: Vikas Publishing House, 1989, pp. 1–3, 12 ff. Cf. Asghar Ali Engineer, *Communalism and Communal Violence in India*, Delhi: Ajanta Publications, 1989, p. 189, etc.

17. See Saral Jhingran, *Secularism in India: A Reappraisal*, New Delhi: Har-Anand Publications, 2000, pp. 232 ff., 236 ff.

18. '[It is a] fact that Islam in India, past and present, unfolds a bewildering diversity of Muslim communities and that there is much variety in their social habits, cultural traits and occupational patterns. [. . .] Much of this discussion [of Muslim identity] tends to centre around imaginary and invented notions of Muslim cultural homogeneity and continuity.' Mushirul Hasan (ed.), *Islam Communities and the Nation: Muslim Identities in South Asia and Beyond*, New Delhi: Manohar, 1998, 'Introduction' by Hasan, pp. 16 and 14 ff.

19. Ibid., pp. 16 ff.; also see Mushirul Hasan, *Islam in the Subcontinent: Muslims in a Plural Society*, New Delhi: Manohar, 2002, pp. 41 ff., 54 ff.

20. Hasan, *Islam, Communities and the Nation*, p. 18.

21. See Hasan Ali, 'Elements of Caste among Muslims in a District of Southern Bihar', and Imtiaz Ahmad, 'Endogamy and Status Mobility among the Siddiqui Sheikhs of Allahabad, Uttar Pradesh', in Imtiaz Ahmad (ed.), *Caste and Social Stratification Among Muslims in India*, New Delhi: Manohar, 1978, pp. 19 ff.; and 171 ff.

22. See Jhingran, *Secularism in India*, pp. 223 ff.
23. It was a big project undertaken by the Anthropological Survey of India, and its results were published in several volumes under the title 'People of India National Series'. The chief editor of the series was K.S. Singh. He later wrote a small book presenting the summary of the project, published by the Anthropological Survey of India, 1994.
24. See Ninian Smart, *The Religious Experience of Mankind*, London: Collins, 1974, pp. 11 ff.
25. Ibid., p. 21.
26. See Saral Jhingran, *The Roots of World Religions*, New Delhi: Books and Books, 1982, chapters 1 and 5, especially pp. 12 ff., 140 ff.
27. Margaret Chatterjee is strongly opposed to any, even minor, changes in the language, liturgy or the cultural milieu of a religion. In her own words, 'If we say as [Reymond] Panikkar does, that Christianity [. . .] is not a culture, we seem to be saying that there is a culture-free core which is available for 'sowing' in different kinds of environment. Religious conceptions in any case do not travel in a disembodied manner.' *The Religious Spectrum: Studies in an Indian Context,* New Delhi: Allied, 1984, p. 191.
28. Smart, op. cit., p. 31.
29. 'Besides the vertical lines suggested by the several traditions set side by side, there are horizontal lines as types of patterns of religious life and thought are traced across the board, cutting through the lines separating one religion from another.' H.D. Lewis and Robert Lawson Slater, *World Religions: Meeting Points and Various Issues*, London: C.A. Watts and Co., 1966, p. 7. This is also the view of S. Radhakrishnan, Mahatma Gandhi and Maulana Azad. The idea here is that the complex and multi-dimensional nature of religions results both in sharp divisions between various religions, as also provides meeting points between them. Religious experience is one such meeting point. I have argued this idea in detail in my earlier work, *The Roots of World Religions*, chapters 1, 5 and 7, pp. 1ff., 126 ff., 210 ff.
30. See Arnold Toynbee, *An Historian's Approach to Religion*, New York: Oxford University Press, 1979, pp. 262–70.
31. See Rajmohan Gandhi, op. cit., pp. 231–3.
32. Toynbee, op. cit., pp. 132 ff., 135 ff., 250–1.
33. 'Truth is the exclusive property of no single scripture.' Mahatma Gandhi, *Young India*, 25 Sept0ember, 1924. 'The one religion is

beyond all speech. Imperfect men put it into such language as they can command, and their words are interpreted by other men equally imperfect. Whose interpretation is to be held to be true?' Gandhi, as given in *Gandhi Reader for 1988*, ed. M.V. Desai, New Delhi: Namedia Foundation, p. 35.

34. 'Two diametrically opposite viewpoints can tolerate each other, but they cannot be expected to respect each other.' Maulana Akhalaq Ahmad Qasmi, quoted in Mushir-Ul-Haq, *Islam in Secular India*, Simla: Indian Institute of Advanced Study, 1972, p. 17; also see his discussion of the Islamic position, pp. 16 ff.

35. Azad, quoted in Muktishree Ghosh, *Concept of Secular Education in India*, New Delhi: B.R. Publishing Corporation, 1991, p. 124.

36. Quoted in Mohd. Sharif Khan, *Education, Religion and Modern Age*, New Delhi: Ashish Publishing House, 1990, p. 28.

37. Quoted in ibid., pp. 37–8.

38. Immanuel Kant, *Fundamental Principles of the Metaphysics of Morals*, tr. Thomas K. Abbott, Indianapolis: The Library of Liberal Arts, 1984, pp. 45–6, 49–50.

39. J.S. Mill, *On Liberty and other writings,* ed. Stefan Collini, Cambridge: Cambridge University Press, 1989, pp. 105–8, 131, etc.

40. Quran 96: 1–5; *The Meaning of the Glorious Koran*, tr. Marmaduke Pickthall, Delhi: World Islamic Publications, 1979.

41. Mohd. Sharif Khan quotes several *hadiths* describing how the Prophet valued knowledge, even declaring it higher than mere ritualistic performance of religion. See Khan, *Education, Religion and Modern Age*, pp. 13 ff.

42. See Leila Ahmad, *Women and Gender in Islam: Historical Roots of a Modern Debate*, London: Yale University Press, 1992, chapters 3, 4 and 5. Her views will be discussed in chapter 5.

43. See the long paper by Asma Afsaruddin, 'Muslim Views on Education: Parameters, Purview, and Possibilities', *Journal of Catholic Legal Studies*, vol. 44: 143, p. 154.

44. Quoted in Syed Ameer Ali, *The Spirit of Islam*, New Delhi: Low Price Publications, 1990, p. 37.

45. See Asma Afsaruddin, 'Muslim Views on Education', pp. 150 ff. 158 ff.

46. See ibid., pp. 153 ff.

47. See ibid., pp. 166–7.

48. See ibid., pp. 157–8.

49. According to Afsaruddin, during at least the tenth and eleventh

centuries the culture of free thinking was supreme 'which held that philosophy, rather than religion was the ultimate guide to perfect conduct'. Ibid., pp. 161–2.

50. See Ameer Ali, op. cit., pp. 365 ff.; and Afsaruddin, op. cit., pp. 150 ff., 161 ff.

51. Hani A. Tawil, 'Al-Ghazzali 1058–1111', in Joy A. Palmer (ed.), *Fifty Major Thinkers on Education: From Confucius to Dewey*, London: Routledge, 2001, pp. 29 ff.

52. See Peter Hobson, 'Aristotle 384–322 B.C.', in ibid., pp. 14 ff. Also see Arthur Bestor, 'Education for Intellectual Discipline', in Philip H. Phenix, *Philosophies of Education*, New York: John Wiley & Sons, 1962, pp. 37 ff.

53. See John Dewey, 'Interest, Discipline, Method and Subject Matter in Education', in William K. Frankena, *Philosophy of Education*, New York: Macmillan Publishing Co., 1965, p. 65 and pp. 53 ff.

54. A.N. Whitehead, 'The Aims of Education', in ibid., pp. 26 ff.

55. R.S. Peters, *Ethics and Education*, London: Allen & Unwin, 1966, p. 25.

56. For a description of the Wardha Scheme of Elementary education see Muktishree Ghosh, *The Concept of Secular Education in India*, pp. 99 ff., also see 'Basic Education and Education for All', at http://www.ncert.nic.in/intro.htm which gives the conception and development of Wardha Scheme.

57. Draft, *National Curriculum Framework 2005*, N.C.E.R.T.

58. Kant, op. cit., pp. 44 ff., especially pp. 46, 50–2.

59. According to al Ghazali, 'Education should be in the service of society and bring up people with high moral standards. [. . .] It [education] should be congruent with the saying of Muhammad.' Hani A. Tawil, op. cit., p. 32.

60. In a recorded interview with the *maulanas* of a reputed madrasa in Old Delhi, I was told that they could not introduce modern science as its assertions, like the solar centricity of the planets, go against the Quranic assertion of the geo-centricity of the world. However, other Islamic scholars have refuted this claim. Yet it is true that the demand for first Islamizing modern sciences before they are taught to madrasa children is a common one. See Shoyeb Ansari, *Education in Dini Madaris: An Opinion Survey*, New Delhi: Institute of Objective Studies, 1997, pp. 96 ff.

61. Quoted in Muktishree Ghosh, op. cit., p. 104.

62. *Harijan*, 23 March 1947, quoted in ibid., p. 124.

63. *Speeches of Maulana Abul Kalam Azad, 1947–55*, New Delhi: Publication Division, Ministry of Information and Broadcasting, 1955, pp. 24–6.

64. Kant, op. cit., pp. 45–6, 49–50; *The Doctrine of Virtue: Part II of The Metaphysics of Morals*, tr. Mary J. Gregor, New York: Harper Torchbooks, 1964, pp. 38 ff., 49-50, 62 ff.,115 ff.

65. *On Liberty and other writings*, pp. 105–7.

2

Reasons for Some Muslims'
Preference for Madrasa Education:
Trying to Understand the
Issues Involved

1. THE NEED FOR SUCH A STUDY

If we want to understand both the madrasa system of education and the relatively fast growth of madrasas all over India, we will have to understand the reasons for the preference of a large number of Muslims for madrasas over modern schools for the education of their children.

Here we may be questioned not only by *ulama* and people involved in madrasa education but also by secular Muslims. Generally it is affirmed that in actual fact very few Muslim children go to madrasas proper (though a large number may be going to maktabs), and hence there is no point in making an issue about them. But so far nobody has been able to give some definite or even approximate figures about madrasas—how many of them exist throughout India, and what percentage of Muslim children go to them for their education. The estimates of Muslim scholars vary largely. While Ghulam Yahya Anjum puts the figure of madrasa-going children at 49 per cent and Fahimuddin estimates it at 36 per cent,[1] there are others who declare that only 1 per cent Muslim children go to madrasas.[2] Now the Sachar Commitee Report on the *Social, Economic and Educational Status of Muslim Community of India* has asserted that madrasa-going children are approximately 4 per cent, while if one considers children of school-going age only, it is about 3 per cent.[3] This is probably not an exact estimate. Of course, challenging the Sachar Committee Report's figures is not based on any personal research on an all-India level on my part, but rather on the general impression gained on visits to Muslim majority areas in and around Delhi and some in Lucknow.

Moreover, the feedback received from frequent talks with madrasa graduates, now studying in Jawaharlal Nehru University or those who have roots in villages, puts the number of madrasa-going children at much higher percentage than that of the Report. Generally they estimate that at least in villages about 12 to 15 per cent of Muslim children go first to maktabs than to madrasas, if only for a few years.

Roughly, the number of madrasas, other than maktabs, is estimated to be 30,000. Liberal Muslims think that it could be higher. Therefore, a study of madrasas in the context of Muslims' participation in and contribution to national life and their own progress does not seem to be uncalled for. Even if one accepts the estimate of the Sachar Report, that is 3–4 per cent of more than 13 per cent of the Indian population, the numbers are still substantial.

Some Muslim academics state that 'poor' Muslim parents send their children to madrasas (here they include both maktabs and madrasas) because 'Muslims have no other option'. Why do they think that? Does it mean that Muslim children have no access to modern schools? The Sachar Committee has contended that it is so, but has not given any figures to support its contention. The impression that Muslim majority areas do not have sufficient modern schools persists without any attempt to support it with well-researched figures. According to one such writer,

Given what is said to be the dismal level of Muslim access to education, and the anti-Muslim bias that has been incorporated into the curricula of government schools, madrasas are often the only available educational option for children from poor Muslim families. Madrasas have thus been playing an important role in promoting literacy among the Muslims, who have the distinction of being the least educated and deprived community in India.[4]

Even some liberal and secular scholars have asserted that:

Rejection of Urdu, the discrimination in gaining admissions, non-recognition of minority institutions, the unsecular school culture, the textbooks which contain material repugnant to beliefs of Muslims and their inherent bias [...] have been perceived by Muslims in India to be a threat to their identity. This perhaps could be an important reason for Muslims opting out of education or else preferring to send their children to traditional centres of education.[5]

It may be taken for granted that the Muslims here are those who mostly belong to either the poor or the lower middle classes, as the parents belonging to middle or richer classes almost uniformly send their children to English medium private schools. It can also be taken for granted that a large proportion of the Muslim population is relatively underprivileged or poor. The task of the present study is to make some attempt at understanding the reality at the ground level and various issues of Muslim children's educational needs and their fulfilment.

Generally Muslims are acknowledged as poor and underprivileged, as well as educationally backward. But since the census till now did not give a community-wise analysis, the facts were sometimes exaggerated also. The Sachar Committee Report has now given definite data. According to it, 'As many as 25 per cent of Muslim children in the 6–14 age group have either never attended school or have dropped out.'[6] Further, 'The literacy rate of Muslims was 59.1 per cent. This is far below the national average (65.1 per cent).'[7]

The Committee however generally puts Scheduled Castes (SCs) and Scheduled Tribes (STs) below Muslims in literacy levels,[8] which goes against the general assertion that Muslims are lowest in all social indices. It also goes against some of the previous sample surveys.[9] Interestingly, the Report also points out that in as many as 10 states out of the 21 selected states, literacy rates among Muslims are higher than that of the states' average. These include Karnataka, Maharashtra, Andhra Pradesh, and Gujarat.[10] However, on the whole, 'The attainment levels of Muslims are close to or slightly higher than SCs and STs and much lower than those of other SRCs [Socio-Religious Categories].' It also affirms that as one goes to higher classes or even higher secondary levels, the representation of all three groups, especially Muslims, declines markedly.[11] This is so because Muslim children drop out of their schools either in the primary classes themselves, or after studying for one or two classes of secondary schools. Thus, according to the Sachar Committee Report, the mean years of schooling (MYS) of Muslim children is the lowest among all social groups.[12] What is worse, at some stage even the SCs and STs have improved their educational level to some extent, so that now Muslim children are lagging behind all other groups.[13]

It would be interesting to note here that before Partition, not only was the proportion of urban middle and landed classes among Muslims quite high, perhaps even greater than other religious communities, but their educational level was also higher than that of Hindus in many areas. Mushirul Hasan gives statistics regarding the relative representation of Muslims (presumably in north India) during the two years of Congress government in 1935–6, and argues that it was mostly higher in proportion to their relative population.[14]

Unfortunately, it was the Muslim middle class that alone migrated to Pakistan, the peasants, artisans and other Muslims who were rooted in the soil and well adjusted to the surrounding society did not think of leaving the land of their forefathers; and it is always the middle classes that value education the most. The result was that an overwhelming portion of the Muslim population that remained in India belonged to relatively socio-economically backward or underprivileged classes. They were left with few liberal leaders (educated in the modern system of education) and at the mercy of religious ones who were naturally not in favour of modern education which was likely to undermine their total hold on the Muslim masses. As Imtiaz Ahmad has observed:

[T]he educational backwardness among Muslims is due not so much to their religious fanaticism or their acute minority complex, but rather to the small size of the social strata whose members can be expected to go in for education as normal activity.[15]

Why could the members of these classes not rise in social mobility? If one could free oneself from a communal point of view, one would notice that the Indian character, perhaps that of all humans, is basically traditional or conservative. That is, the law of inertia is generally inherent in all social structures. Social mobility takes place only through individuals and families, which in the long run includes in its sweep the neighbourhood or community. No such social mobility took place till almost the nineteenth century even in the West. In less developed countries like India, this inertia, and as we shall see, the retrograde influence of the neighbourhood or community played a prominent role in dragging down the individual's or family's socio-educational ambitions and mobility.

2. THE ECONOMIC DEPRIVATION OF MUSLIMS: SOME ESTIMATES AND FACTS ABOUT POVERTY AND RELATED ISSUES

2.1. POVERTY OF MUSLIMS

The most frequently cited reason for Muslims' preference for madrasa education rather than a modern one is their extreme poverty. It is contended that Muslims being extremely poor cannot afford even a minimum expenditure on the education of their children. Generally it is simply said that being too poor, Muslim parents cannot send their children to any schools other than madrasas, as the latter not only do not charge any fees, but they also do not expect any expenditure on uniforms and books, and even provide food, clothes and hostel accommodation.

Though so far such assertions were made on vague, often exaggerated estimates, the Sachar Committee Report has apparently confirmed the earlier estimates. According to the Sachar Committee, the unemployment rates of Muslims are higher than other social groups, and their representation in high-salaried jobs is very low. The participation of Muslims in security jobs or high-salaried jobs in both public and private sectors is minimal.[16] Even the work participation of Muslims in larger industries and other market jobs of the formal sector is generally low. Muslim workers are most often engaged in self-employment in traditional manufacturing and trade, or they work as low-salaried labour.[17] On the indices of wealth and consumption, Muslims are lowest in all social groups. A substantially large proportion of Muslim households come under what is known as the BPL (below poverty line) category. There has been no determinate criterion to judge the level that divides those who belong to the BPL category and the rest of the population; it generally refers to the poorest sections of society. The Report concludes that the incidence of poverty among Muslims in urban areas is highest, even though this extreme inequality is relatively lower in rural areas.[18]

The National Council for Applied Economic Research Study, (NCAER), 1999, has also recorded lower household and per capita income among Muslim households compared to other religious communities. Azra Razzack and Anil Gumber have given a detailed analysis of household incomes and per capita consumption among different religion-based groups. At the same time if one goes into the details of the Study, the difference between the two religious groups is either marginal, or varies from region to region and on the basis of different indices.[19] Very generally speaking, it can be said that Muslims are relatively poorer and educationally backward as compared to other religious communities. The majority of Muslim families in rural areas do not own land and work in farms on daily wages. Many of them are petty craftsmen or traders. Since with rapid industrialization the market for the products of handicrafts is dwindling fast, those who were so far employed as craftsmen are also turning into wage earners. Muslims are also educationally among the most backward communities in India. These facts have been confirmed by many studies, including those of Razzack and Gumber and Sachar Committee.

Jyotsna Jha and Dhir Jhingran have taken up five villages of three of the most backward states—Uttar Pradesh, Bihar, and Assam—for a study of the correlation between poverty and backwardness in (modern) education. They observe that the proportion of BPL families in the total Muslim population is about 40 per cent in those districts at least. Even the upper-caste Muslims have 32.7 per cent families below the poverty line. About 40 per cent of the Muslim families from all groups are landless, while both parents are illiterate in 80 per cent of the lower-caste Muslim households. This proportion of both poverty and illiteracy among Muslims is higher in all social groups. Being landless, most of the families either work in the farms as labourers, or cultivate land on the basis of sharing the crop. They are out of work during the season when there is no farm work, these periods being often quite long. Sometimes whole families migrate to the cities in search of work, but most often only the males of the family go to cities or other places in search of a livelihood. In addition, excessive poverty, deprivation, and the consequent ill health of either children or parents adversely affect the participation of Muslim children in schooling.[20] Children's education is probably the worst affected in this scenario of poverty and deprivation. In the five villages, the overall enrolment rate of Muslim children at 51.6 per cent is the lowest among all social groups. Worse still, only about 38 per cent of the enrolled children are reportedly regular in school attendance. This proportion is even lower than that of SC and ST children. In all, about one-fifth (19.3 per cent) of Muslim children attend school regularly. The dropout rate of Muslim children is also the highest amongst all social groups.[21] Significantly, about 18 per cent of Muslim children attend maktabs/madrasas for their education in the districts studied by Jha and Jhingran. There are some children who get enrolled in school but attend only maktabs; very few of them attend both.[22]

However, this particular description of poverty among Muslims need not be taken as the 'truth' about Muslims in general, as Jha and Jhingran's aim was to study the educational status of the poorest and other deprived groups, and naturally they selected the districts that were already declared as being among the poorest and most underdeveloped districts in India. It should also be remembered that even though the particular chapter of the study refers only to Muslims, the remaining population of the districts studied is equally poor and disadvantaged, as the authors have repeatedly acknowledged.

Economic hardship is the root cause of many problems. If a family is not sure of where its next meal will come, or if it comes at all, it can hardly think of the education of its children. It is a question of priorities. Long ago, Swami Vivekananda declared that you cannot give religion to the hungry, as for them bread is their religion. Substitute education for religion, and the result is the same.

A major reason for the non-attendance or irregular attendance of children in schools, or a very high dropout rate among the children of economically underprivileged families, is the annual migratory routine. In the villages those who are either engaged in share-cropping or work as farm labourers are out of work for long periods when there is no farm work. Their meagre incomes not being sufficient to carry them through the lean period, they often migrate to nearby cities in search of work. There is also an opposite migration from cities to villages. The village people who work in industries, big or small, and live in slums are mostly homesick, and whenever they are out of work or there is some family need they go back to their villages. Children's school days are not their prime concern. Such frequent visits to villages or to cities disrupt the children's schooling, and generally they do not rejoin schools on their return. Here it must be remembered that though we are discussing the situation of Muslims alone, these are exactly the conditions of all landless labourers, and daily wage earners, whatever religion or caste they may belong to.

Azra Razzak and Anil Gumber have made two very interesting observations. First, 'There also does not appear any relationship between income and literacy levels of Muslims in the five states (studied by them).' They also contend that this non-correlation between poverty and education is true for both Muslims and Hindus.[23] Second, it is quite possible that those Muslim parents who cannot afford private schools could still have sent their children to government schools had they more confidence in them. In a very significant observation, the authors point out that a larger number of Hindus (70 per cent), SCs (71 per cent) and STs (67 per cent) than Muslims (49 per cent) go to government schools. A larger percentage of Christians and Muslims go to aided or even private schools. The percentage of Muslim children who go to private schools (13.3 per cent) is highest among all social groups. However, in Kerala and West Bengal more Muslims go to government schools as against the three northern states, which indicates a lack of confidence or faith in the government schools in these states.[24]

It appears that the assertion that 'the poor Muslims have no other option but to send their children to madrasas', does not reveal the whole truth about the complexities of the ground reality. It is strange that there is constant discussion of the financial difficulties of Muslims due to which they are unable to send their children even to government schools where expenditure is minimum, and yet the percentage of Muslims sending their children to expensive private schools (13 per cent) is much higher than that of other religious communities.

2.2. THE ROLE OF THE FAMILY IN CHILDREN'S EDUCATION

Generally fathers leave home and go to cities in search of work, leaving mothers to cope with all household responsibilities. In the absence of the father and with the mother being constantly busy in other responsibilities, it becomes easier for children to abscond from schools.

Of course, economic hardship affects children's education in other ways also. Not all poor live a hand-to-mouth existence. And yet all BPL families and most of those marginally above the poverty line have to work very hard to earn their livelihood. Womenfolk either work outside their homes or have large families to attend to. In the absence of the fathers they have to bear the double responsibility involved in the running of a household. Therefore, they have neither the time nor the inclination to worry about children's education, or even their whereabouts. Most children in slums or villages spend all their time in roaming the lanes or playing in extremely unhygeinic surroundings. They play among the garbage and squalour surrounding the slums, especially the Muslim ghetto areas and even village *bastis*. They spend very little time at home, as the home is mostly a small, single cluttered room with hardly any windows and no bathroom.

Generally speaking, this holds good for all families, whatever religious community they may belong to, who happen to belong to the extremely underprivileged category. There is a big difference, though, that unfortunately the relative number of such families is higher among Muslims than other groups, excepting, of course, the SCs and STs whom the Sachar Committee has constantly kept at par with the Muslims. The compulsion of wearing the veil sometimes adds to the woes of Muslim women; but most women of the poor classes do not generally adopt the *purdah*. Still, for various sociological reasons, as reported by the Sachar Committee, the work participation of Muslim women is much lower than that of other groups. That may be increasing the level of poverty among the poorer sections of Muslims.

Sometimes these children are admitted in local schools. But for various reasons their attendance becomes irregular, and finally they drop out of school altogether. Parents, or rather mothers (as Indian fathers take even less interest in their offsprings) do not pay much attention to whether the children have gone to school or, having started for school, stopped midway.

However, one need not concentrate on BPL families alone, though their living conditions are of greater concern for the overall welfare of the children. While a relatively large percentage of the Muslim population belongs to the BPL category, the rest of the population is distributed along the wider spectrum of different economic groupings, concurrent with the rest of the Indian population.

Parents belonging to the lower middle class are more ambivalent regarding the choice between the two systems of education for their children. While in villages and small towns, this choice is heavily tilted towards madrasa education, in the cities school is a very important option. In fact, factors other than poverty influence the decision of this class. The proporation of parents in this economic category who send their children to either of the institutions is about fifty-fifty, depending upon these other factors. Often the Muslims belonging to lower or marginal middle classes send their children to both school and maktab (either morning or evening). They understand the worth of modern education, but are also eager to give their children religious education. It is also found that the category of small traders or craftsmen, who are relatively better off economically, are more conservative in their outlook and are even more particular about their religious identity.

The family plays a strong role in the decision whether the children are to be sent to a madrasa, school, or neither. In Indian extended families, among both Hindus and Muslims, grandparents or even other elderly relations have a strong say in family matters, including children's education. This culture is fast disappearing from big cities but is still prevalent in the rest of India, especially in the towns and villages of the North. Grandfathers, who are either illiterate or have studied in madrasas, insist upon children going to madrasas for their study. There is no other reason for this insistence except the inherently conservative or traditionalist human nature that makes the old people assert that, 'If madrasa education was good enough for us, it should be good enough for our children'.

The size of the family is equally important. In larger families there are so many other concerns relating to various members of the family and their problems or even diversions, as child birth marriage or illness of someone in the family, that children's education is often neglected. Families can be divided according to their size into small, middle, and large. In large or very large families of both Hindus and Muslims, women and children are neglected and children's education and general development suffer the most. They fare better in middle-size families, and are best cared for in small families. Generally, larger families prefer madrasa education for their children because first, the presence of elders ensures a traditional approach to all practical issues, including children's education; and second, the fewer number of hours of attendance required, as well as the informal nature of madrasas, makes them a more viable option for their children, as it leaves them free for other family engagements for the rest of the day.

Moreover, children's education and general welfare are inversely proportional to the number of children per family. The greater the number of children, the fewer the chances of their overall development being taken care of properly by their parents. In families with a relatively large number of children, elder siblings, especially girls, are regularly made to look after their younger siblings, and that leaves no time for school. Sometimes they may continue in maktabs with irregular attendance. Nuclear families with two, three children are in the best position to take care of their children's education and future prospects.[25]

Parents' educational status is often responsible for the level of education of their children. Illiterate parents are usually not bothered about educating their offspring. 'What would they gain by going to school, as in the end they would have to work as labourers or farmers as we do?' Or, they enrol their boys and girls in schools, but being uninterested in education themselves, do not bother whether they go to school at all or not.

Mothers' education level is often even more important. There is a very deep-rooted bias against girls' higher education among Indian masses of all religious communities, the popular argument being that in the end they have to be married and look after the home and hearth in which all this theoretical education

would be of no help. And yet generally girls study more and
even go up to relatively higher classes than boys. Boys, being
pampered in Indian homes, are more apt to take things lightly,
and drop out of school easily, while girls persist. The Sachar
Committee has observed that as compared to males, Muslim
women's educational level is equal to the national average in
villages. Often mothers are educated to some substantial level,
while fathers are not. Such mothers, and even many uneducated
ones take the initiative in sending their children to school and
ensuring that they attend it regularly. However, in villages, girls
are educated mostly in madrasas. Madrasa-educated mothers
generally opt for a madrasa education for their sons and daughters. Some, when they are exposed to liberal influences through
anganwadi workers or some other NGO, may choose, in spite of
their madrasa background, school education for their children.
Unless there is a grandparental diktat, mothers can influence the
decision regarding children's education, as the males of Indian
families (fathers) are generally disinterested in family affairs (including children's education).

An important factor in this context is the family profession. A
large proportion of the economically disadvantaged Muslim families are engaged in small handicrafts and other family trades in
which their forefathers were engaged. In Uttar Pradesh and
Rajasthan, *bidi*-making and carpet-weaving are such handicrafts.
Children are often initiated in these crafts at an early age, which
puts an end to their schooling. Alternatively, many children of
poor families are employed as casual labour which leaves no
time for education.[26] Such families find modern education useless, as the refrain is always the same, 'What would they gain by
education since finally they would have to work for their living
as we do'. The cost-effectiveness of education is an important
factor in parental decisions regarding their children's education.
The masses, whether Muslim or Hindu, are generally convinced
that the minimum school education that is available in their
neighbourhood, or which they can afford, is not going to help
their children in any way to earn their livelihood.

Madrasa education is preferred by rural Muslims and those
engaged in hereditary crafts, because: First, those people who are
following their family profession and have not moved out of

their old environment are much more traditional and conservative and value religious education much more than their counterparts in cities. Second, madrasas being more or less informal institutions, children have sufficient time for the family profession. And third, madrasas, are often situated in or very near the locality itself; their *maulavis* are an integral part ot the community; therefore both children and parents feel more comfortable in the milieu of the madrasa.[27]

Families living in the cities, even those who belong to the migratory labour class are out of their ancestral milieu, and have come into contact with the wider society. These families, though they come under the category of BPL, do find a certain amount of education or formal schooling useful, and want their children to have it. They find it worthwhile for their children to have a modicum of modern knowledge which would include Hindi, a little English, and arithmetic which would make their transactions in the everyday world easier.[28]

3. THE PAUCITY OF MODERN SCHOOLS IN MUSLIM MAJORITY AREAS, SCARCITY OF GIRLS' SCHOOLS

3.1. NON-AVAILABILITY OF GOVERNMENT SCHOOLS IN MUSLIM MAJORITY AREAS

It is often argued that since economically underprivileged Muslims cannot afford to send their children to private modern schools which charge from moderate to high fees, and since there are very few government schools in the vicinity of Muslim majority areas, they have no option but to send their children to madrasas.

There are no definite statistics available for whether or not there are adequate government schools available in the Muslim majority areas at any disaggregated level. To study the adequacy or otherwise of physical access to schooling facilities, an internal study was undertaken by the ministry of Human Resource Development (HRD) in the districts which have been identified as having a higher proportion of Muslim population in 2006. For this purpose 86 districts with 20 per cent or more Muslim population (Census 2001) across the country were identified. The following indicators were used to assess the level of availability of educational facilities:

i. Number of government primary schools (classes I to V) per 1,000 population.
ii. Number of government-aided primary schools per 1,000 population.
iii. Number of government upper primary schools (classes VI to VIII) per 1,000 population.
iv. Number of government-aided upper primary schools per 1,000 population.

The information on schools was taken from the Districts Information System on Education (DISE) data of 2004–5. DISE is a huge database of a large amount of information regarding each of the approximately one million primary and upper primary schools in the country. Government-aided schools are included because they get grants of about 80 per cent of their cost, generally follow the state board curriculum and are not supposed to charge any tuition fees.

The values of the above indicators for high-Muslim-population districts were then compared to the state average for each of these indicators.

The study found that, in a total of 86 districts with the Muslim population higher than national average about half the districts had a fewer number of government or government-aided schools than the state average. The ratio of upper primary schools (from classes VI to VIII) shows a similar pattern as that of primary schools (classes I to V) in those districts. As its corollary, about half the number of districts have the same number of schools as the state average.

More importantly, the fact that in certain districts the number of schools is less than the state average does not mean that the lack of adequate number of schools refers only to Muslim majority areas and not to the rest of the areas in those backward districts, because invariably the same ratio of schools prevails in those areas of identified districts that do not have a Muslim majority in the population. This fact means that the reason for the fewer number of schools in those areas lies elsewhere other than that there are some relatively larger proportions of the Muslim population.

However, statistics can hardly tell the truth about very complex social realities. For example, the above conclusion on the basis of those statistics neglects the fact that in those districts the Muslim population is 20 per cent or little more, the rest of the population comprises either Hindus or other religious groups. Now, if schools are fewer in those districts, this fact adversely affects the educational opportunities of all children living in those districts. The scarcity of schools may not be related to the presence of a Muslim population but might be due to many other socio-political or administrative reasons. The districts that have fewer schools are mostly those that are acknowledged to be 'backward' on all scales of socio-economic development. Hence the lack of schools in them is a part of the overall deprived conditions of those districts.

Life and society are complex phenomena and should be understood holistically and not selectively. One more aspect of this argument, which is always overlooked, is that while Muslim children go to madrasas if there are no government schools in the vicinity, children of other religious communities are left without any educational institution.

If we must have the data on the availability of schools in Muslim majority areas, then two more detailed studies are also necessary. First, a study covering the districts under discussion must collect data not only at the district level but also at the block level in villages and at the level of small localities in cities. Of course, this is a near impossible task given the nation's large population, geographical spread and diversity. Second, there must be very detailed analytical data regarding the various dimensions of the backwardness of those districts, such as lack of development and industries, and that of infrastructure, such as roads, electricity, primary health centres, etc.

Then it is important to try to understand and analyse the causes of that local or district-level backwardness. They can be socio-political, economic (lack of industries and development) and even natural (frequent droughts or floods resulting in the spending of all state energies and resources in relief work), or geographical (the inaccessibility of the region). So far no statistics, not even those of the Sachar Committee, have proved that only the small pockets with definite Muslim concentration have been left without schools and economic development, while the rest of the surrounding areas have seen full development in all fields, including educational. On the contrary, the number of Muslim majority areas with relatively fewer schools includes districts in Maharashtra, Gujarat, Karnataka, Kerala, and Tamil Nadu, though according to the Sachar Committee, the literacy rate of Muslims is higher in these states than the state average.[29]

In order to arrive at some definite assessment of the overall situation not only do we need data on whether an adequate number of government or government-aided schools is available in Muslim majority areas, but also whether Muslim parents send their children to modern schools and not to madrasas, in areas where government and government-aided schools are available. So far, neither the number of madrasas in the country nor the number or percentage of Muslim children going to madrasas or modern schools are known. It would be too arbitrary to contend that most Muslim majority areas do not have government or government-aided schools; and that is why poor, neglected Muslim children have no other option but to go to madrasas.

Moreover, unless there is definite information regarding the Muslim children's attendance in modern schools in areas where government or government-aided schools are available; the number of madrasas in those areas; the number of madrasas in areas where government schools are scarce, and the percentage of Muslim children going to modern schools and those going to madrasas in those areas, we cannot arrive at any conclusion. Suppose the number of madrasas is more or less evenly distributed across the country, which is a more likely scenario, that is, we have madrasas with a large number of children attending them in areas where government or aided schools are available, then, can we still argue that Muslim children go to madrasas because they have no other option?

The point here is that the data should be very detailed as well as comprehensive, that is, covering all dimensions of a given life situation; one must not derive any conclusions from limited data. Those, who declare that Muslims send their children to madrasas and not modern schools because they have no other option are basing their argument on prejudice and not on facts.

We will further submit that if government or aided schools are fewer in Muslim majority areas, the duty of all concerned citizens, not of Muslims alone, should be to insist on the right of the people of that area to have proper government schools and to bring pressure on the state to correct the lapse immediately, and not merely to complain that poor Muslim children have no other option but to send their children to madrasas.

According to the government claims, in the past decade or so, there has been a tremendous expansion of educational facilities in every state of the country. The aim is to make available to every segment of the population proper government primary and upper primary schools within 1 km. Authorities of the Sarva Shiksha Abhiyan (SSA) assert that since 2004 about 1,00,000 primary and upper primary schools have been sanctioned throughout India, and most of them have started functioning already.

The central government has taken up the scheme of midday meal as an integral compulsory part of universal elementary education. This programme is claimed to have been a total success, that is, all government schools provide noon-time meals to their children.[30] This is an accomplishment worth acknowledging. Its aim is to attract or motivate really poor children to attend the school on a regular basis, and there is no reason why Muslim children should not benefit from this, or why this should not motivate them to attend government schools regularly, as it does in the case of underprivileged sections of other religion-based groups. (Of course, one cannot be sure of the extent to which this ambitious government programme has been successfully carried out throughout the length and breadth of this vast subcontinent.)

3.2. LACK OF SEPARATE GIRLS' SCHOOLS AND FEMALE TEACHERS IN COMMON SCHOOLS

Traditional Muslims believe in the need for segregation of the sexes and insist on strict observation of *purdah* by all females after puberty. Those who do not wear the *burqa* are expected to at least not mix freely with the males. They willingly allow girls to study till primary school, after which girls are not supposed to mix with boys. They rightly complain that there are very few separate government or government-aided middle and secondary schools for girls. Frequently, there are no female teachers in common government schools either who could ensure Muslim girls' safety.

The problem is genuine. Even Sayyid Ahmed Khan had to give in to the pressure of the orthodoxy and disallow co-education in his Mohammaden Anglo-Oriental College (now, of course, there is co-education in the Aligarh Muslim University). As we shall see in chapter 5 on *Shari'a*, the general Muslim view had been that girls do not need detailed education, especially a modern one, as they do not have to go outside for work. All that they need is some form of religious education so that they can read the Quran, and fulfil other requirements of being a true Muslim. They also need some instruction in being good wives and mothers. All this they can get in a girls' madrasa. In the nineteenth century there developed a liberal view that Muslim girls should also be given modern education. However, these Muslim liberals, like Sayyid Ahmed cited above, gave into the orthodox opinion that the two sexes should be segregated, and there should be separate schools and colleges for girls.

Given this Muslim belief, what can the state do to ensure that Muslim girls also get educated? Unfortunately, nothing much can be done about it at the present stage as already there are fewer upper primary or middle schools than primary schools, especially in the countryside. While the goal of having a primary school within 1 km of any habitat has almost been achieved, an equal number of upper primary or middle schools are not available in the vicinity of every habitat. Though boys in the villages walk for a longer distance to reach their school, it is inconvenient for girls to do so. The first goal of the SSA and the state governments is at present to open more middle schools to ensure that every child up to the age of fourteen gets an education. This goal will take quite some time to be fulfilled. Also, opening more higher schools in a hurry without sufficient resources and educated and trained teachers, as well as in view of the limited capacity of the government machinery, would result in a further fall in the standard of education provided in government or government-aided schools. In these circumstances, and also since the Muslim population is spread in every nook and corner of the country, it is impossible to establish separate middle and high schools near every habitat of this vast country. There are some separate girls' schools in towns and cities, but they cannot serve the entire Muslim population.

However, this does not absolve the government from its responsibility to ensure that Muslim girls get their constitutional right to education, or to ignore Muslim sensitivities. It may be pointed out here that in spite of religious differences, the cultural norms of any given region are similar in the entire society. That is to say, Hindus also do not want free mixing of sexes; they also do not want their girls to walk long distances alone, or to study in schools with a majority of boys and no female teachers. But they seem to have adjusted to the situation and often send their girls to common schools. But at the same time Muslim sensitivities also have to be considered.

At present, the only sensible thing that can be done is separate seating arrangements for boys and girls, which is even now the general norm. More importantly, the government must see to it that every school gets a few women teachers. At present, many women teachers, not finding it convenient to travel to village schools, manage to secure postings in city schools so that often there is no woman teacher in village schools. In view of the incidence of increasing sexual harassment of girls by male teachers, placing a few female teachers in every upper primary and secondary school is a necessity. This one fact alone would go a long way in reassuring the parents of girls.

Imtiaz Ahmad has suggested that if those middle schools that are situated at a distance from the village or hamlet are provided with a female *bai* (attendant) who could accompany girl students to school and back, it would greatly reduce the resistance to common schools. The above two suggestions can be implemented even at present without the need for further resources.

4. THE COST OF MODERN EDUCATION AND THE POOR QUALITY OF GOVERNMENT SCHOOLS

4.1. Cost of Modern Education

The second argument against the option of modern schools for their children before Muslim parents is that sending children even to government schools involves incurring expenditure on some, however minimal, fees, books, and uniforms, which poor Muslims cannot afford.

How far is this argument against the option of government schools correct? Since education is a state subject no generalizations can be made. The Central government, however, has taken a strong, successful initiative in its scheme of universal education, called the SSA as mentioned earlier. Under this scheme no fees are charged till the primary level and all girl children and SC, ST children are exempted from paying fees till class 8 (that is estimated at 14 years of age). Under the SSA, all girls of all communities and castes, as also all male children of SCs and STs are given free books till class 8.[31] Some state governments, like that of Madhya Pradesh, have gone beyond SSA guidelines and aid and have started giving the uniforms to all girls, and boys of SCs and STs. (About the correct implementation of these guidelines one cannot be completely certain.)

How much does it cost to send a child to school? In any given area there are three types of schools: government, government-aided, and private. Private schools, in turn, are of innumerable levels and variety. While in certain urban areas they are extremely expensive charging fees up to several thousand rupees per month, in small towns, private schools are relatively less expensive. These private schools or teaching shops have mushroomed throughout the country. However, they are still beyond the means of an average poor household.

Leaving these private schools, there are the two options of government and government-aided private schools for average Indian families. Here by government schools is meant all schools run by the state, municipality, panchayat, or zilla parishad. A study by the NCAER gives the approximate expenditure on a child's education if the child is being sent to a government or government-aided school. According to it, a household has to spend Rs. 341 per child per year on his or her primary education, that is, approximately Rs. 28 per month. The expenditure would come to Rs. 474 for a child studying in upper primary school, and Rs. 788 for secondary education. Other surveys have given a lower amount as needed for the free education of a child. The

52nd National Sample Survey Organization's (NSSO) survey for 1995–6 has given the figure of Rs. 297 per annum.[32] Generally speaking, the expenditure on books, stationery and uniforms constitutes 80 per cent of the total expenditure of Rs. 300 plus per annum, per child in government schools. The above studies contend that approximately only 12 per cent of the total expenditure is on fees in government schools. The expenditure is actually more on uniforms, books, etc.[33] Though no tuition fee is charged in government schools, some sundry fees for examinations, etc., are still taken. Very generally speaking, one can say that a household has to spend Rs. 28–30 per month on every child's primary education. If there are 4–5 children in a family, the expenditure on education would become considerable. It would be higher for children studying in secondary classes, as the expenditure on secondary classes is substantially more.

The expenditure on the education of children differs on two counts: First, depending on whether a child is being sent to government, or government-aided, or private school, expenditure would differ drastically. Leaving private schools, even educating a child in government-aided schools incurs expenditure. As those areas in which a government-aided school is there the government or other state agencies generally do not open additional schools, which may mean that many areas have only government-aided schools and not government schools. These schools do not charge any tuition fee; but often ask for money under different heads. They also emphasize proper uniforms and books which would involve further expenditure, higher than that in purely government schools. Thus, overall expenditure involved in educating a child in them is considerably more.

It means, a household with 2 to 4 children of school-going age would have to spend a considerable amount on the education of their children, especially if the area has only government-aided schools. Second, the cost of secondary education is relatively higher, which can be a reason of parents' unwillingness to send their children to secondary schools.

The cost of uniforms and books, though not very high, is still the largest portion of the expenditure on school education. While girls and children of SCs and STs are given free books, the rest of the children have to purchase them. The irony is that the country's politically determined national policy of affirmative action is undertaken on the basis of caste and not economic condition. It should and must be based on economic condition; then all those families, whether of Hindu upper castes, SCs, and Muslim, who belong to the BPL category would have the advantage of affirmative action. That is, all children from BPL families must not only be exempted from tuition but all kinds of sundry fees; they must also be given free textbooks and two sets of uniforms, including shoes. Preferably, even the distinction between BPL and poor families must be done away with, as the finances of most families in the 40 per cent lower strata of Indian society keep on changing. Families which are above the poverty line often slide into even lower levels of poverty due to ill health or other family problems. In fact, the poverty line is not a magic line which can once and for all create a divide between those who are above and those who are below it. In any case of financial strain, it is the education of the children that is generally the first casualty.

The government must not take any chances, and must make the entire primary and secondary education completely free, and this includes all expenditure, including that on uniforms and books. Moreover, this free quality education must be available to the entire young Indian populace, which would not only include all Muslim families, but also those with other religious affiliations on the singular condition of their being economically underprivileged.

A possible reason for the reluctance of poor Muslims to educate their children in modern schools is their consideration of the cost-effectiveness of education, that is, whether the education they are providing to their children (here mostly boys) at— from their point of view—considerable cost, can get them jobs. Though they are justified in thinking thus in their circumstances, the same circumstances are true for all poor parents, irrespective of their religious affiliation. The only difference is that sometimes under the influence of their communalist leaders the Muslim masses doubt the very possibility of their children getting jobs even if they are well educated. Interestingly, this distrust of the government is also indicated by the findings of Razzack and Gumber, quoted earlier, where they observe that the relative number of parents sending their children to private schools is much higher among Muslims than other groups.

It may suggest a lack of confidence in the government and the larger society in general, rather than poverty which is often considered the cause of fewer Muslim children studying in government schools. It may imply that perhaps a bias against Muslims in the larger society is directly or indirectly responsible for the relatively fewer opportunities for the Muslim youth to procure good jobs or advance themselves in the society. This seems to be confirmed by the Sachar Committee Report which observes that the share of Muslims in salaried jobs is very low. And more importantly, 'unemployment rates among Muslim graduates is the highest among SRCs'.[34]

4.2. POOR QUALITY OF EDUCATION IN GOVERNMENT SCHOOLS

Another reason advanced against the desirability of sending Muslim children to modern schools is the extremely poor quality of education that is available in government schools. There is no denying that government schools are mostly in a very poor state as regards building and the availability of drinking water and toilets on the one hand, and the frequent absence of teachers on the other. There is no dearth of central government grants, but they either remain underutilized in many states, as in Bihar or West Bengal, or are misused by politicians and bureaucrats. Since there is no participation of parents or local people in the functioning of the education machinery, there seems to be no accountability of the officials involved, often resulting in the tardy implementation of programmes.[35]

Most government schools, especially in villages of the North and North-East, are situated in damaged buildings which need urgent repairs, or they function out of tents. It so happens that even the government grants for building repairs reach those schools that are in better condition but have local politicians with influence; or they are distributed equally without considering the needs of different schools. Equally, or more importantly, clean toilets and drinking water are rarely available in most village schools. The absence of toilets is especially inconvenient for girls. As regards other infrastructure facilities, one need not even expect them.

The worst aspect of government schools is the frequent absence of schoolteachers. Most teachers are educated in cities and live in cities and towns. Very few teachers in this category are ready to work in villages as it involves either living in villages— not a very agreeable option to the city bred—or commuting daily from cities or towns to villages. A large number of them 'manage' to be posted in city schools, where the number of teachers is always disproportionately high as compared to rural schools. If the teachers are sent to rural schools, they commute daily to their schools and are invariably late, or they are habitually absent. They also take very little interest in their teaching duties. Unfortunately, the government has also been misusing these teachers, deputing them for census work, election duties, and even its family planning programme! A countrywide study in 2004 estimated that on any given day at least 25 per cent of the teachers remain absent; and those who are present hardly take interest in their teaching duties.[36]

There is no doubt that most government schools, excepting probably those in the metropolitan cities, are in quite a bad shape. Until recently no attention was paid to this situation. Now, however, the central government at least has made some attempts to improve the situation. But these efforts do not seem to have made a substantial difference in the overall condition of government or aided schools, excepting in a few states like Rajasthan, Madhya Pradesh and possibly Karnataka. However, when it is said that madrasas are the only option before the poor Muslim parents for the education of their children since private schools are beyond their reach and government schools give such poor education and are in a bad condition, does it mean that most other equally poor Indians have other options? All Indian children whose parents cannot afford to send them to high fee private schools go to government schools. The real need is to improve the condition of these schools through better public awareness and public action, which can bring to the attention of the authorities the lack of proper school in a given neighbourhood, or the poor conditions and functioning of their schools. If need be, the public must put pressure on the schools to improve; but to reject them altogether is no solution. In this venture, unless the entire local population takes personal interest, success may elude the few who try.

The situation was always somewhat better in the South. However, there is an even greater demand for English medium schools there than in the North which only private schools can provide. Unfortunately, the standard of education in these English medium, but relatively low fee-charging 'public', schools is no better than that in government schools.

The overall situation in the field of primary education has improved considerably throughout India, though the state-wise differences remain. Primary and secondary education, so far the most neglected field in the Indian state's planning, has received a great boost under the SSA. Considerable effort is being made not only to engage more teachers but to select them from the local populace. The greatest drawback to good education in government schools has been the regular absence of teachers living in cities, as mentioned earlier. There is also hardly any supervision of these schools. Now there are strict guidelines that the teachers must be appointed from the village community. The teachers selected for Muslim majority areas are preferably from the same locality. However, the same cannot perhaps be said for upper primary and secondary education. Secondary schools are relatively fewer in number and the cost for upper primary and secondary education is relatively higher. Teachers for these schools are required to be better educated and cannot easily be recruited from the local community.

To reiterate: First, government schools, whether poor or good, are the same for a segment of the population of a given region belonging to various religious communities, and not for Hindus or Muslims alone. Second, the awareness and active involvement of the local community, whether Muslim, mixed, or Hindu, would make a great deal of difference to the quality of education being imparted in government schools. The shortcomings of government schools are an occasion for focused protest and demand for better schools rather than rejecting them and opting for madrasa education for Muslim children.

Could it be that there is discrimination against Muslim children in admission, or later on in their general treatment by school authorities or teachers? Discrimination is something which cannot be estimated on a statistical scale. My experience in my limited field research for the present study in and around Delhi did not support any such hypothesis. Even during casual talks with the parents—mostly mothers—no one ever suggested that they did not want to send their children to government schools because of discrimination being practised there. In the interior villages its possibility cannot be ruled out. Still, even there discriminatory practices are more marked against the 'lowest' castes in the Hindu hierarchy than against Muslims. But exceptions cannot be ruled out, and there might be instances of discrimination against Muslim children.

Possibly the reasons why some Muslim parents prefer to send their children to madrasas instead of modern schools could be the non-availability of government schools in the Muslim majority areas, or the cost of education in government or aided schools, or the poor quality of those schools. However, neither poverty nor the poor quality and cost of modern education are alone responsible for those Muslim parents' choice of madrasas for the education of their children, though they also are important factors which decide the choice.

4.3. SCHOOLS *VERSUS* MADRASAS

It has been rightly pointed out that while government schools are mostly in a pitiable condition, with no water, toilets or even teachers, madrasas function regularly. They are cleaner, have toilet and water facilities, teachers who are not only regular, but also provide a better example of personal integrity than government school teachers who are hardly interested in their jobs. The contrast between the two types of institutions makes Muslim parents favour madrasas over modern schools for their children.

It is further pointed out by the advocates of madrasas that not only do madrasas not require any expenditure on uniforms and books, they also provide free boarding and lodging. While it is true that madrasas do not require uniforms, and books are not needed at least for maktab-level education and are later provided by madrasas, the assertion that they also provide boarding, lodging, and clothes free to all children is not correct. There are several kinds of madrasas, which will be discussed in the next chapter. However, a basic difference between madrasas can be made on the basis of provision for lodging and food. Only the bigger madrasas provide lodging and food, and mostly for those children learning *Hifz* (memorization of the Quran). A large number of madrasas have two sections, the first teaching normal subjects of the Arabic course and the second teaching *Hifz*. Madarasas also make a distinction between residential students (*rihaishi*) and local (*bahari* or outsider) students. Food and lodging are provided only to the former category of children. Madrasas, excepting those teaching *Hifz*, usually teach for about four hours. By noon or 1 p.m. the children go back to their homes; so the question of providing food for them does not arise. Importantly, maktabs never provide food. And most Muslim children belonging to poor or lower middle-class families go to maktabs in their early years. From there they generally do not go to school at all but just drop out.

The reason for many Muslims' preference for madrasa (including maktab) education for their children cannot therefore be that madrasas take care of everything, including lodging, food, and clothes. Granted that there are a large number of madrasas that do provide all these, but the percentage of children studying in them would be quite small (though the figure is not known) compared to the number of children studying in thousands of other madrasas and the innumerable maktabs all over the country. Of course, expenditure on madrasa education, even if food and lodging are not provided, is still nil, as they do not demand any expenditure either on uniforms or on books. The local students are not expected to wear any specific uniform, while residential students are provided with two sets of what is considered Islamic dress. Significantly, very few books are needed as most of the learning is by rote; where books are needed, they are provided by the madrasa and taken back at the end of the year.

Perhaps one of the main reasons for many Muslims' choice of madrasas rather than modern schools for the education of their children is the psychological fact that while they feel closer to and at home in madrasas, they find the ambience of modern schools as unfamiliar or un-Islamic.

5. THE RELIGIOUS REASONS FOR MUSLIMS' PREFERENCE FOR MADRASA EDUCATION

5.1. EMOTIONAL CLOSENESS WITH MADRASA AMBIENCE

Madrasas, especially maktabs, being closely linked with mosques and being situated inside the Muslim concentration locality, are seen as an integral part of community life. *Maulavis* or teachers at the madrasas dress and speak the same way as common Muslims do. Muslim clerics and other traditionalist leaders have been constantly telling the masses about the need to adopt a way of life according to the *shari'a*. The *maulavis* of the madrasas seem to be the living embodiment of the ideal Muslim way of life. And hence the emotional closeness that the Muslims feel for madrasas and the values they embody.

Maktabs as well as madrasas are usually situated within or very near the Muslim majority areas, and are part and parcel of the Muslim community. On the other hand, modern schools are seen as something outside the Muslim milieu. Government schools are generally situated near but not inside the Muslim locality. Till recently, most of the teachers at these schools were outsiders. There are efforts now to rectify this situation and local teachers are being recruited. But it will take time for all Muslim majority areas to have conveniently located government schools with locally recruited teachers. Till that time perhaps a relatively large number of Muslims will regard government schools as something 'other' or external, and madrasas as their very own.

Most Muslims have a soft corner for madrasas. Even middle-class Muslims who do not send their children to madrasas are very protective about them. They often give apologetic rationalizations in defence of madrasas. Their partiality to madrasas is most evident when they confront anyone who seems to be critical of the madrasa system, especially if that person is a non-Muslim. Their refrain always is 'Madrasas are doing an excellent job'; or, 'They are doing the work they are meant to do'. When middle-class Muslims who send their children to English medium schools want to do some charity they often choose a madrasa as the recipient, citing the good work being done by them. While some of these arguments are valid, most are expressions of a sentimental perception of madrasas as embodying Islamic religion and culture and preserving them, or as imparting Islamic knowledge.[37]

The readiness of the Muslim masses to adhere to the dictates of *maulanas*, their growing attachment to a separate religious identity, their attempts to follow the norms of *shari'a* (especially with regard to the womenfolk) seem to suggest that religion is very important for them. Researchers have also recorded that a greater number of Muslims more than the followers of other religions, claim that Islam (or rather Islamic identity) is the most important thing in their lives.[38] Their attachment to Islam is translated into their choice of madrasas, perceived as religious institutions, for the education of their children. Madrasas are seen as symbols of Islamic religion, knowledge and glory. This perception is strengthened by their belief that persons who get Islamic knowledge in a madrasa earn merit *(sabab)*. Such individuals not only ensure a better life after death for themselves, but they also become capable of interceding on behalf of their family members on the Day of Judgement. This belief has made parents opt for madrasa education for their children. Alternatively, one boy in a family is sent to a madrasa even when the other children were being sent to modern schools. This belief in the merit of madrasa education as an insurance for the other world has resulted in the strong attachment of a large number of Muslims to madrasas.[39]

5.2. The Muslims' Need for Islamic Education

As we have seen in the first chapter, at least at the theoretical level it is asserted that Islam is not only the perfect religion, it is also a complete guide to a Muslim's life, in all eventualities of life. It not only leads Muslims to the way of God, but also makes them better human beings, responsible citizens and morally upright persons. An ethical way of life, it is argued, is impossible without the individual's being firmly grounded in the teachings of Islam. Further, Islamic *shari'a* is often declared to be 'divine'. At least it is inviolable.[40] *Shari'a*, as will be seen in chapter 5, is constituted of both the Holy Quran and the *sunna*. Though the *ulama* generally affirm that maktab education is sufficient for the masses, as this ensures their own role as the sole interpreters of Islamic *shari'a*; some academics believe that the Quran alone is not sufficient as a total guide to the entire Muslim life; and therefore every Muslim must know the *sunna*, that is, the records of the sayings, approvals and disapprovals of some acts of others by the Messenger of God, as collected in various *hadiths*. According to them, the education provided in maktabs is not sufficient, and Muslim children need more detailed religious education.[41] Whether this argument for the need for detailed religious education implies that madrasas are the correct institutions for the education of Muslim children, or whether it is just an expression of the religious needs of Muslims is not clear. To find some viable answers to the problem of how to satisfy the religious needs of Muslims, while at the same time ensuring that Muslim children are not deprived of their constitutional right of getting a good modern education is one of the main tasks of this study.

5.3. Alien Ambience of Modern Government Schools for Muslims

Education is a state subject and the teachers, supervisors and even the policy makers are mostly Hindu. Though on paper the Indian Union is declared secular, in practice it is not so. The morning assembly mostly or fully consists of Hindu prayers, including Saraswati Vandana. As Saraswati is regarded the goddess of knowledge, the prayer, often in Sanskrit, is a regular feature in schools. In most schools pictures of Hindu gods adorn the office walls. Often the teachers and others greet each other with some form of Hindu greeting (*Jai Ram ji*, etc.). This atmosphere presents an alien culture to Muslim parents and even to children as they have been taught from the beginning that there is no God but Allah. Muslim girls may find the free manners of Hindu girls strange and, coming from a sheltered atmosphere, may feel alienated.

A large number of Muslims object to the singing of Saraswati Vandana and having to attend yearly Saraswati Puja in government schools. Imtiaz Ahmad reasons that the state has failed in achieving any measure of secularization. These secular academics give the example of Western nations where no religious symbol is allowed inside schools. However, there is a difference between the West and India. In the former, religion has become an occasional attendance of the church on Sundays, while in India religion is an integral part of most people's lives. It may be more so for Muslims, but it is almost equally important for Hindus. I feel that some influence of the culture of the numerical majority is bound to seep into the public places and schools as well.

This is not at all meant to justify any attitude of aggressive Hinduism. Any religious symbols, like pictures of Hindu gods, must not be brandished about. Also, attendance at the Saraswati Puja, or singing of the Saraswati Vandana must be totally optional. Unfortunately, this is not the case, especially in the NDA-ruled states. For example, in Madhya Pradesh the government is planning to introduce Sanskrit language from class one. In Gujarat there is not only compulsory yoga training (which is not such a bad thing) but also some special practice of *Surya namaskar*, which is a purely Hindu ritual. A clear central directive is needed to reinforce the need of avoiding all emphasis on Hindu symbols and ensure that no one is forced to participate in any ritual or function which they find offensive to their religious feelings. At the same time, efforts must be made by both teachers and students to free the Muslim children from the feeling of cultural alienation and make them feel at home.

These are complex issues and cannot be taken up casually. However, the issue of Vande Mataram is different. The word *vande* does not mean bowing down but rather hailing and some form of saluting the motherland. The lyric rendered by A.R. Rahman, '*Ma Tujhe Salam*', catch the spirit of the song wonderfully. I feel saluting the motherland is not against Islam. Even if it is declared to be so, those students whose parents object can stand without singing the song, though I do wish that those Muslims would here show a more liberal attitude. At the same time an aggressive Hindu campaign that all must sing the song, as witnessed in Gujarat, becomes counter-productive. One can expect but not force a person to do something in a secular democracy.

5.4. OBJECTIONS AGAINST THE CONTENTS
      OF TEXTBOOKS

Another genuine grievance of orthodox Muslims is that there is a Hindu bias in school textbooks. Though such biases have a tendency to creep up even in supposedly objective statements, any such pro-Hindu and anti-Muslim bias is unfortunate and must be avoided with utmost sincerity, as it would cause further resistance to modern education among a particular section of Muslims.

Although NCERT books have been thoroughly rewritten in an unbiased manner, it is the books of state boards that are mostly prescribed in government and government-aided schools. In Uttar Pradesh, Madhya Pradesh, Rajasthan, Gujarat, Maharashtra, and now perhaps Karnataka Hindu sentiments are quite strong. This has resulted in some bias creeping into school textbooks. This bias is not generally offensive and is mostly expressed in the form of idealization of the Hindu past and of some of the Hindu heroes such as Rana Pratap and Shivaji who are hailed as the saviours of Hindu honour and culture, but such an idealization implies that Muslims are enemies.

There is urgent need to filter out all those biased passages or stories that are likely to offend the Muslim sentiments, or which simply present a biased or one-sided picture of some historical facts. For example, the battle of Haldi Ghati between Akbar and Rana Pratap is portrayed in Hindi literature and even in the history textbooks of state boards as a battle to save the glory of Hindu *rashtra*, despite the fact that Akbar's army included forty thousand Rajputs and sixty thousand Mughals or Muslims; or that there were a large number of Pathans, including the one thousand presented by a Pathan King, Taj Khan, in Rana Pratap's army![42] The same is true for Shivaji. He was a great man in his personal life, but when he is given a status equal to gods in Maharashtra as the symbol of Hindu glory and the hero fighting for Hindu *rashtra*, it gives a biased picture of Indian history. Such projections are likely to offend Muslim sensitivities. Life and history are complex phenomena, and though difficult, Indian history needs to be presented in a comprehensive perspective which welcomes the diversity of India and equally hails its underlying unity.

The Dini Anjuman Council of UP and Jamaat-e-Islami-Hind have taken up the task of pointing out objectionable passages in school textbooks. Secular organizations and other concerned citizens should also take up the job of scrutinizing the textbooks of state boards and getting them edited or rewritten.

An allied allegation is the Hinduization of Hindi textbooks, by which is meant the references to Hindu religious beliefs, and Hindu gods, and the inclusion of Hindu *bhakti* poetry in Hindi literature. According to some secular intellectuals like Bipan Chandra, *bhakti* poetry is an integral part of Hindi literature and need not be removed. I can say from my experience of student days that *bhakti* poetry is so sublime that it can offend no one. Certainly, it has constant reference to Hindu mythology; but it must be remembered that the Muslim poets of medieval period, such as Kabir, Abdul Rahim Khankhana, and Malik Mohammad Jayasi, too made constant references to Hindu mythology, so much so that for a non-biased person it is impossible to identify these poets as Muslims. In the medieval period, especially during Mughal times, the two major religious communities lived in greater harmony than at present.

Still, if some contemporary communal-minded Muslims feel offended by *bhakti* poetry, this can be easily remedied. Already the NCERT and some state boards have developed a Hindi 'B' course which does not include Hindi literature in detail, including *bhakti* poetry. So, those who so wish can opt to take B group Hindi. But there are practical difficulties in this suggestion. Even private schools offer only one course, either Hindi A or B. For government schools it would be impossible to teach both courses simultaneously. If only the B course is taught, it would deprive Hindi-speaking children of learning the rich literature of their language.

To conclude, the choice of madrasa, rather than modern schools, by Muslim parents is determined by a large number of factors, such as general poverty which results in their unwillingness or incapability to spend on their children's education, or even forces them to make their children work as casual labour; the usefulness of children at home or in family profession; the influence of *beradari* or other conservative but more vociferous members of the community or locality; the inherent perception of madrasas as a symbol of Islam and Muslim culture; and, above all, the belief in the need for Islamic education for all Muslim children. Generally, it is a combination of all these causes which leads to the choice of madrasas rather than modern schools by many Muslim parents for their children.

6. MUSLIM CHILDREN'S NEED FOR URDU AS A MEDIUM OF EDUCATION

6.1. DEVELOPMENT OF URDU AS THE LINGUA FRANCA OF NORTH INDIA

Urdu is the biggest contentious issue in madrasa *versus* school controversy. It is argued by most Muslims, especially middle-class intellectuals, that Urdu is the mother tongue of the Muslims of India; and it is a well-accepted fact that children must be taught in their mother tongue.

A digression here about the genesis of the Urdu language would be in order. First, it is an Indian language which was developed in the army and marketplace of the cities during the later period of Mughal rule. Hindus and Muslims had mostly lived together harmoniously and there was constant interaction and give-and-take between the two religious communities, especially in the marketplace. The Persian language of the Mughal court could not serve as the *lingua franca* of everyday life. Hindi as it is spoken today (*khadi boli*) was not yet developed. Instead, there were various Hindi regional dialects, as Brij, Awadhi, and a common dialect in which Hindu and Muslim *bhaktas* (devotees) communicated known as Hindwi.

Urdu gradually developed at first as a medium of communication between various communities and peoples. It was a combination of Arabic and Persian on the one hand and the grammar of Hindi dialects on the other. In the initial stage it used the vocabulary of the three languages freely. In all probability there were more local Hindi words and even the Arabic and Farsi words that were used were easier or simpler ones. Its script, of course, was a mixture of Arabic and Farsi scripts. During the declining period of the Mughal empire it was decided to substitute Persian with Urdu as the court language. Naturally as the court language it must have gained more sophistication, and more Arabic and Persian words would have been included in it.

The present Hindi language developed much later in the late nineteenth century. Earlier than that Urdu was the *lingua franca* of all north Indians. There was hardly any talk of Urdu being the language of Muslims only. Interestingly, till English language took the place of a guarantor of jobs, and Indians, especially Hindus, took to English education, Urdu was the language of educated people. Urdu was popular not only because it was the official language for all purposes, but also because knowledge of Urdu language and literature was a sign of culture. Many writers and poets of Urdu literature, such as Krishan Chandar, Krishna Sobti and Firaq Gorakhpuri, as also Premchand in his early years, were Hindus. To repeat, no one thought of Urdu as the language of Muslims alone.

Imtiaz Ahmad opines that this Urdu was used in three forms.[43] The first was the literary language. But even this literary Urdu was written in two forms, a simple one which used words from Hindi and local dialects liberally, such as the works of Saadat Hasan Manto, and a more Persianized Urdu used by other writers. The second form was the spoken Urdu. And let us be honest here that the spoken Urdu is indistinguishable from Hindustani, the language spoken by all north Indians. Recently there were several serialized TV shows in which several Pakistani Muslims not only took part but won laurels. It was impossible to find a single word in their language which is not used in everyday language on this side of the border. A large number of Arabic and Persian words are used in Hindi speech and writings without the users being conscious of their origins. Similarly words from Hindi or local dialects have been an integral part of the Urdu language. It is so because there has been a constant give-and-take between the two languages: Urdu and Hindi.

The main difference between the two sister languages is in their respective scripts. Urdu, using the Arabi-Farsi script, naturally incorporates their vocabulary and is influenced by their general conceptual framework. Hindi using the Devanagari script is much closer to Sanskrit. A large portion of its vocabulary is derived from, or is a simplified version of, Sanskrit words. It is only Arabized and Persianized Urdu and Sanskritized Hindi which differ from each other markedly, and not the Hindi–Urdu–Hindustani that is not only spoken but also used in everyday writings and journalism.

The third kind of Urdu is the one that is used in madrasas. There it is not used in its capacity as a sensitive language capable of expressing profound emotions and having a rich literature, but just as a means of explaining difficult Arabic texts. As it happens, the Urdu used for the purpose is overloaded with Arabic and Persian words which makes it almost a different language. Another thing, as Ahmad suggests, Urdu's intimate association with madrasas makes it the language of Muslims only, but not of modern or 'educated' Muslims, and not of others as was the practice earlier in the North.

Ahmad further contends in the same article, that because at the present time Urdu is being used only by madrasa educated persons, its natural development is thwarted and it is perceived as the language of Muslims. Therefore, the need is to bring it in the secular field. This can best be done, according to Ahmed, by 'mainstreaming Urdu in the secular syllabus'.

6.2. The Need for Introducing Urdu Medium in Modern Schools

To return to the original issue that Urdu is the mother tongue of Indian Muslims; that since Urdu medium schools are rare, Muslims are 'forced' to send their children to madrasas. But is it so? At most Urdu is the language of a few elite Muslims in Delhi, Uttar Pradesh, and Bihar. In the North-East and West Bengal no one knows, far less speaks Urdu (though in most madrasas it is taught religiously with the assumption that it is the language of Muslims!). In the Hindustani-speaking belt of the North, including Uttar Pradesh, Bihar, Madhya Pradesh, Rajasthan, and also Gujarat, Urdu is not spoken by the Muslim masses who communicate in local languages or dialects. The most important fact to be remembered in this context is that the 'real' Urdu is the language of the elite only; and they in any case send their children to English medium schools! The Muslim masses speak either Hindustani (a welcome combination of Urdu and Hindi) or the local dialects, especially in the villages. Even in Lucknow proper, the heartland of Urdu culture, they speak some form of Awadhi (a dialect of Hindi).

The argument, that Muslims do not send their children to modern schools because primary education at least must be provided in one's mother tongue, and there is no proper provision for Muslim children's education in their mother tongue (Urdu), is not perhaps fully based on facts. It is commonplace that Muslim parents and children in the North do not generally have any objection to studying in Hindi medium. Sometimes those who are actually in the field have noticed that parents are eager that their children learn the language of the area, especially if it is used at the state level. At the same time when they are offered the option of taking Urdu as a subject they are very pleased.

In Rajasthan, under the Lok Jumbish Project, attempts were made to bring Muslim children to modern schools in educationally backward blocks. This project was launched in 1992 and was jointly funded by the Government of India, the Government of Rajasthan and the Swedish International Development Agency. But its efforts for universal elementary education faltered in areas with a Muslim majority. The Kamma Block in Bharatpur district is largely inhabited by the Meos who are Hindu converts to Islam. They used to speak the local dialect and were almost indistinguishable from other Rajasthanis in their dress and customs. But the *Tablighi* movement changed all that. These people turned away from school education preferring to send their children, especially girls, to madrasas. They also objected to education through the Hindi medium. All reasoning and cajoling by the volunteers of Lok Jumbish failed to have any tangible effect. Then Urdu was included as a subject while the medium of instructions remained Hindi; and enrolment to modern schools increased substantially. NGO workers say that most Muslims are content to study in Hindi medium as it is the official language and are not very eager for eduation in the Urdu medium, but want to learn it as an additional language.[44]

Interestingly, Muslims in some parts of Andhra Pradesh, Maharashtra and Karnataka declare their mother tongue to be Urdu. Most other Muslims in India speak the local language. But in regions where because of some historical circumstances Muslims have not taken to the regional language, they prefer to learn

Urdu rather than the regional language. Their spoken Urdu may be mixed with the local dialect; for example, in Hyderabad common folk among Muslims speak an interesting combination of Urdu and *bambaiya* Hindi. Thus, Urdu is declared as the mother tongue in some southern states much more frequently than in the North, whereas all the clamour for Urdu emanates in the North.[45] In Uttar Pradesh and Bihar the reasons for the demand may be political or emotional; but it would be best to accept this demand wherever it is made if the government is interested in drawing Muslims into mainstream modern education.

Since the mid-twentieth century, when the Deeni Talimi Council was established in Uttar Pradesh, it has been actively implementing a two-pronged programme. First, it is promoting the establishment of maktabs and even madrasas which try to combine the two kinds of subjects, Islamic and modern. And second, it puts demands before the government for redressing the various educational problems of Muslims. Some of its chief demands are provision for separate Urdu medium schools for Muslim children and provision for religious education in common government schools. These demands are enthusiastically endorsed by various other Muslim organizations.[46]

Starting Urdu medium schools should not have been difficult, since as early as 1949 the Conference of Chief Ministers had declared that at least primary education should be in the mother tongue and, given that a certain number of pupils' mother tongue may be different, arrangements should be made for their education through their respective mother tongues. The central government had issued a statement to that effect in 1958. It further said that facilities should be provided for teaching in Urdu at the primary stage to the children whose mother tongue is Urdu. As far as possible, this facility should be carried forward to secondary education also. The Bihar government even promised to either open Urdu medium schools or appoint Urdu teachers for a class where there were ten or more Urdu-speaking children.[47] But these intentions were never carried out, though some efforts were made from time to time.

Since 1961 the government has accepted the three-language formula for all school children, according to which every child must learn Hindi, English, and a third Indian language. Alternatively, if the mother tongue is some other Indian language, then that language must be taught, followed by Hindi and English. However, in the Hindi belt and some other states, the third language is mostly Sanskrit. From my point of view, Sanskrit (as also Arabic) should be learnt only by those who want to specialize in their respective religions. There are Sanskrit universities that teach Sanskrit; as for Arabic there are a large number of madrasas where it is taught. The time spent by students in learning Sanskrit in modern schools, at the end of which they promptly forget it, is a sheer waste of energy. In fact, Urdu should have been introduced as an optional third language in the northern Hindi belt; and non-Muslim children too should have been encouraged to learn it. Perhaps then the demand for Urdu as a medium of instruction would not have been so strong; and a rich Indian language would have been preserved.

I am in favour of a provision of Urdu medium sections for Muslim children in common schools, wherever there is a demand for it. It may not be factually correct that the mother tongue of Muslims is always Urdu, but it is an emotional issue, a question of their beliefs and feelings, in fact their legitimate desire to maintain their separate identity, and this must be respected.

However, the question remains, are separate Urdu medium schools ideal? From the beginning we have taken the stand that all Indian children should study together in common schools. This would be especially true in villages where to run one school is difficult enough, to run two schools, one Hindi medium and another Urdu medium, would be impossible. At the same time, it would be easy to create separate sections with Urdu as the medium of instruction in those schools that are in the vicinity of Muslim majority areas.

Then there is the need for Urdu textbooks. So far Urdu textbooks have betrayed the same pro-Muslim and traditionalist bias as their Hindi counterparts. Till the time of writing both Hindi and Urdu textbooks are full of communal biases; in fact this is more true of Urdu language books. They are also outdated, and therefore it is important that they are totally re-written. Care must be taken that these Urdu textbooks are written strictly according to the guidelines and prescribed syllabus of central or state boards. The same holds true for the southern states, where for historical reasons Muslims prefer to learn Urdu. There Urdu textbooks should be written according to the strict guidelines of the state board, almost exactly as the regional language textbooks.

My second reason for favouring teaching in Urdu in schools is that it has become a neglected language for various reasons. It is high time the government relized and became conscious that an Indian language with a rich literature and its associated culture is whithering away out of sheer neglect. Urdu has been included in the VIIIth Schedule of Indian Constitution, as also Sanskrit. But since Muslims are not a regional secular group and are spread throughout India, Urdu cannot be acknowledged as the state language of a particular region. As a result it is neglected in all states, including UP and Delhi where it was first developed. The intention of the VIIIth Schedule of the Constitution was to give recognition to Indian languages, and Urdu is an Indian language, without doubt. Not to give it proper recognition and encouragement is contrary to the spirit of the Constitution.

Perhaps the greatest hindrance to the further development of Urdu and its literature was the loud declarations by Muslims that Urdu is the language of Muslims alone, and that is why it was being discouraged by the Hindu majority. In a sense it is true that Muslims use Urdu much more than Hindus; also that somehow Urdu has become a symbol of Muslims' separate identity, and hence is very dear to them.

The best way to rejuvenate Urdu is to bring it into the secular field. And that can best be done by first freeing it from communal politics, and second, by making it a medium of secular modern education, at least up to the primary level. The third and best way to encourage the development of Urdu is to make it one of the three languages. School children should study in their respective mother tongues, and then given the option of English and Urdu as their second and third languages. If non-Muslim children take Urdu as a third language it would both introduce them to a rich and sensitive literature and also promote the earlier communal harmony, lost somewhere during this period. Arrangements for the teaching of Urdu can be made in those areas where Muslims are in the majority who have chosen Urdu as their mother tongue. In such areas it would be good if children of other religious communities also learn Urdu. There would be some difficulty in those areas where the regional language is the mother tongue. There the number of additional languages to be learnt increases. But Urdu, especially in the North, would be a far better option than either Sanskrit or some foreign language (as in some elite private schools).

Another suggestion of our own is that Hindi books should be totally overhauled, especially their language; they should not use Sanskritized Hindi, nor should they try to translate modern scientific terms in Sanskritized Hindi. This holds equally good for books in Urdu and other regional languages. They should use simple language so that the child's energies are not wasted in understanding the language itself, thus losing the thread of the content. Scientific terms can be transliterated in the script of the mother tongue. Or, as a less desirable option, some easier translation of the term may be used with the original term given in brackets.

7. MUSLIMS' 'ALIENATION' FROM THE 'MAINSTREAM' AND GHETTO LIVING

7.1. ARE MUSLIMS AN ALIENATED PEOPLE?

The Muslims are said to suffer from a minority complex which involves a sense of insecurity and of feeling discriminated against. This, in turn, makes them cling to those they perceive as their own people. It also makes them desperately eager to cling to their 'separate' identity as Muslims. And for this purpose they, under the leadership of their more conservative, even fundamentalist leaders, have to reject all that they share with the wider society, such as customs and practices associated with the life cycles of birth, marriage, etc. A communitarian identity, in order to be concrete, would have to be based on outward symbols and customs, and not on inner faith which is in conflict with none. Muslims, regularly praying together in the mosques, have always had a distinct religious identity.

But their communal leaders want a stronger affirmation of

their separate sociological identity, so they seek it in everyday customs and practices, and these the Muslims often share with the rest of society. That is why the 'reformists' have emphasized a drastic Islamization of their life, customs, and even dress and language. Their efforts have resulted in even the simple Muslim folk now asserting their separate Muslim identity. Muslim religious leaders further assert that Muslims are discriminated against which has resulted in their alienation from the wider society. But how far is this assertion true?

Muslims have not been an alienated community. Life and society are complex, multifaceted phenomena, and generalizations cannot tell the whole truth about them. There are reasons to believe that Hindus and Muslims lived quite harmoniously together at least till the establishment of British rule. The composite culture that secular historians talk about is not a figment of their imagination.[48] There were three reasons for the peaceful existence of the two religious groups. First, the majority of Muslims were Hindu converts who did not leave behind all their old beliefs, customs, and practices when converting to Islam. They continued to share these beliefs and practices with their Hindu neighbours. Second, there was mutual interdependence in day-to-day living which made both communities feel at home with each other. Society was divided not between Hindus and Muslims but between the urban elite and the rural landlords on the one hand and the masses of peasants and craftsmen on the other. Hindus and Muslims belonged to both groups and shared identical conditions of living and culture. Third, there was a vast amount of religious toleration. Though Hindus and Muslims did not intermarry or even inter-dine, yet they shared each other's religious festivals and social occasions.[49]

In the nineteenth century, for various historical reasons, Muslim revivalist leaders became aware of the religious laxity of the Muslim masses and set out to correct what they perceived to be aberrations. Earlier from Sheikh Ahmad Sirhindi (sixteenth century), Shah Walliullah (eighteenth century) to leaders of Tablighi movement (nineteenth and twentieth centuries), various Muslim leaders have tried to make the Muslim masses adhere to *shari'a* rules and norms and give up all those practices that they shared with the local populace. This has even involved giving up common dress and language in certain areas where Tablighi leaders are more active.[50]

In the nineteenth century this revivalist movement became further entwined with communalism. Somehow the Western ideas of equality and democracy had a negative impact on the Indian psyche. The people started counting numbers and Indian society became divided into the majority and the minorities who competed with each other for tiny bits of favours from the British rulers. The communalism of Hindus, Muslims, and Sikhs fed upon each other, and finally divided India.[51]

After Independence, the earlier harmonious relations are gradually being reestablished. In the economic field, that is, in everyday transactions, both Hindus and Muslims show no discrimination against each other or a preference for people of their own religion, which is good business sense. Significantly, Muslim craftsmen and sculptors have always helped to construct Hindu temples; they also sell things required for Hindu worship before temples. The two communities share the same conditions of life and have identical regional cultures. They mostly speak the same regional language, whether it is Tamil, Malayalam, Kannada, Bengali, Marwari (Rajasthani), or Awadhi (dialect of Hindi). The dress and food habits, as also innumerable social customs and norms, are common to both religious communities, that is, Hindus and Muslims.

Generally speaking, Muslims, at least the common folk among them, are not an alienated group. In a very perceptive and well-planned study Peter B. Mayer has discussed the Muslims' attitudes and patterns of response in two cities, one each from the North and the South, i.e. Jabalpur (Madhya Pradesh) and Tiruchirapalli (Tamil Nadu). He correctly observes that the historical circumstances of the introduction of Islam in various parts of India were very different. Islam came to the South through traders, and Muslims were not the rulers in large areas of the South. Therefore, no antagonism developed between the two major religious communities. On the other hand, Islam came through invaders in the North. Also, Hindu organizations are more active and aggressive in the North. Therefore, the feeling of mutual antagonism and of alienation in Muslims are more prominent in the North.[52]

Mayer argues in his study that the differences in the responses of Hindus and Muslims to emotionally loaded questions are not as marked as those between inhabitants of the two cities. In Tiruchi, both Muslims and Hindus favoured India above any other thing (36 per cent and 37 per cent respectively), though religion was also the most important thing for a large number of Muslims (19 per cent) there also. In Jabalpur, India was import-ant for 29 per cent Hindus (much less than in Tiruchi), and for 20 per cent Muslims only. Religion was important only for 3 per cent Hindus and 19 per cent Muslims in Tiruchi. But it became important for 32 per cent Hindus and 68 per cent Muslims in Jabalpur.[53] It does not mean that Hindus and Muslims are far more religious in Jabalpur than in Tiruchi. Rather, the commu-nal atmosphere and politics of Jabalpur have vitiated the emo-tional perceptions and responses of both Hindus and Muslims of Jabalpur. More significantly, in both cities Muslims accepted the value of religious toleration far more than Hindus. Mayer observes, 'Muslims in India have a heightened awareness of the importance of religious freedom in a secular democracy.'[54] An alienated people do not express such positive attitudes.

Significantly, Mayer found that Muslims have the same ex-pectations from the government and are equally confident as Hindus of the possibility of their grievances being attended to by government officers. Equally significantly, the responses of Tiruchi Muslims were more confident and positive than those of Muslims in Jabalpur. Not only that, Tiruchi Muslims were even more enthusiastic about their socio-political involvement than Hindus. Mayer contends:

It is poverty, rather than religion, which is responsible for the low level of political awareness in Jabalpur. [. . .] The responses of Muslims and Hindus are remarkably parallel [in Tiruchirapalli], with Muslims, if any thing, more interested in public affairs.[55]

Other researchers and scholars have corroborated Mayer's observations. They have asserted that the feelings of frustration or alienation among Muslim youth are not more than those found among Hindu youth. Talmeez Fatima and N. Hasnain, after a comparative study of Hindu and Muslim adolescents, conclude: 'All comparisons between [Hindus and Muslims . . .] came to be insignificant. So Muslims can not be said to be alienated, neither from themselves, nor from the society.'[56]

While the Muslim masses are far less alienated from, and far more integrated with, the society around them, certain segments of the lower middle class and middle class among them feel alienated for various socio-economic reasons, and project this alienation on the entire community. The lower middle class consists of those families that are mostly successful craftsmen and small businessmen. Often advance in business or enhancement of family income due to remittances from the gulf countries by Indian Muslim expatriates result in a drastic change in family fortunes; but they generally do not change either their lifestyle, or their attitudes. They are also the most conservative group among Muslims. They send their children to madrasas, and seek and abide by the *fatwas* of the not so learned and extremely traditionalist *muftis* and *maulavis*. Remaining aloof from the rest of the society and sentimentally attached to their Muslim identity, these Muslims insist on their women observing *purdah* and not getting any modern education, or procuring jobs. They also insist that all customs and practices that the Muslims have been sharing with their Hindu neighbours must be discarded. Insisting on their separate identity, they keep minimal contact with the outside society; and naturally feel alienated from it.[57]

Muslims who have acquired modern education and have also acquired jobs and social status show an ambivalent attitude towards this issue of alienation. They adopt modern ways, live in mixed colonies, and socialize with families belonging to their socio-economic status. However, increasing population and the city culture of cut-throat competition results in a certain amount of frustration in most educated Indians, including Muslims, these days. Some of the middle-class Muslims misconstrue their personal frustrations and translate them into a sense of being discriminated against, resulting in a sense of alienation with the larger society. Then they superimpose these personal feelings on the entire Muslim population and declare that Muslims as such are alienated from the 'mainstream' society.[58] (By 'mainstream' I do not here mean Hindus alone.) It would be better if one were to keep in mind that the entire population of educated Indian youth, excepting a few top ones, are presently feeling the same frustrations and rage against the politico-economic system.

The vociferous protestations and affirmations of alienation by a section of the Muslim community, mixed with the traditionalist emphasis on *shari'a* rules and norms, as also the misplaced emphasis on a separate Muslim identity, percolate down to the masses. The latter, who earlier may not have subscribed to any of these ideas, interiorize the feelings of their elite. Thus, the entire atmosphere is vitiated. The aggressive stance of the advocates of *Hindutva* since the 1980s has further resulted in strengthening the sense of alienation and a greater emphasis on a separate Muslim identity.

It is not our intention here to argue that Muslims are not sometimes discriminated against, or that whatever is being done to ameliorate their socio-economic and educational levels is sufficient, or that the wider Indian society, as well as the state, does not have a duty to ensure the welfare of Muslims and make them feel integral to the society. The point being made here is only that if those sections of the Muslim middle-educated class who have benefited from the non-discriminatory attitude of the state and society would cease to indulge in unnecessary frustrations, then perhaps Muslims in general, who are otherwise quite well-adjusted to the wider society, would feel less alienated.

At the same time, the fact that Muslims, even the common folk among them, often feel discriminated against or feel uncertain as to whether even with qualifications they can get jobs cannot be denied. Nepotism is rampant in Indian society. Not only Muslims who feel discriminated against in the present Indian society but also anyone belonging to a different caste who may be seen as a competitor in the limited market for jobs. is often discriminated against. But as often as not, Muslims are not necessarily discriminated against. However, as Imtiaz Ahmad pointed out long back:

> [T]he important thing is not that there is discrimination against Muslims in the economic structure. What is important is that Muslims have felt so insecure as to believe themselves to be the target of continuous economic discrimination. The fact of their belief has been crucial to their social adjustment in the country.[59]

7.2. THE INFLUENCE OF GHETTO LIVING

A majority of Muslims live among their own community. The sociological reasons for this fact are various and complex. All over India there is a tendency of various 'communities', i.e. professional, caste, or religious groups, to live together in some part of the village or city. In recent decades Muslims have begun to feel more insecure, and their Muslim identity threatened, which may not be based on facts but is a mere psychological perception, what is generally called a 'minority complex'. Sometimes this feeling is caused by the occurrence of communal riots, or it may be due to some political mobilization, but the fact is the feeling exists. There is also a growing emphasis on religious identity, especially in the lower middle class. There is both strength and regressive pull in numbers. People living in a city *mohalla*, or other Muslim majority areas in villages, are cut-off from the rest of society. They perceive themselves only as members of their extremely limited community and not of a wider nation-society.

Muslim womenfolk living in these *bastis* (limited localities) are often expected to observe *purdah* (veil), and rarely go out and interact with others of the wider society. Under the constant oppressive influence of the more assertive and conservative members of the neighbourhood community, these Muslims behave as part of the community and not as individuals. Constant contact only among members of a certain limited religious group, and the influence of traditionally inclined elders and the more aggressive religious leaders make the people living in these Muslim majority localities more tradition-bound and eager to preserve the 'Muslim culture' and *shari'a* at any cost. As a result they force their womenfolk into *purdah*, and send their children to madrasas. The latter, in turn, make the children even more conservative from their childhood. The result of all these factors is a ghetto mentality. To quote J.M. Khan:

The ghetto living promotes poverty, hunger, fear, communalism, and religious dogmatism. While this kind of living saves the individual from loneliness, it also separates him from the mainstream progress and development. A large number of children from this group go to madrasas and maktabs. The imparting of religious education leads to mental isolation of groups and promotes craving for identity and exclusiveness [. . .]. This type of education generates religious and communal prejudices.[60]

Muslim *bastis* are further subdivided into sub-groups or *beradaris*. The influence of and solidarity among the members of *beradaris* and *mohallas* had been uniformly strong in north Indian society (first-hand knowledge of the south Indian social structure is not known to me). Some time after Independence younger generations of Hindus started moving out of these *mohallas* and small villages in search of social mobility. This resulted in the erosion of certain old time values, such as the family-like relationship among neighbours, respect for elders, and latter's involvement in the younger generations' decisions and lives. However, it also set the younger people free from the constraining traditional mindset, and paved the way for the adoption of modern liberal values and scientific approach to life and its various issues. Nothing like this happened in a greater part of Muslim society. The regressive influence of *beradaris* has remained very prominent among a majority of Muslims.

Muslim *beradaris* often act like Hindu castes. Four broad characteristics of Muslim *beradaris* in the Indian subcontinent are significant for the present discussion. First, the *beradaris* are necessarily endogamous. Second, excepting the so-called higher castes of Ashrafs, most other castes or *beradaris* reflect hereditary occupation, which they have been pursuing for generations and which they are not easily ready to forsake, either due to their conservatism or due to their lack of professional options. Significantly, these caste categories, as nais, manihars, etc., are the same as those among Hindus and have nearly the same customs and social norms. Third, these caste groups or *beradaris* have their separate panchayats which have a determinative say in their lives, especially in matters of marriage, divorce, and inheritance. They even have their own separate mosques and madrasas. Finally, the status of a given *beradari* is often determined by the degree of the observance of *purdah* by its womenfolk, and the strictness of the observance of religious practices by its male members.[61]

The continuing process of Islamization encourages the rejection of all those practices at the mass level that Muslims share with their Hindu compatriots, and the adoption of strictly *shari'a* based Islamic ways. Common customs and practices, such as singing songs and distributing sweets on auspicious occasions, however dogmatic and apparently un-Islamic they may appear, bring an element of freedom, joy, and liberality in the lives of common Muslims. The champions of the purity of Islam have been working hard to wean the Muslim masses from these practices.

Though certain *maulanas* and apologetic writers on Islam may not admit it, the social structure in India is more or less the same across different religious communities. Thus *beradari* or caste panchayats have a similar strong say in the lives of both Hindus and Muslims. More importantly, these panchayats mostly consist of elders of the group or caste, thus ensuring continuance of traditional, restrictive ways. In fact, these elders act as a strong regressive pull for the entire community, invariably condemning and censoring any individual freedom and any introduction of modern ways or values. As observed by Douglas E. Goodfriend,

The primary function [of these community *panchayats*] is to regulate social behavior and maintain social norms. [. . .] If the rules are violated, the association has the authority to punish the offending persons with varying degrees of social ostracism or outright social boycott as the offence requires.[62]

These *beradari* associations decide matters of marital discord, and may take the help of *muftis* or *maulanas*. *Beradari* leaders have now started dictating whom to vote for in general elections. The *Imams* of neighbourhood mosques often play a similar role and the ordinary folk obey the dictates of the *Imam*, or *beradari* heads. The latter further manages and maintains the locality mosque, maktab and madrasa. As a result of the activities of these *beradari* panchayats or *mohalla* (locality) committees, the Muslims living in the confined space of a *mohalla* or slum feel a sense of strong solidarity, of belonging together. They are open to the influence of the more orthodox members of their *beradari* or *mohalla* (locality), both in villages and in cities. The caste or *mohalla* panchayats have no legal or even religious binding, but they have an irresistible socio-psychological impact. Since their verdicts or dictates are invariably traditionalist, their influence is always regressive and nips in the bud any effort towards modernization.

When religion and religious law (*shari'a*) are that important, it puts a premium on religious education. Another factor in favour of religious education is that madrasas along with mosques are seen as an integral part of the life of the community. Going to mosques and sending one's children to madrasas become two sides of the same coin, as a natural part of community life. Both religious knowledge and religious practices, such as regular attendance in *namaz,* are highly respected which in turn tilts the scales heavily in favour of madrasa education for children living in such Muslim concentration areas.

In contrast, Muslims living in mixed colonies almost always send their children to modern schools, though some of them may also send them to morning and evening maktabs/madrasas. Their womenfolk do not observe *purdah* and often go out of their homes for jobs. They also do not so frequently ask for *fatwas* from *muftis,* though they may still be as religious as their co-religionists in Muslim majority areas.[63]

Thus, we have seen how various factors combine to influence the decision of parents or the family regarding the type of education their children are going to receive. Only a holistic approach to the educational backwardness of Muslims can understand the issues involved and successfully respond to them.

NOTES

1. Ghulam Yahya Anjum has been frequently quoted in this context, but his own source is not reliable. On the other hand, Fahimuddin had conducted some research and came out with the result that around 36 per cent of all school-going Muslim children in the age group of 6 to 18 yrs. study in madrasas. Quoted in Amir Ullah Khan, Mohammad Saqib, and Zafar H. Anjum, 'To Kill the Mocking Bird: Madarsah System in India: Past, Present and Future', found on the website: http://www.chawk/article/6216/5August,2003/

2. I was told this by a *maulana* in a special get-together of several professors from various disciplines and two or three *maulanas* to discuss 'Madrasa Education in India' at Jamia Millia Islamia, very kindly arranged for me by its Vice-Chancellor Professor Mushirul Hasan.

3. The report is a government publication, November 2006. See pp. 76–7.

4. Muhamadullah Khalili Qasmi, *Madrasa Education: Its Strength and Weakness*, Mumbai: Markazul Ma'arif Education and Research Centre, 2005, p. 194. Saiyid Hamid says that it is 'misapprehension that the admission to the madrasas is "by choice". This is so only in a very few cases. Otherwise the children who do not get or afford admission to mainstream schools find a refuge in madrasas where it is all found.' From a personal letter from S. Hamid in response to the author's queries to him, 10 September 2003.

5. See Azra Razzack and Anil Gumber, *Differentials in Human Development: A Case for the Empowerment of Muslims in India*, Study commissioned by the Department for International Development, United Nations, New Delhi, and conducted by National Council of Applied Economic Research (NCAER), New Delhi: NCAER, 2006, p. 15 (published for circulation).

6. *Social, Economic and Educational Status of the Muslim Community of India: A Report* (henceforth *Sachar Committee Report*) by Prime Minister's High Level Committee, November 2006, (published for a limited circulation) also found on the website www.indianmuslims.info/reports...2006sacharcommitteereport. htm p. 58.

7. Ibid., p. 52.

8. Ibid., pp. 52–3, 60–3.

9. Razzack and Gumber, op. cit., pp. 12 ff.

10. *Sachar Committee Report*, p. 53.

11. Ibid., pp. 62–3, 72–3.

12. Ibid., pp. 56–7.

13. Ibid., p. 67.

14. Mushirul Hasan, *Islam in the Subcontinent: Muslims in a Plural Society*, New Delhi: Manohar, 2002, pp. 208–9. Of course, Hasan's analysis cannot be applied to the entire subcontinent. Like all our population, Muslims differ in their socio-economic conditions from region to region. While Muslims were in a far better position in pre-partition Uttar Pradesh, they were worse off in Bengal, and so on.

15. Imtiaz Ahmad, 'Muslim Educational Backwardness', in Amrik Singh and G.D. Sharma, *Higher Education in India: The Social Context*, Delhi: Konark, 1988, p. 183.

16. *Sachar Committee Report*, pp. 66–75.

17. Ibid., pp. 90 ff.

18. Ibid., pp. 154 ff.
19. Razzack and Gumber, op. cit., pp. 26 ff.
20. Jyotsna Jha and Dhir Jhingran, *Elementary Education for the Poorest and Other Deprived Groups: The Real Challenges of Universalisation*, New Delhi: Manohar, 2005, pp. 142 ff.
21. Ibid., p. 140.
22. Ibid., pp. 140, 155–6.
23. Razzack and Gumber, op. cit., p. 26, also see p. 22.
24. Ibid., pp. 23–4.
25. J.M. Khan, in an excellent study of madrasa education, asserts the role of family and its size as one of the important factors determining the choice of madrasa or modern education for children. See J.M. Khan, *Education Among Muslims*, Jaipur: Classic Publishing House, 1993, pp. 61 ff., 87 ff., 92 ff.
26 There is evidence all around us of children engaged in casual labour at Petrol pumps, roadside *dhabas*, etc. This is true for all religious communities. Thus the parents' decision of withholding their children from schooling is determined not only by the cost of school education but also by the resultant loss of income from children's labour. See Santosh Malhotra, ed., *The Economics of Elementary Education in India: The Challenge of Public Finance, Private Provision and Household Costs*, New Delhi: Sage, 2006, p. 150.
27. See Khan, *Education Among Muslims*, pp. 64 ff.
28. See Zakir Hussain, 'Analysing Demand for Primary Education: Muslim Slum Dwellers of Kolkata', *Economic and Political Weekly*, 8 January 2005, pp. 139 ff.
29. *Sachar Committee Report*, pp. 53, 57.
30. See central education department website www.education.nic.in/ mdm (midday meal).
31. See www.ssa.nic.in/framework.
32. See Jandhyala B.G. Tilak, *Determinants of Household Expenditure on Education in Rural India*, NCAER, 2003, pp. 11 ff; also see Santosh Mehrotra, ed., *The Economics Elementary Education in India*, pp. 144 ff.
33. Tilak, op. cit., pp. 12–13; Mehrotra, op. cit., pp. 146–7.
34. *Sachar Committee Report*, p. 73, also pp. 87 ff.
35. See Dhir Jhingran, 'Cess Appeal: Go beyond it', *The Indian Express*, 12 July 2004.
36. M. Kramer, M. Murlidharan, N. Chaudhary and N. Hammer, 'Teacher Absence in India: A Snapshot', in *Journal of the European Economic Association*, no. 3. April–May 2005, pp. 658–

67. Also see SSA website: ssa.nic.in 'Some Finding by External Agencies on Primary Education'.

37. 'First, madrasas have been established for a particular purpose of producing *Ulama*, having command over Islamic Sciences that require full time and attention. [. . .] That is why it is not proper for madrasas to impart modern arts. [. . .]

'Second, doesn't the Islamic society need Ulama who can guide it in religious field, educate Muslim children, defend Islam and devote their life to safeguard Muslims' future.' Mufti Taqi Usmani, *Hamara Talimi Nizam*, quoted in Muhamadullah Khalili Qasmi, *Madrasa Education: Its Strength and Weakness*, pp. 151–2. Qasmi himself advocates this view.

Also see, 'Islamic education is much broader in its scope than the education system of the democratic West [. . .]. It aims to train the sensibility of the pupils [. . . .] to all kinds of knowledge [that] they are governed by the spiritual and ethical values of Islam.'

And,

'At present, there are more than 30,000 such non-governmental educational institutions. [. . .] Their contribution towards mass literacy, theological education and maintenance and deepening of Islamic identity has been incalculable and invaluable.' Manzoor Ahmad, *Islamic Education: Redefinition of Aims and Methodology*, New Delhi: Qazi Publishers and Distributors, 1990, pp. 5–6.

38. In an excellent comparative study of the responses of two religious communities, Peter B. Mayer, points out that though the percentage of Muslims who affirm that their religion is the most important thing in their lives is much higher than that of Hindus, they are even more tolerant of others' religions than other religious communities. 'Tombs and Dark Houses: Ideology, Intellectuals, Proletarians in the Study of Contemporary Indian Islam', in Imtiaz Ahmad (ed.), *Modernization and Social Change among Muslims in India*, New Delhi: Manohar, 1983, pp. 14 ff., 19 ff.

39. See Mushir-Ul-Haq, *Islam in Secular India*, Simla: Institute of Advanced Study, 1972, p. 25; also J.M. Khan, *Education Among Muslims*, p. 56.

40. All or at least most *ulama* and *maulavis* believe in the 'divinity' of *shari'a*. But *shari'a* is based not only on the *Quran* which is a 'Divine revelation', but also, perhaps even more so, on the *sunna* or *hadiths*. As will be seen in a later chapter 5, the *hadiths*,

written long after the demise of the Prophet, can hardly be called 'divine'.

41. Saiyid Hamid, perhaps the most well-known academic in the field of madrasa education and 'modernization of madrasas', said in a personal interview long back that every Muslim should learn not only the Quran but also the *sunna'*. Although there has been an exchange of letters between Sayyid Hamid and the author but I am not yet clear whether he is talking of only the madrasa curriculum or about all Muslim children. If it is the latter, then all Muslim children will have to go to madrasas, which is definitely not his intention.

42. See Kuldeep Kaur, *Madrasa Education in India: A Study of Its Past & Present*, Chandigarh: Centre of Research in Rural and Industrial Development, 1990, p. 271.

43. Imitiaz Ahmad, 'Urdu and Madrasa Education', *Economic and Political Weekly*, 2007, vol. 37(24): 2265–7.

44. See details of the Lok Jumbish project on the following website: www.unesdoc.unesco.org/images/0011/pdf.

45. See *Sachar Committee Report*, p. 80.

46. See Kuldeep Kaur, op. cit., pp. 203 ff., 211ff., 227 ff., 234ff.

47. See ibid., pp. 237 ff.

48. Jawaharlal Nehru, S. Abid Husain, Maulana Azad, Bipan Chandra, Mushirul Hasan, and a host of other secular Indians have argued strongly in favour of India's composite culture which consists of a shared space, lifestyle and values between Hindus and Muslims. To quote just Nehru: 'Partly because the great majority of Moslems in India were converts from Hinduism, partly because of long contact, Hindus and Moslems in India developed numerous common traits, habits, ways of living and artistic tastes. [. . .] They lived together peacefully as one people, joined each other's festivals and celebrations, spoke the same language, lived in more or less the same way and faced identical economic problems.' *The Discovery of India*, New Delhi: Oxford University Press, 1989, p. 268.

49. Mushirul Hasan is another enthusiastic supporter of this composite culture: 'Indian society was at no stage structured around religious solidarities, or polarized along "communal" lines [. . .] intercommunity conflicts, as and when they occurred, were counterpoised to the quiet, commonplace routines in which communities intermingled.' Hasan, op. cit., 2002, p. 54. He also quotes from various English observers how Hindus and Muslims shared a common socio-economic life together. Ibid., pp. 41 ff.

As an example of this syncretism in culture, see Shail Mayaram, 'Rethinking Meo Identity: Cultural Faultline, Syncretism, Hybridity or Liminality', in Mushirul Hasan (ed.), *Islam Communities and the Nation: Muslim Identities in South Asia*, New Delhi: Manohar, 1998, pp. 283 ff.

50. See http//en.wikipedia.org/wiki/Tablighi_Jamaat; and Mohammad Talib, 'Tablighis in the Making of Muslim Identities', in Hasan (ed.), *Islam Communities and the Nation*, pp. 307 ff. For details of the Tablighi movement, see Shail Mayaram, 'The Indian National Congress and the Ulama', in Iqbal Narain (ed.), *Secularism in India*, Jaipur: Classic Publishing House, 1995, pp. 125 ff.

51. See Bipan Chandra, *Communalism in Modern India*, New Delhi: Vikas Publishing House, 1989, pp. 78 ff., 122 ff., etc.

52. See Mayer, 'Tombs and Dark Houses', in Imtiaz Ahmad (ed.), *Modernization and Social Change among Muslims in India*, pp. 14 ff.

53. See ibid., p. 17.

54. See ibid., pp. 17 ff.

55. See ibid., pp. 28 ff., 32.

56. Talmeez Fatima and N. Hasnain, 'Adjustment, Alienation and Defeatism in Muslim and Hindu Adolescents', in N. Hasnain (ed.), *Social Psychological Dimensions of Muslims: The Post Independence Scenario*, New Delhi: Institute of Objective Studies, 1998, p. 71, also ibid., pp. 61 ff.; and the article by Qamar Hasan, 'Indian Muslims: Identity and Outlook', in ibid., pp. 2 ff.

57. The lower middle class of Muslims generally live in Muslim-dominated *mohallas* (localities) in cities. For a discussion of their lifestyle, see Douglas E. Goodfriend, 'Changing Concepts of Caste and Status among Old Delhi Muslims', in *Modernization and Social Change Among Muslims in India*, pp. 119 ff.

58. 'The prevalence of a greater sense of alienation among Muslim elite—better educated, having more experience of public life, and with high socio-economic status—than among Muslim mass public, as reported by (Gopal) Krishna, is a matter of concern.' Qamar Hasan, 'Indian Muslims: Identity and Outlook', in *Social-Psychological Dimensions of Muslims: The Post-Independence Scenario*, p. 12.

59. Imtiaz Ahmad 'Secularism and Communalism', in *Economic and Political Weekly*, 5, 1960 (special number), pp. 1137–58.

60. Khan, *Education Among Muslims*, p. 129.

61. See Goodfriend, 'Changing Concepts of Caste and Status among

Old Delhi Muslims'; Hasan Ali, 'Elements of Caste among the Muslims in a District in Southern Bihar'; Imtiaz Ahmad, 'Endogamy and Status Mobility among the Siddiqui Sheikhs of Allahabad, Uttar Pradesh', in Imtiaz Ahmad (ed.), *Caste and Social Stratification among Muslims in India*, New Delhi: Manohar, 1978, pp. 19 ff.; 129 ff.; 132 ff; 171 ff.

62. See Goodfriend, op. cit., p. 134. We need not look at any authoritative source for confirmation. Everyday we get news of some atrocious decision or the other of such panchayats among both Hindus and Muslims, especially those in villages.

63. We—my husband and I—have been closely associated with a Delhi slum in Shadipur. There are parts in this vast area where Hindus and Muslims live separately. But the largest part of the slum is one where the families belonging to the two religions live adjacent to each other very comfortably. Especially, the children study in common schools and are totally integrated.

While the poor of all 'communities' live mostly harmoniously together, the problem comes with lower middle class, who are most influenced by fundamentalist ideologues and political leaders, and insist on their separate Islamic identity, and who may prefer to stay with their co-religionists. On the other hand, it seems that those middle-class Muslims who want to live in mixed colonies are finding it difficult to do so in some communalized cities and towns. Actually mixed colonies are the panacea for all the evils that are plaguing our society these days.

3

Historical Background of Madrasa Education

1. THE IMPORTANCE OF *ILM* IN ISLAM

Every work on madrasa education gives a detailed and comprehensive history of the madrasa system of education from the Prophet's time up to the contemporary period. It, therefore, seems to be a waste of time and space to repeat almost the same things here. However, any study of a phenomenon or system would remain incomplete unless put in a balanced historical perspective.

It is a well-acknowledged fact that Islam gives the greatest importance to knowledge. The very first verse of the Holy Quran starts with the word *iqra* (read).[1] In fact, this *sura* comes quite late in the Quran, but arrangement of the *suras* apart, it is unanimously regarded as the first verse of the holy book. It is said that the word *ilm* is the second most repeated word in the Quran. Here are a few verses of the Quran hailing knowledge:

Say, O Muhammad, 'My Lord increase me in knowledge.' (XX. 114)

Mankind having hearts understand not; having eyes they see not; having ears they hear not. These are as the cattle, nay they are worse. These are the neglectful. (VII.179)

Our revelation is for people who have knowledge. (IX.11)[2]

The Quran repeatedly asks us to observe nature and its laws. Of course the aim of observation is to understand the greatness of the Lord who has created all this.[3] Prophet Muhammad, though illiterate, was a man of wisdom and respected men of knowledge. He asked all men to send their children to educational institutions. He freed slaves who could teach his people. It is said that the Prophet preferred knowledge even to piety. An often-quoted saying of the Prophet is 'Seek knowledge, though for it you may have to go to China'.[4]

Prophet Muhammad himself established the first maktab (elementary school) in a mosque. Gradually these maktabs were established throughout the Muslim world. The word maktab is derived from the Arabic *kitabat* which means a place of teaching, especially religious teaching. The maktabs taught reading of the Quran and various rituals associated with *namaz*. Perhaps some writing and basic arithmetic were also taught. Mostly the *maulavi* of the mosque served as the teacher.

The early years of Islam lacked regular arrangement for higher learning, so the seekers of higher knowledge studied under various teachers who were experts in particular fields of knowledge. Having studied with one teacher, specializing in a particular subject or book, the students went to another teacher who was an expert in another subject, and so on. There were also study centres and libraries consisting of hand-copied books, maintained by princes or other feudal lords. Different from these were madrasas or institutions of higher learning. The word 'madrasa' is derived from the root *dars* which means to teach or impart knowledge; thus madrasa is a place where knowledge is imparted. Madrasas came into being quite late. The first formal madrasa was established in Nishapur in Khurasan; the second was the Nizamia madrasa in Baghdad, both established in eleventh century. Madrasa Al Azhar (now called University) is said to have còme up even earlier. There were not many madrasas, though they, as also the scholars who taught students at home, were often given generous grants by the rulers. Education, therefore, was totally free. Gradually, the bigger madrasas started giving free boarding and lodging to their students. Some of these madrasas, as well as the houses of scholars and *amirs*, had libraries with large collections of books. These books were copied by hand and therefore few in number. So learning was mostly done by memorization of whole texts.[5]

Islamic learning flourished in the Umayyad and Abbasid periods as a result of state patronage. Of course, there was no arrangement for the further education of the masses and women of all classes. Women of higher classes took private tuitions from *maulavis* at home, while the rest were left out. The boys who attended madrasas or went to independent scholars for learning were sons of the elite who were expected to become *qazis, muftis* (judges) and fill other government posts. That is why the subjects taught in these institutions were mostly secular or dealing with this world with very little *dini* (religious) content. *Fiqh* (Islamic jurisprudence) was the most important subject, and it is even now regarded as an integral and almost the central subject of education in *dini madaris*. It is generally asserted that there was no restriction against the poor getting full Islamic education which was free. Though true, we can well imagine that very few among the poor would have thought it worthwhile to spend so many years on an apparently non-productive education.

Islam's high praise of all kinds of knowledge gave a great impetus for gaining knowledge even from foreign lands; so logic came to the Muslim world from Greece and astronomy and mathematics from India. As a result, Arabs and Arab culture became perhaps the most prosperous and advanced of that time.

However, to claim that the pioneer Arabs who excelled in various walks of life could do so because of madrasa education is not fully true. They did study in madrasas but they went much beyond the traditional education taught in them. Greek philosophy, logic, and Indian mathematics were made acceptable and were included in madrasa curriculum because the real seekers of knowledge had first explored and accepted them.[6] This shows that the then Arabs in general and even madrasa *maulavis* were much more open-minded than their present counterparts.

In Islam there is no difference between religious (*dini*) and secular (*duniyavi*) education (*talim*). God created both the universe and man. His Will rules the world, and it is the duty of man to obey His Will in everything. At the same time, a Muslim is expected to have a positive approach towards the world created by Allah. He is also expected to respect nature and its laws as signs of the glory of God.[7] That is how the medieval Muslims could include all sorts of secular subjects in their madrasa curriculum.

2. MADRASA EDUCATION AND ITS CURRICULUM IN INDIA

2.1. Sultanat Period

In the Indian context, early Muslim conquerors were too busy conquering new lands; only when they settled down did they pay attention to Islamic education. Sayyid Manazir Ahasan Gilani describes, albeit in a rhetoric manner, how good Islamic education was during the Sultanat period.[8]

There is no record of what the maktabs used to teach. It is, however, definite that they catered to the needs of the masses. The elites taught their sons and daughters at home at the elementary stage. Maktabs probably taught memorization of some *paras* of the Quran, basic rules regarding preparing for and performing *namaz*, and possibly basic reading and writing of Arabic and elementary arithmetic. The same curriculum continues even now, almost nine or ten centuries later.

Gilani and others have divided the development of madrasa system of education in India into four stages.[9] One important development that happened during the early period was the influence of Mir Fathullah Shiraji during Akbar's time. He introduced and popularized various rational sciences (*ma'qulat*) which became a major part of madrasa curriculum.[10] The demarcation between the first three stages of madrasa evolution is a little fuzzy as there is neither any reliable material to confirm the division, nor does there seem to be any basic difference between them as described by these scholars. It is the fourth stage that concerns us which starts with Aurangzeb's time. However, we must take a cursory look at Islamic education prior to that time.

Apart from maktabs, there were probably very few madrasas. Though education was free, only the sons of the elite went to madrasas because they were expected to become *qazis, muftis* and other government officers after completing their education and these posts were possibly not open for common men.

Other than madrasas, there were independent Islamic scholars who taught students at their homes. Students who were really desirous of knowledge went to more than one teacher, as each scholar's specialization was different. In addition, there were Sufi *khanqahs* (a form of monastery) where traditional Islamic teaching was imparted, in addition to their own mystical knowledge (*tasawwuf*). As in the rest of the Islamic world, there was no arrangement for higher education of masses or of women. Women of higher classes took their education at home under a *maulavi*, and some of them excelled in literature and the arts. However, the rest of the populace was left out. Though theoretically the poor could study in madrasas—and there are persons who argue that they not only studied in them, but that higher education helped them gain social mobility.[11] Other Muslim scholars accept that class distinction existed in the then society. The orthodox *ulama* and even many elite, such as Ziauddin Barani, believed that the gems of knowledge should not be carelessly thrown to the undeserving.[12]

Fiqh (Islamic jurisprudence) was the most important subject in early Islamic education because the future magistrates (*qazis*) and governors were expected to pass judgements and administer their state according to Islamic laws. *Fiqh* is still a very important subject of Islamic education in India. Along with it *usool-e-fiqh* (principles of jurisprudence) was and is taught.

Arabic was the second most important subject, and was taught with elaborate grammar, consisting of *sarf* (etymology) and *nahw* (conjugation). They continue to be important and integral parts of the modern madrasa system. There was, and is, a lot of emphasis on teaching flowery Arabic language consisting of *Baya'n*, *Ma'ni*, as also *Balaghat* (rhetoric).

Later on, when Persian became the official language of the court, it was included in the Islamic system of education. The *tafsirs* (commentaries) of the Holy Quran were perhaps also taught, along with *mantiq* (Greek logic), *falsafa* (mostly Greek philosophy). These are still being taught. Other subjects, being taught were perhaps *kalam* (scholastics), *tasawwuf* (mysticism), *tibb* (Unani medicine), *riyazi* (mathematics), *hindsa* (engineering) and *haiyat* (astronomy).[13]

If one wonders how any person can study and gain expertise in so many subjects, it is almost certain that all these subjects were not taught in the same madrasa. Each madrasa had its own curriculum which included different subjects, with a few common ones like detailed knowledge of Arabic, *tafsir* of the Quran, and so on. Moreover, as referred to above, various scholars were renowned experts in different disciplines, or rather books. So if any one wanted to gain expertise in one or the other subject, he would choose an appropriate teacher and go to him. Three things are however clear. First, even though free, this education was meant for the elite and not for the masses. Second, it follows that the students who laboriously learnt the vast course did so not for the sake of knowledge alone, but more for the sake of securing prestigious jobs. When it is contended by modern Muslim scholars that Islamic education is not meant for earning money but for gaining knowledge, it is perhaps not true. In fact, except *fiqh* (Islamic jurisprudence) and *tafsir* (commentaries on the Quran), *dini* (religious) content in the then madrasa system of education was much less, its greater part consisting of various secular or this-worldly (*duniyavi* or *ma'qulat*) subjects.

Third, if the above brief discussion gives the impression that there was a regular chain of well-established madrasas with well-defined curriculum, then it is not the case. There is no definite information about the number of madrasas; but it is clear that they were all autonomous and had their own *nisab* (curriculum). There was no class-wise division; students progressed from one book to the other according to their respective capabilities, and were promoted according to their capacities. The education was book-centered and distinction among students was made according to the book they were studying. Examination simply required the student to recite the book he had learnt (memorized).[14] There was no specific syllabus in madrasas. Each madrasa, big or small, decided its own syllabus or rather books it intended to teach. So did the individual scholars.

2.2. MADRASAS FROM AURANGZEB'S TIME
TO THE COMING OF THE BRITISH

It was Aurangzeb (seventeenth century) who, for the first time set up a team of scholars to prepare a digest of Islamic law, later on called Fatwa-i-Alamgiri. He granted Mulla Nizamuddin a mansion in Lucknow, known as the Firangi Mahal, where he established a madrasa. It was the predecessor for later madrasas and became a renowned centre of Islamic learning.

Under Aurangzeb's patronage Mulla Nizamuddin developed for the first time a systematic syllabus meant for all madrasas. It was named *Dars-i-Nizami*, in honour of its creator. We will study this syllabus in detail in the next chapter. For now, it will suffice to say that the focus of this syllabus was on so-called rational sciences (*ma'qulat*), Arabic and Persian languages with special emphasis on grammar (*sarf* and *nahaw*), *fiqh* (Islamic law) and *mantiq* (logic). This *nisab* laid greater emphasis on rational sciences than on religious subjects. Clearly the aim was to prepare the students for government jobs since all state functionaries, not just the judges, were expected to follow the *shari'a* (Islamic way of life, also understood as law) and *fiqh* (Islamic jurisprudence) in every department of governing.

2.3. The Impact of Usurpation of Power by the British

After Aurangzeb, Mughal empire's power declined and several small Muslim and non-Muslim kingdoms came up. On the one hand, the Marathas and the Sikhs fought with subsequent Mughal emperors, on the other, the British East India Company, which was granted the right to trade by the Mughal emperor Jahangir (early seventeenth century) started building its own empire at the cost of local powers, both Hindu and Muslim. In nineteenth century, Indians decided to organize and execute a revolt against the British. It is heartening that all petty princes and army heads went up to Delhi (*Dilli chalo* was their slogan), and formally asked the old and frail Mughal emperor Bahadur Shah Zafar to lead the revolt. Many *ulama* took active part in the revolt and suffered or were killed in retribution. The revolt was crushed cruelly. In the aftermath of the revolt, the British systematically slaughtered the local populace and destroyed its culture. In this wild spree of revenge Muslims, especially the *ulama*, seem to have suffered the maximum. However, this persecution did not continue for long.

At first, the English conquerors were accompanied by Christian missionaries who insisted on their right to preach the only 'true' religion of God. This involved condemnatory criticism of Indian religions (i.e. Hinduism and Islam). In the beginning, the missionaries' evangelical practices were both encouraged and funded by the British rulers. Gradually the English realized that the missionaries' activities went against the overall interests of the British rulers. So the latter started distancing themselves from the missionaries' activities, and even discouraged them. It was only afterwards that the British policy of religious neutrality was clearly defined and asserted.[15] The English tried to placate the local people, both Hindus and Muslims, by asserting that their religions, including personal laws and culture, would not be interfered with either by the administration or the missionaries.

Meanwhile, Warren Hastings established a madrasa in Calcutta (Madrasa-i-Aliya) as early as 1782, quickly followed by the establishment of the Banaras Hindu University. The aim of setting up these institutions was to produce scholars proficient in Arabic, Persian and Sanskrit who could then help the courts in deciding cases according to Muslim and Hindu personal laws.

While the Hindus remained passive, accepting the new order at least for the time being, and went about their ways as if unconcerned, the Muslims were traumatized and unable to accept the new ground realities. The first reason for this must have been that while the Hindus were used to and reconciled with the idea of being ruled by non-Hindus, the Muslims thought themselves as the rulers and were emotionally upset when they found that their power had been usurped by foreigners. However, a point to note is that the Muslims as such were never the rulers; only their elites were. There was always a vast distance between the urban elite who had some foreign blood and the Muslim masses who were mostly Hindu converts and who did not seem to have profited much by the fact that the rulers and feudal lords were Muslims. But the slipping away of power left the *ulama*, the landed gentry and other urban elite who had enjoyed the Mughal court's privileges with a sense of deprivation of their legitimate right. The masses, blindly following them, appropriated their feelings.

Second and a related factor was that the British usurpers and the Muslims saw each other as enemies. Some of the Muslim *ulama* and feudal lords had taken active part in the first freedom struggle of 1857 because they felt threatened by the foreigners. Post the revolt, the British, many of whom were from the peripheral sections of the English society, took terrible vengeance upon the local population. It is another thing that the vengeance was wrecked indiscriminately both on Hindus and Muslims, but the Muslims nevertheless believed, and some of them even now believe, that only Muslims were selected for vengeance. This resulted in a strengthening of the sense of being wronged which, in turn, made Muslims wary of the English and keep away from them. An unrecognized factor in the difference between the Hindus' and Muslims' responses to the British is that while Muslim consciousness was generally dominated by their religious identity, Hindus were a much diversified lot and did not possess a sense of a unified communal identity. As such, while Hindus could accept the English rule, Muslims could not.

The last straw for Muslims was the removal of Persian as the court language and its substitution by English, following Macaulay's famous debate over the issue of administrative language. Though his interest was only administrative convenience of the British and what he called the need for clerks or *babus* from the native people who could be employed by the English, the substitution resulted in a shift from Persian (and Urdu) to English in the perspective of employment seekers. Not only Muslims but even Hindus had been seeking proficiency in Persian with a view to not only secure administrative jobs but also to approach the court or other departments of the government. While the Muslims learnt Persian as if it was their own, even though it was not the mother tongue of any of them, Hindus learnt it as a matter of necessity or convenience. It was therefore easy for the latter to shift from Persian to English, as neither was either their mother tongue or the medium of their religion. Even though the same was true of the Muslims, and in practice Urdu was mostly employed as the court language in the pre-British period, Muslims had accepted the Persian language as their own. They now rejected the English language as foreign and a symbol of alien culture, and mourned over the loss of the Persian which had given the elites an edge in administrative and other matters.

Once the official language was decided to be English instead of Persian, Warren Hastings issued the order (in 1785) that the madrasa graduates were not to be given employment. Before it, the East India Company had appropriated the properties of Wakf boards.[16] These acts finally broke all possibilities of Muslims ever accepting the English as rulers, as they seemed to have been denied not only the power and majesty of being the rulers but also some share in the governance. This sense of deprivation and injustice played a very important role in the future attitude and activities of Muslims and their relations with the English.

Over time the Muslims' opposition not only to British rule but also to every thing Western, especially English education, hardened. Along with the perception of English education as being antithetical and a danger to Islam and Islamic values and culture came the realization of the urgent need to preserve these. This led to an active interest in the establishment of madrasas, as they were perceived as the only institutions which could preserve and strengthen Islam and its culture. The Muslims thus started establishing madrasas with the sole purpose of preserving Islam as a religion and a culture. Not only the *ulama* but the landed gentry too took active part in the establishment and maintenance of various madrasas.

Here it may be noted that Islam has never distinguished between the *dini* (religious) and *duniyavi* (worldly) life and values, so that Islamic institutes of learning in various forms always included both religious and secular subjects. That is the reason madrasas taught worldly subject from Arabic grammar and flowery prose to chemistry, physics astronomy and medicine. All the pre-modern luminaries of the Arab world, as well as of India, were the products of madrasas. What is more, since Islam as a religion did not form the core of madrasa syllabus, non-Muslims (Hindus) equally participated in madrasa education. Rammohun Roy, the great Hindu liberal thinker and reformer, had his initial education in a madrasa, and his ability to argue his point convincingly was probably the result of his madrasa training which emphasizes both logic and rhetoric.

Why did Hindus join the *madaris*? As the rulers were Muslims (whom Hindus acknowledged willingly), and the language of the court and administration was Persian, Hindus as well as Muslims studied that language, as also other subjects fashionable at that time in *madaris*. They did so because a madrasa education enabled them to get employment, as well as social prestige.

However, while the so-called rational sciences (*ma'qulat*), such as Arabic, Persian, logic and rhetoric were valued and respected in the Mughal courts, they were found to be useless in procuring jobs or prestige in the new political order. These subjects continued to be taught in the madrasas, but soon it was realized that the more valuable and essential part of madrasa education was the one concerning religion and religion-based culture. Under these circumstances, the orthodox seem to have appropriated the Christian-Western dichotomy of the sacred and profane or secular, which was foreign to Islamic thought. Though madrasas continued to teach the *ma'qulat* or rational (secular) sciences, they at the same time, began perceiving themselves as purely religious institutions. Thereafter the *madaris* on their own started to call themselves *dini madaris*.[17]

In the eighteenth century, Shah Walliullah made pioneering efforts to 'reform' Islam. His ideological campaign included: First, a call to go back to the original purity of Islam which meant discarding all those beliefs and customs which had some Indian (Hindu) influence. This ideology was adopted by *ulama* and certain other Muslim leaders in a big way in the nineteenth century. Second, Shah advocated that the Holy Quran should be read in one's mother tongue or any language one is most familiar with. This suggestion has not been accepted by most Muslims till date. The third suggestion of Shah was even more important. He advocated greater emphasis on the study of *hadiths* (the accounts of the approvals, disapprovals and other sayings of the Prophet Muhammad) in the madrasa curriculum. Though at that time this advice was not heeded to, *hadiths* were included in the syllabus of madrasas established in the nineteenth century.[18]

3. NINETEENTH-CENTURY REFORM MOVEMENTS AND THEIR IMPLICATIONS

3.1. INDEPENDENT MOVEMENTS FOR 'REFORM' IN DIFFERENT RELIGIOUS COMMUNITIES

Nineteenth century saw tremendous intellectual turmoil around the globe. Some of the intellectual movements, such as those of Rammohun Roy and Sayyid Ahmad Khan were directly influenced by Western thought, while many others, such as that of Dayanand Saraswati among Hindus and those of *ulama* for the revival of old pristine Islam, were fully indigenous. Most of these movements were aimed at reforming the society around them. As these reform movements were directed at different religious communities, and as the reformers could not address the evils of another religion or religion-based community, they resulted in the defining of a separate identity of various sections of the populace exclusively on the basis of their religion.

Perhaps it was the catholicity of Hindus, or perhaps it was the largely diffused or heterogeneous character of Hinduism, or perhaps it was the fact that Hindus had already confronted a 'foreign' religion—Islam; whatever the reason, they did not feel traumatized by either the introduction of Christianity or of English education in India. The middle class or the upper castes among them took up English education. Perhaps the original motivation among Hindus was to get employment as *babus* (clerks), but once they took up English education, they benefited from the flow of the ideas of the Enlightenment (eighteenth century) and Liberalism (nineteenth century).

Luckily for Hindus, their introduction to Western liberal thought through English education generated in them an admiration for freedom of thought and liberal ideas. That, in turn, gave birth to several religious-social reform movements which together generated a Renaissance of sorts in Hindu thought and practice. These Hindu reform movements mostly tried to bring in social change by introducing Western ideas of social equality and freedom of thought, and most of them were directed towards the rejection of caste distinctions and improvement in the lot of women.

Unluckily, the Muslim reform movements aimed at going back in centuries to the pristine purity of Islam by rejecting English education and the Western ideas that it stood for. There were several reasons for their rejection, as suggested above. The Muslim leaders thought themselves to be the legitimate rulers of India and regarded the Englishmen as usurpers of that power. *Maulanas* and some fundamentalist leaders among Muslims had, and still have, the sense of being in possession of God's supreme and final religion, as the chosen people of God's final 'revelation'.[19] Therefore, they were not ready to admit that the Western people had something to teach them. Above all, they perceived the British as representing a culture and religion which were opposed to and destructive of their own religion, culture and values. The *ulama* and other elite of the Muslim society had not so far felt threatened by the presence of Hindus and Hindu religion as the latter, being polytheistic and idolatrous, at least in practice, was perceived as an inferior religion. But here was another Semitic religion, a religion of the Book which also claimed to be the highest and final religion. (Hinduism does not always make this claim.) Muslims saw in it a danger to their religion. Muslims were and are so totally convinced of the truth of the Word of God that hardly any followers of Islam converted to Christianity. So, in fact, they need not have worried about the challenge posed by Christianity.

Earlier, Shah Walliullah had started a movement in the eighteenth century to purge Islam of all its supposed accretions. It was a momentous occurrence in Islamic history. Islamic reform movements of later nineteenth century took the form of revivalism, through which they sought to bring back the 'pure' form of Islam, as it was understood in the times of the first four pious *Khalifas* and the Companions of the Prophet. The right Islamic way was conceived as one that follows the *shari'a* unquestioningly (*taqalid*). The *ulama*, who were until now preoccupied with the feudal lords and the landed gentry of Muslim society, suddenly found themselves deprived of their patronage, as the latter themselves had lost their privileged positions. The *ulama*, for the first time turned their attention to the common people for patronage and field of influence. They found that what the Muslim masses were practising was very different from what they knew the 'true' Islam to be. They at once set about correcting the ways of the masses and teaching them the true religion. They also realized that Islamic education was urgently needed to tell the common people about Islam and above all Islamic *shari'a*.

3.2. NEW MADRASAS IN THE BRITISH PERIOD

As we have seen above, the greatest impetus for establishing madrasas came from the Muslim perception of the threat to their religion and culture from the British. This resulted in the urge for preserving Muslim culture. It was thought that well-planned madrasas, which would give the knowledge of Islam, its culture and values in such a way that the students would become fully convinced of the ultimate 'truth' of Islam, was the best way to preserve the religion. A second factor, mentioned earlier, in determining the nature and set up of these madrasas was that the secular education given so far in the madrasas was found to be of no use. So madrasas were reduced to *dini* madrasas, which were expected to teach only Islamic religion and related subjects. Madrasa authorities and teachers were not averse to this new classification.

So far the madrasas were few and they were known on the basis of the specialization in any one or the other field of knowledge. For instance, the madrasa of Khairabad specialized in Iranian philosophy; the Firangi Mahal of Lucknow specialized in *fiqh*; a few other madrasas mainly taught Arabic grammar. The Madrasa Alia of Calcutta, and later Delhi College under the influence of English Company officers stressed on the learning of literature and history. Shah Walliullah had earlier emphasized the need for teaching religious subjects proper, like the Quran, *tafsirs* (commentaries on the Quran) and *hadiths*. Though his views were not adopted at that time, now the *ulama* started accepting the worth of his views.

Gradually, other madrasas started coming up as a response to the challenge posed by the British rule and English education.[20] It was in these circumstances that the Darul-Uloom was established in Deoband, near Saharanpur in Uttar Pradesh in the year 1866. Maulana Qasim Nanautawi and Maulana Rasheed Ahmad Gangohi, especially the former, were among the chief founders of the Madrasa. Nanautawi tried to reconcile several traditions of his time which were used for madrasa teaching at Khairabad, Firangi Mahal (Lucknow), Delhi and Punjab. As a result, the syllabus of Deoband became lengthy and heavy.

In spite of its length the Deoband syllabus remained mostly confined to what are called intellectual sciences (*ma'qulat*), such as Arabic grammar, the art of flowery language both in oratory and writing (*balaghat, ma'ani, baya'n*). At first religious subjects were not very important. It was only gradually that they were added and became integral to the madrasa syllabus. Darul-Uloom was not only the first madrasa with a regular curriculum and syllabus in India, but also possibly the first in the world. Its chief stress was on *fiqh* and learning of Arabic and Persian. Thus, in its original form, its syllabus not only accepted the traditional subjects and contents of old Islamic studies but also undermined the importance of *dini* subjects proper in preference to the 'rational sciences'. It refused to recognize the changes that had come in the world and in India in that period. However, it emphasized the central role of religion in personal and social life and sought to preserve and advance the Islamic way of life (*shari'a*).[21]

The approach and views of the Deoband *ulama* came to be known as the Deobandi movement. It tried hard to preserve and emphasize the religion and traditional values of Islam, and affirmed that religious education alone can give Muslims firm grounding in Islam. These *ulama* also encouraged the setting up of other madrasas, mainly in north India, which were expected to follow the Deobandi curriculum. Madrasas were established in Saharanpur and Rampur soon afterwards.

During the middle ages in the Islamic world, and later on in India till the Mughal rule lasted, the chief motive for madrasa education was worldly, not spiritual. It was not that those who went in for madrasa education undermined their religion; only that acquiring religion was not their first priority. Contemporary *ulama* and other scholars repeatedly assert that teaching students to earn one's livelihood is not one of the goals of madrasa education; it is chiefly, and perhaps solely, to train them to become righteous and devoted Muslims (*momins*).[22] Perhaps this was not the case with medieval madrasas which trained their students to be efficient *qazis, muftis* and administrators. Perhaps it is not the case even now, as the pass-outs of madrasas do want to earn a decent living through their laboriously acquired education.[23]

With the coming of the British the situation changed drastically. English schools became the instrument for students to earn livelihood and status in society. The role of *madaris* was confined to one of providing religious education. Thus the *madaris* which were the providers of comprehensive over-all education, became *dini madaris*. The duality between the secular or worldly and the religious was firmly established.[24] No one seems to have noticed it, or the leaders of the Muslim community could do nothing about it. However, though their role was confined to religious (*dini*) education, the *madaris*, especially those following the Deobandi syllabus, continued to stress on worldly sciences (*ma'qulat*). It was only gradually that *sirat* (biography of the Prophet), *aqeeda'* (fundamental Islamic beliefs) and *hadiths* were added.

Meanwhile Sir Sayyid Ahmad Khan realized that the Muslims were being left behind in the race for worldly advancement as a result of their rejection of English education. He therefore established Muhammaden Anglo Oriental College (MAO) at Aligarh in 1875 which developed into the Aligarh Muslim University in 1920. He also actively advocated English education among Muslims, contending that instead of opposing the British, Muslims should reconcile with the ground realities and learn the English language which had now become the means of social, political and economical upliftment. His approach to education came to be known as the Aligarh movement. Sir Sayyid was not against religious education but according to him, an ideal system of education in modern times should be that of the type of English schools, though religious education may be imparted along with it. Apart from advocating and actively working for modern education for Muslims, he also had relatively heterodox views on matters of *shari'a*, advocating *ijtihad* (reasoning in accordance with scriptures) in doubtful matters. He advocated the adoption of both Western education and ways which need not oppose *shari'a*.[25]

Subsequently Sir Sayyid gave up efforts to interpret Islam and devoted himself to the MAO College in Aligarh. He visualized the college not as a vehicle for reforms but as a place where Muslims may acquire English education without prejudice to their religion. Therefore, women were not considered for admission because of the opposition of the more fundamentalist Muslims. Importantly, MAO was not meant only for Muslims: Hindus were equally welcome. However, scholars as M. Mujeeb and Rajmohan Gandhi have bemoaned the fact that in order to establish an English-medium college, Sir Sayyid had to give up his modernist views and goals of religious reforms, so that he could get Muslim boys to learn Western education.[26] Moreover, to achieve the goal of uplifting his community through English education, he also denounced the national movement, and asked Muslims not to participate in it.

At first there was a strong opposition to his views, especially since he had adopted Western dress and lifestyle along with his Western education. At the same time his strong advocacy for modern education had some effect on the traditionalist *ulama*. It prompted them to question for the first time whether their system of education in vogue so far was sufficient for modern times. A large convention of Muslim *ulama*, both traditionalists and modernists, was held at Kanpur in 1894; it was followed by several other conventions. Both groups of *ulama* agreed that the purpose of Muslim education was not being served rightly either by Darul-Uloom, Deoband, or by MAO College. Darul-Uloom Nadwatul Ulama was thereafter established in Lucknow as a 'model educational institution' in 1898. Maulana Muhammad Ali Mungeri and Allama Shibli Noumani were the most important ideologues and activists among the founders of Nadwatul Ulama, which was supposed to create a fine balance between the educational systems of Deoband and MAO College. Its basic aims were: extensive and intensive change/reform in the syllabi of Islamic studies and preparing a new syllabus; producing a new generation of religious scholars (*ulama*) having wide and deep knowledge of Islamic studies as well as modern thoughts who must also know the requirements of modern times; developing consensus and brotherhood among Muslims; and propagation of Islamic teaching, especially among the non-Muslim brothers.[27]

Maulana Sayyid Hasan Ali Nadwi has been a prominent scholar of Nadwa. He has observed that though the syllabus and approach of the *madaris* had been changing in earlier centuries, it suddenly became stagnant in nineteenth century, when due to global transformations, change in human approach was required all the more.[28] We will have occasion to discuss Nadwa's syllabus in brief in our next chapter. There is some teaching of modern subjects but only at the primary stage. English language is taught throughout. However, other than English, there is no basic difference between Nadwa's syllabus and that of Deoband, or most madrasas in India.

The movement for reform in the madrasa system became stag-

nant immediately after the establishment of Nadwa. Shibli
Noumani, who was a prominent figure in pro-reform movement, resigned from his post in Nadwa in frustration. Maulana
Abul Kalam Azad, another distinguished scholar from Nadwa,
acknowledged the failure of this thrust for reform in Nadwa
experiment.[29] Noumani then went to Azamgarh and helped in
establishing, along with others, Madrasat-al-Islah in Sarai Mir,
Azamgarh, in 1909, as an institution which aimed to combine
the two systems of education. It is continuing on this course
even now, though perhaps not very successfully. Noumani also
established Dar-ul Musannifin (House of Authors), a publication house in Azamgarh, that is still functioning. He was a renowned scholar of Islam. Noumani, as also Qasim Nanautawi,
strongly supported the cause of communal harmony.

The fourth major madrasa was established after a few years of
Nadwa. Maulana Nanautawi was also not satisfied with the
way Deoband's madrasa was shaping up, and realized that the
syllabus of Deoband still put greater emphasis on the (so-called)
rational sciences and less on *dini* subjects. Therefore he went to
Azamgarh and was one of the pioneers of the Madrasa Jamiatul
Falah in Balariaganj, Azamgarh. His intention was to create
an institution for Muslim boys which would give them genuine
religious education and also some elementary knowledge of
modern subjects. Now, the madrasa follows the curriculum of
Jamaat-e-Islami, and has some amount of modern subjects in
its curriculum. We will briefly discuss its syllabus in the next
chapter.

There are several other important madrasas in Azamgarh. Almost all the schools of Islam have established their own distinct
madrasa in the city. There is also a women's madrasa, a branch
of Jamiat-ul Falah. The fifth important madrasa is Darul-Uloom
Manzar-i-Islam, Bareilly, founded by Maulana Ahmad Raza Khan
in 1904. Its founder was strongly opposed to Deoband's conception and teaching of Islam. He even issued *fatwas* against
the founders of Deoband madrasa. This school calls itself Ahl-e-
Sunnat. It regards all other schools of Sunni Islam as misrepre-
senting the religion, while declaring itself as the true Islam. Ahl-e-
Sunnat followers are popularly called Barelvis, though they do
not accept this nomenclature. They are in favour of retaining

certain Sufi customs like saint worship (including visiting *mazars*), idolization of Prophet Muhammad and celebration of his birthday. However, acceptance of certain popular customs does not make them liberal. They are quite fanatic in their views and even condemn followers of other schools of Islam as *kafirs*. Unlike the Deoband *maulanas*, Ahmad Raza opposed Khilafat movement, and supported the Muslim League.[30] We will discuss its curriculum in the next chapter.

Apart from the above, several other important madrasas were established in the same period:

- Mazahar-al Uloom, Saharanpur, established in 1866.
- Madrasa Baqyatris Salehat, Vellore, Tamil Nadu, established in 1883.
- Jamiat-ul Falah, Balariaganj, Azamgarh, established in 1889.
- Jamia Mazjharul Uloom, Banaras, established in 1893.
- Madrasa Ameenia, Delhi, established in 1897.
- Darul Uloom, Khalilia Nizamia, Tonk, established in 1899.
- Jamia Arabia Hayatul Uloom, Mubarakpur, Azamgarh, established in 1899.
- Jamia Ashrafia, Mubarakpur, Azamgarh, 1905.
- Madrasat-ul Islah, Sarai Mir, Azamgarh, established in 1909.
- Jamia Darus Salem, Umnabad, established in 1924.

The sudden spurt in the establishment of and support for the madrasas after the 1857 revolt might have been due to the Muslims' perception of threat from the English who not only usurped Muslim kingdoms but also epitomized an entirely opposite thinking and way of life. The British at first hardened their attitude towards Muslims and persecuted them. However, gradually they tried to be neutral in religious matters.

During the late nineteenth and early twentieth centuries Muslim leaders were constantly preoccupied with the 'correct' education of their youth. Many of them even favoured modern education through English medium. Anjuman-i-Islam, an education society of Muslims, was established in 1876 in Bombay. Badruddin Tayyabji was closely associated with it and encouraged modern education for Muslims. Ameer Ali also worked actively for the spread of modern education among Muslims of eastern India. Whatever the efforts of such leaders, children of the Muslim masses still largely went to madrasas. The main reason for this was that most of them did not like the idea of sending their children to missionary-run schools which were so far the main vehicles of modern education.

Thus, there emerged two parallel trends among the Muslims—first of those advocating modern education and second of those who were making all out efforts to promote traditional education. There was also a renewed effort to assert separate Islamic culture and values. For the time being it appears that, the number of Muslims favouring traditional education for their children increased with time due to the persistent efforts of *ulama* and other leaders to bring the Muslims to the fold of orthodoxy.

So far at the level of masses Hindus and Muslims were living in harmony, having close contact at the social level. Neither the Muslim nor the Hindu masses cared much for education, as they were too busy making two ends meet. However, if they ever thought of educating their children, while the Muslims sent them to maktabs, Hindus sent them to government or even missionary schools. Significantly, very few Muslim leaders were, and even now are, bothered about the conditions and educational level of maktabs, the educational institutions integrally associated with mosques, to which the majority of children of poor Muslims go. A very small number of them pursue further studies in madrasas or common schools. But the emphasis throughout in Muslim thinking and writing has been on madrasas which give detailed Islamic education. Maktabs of today, like those of medieval times, still continue to teach memorization of some verses of the Quran, basic Islamic rituals, Arabic and Urdu alphabets. (Some maktabs in modern times have introduced Urdu, Hindi and arithmetic, but there is no proper information as to the number of such maktabs and the level of their teaching.)

3.3. OTHER 'REFORM' MOVEMENTS AMONG MUSLIMS

Unlike among Hindus, reform movements among Muslims took an entirely different shape. They were not directed at improving the lot of women or encouraging education and liberal ideas; rather, they called for bringing Islam back to its pristine glory, and purging it of all accretions, that is, those beliefs and practices which Muslims have unconsciously taken from their Hindu compatriots.

Tablighi Jamaat was founded by Maulana Muhammad Ilyas and his supporters in the Mewat region of Rajasthan in the 1930s. Its avowed aims were and are propagating belief in the oneness of God; perfection in religious observances; acquiring (religious) knowledge and remembrance of God; good behaviour towards others (in practice it means towards Muslims); purity of intention; and spending time in preaching (*da'wa*). This Jamaat is a mass-based organization, and its objectives are to free Muslims from their acquired non-Muslim practices emphasize purely Islamic beliefs and practices, and preach Islam among the non-believers. Its members are spread all over north and central India. They stay at mosques and work among the people for religious reform. Though it is a mass movement, the role of *ulama* who know the *shari'a* is prominent.

Jamaat members have paid special attention to those regions where there was a close contact between Hindus and Muslims, who together created a composite, shared culture, such as Mewat and some areas of Bengal. As a result, most rituals and practices that resembled Hindu ones, as well as the worship of saints and *pirs*, which brought Hindus and Muslims together, have been either discarded, or are on the verge of being discarded. There is also an emphasis on a centralized Islam which rejects regional cultural variations. Proselytizing is also undertaken regularly. As a result, a large number of Muslims in areas where the Tablighi Jamaat is active have abandoned their local dress and language as well as many of the practices and customs which were common to Hindus and Muslims. In place of the composite culture they adopt an Islamic culture based on the *shari'a*. This results in a distinct identity marked by an intense awareness of the 'otherness' of rest of the population. The Jamaat, as well as other *ulama* engaged in 'reform' movements, stress the unity of the *millat* that transcends all national boundaries. They insist on applying *shari'a* to every Muslim in every possible circumstance.[31]

Unfortunately, the Tablighi Jamaat believes in conversions of non-Muslims. It has set before it the goal of 'an overall spread of Islam in the whole of India', and declares non-Muslims as the 'field of action of Tabligh', and 'the raw material for this splendid activity'. Though the Tablighi activists do not take part in political activity, they believe that Islam can best be preserved and strengthened when the state is Islamic.[32]

The Tablighi movement and the Deobandi approach to both religious and socio-political matters have brought *ulama* to the forefront of Muslim society. Theoretically, Islam provides for a direct relation between the creature and the Creator which needs no mediators. But in practice, the *ulama* being the experts of *shari'a*, have always been very important. The Muslim masses always turn to them for guidance and judgement in any practical problem.

However, while the Jamaat is an apolitical organization, Deobandi *ulama* took active part in the struggle for independence (in 1920s), especially in the Khilafat movement, which Mahatma Gandhi combined with the non-cooperation movement and which saw an unprecedented, though temporary, unity between Hindus and Muslims. Significantly, till that time not only the *ulama* but also Muslims in general had kept aloof from the movement for independence. Sayyid Ahmad Khan had emphatically rejected the idea of Muslim participation in politics (i.e. any agitation against the British).

Within the Muslim community the two groups of English-educated elite and the rest of the populace, a large number of whose children went to maktabs and madrasas, were quite distinct. During the Khilafat movement the two groups came together. Both, the English-educated Muslims and Gandhi wanted the cooperation of *ulama*, as they knew that their support would also mean the support of the Muslim masses. While conjoining the two rather different agitations, Gandhi knew that if he wanted to involve the Muslim masses the motivation would have to be religious.

Khilafat movement was the first mass movement in which Muslims participated, and its leaders were largely *maulanas*. These *ulama* reached the remote parts of country and told the Muslim masses that Islam was in peril due to the threat to the last Muslim empire in Turkey. Alongside they exhorted their audience to mould their life according to the teachings of the Prophet and *shari'a*. Outward signs of religiosity or Muslim identity were encouraged, such as the Islamic dress and the beard.

The *ulama* came to hold a position in the public arena that they had never enjoyed before. Not only the *ulama* but even other Muslim leaders like Maulana Azad constantly used religious idiom and textual references in order to exhort the masses to actively oppose the British.[33] Without going into the details of history, suffice it to say that the Khilafat movement vastly increased the importance of the *ulama* and other religious leaders. At every juncture of this movement, *fatwas* were sought and pronounced. The attitude and approach of Muslims in this period was similar to the Deobandis. Deobandi *maulanas* have always been conservative, and have emphasized the role of *maulavis* in guiding and even determining the lives of Muslim masses. The Khilafat movement put this philosophy in practice.

Since madrasas were the place where *ulama* are prepared, their importance too increased. It goes to the credit of Deoband *ulama* that they were (and are) staunch nationalists and rejected the Muslim League and Jinnah's Two Nation theory. They opposed the Partition of the country and most of them opted to stay in India at the time of Partition. At the same time, not only the *ulama* but even other Muslim leaders thought in terms of a global Muslim *millat*. That is why, Muslims were so eager to fight for the retention of Khilafat as a symbolic head of the entire Muslim world. The brotherhood of all Muslims of the world transcending national boundaries became the goal and dream of pious Muslims.

Hamza Alavi has argued intelligently and persuasively how the entire institution of *khalifa* is based on a misrepresentation of Islamic traditions and even history. She also argues that it was mainly spearheaded by *ulama* and other dissatisfied elites among Muslims, and in no way addressed itself to the real issues of Indian Muslims.[34] It is difficult to understand why Indian Muslims should have been agitated over the preservation of Khilafat in Turkey if they could not be emotionally involved in India's freedom struggle. Obviously the clerics and others leaders of the Khilafat movement wanted to drill into the Muslim psyche that they first belonged to the universal *umma* and the latter's concern were their primary concern, and by implication India's concerns were secondary.

Let us remember that the first unorganized struggle for India's freedom in 1857 was fought under the banner of Bahadur Shah Zafar. Various petty kings, most of them Hindus, and their armies marched to Delhi, acknowledging Bahadur Shah Zafar as their true ruler, even though he was only nominally so. He, in turn, not only sacrificed his two sons to the cause of freedom, but at the end of the day mourned that he could not even get two yards of ground in his dear homeland (*do gaz zamin bhi na mili kuche yar main*).

By identifying themselves with the past glory of other Muslim nations, the Muslim leaders started a wave of pan-Islamism which was possibly not endorsed by other Muslim countries. That is why the saving of the Khilafat in Turkey became such a big issue for them. Even before that, Iqbal, the poet of *Qaumi Tarana*, became a pioneer advocate of pan-Islamism. We cannot go into the details of his conversion to an entirely different ideology exemplified by his lament for the glory of the Muslims' past at the sight of Sicily; and his *Shikwa* to God who seems to have forsaken the Muslim race.[35] His later poems reflect a conceptual framework in which the entire population of Muslims in the world forms one *umma* transcending all national boundaries. More importantly, he rejected the relevance of nationalities:

The expression Indian Muhammedan, however convenient it may be, is a contradiction in terms, since Islam in its essence is above all conditions of time and space. Nationality with us is a pure idea; it has no geographical basis. But inasmuch as the average man demands a centre of nationality, the Muslims look for it in the holy town of Mecca.[36]

Almost all the leaders of Khilafat movement were pan-Islamist, Maulana Abul Kalam Azad being the foremost. He edited the paper *Al Hilal*, and declared that:

The fundamental mission of *Al Hilal* is to invite the Muslims to follow only the Book and the Tradition of the Prophet in all their activities and beliefs. Be it the field of education, culture, or politics, it is subject to religion. The *Al Hilal* wants to see the Mussalmans only as Mussalmans.[37]

Azad went on to develop the theory that all Muslims together constitute one *umma*, *khalifa* being their head. Thus, to fight for the preservation of Khilafat became the duty of every Muslim.[38] Since the masses could not have been bothered about the *khalifa* in a far off land, the *ulama* took upon themselves the responsibility of going to villages and towns and exhorting them to defend it. Though it is difficult to reconcile pan-Islamism with nationalism, Indian Muslims have been successfully trying to do the same for the last century or so.[39] Most leaders of the movement were equally devoted to the cause of national Independence.

Again, Azad was in the forefront of these leaders. He modified his pan-Islamism under the influence of Mahatma Gandhi, and declared that 'It is one of the greatest frauds on the people to suggest that religious affinity can unite areas which are geographically, economically, linguistically and culturally different.'[40]

During the same period as the Khilafat movement, the Jamiat-e-Ulama Hind was founded in 1919, under the leadership of Husain Ahmad Madni. It allied itself to the Congress, opposed Partition and supported India as the nation of all communities with a composite culture. Later on in 1940 Jamaat-i-Islami was founded under the leadership of Abul Ala Maududi. It was close to the Muslim League. Maududi and his followers migrated to Pakistan. Both the Jamiat and Jamaat are still functioning in India. In spite of their different attitudes to the integrity of India, they are both extremely conservative and have influenced the Muslim masses, as well as popularized madrasa education. According to Mushirul Hasan,

The Jamaat has remained [. . .] a retrograde and reactionary force, deriving ideological and financial support from conservative and semi-feudal regimes of West Asia. It is opposed to social reform, enforces strict adherence (*taqlid*) to the tenets of Islam through their vast network of *madaris* and *makatib*, and has stalled Muslim participation in the democratic process.[41]

At the same time, Jamaat is interested, like Sayyid Ahmad Khan, in the material progress of Muslims, and accepts that this is not possible unless Muslim children become conversant with modern world and knowledge. Since it is both conservative and in a way anti-government, it does not encourage Muslims to send their children to common schools. Instead, it has developed a curriculum which seeks to combine both religious and modern

subjects, and actively promotes it. The curriculum is now followed in various madrasas, including Jamiat-al-Falah, Azamgarh.
We will have an occasion to discuss this curriculum in the next
chapter.

4. MADRASAS AND ORTHODOX MUSLIM ORGANIZATIONS AFTER INDEPENDENCE

Following Independence and the trauma of Partition, the entire
nation, especially the Muslims, remained in a state of shock.
Most Muslim middle class who were educated in the modern
way and were relatively liberal, and a number of noted Islamic
scholars and *maulanas*, migrated to Pakistan. On the other hand,
Muslims engaged in agriculture and hereditary craft, who were
rooted in the soil, opted to stay in India. The latter were left
without any worthwhile modern leaders and completely at the
mercy of the *ulama*. The common Muslims would have adjusted
well but for the remaining middle class, and the *ulama*. They
started the bogey of Muslims being a minority and Islam as a
religion and culture being in danger. Deprived of the guidance of
the earlier educated, liberal middle class, Muslim masses have
learnt to rely more and more on the *ulama*. Apart from the
feeling of 'Islam in danger' there have been a few other irritants
for Muslims. They are related to certain aspects of modern education as it is being offered in government schools.

Suffice it to say that both Muslim clerics and some sections of
middle class are misleading the masses. The *ulama* are constantly
pulling them towards more conservative practices; and the middle
class Muslims, while they themselves mostly send their children
to English-medium private schools, talk of how Muslims are
neglected, how modern government school education is biased
against the Muslims, and so on. As a result, the role of *ulama*
and madrasas has been constantly increasing among Muslims.
On every issue, from the pettiest to most relevant ones, a large
number of persons among the poor and relatively uneducated
Muslims seek the *fatwa* (judgemental opinion) of the *muftis* of
Deoband and other madrasas who pass thousands of *fatwas*
every year, thereby determining almost every detail of a majority
of Muslims' lives.

Orthodox Muslims were and even now are opposed to English education. They fear that modern education would destroy the religious faith and ethical character of Muslims. Even now the dangers of modern education for Islamic religion and ethics are rhetorically pointed out.[42] Not only the *ulama*, a large number of educated middle-class Muslims are convinced that Muslim youth need Islamic education, and madrasas are doing a fine job in this field.[43]

There are two basic factors which have resulted in the mushrooming of madrasas all over the subcontinent. The first, as mentioned above, is the orthodox *mullas'* obsessive fear that modern education, and its accessory Western culture, will erode and finally destroy Islam and Islamic values. It seems to make Huntington's theory of Clash of Civilizations stand on its head! The *mullas* in effect seem to be saying what Huntington says, only the 'other' in their case has changed. The fear is exaggerated, as the children of other communities are studying Western curriculum for almost the last one and a half centuries, and excelling in it, without any danger to their religion and culture.

A second factor is the post-Partition feeling of alienation, the fear of being absorbed in the mainstream mostly dominated by Hindu ethos. However, until the Khilafat movement when pan-Islamism was invoked and instilled in the minds of the masses, Hindus and Muslims lived together peacefully in the same society. After the Partition, the consciousness of being a numerical minority, strengthened by the aggressive stance of Hindu chauvinists, has made Muslims cling to their distinct religious and cultural identity even more.[44] And what better means to preserve and assert that identity than through madrasa education. To quote one such writer,

At present there are more than 30,000 such non-governmental eduational institutions, spread all over the Indian Union. This is the largest peoples' endeavour, on absolutely voluntary basis, in the field of education in history, any where in the world. These madaris do not accept government aid for the fear of dilution of their character and charter. Their contribution towards mass literacy theological education and maintenance and deepening of Islamic identity has been incalculable and invaluable.[44]

With the same purpose in view, a Dini Talimi Council was established in Uttar Pradesh in the 1950s. This turned into a full-fledged movement for establishing *dini* madrasas, first in Uttar Pradesh, and then throughout the North. Its main opposition has been to what some Muslims perceive as Hinduism-based education being imparted in government schools. It has asserted the need of education through the mother tongue, which it claims to be Urdu for all North Indian Muslims. It also insists on the need for religious education for Muslim children. With a view to these perceived needs of Muslims, the Council has tried to establish maktabs in every Muslim majority locality, both urban and rural. These maktabs provide the basic knowledge of Islamic teachings and reciting the Quran, as also some elementary knowledge of modern languages, arithmetic and other basic modern subjects. It has also established some primary schools where along with modern subjects through Urdu medium, religious instructions are given.[45]

The Dini Talimi Council has further demanded that religious education be imparted in government schools. From time to time Muslim conferences have been organized which demand from the government the introduction of religious education in schools; making arrangement for the publication of religious literature in Urdu, and so on.[46] The council has further proposed that Muslims alone take up the task of educating Muslim children; and maktabs and madrasas should not take any government aid. Like the Tablighi Jamaat, the Dini Talimi Council is a full-fledged movement, and not merely an organization.

Since Independence and Partition, orthodox Muslims have been working with zeal for the establishment of madrasas and maktabs. In the 1980s there was a fresh spurt in the efforts to establish more madrasas. This renewed religious enthusiasm is a part of a similar wave sweeping through the entire South Asia, as well as a response to the Hindutva movement. One thing is clear, however, that these madrasas have not come up spontaneously in response to the need of Muslim masses, but have been deliberately, systematically established and promoted. Many Muslim authors hail the efforts of the *ulama* in spreading madrasas to the far corners of the subcontinent. In the words of one such author:

The persistent efforts of *Ulama* in the post-independence period to resuscitate madrasa education ultimately brought it back on the track and, ever since, it is steadily progressing and refurbishing. On the one hand, the number of madrasas now stands increased considerably and on the other, many new experiments in their curriculum and mode of instruction have been initiated.[47]

Various Dini Talimi Councils, Tanjeems and Jamaat-i Islami Hind are working with the goal of spreading Islamic learning throughout the country. Qamr Uddin of Hamdard Education Society has expressed a pious hope that once some minimal reforms in the examination system, etc., are carried out in the madrasa system of education, then even the children of English-educated upper classes would come to madrasas for their education![48]

Even after so many years of Independence and the declaration of equal rights for all Indian citizens, as well as the special rights of minorities in the Constitution, a large number of Muslims, not only the *ulama* but also intellectuals, harp on the separate identity of Indian Muslims. They are supposed to be an integral part of the international *umma* which separates them from the rest of the population of Indian nation. They further use the terms 'we' and 'our society' not for Indians but for Muslim *umma*. To quote one such writer:

It [madrasa systems] has also to educate the young people about the dangers of fragmentation of the *Ummah*, the world over. That the unity of *Ummah*, in the face of challenges, both from the West and the East, is a prerequisite for our survival as a free people....[49]

And

We have to recognise the existence of a community which, amidst the variety of nationalities and cultures, of political options and degrees of developments, is aspiring for the solidarity of its people.[50]

It is significant that madrasas get maximum financial help from petty local merchants and bourgeoisie generally belonging to the lower middle class. Madrasas are also more popular among these classes. While the rich and modern-educated Muslims are not interested in madrasas, the poor, at least in cities and towns, are willing to send their wards to modern government schools.

Any way, they are in no position to donate to madrasas. This is especially true for madrasas established by Jamaat-i-Islami which, as a matter of policy, charge a certain amount of fee and encourage the children and youth of businessmen to get their education in madrasas. The Jamaat further tries to involve the parents of its students in its *tablighi* (proselytizing) activities. Madrasas in general and those of Jamaat in particular are thus integrally related with the relatively more conservative and less educated lower middle or middle class of craftsmen and petty merchants. They derive sustenance from these classes, and in turn strengthen their conservativeness and dependence on the *maulanas*.[51]

5. THE NUMBER AND VARIETY OF MADRASAS

5.1. THE NUMBER OF MADRASAS

Nobody knows the approximate number of madrasas in the country. The Hamdard Education Society attempted an all Indian survey but failed to come out with even a vaguest estimate. The estimates vary from a few thousand to even lakhs. Generally, the figure of 30,000 is accepted, though no proof is given; the number might well be more. In addition there may well be lakhs of maktabs, as a maktab is generally attached to a mosque, and there is a mosque in every village and urban Muslim majority area.

Similarly, the estimate of the number of Muslim children going to madrasas ranges from 1 per cent to 36 per cent![52] The Sachar Committee Report puts the number of madrasa-going children between 3 to 4 per cent. The latter estimate is very important because we must know how many Indian children are deprived of modern education before we can even think of helping them.

5.2. DIFFERENT LEVELS OF MADRASA EDUCATION

Various scholars talking of or writing on madrasa education often work with a conceptual framework which confuses between several branches or divisions of learning which are all juxtaposed and named madrasas. The madrasa system of education is divided into several types of institutions. They are:

(a) *Maktab*: Maktabs (or *makatib*) are a form of elementary school. Therein a child is expected to be admitted at the age of 4 years and continue his/her education till the age of 8 years. However, generally children admitted in maktabs are older. Generally the maktabs teach recitation of a few fundamental verses of the Quran, reading (and perhaps writing) of Arabic Alphabets (*Arabi Quaida*), as well as those of Urdu (*Noorani Quaida*). Students are taught some fundamental tenets of Islam orally. Above all, they are taught the correct rituals for performing the *namaz*, such as the right way of performing *wuzu* (washing before *namaz*), and the various rituals and verses of the Quran required for performing the *namaz*. The maktabs also generally teach basic arithmetic, Urdu and sometimes Hindi. All these subjects, however, are entirely voluntary and the standard and content of teaching varies from maktab to maktab.

These institutions take both boys and girls; often the number of girls is larger than that of boys. Maktabs are almost always affiliated to the local mosque. The *Imam* of the mosque generally is also the teacher (*maulana*) of the maktab. He teaches all the subjects to all the students belonging to different age groups, many of whom would already have learnt the subject or ritual being taught. Some city maktabs are independent. They hold classes in the morning and evening to facilitate the children to attend common schools. These independent maktabs also mostly have only one teacher for all subjects, as well as all students. Children are irregular and are not always attentive. However the atmosphere is disciplined and congenial.

(b) *Darul Quran* or *Hifz madrasas*: These are institutions which especially train boys *hifz* or complete memorization of the Quran and *tajweed* (*tajweez*) or the correct manner of reciting the Holy Text. There is no fixed duration for the memorization of the Quran. It depends on the personal ability of students; generally it takes between 2 to 4 years. Most *Hifz* madrasas do not teach anything else, not even the meaning of the verses being memorized. It is argued that trying to understand the meaning would divert the students' minds from the task of memorization. Most madrasas, other than those exclusively dedicated to *Hifz*, also have *Hifz* sections. *Nazira* (correct reading of the Quran) is also taught in most madrasas. Since the memorization of the Quran is a source of *sabab* (merit) for the faithful, a large number of Muslim boys go in for *Hifz*. While the other madrasas mostly teach in mornings, the *Hifz* children practice memorization from early morning to late night.

(c) *Madrasa*: These are the typical institutions of Islamic learning. They generally have an eight-year course culminating in the degree of *Fazil* (*Fadil*). Students passing out from maktabs or *Hifz* madrasas are admitted to Arabi Auwal (class 1) and study for eight years till *Arabi Hashtum* (class 8). Better organized madrasas also have a preparatory class, as the students coming out of the above institutions are often not capable of pursuing the demanding Arabic course. The books are in Arabic in most madrasas, while in Shi'a madrasas they are in Farsi (Persian). However, usually the teaching or explanations are in Urdu. In the states of Bengal, Assam, Tamil Nadu and Kerala, the local language is frequently employed for explaining the Arabic text.

Not all madrasas are up to Arabic eighth class, rather they have provision for teaching up to class 3 or class 4. After that either the boys drop out, or they go to other madrasas for continuing education. A few of them even join modern schools. Many of these madrasas also have elementary sections, thus providing education from the beginning. However, these primary sections are mostly independent of the main madrasa.

(d) *Jamia*: There are some madrasas which provide specialization in a certain fields and are called Darul-Uloom or even Jamia. Thus madrasas may be ones which teach up to 3rd or 4th Arabi classes, and ones which teach up to Arabi eighth class, equivalent to graduation; and ones which are actually Jamias. The latter teach specializations in various Islamic subjects such as *hadiths*, *fiqh* and so on after which one gets a post-graduate degree.

(e) *Madrasas for Girls*: They are a class apart. Muslim girls are not expected to study in common madrasas after they finish their maktab studies, by which time they are expected to have reached puberty. Hence after, they are expected to remain in seclusion. Therefore some girls' madrasas have been established which definitely are not sufficient if all Muslim girls are to be educated in them. They may be big, like the girls' branch of

Jamiat-al-Falah at Azamgarh, or very small in some towns. Importantly, though their syllabus is also Dars-i-Nizami, it is mostly shortened 'to suit girls' (supposed) limited capacities', and some subjects like housekeeping are added.

The confusion in the terminology leads to several other confusions. It also makes it easier for both the supporters and critics of madrasa system of education to make any assertion about it, thus glossing over the large variety of madrasas.

For example, there are two almost deliberate confusions regarding girls' access to madrasas, and modern subjects being taught in them. They are made possible because of the use of the common word 'madrasa' for these varied institutions. Many Muslim writers claim that girls' education is equally taken care of, while the fact is that either the girls are taught in maktabs alone, or in madrasas up to a very elementary level; or they are expected to study in girls' madrasas which are very few in number. Likewise, when it is claimed that modern subjects are regularly taught in madrasas, it is not acknowledged that this is the case in very few madrasas affiliated to some state Madrasa Board, while almost 90 per cent or more do not teach modern subjects; or they are taught only at the elementary stage, and that too in a very shoddy manner.

5.3. THE VARIETY OF MADRASAS

There is an extensive variety of madrasas. There are madrasas which have only 15–20 students; others like those at Deoband, Lucknow and Azamgarh have thousands of students. There are a large number of madrasas which cater to the needs of local children and do not have hostels for residence. There are many which have residential facilities and provide not only food to their students but also clothes, bedding and medical care. There are still others which have some residential boys from outside, as well as local students who come for a limited time. Most *Hifz* madrasas have arrangements for the stay of students as learning goes on from early morning to late night. Madrasas which have both *Hifz* section and usual teaching may have both arrangements. In almost all madrasas education is free, though a few, especially those established by Jamaat-i-Islami, charge a small fee. Therefore to say that Muslims prefer to send their children to madrasas instead of government schools because the former provide free education as well as free boarding and lodging, is only partially true. Then there are girls' madrasas which are wholly different. Both the syllabus and the extreme level of discipline make them different from those of boys.

This confusion in terminology results in several other confusions. While all madrasas are more or less autonomous, the bigger ones have a clearly defined curriculum and syllabus; all the rest work arbitrarily. They have very varied syllabuses, even though a large number of them formally follow the Deobandi curriculum. Some of the books, especially in *mantiq,* prescribed in the Deobandi syllabus are often not included in the syllabus of many madrasas as they are too many and too difficult. Since no *hadith* is taught in full in the Deobandi syllabus, there may well be difference in the amount of prescribed portions in different madrasas of this order. Greater difference lies in the teaching of Arabic. While it may be taught in bigger madrasas to a level where students become proficient in Arabic speech and writing, it is not so in smaller madrasas whose students can hardly understand the language. Most madrasas explain Arabic books in Urdu or the local language; in bigger madrasas the emphasis is on understanding the Arabic language.

It should be remembered here that girls are not educated in common madrasas. Maktabs are coeducational, but once girls are near puberty they are not allowed to go out. Some smaller madrasas accept girls for one or two years more. There are a few madrasas which admit girls provided they are in *purdah.* But their number is very small. However, the need for the education of girls was felt quite early. At first Sayyid Ahmad Khan intended to admit girls to MAO College, but due to strong protests from the *ulama* he gave up his proposal. The only alternative left was to establish separate madrasas for girls.

The girls' madrasas may be affiliated to some particular sect, but their syllabus and functioning would still be different from other madrasas of the same order. Jamiat-al-Falah, Balariaganj, (Azamgarh) was the first girls' madrasa, followed by another madrasa in Rampur. The number of girls' madrasas has increased since then. Earlier orthodox Muslims insisted on two things: first, girls do not need detailed knowledge either of the modern or of the traditional kind. After all they were not supposed to do jobs outside their homes. Second, girls must not come in contact with the male members of the society except their family members. Liberal Muslims of that time seemed to have found a via media. Girls should be given education; but for acquiring this education they need not go to common madrasas or schools. Therefore, separate girls' madrasas must be established. In Delhi alone we have seven relatively large girls' madrasas. There are a few others which seek to combine Islamic education with modern education. Sometimes there are local level girls' madrasas even in small towns such as Mau in UP and Tonk in Rajasthan. Though the number of girls' madrasas is not known, it is at most about 100 all over India. Even if there are more, their number is too less as compared to approximately 30,000 or more madrasas for boys. Significantly, the syllabus of girls' madrasas is kept easier 'in view of the limitations of their capacities'! Moreover, they are often far from the residence of the girls' families, and not many like to send their daughters so far away.

Even greater difference lies in madrasas belonging to different schools of Islam. The main difference is not in the syllabus which is almost always the Dars-i-Nizami; rather it lies in the interpretation, relative emphases, the selection of books for various courses, and above all general approach to secular life, *shari'a*, society and other schools of Islam. Below is given only the bare outlines of their religious approaches and syllabuses, as we will discuss them in greater detail in the next chapter.

Most madrasas in India and the subcontinent are not only of the Sunni sect of Islam but also belong to what is popularly known as the Deobandi order. It teaches Dars-i-Nizami, an almost universal syllabus of the madrasas of the subcontinent. The syllabus was prepared during the time of Aurangzeb, and importantly, there have not been any significant changes in it since then. Its main emphasis is on various 'rational sciences', Arabic language and *fiqh*. Of course, the present Deobandi syllabus also teaches *hadiths* in considerable detail as also the biography of the Prophet (*sirat*). The Quran is not taught directly but through various *tafsirs* (commentaries).[53]

Ahle-Hadees (also written as *Ahl-e-Hadith*) is a very important sect of Islam. Though they are Sunnis, they have their own
unique philosophy and identity. They do not believe in confining themselves to one school of *fiqh*, and have therefore decided
to teach all schools of Sunni *fiqh*. But since it is not possible to
teach all schools of *fiqh* to students; and since in case of conflict
between the laws of various schools, there is no way to decide
which viewpoint is right, the followers of Ahle-Hadees assert the
need to go directly to the Holy Quran and various authenticated
ahadis (*hadiths*). It seems to be a reasonable approach but not
so in reality. Ahle-Hadees emphasizes the need to adhere to the
'pristine monotheism' of Islam which includes whatever was believed and practised by the Arab society during the time of the
Prophet; and 'to regenerate the Muslim society by eradicating
innovations and un-Islamic practices'. It also emphasizes the need
for proselytizing.[54] As a result, the *maulanas*, teachers and other
ideologues of this school are even more fundamentalist and strict
than those of other Sunni schools.

The Salafiyya madrasas also belong to Sunni Islam. The term
Sala'f means 'reform'. Salafiyya sect of Islam wants to 'purify'
Islam to the level at which it was practised by the 'Pious Forefathers', that is, the Companions of the Messenger of God. In
India the extreme version of this philosophy is not very popular,
and it is merged into the Ahle-Hadees version of Islam. One
important madrasa of this school is in Varanasi.

The leaders, ideologues and followers of Ahle-Sunnat, another
school of Sunni Islam, popularly known as Barelvis, are even
more fundamentalist in their approach. The popular conception
of Barelvis, not only among non-Muslims but also among a
majority of Muslims, is that they are the most liberal of Sunni
sects as they accommodate popular Islam, especially the tradition of praying at Sufis' and other saints' *mazars* (graves). They
do allow it, though perhaps not in the extreme form in which it
is practised but other than that, they have a very strong view of
Prophet Muhammad's person and his role in the scheme of things.
They believe *Rasool* Muhammad (the Messenger of God) to have
had supernatural qualities; and assign to him the role of medi-
ating for his folk with Allah on the Last Day of Judgement. The

proponents of Ahle-Sunnat declare that they alone are the true Muslims, and all others, including Sunnis of other sects, especially Deobandis, and Shias, are *kafirs* (heathen)![55] The higher madrasas of Ahle-Sunnat do not even take pass-outs of other Sunni madrasas.

The madrasas established and run by the Jamaat-e-Islami Hind follow more or less the same ideology of 'reforming' Islam as that of Ahle-Hadees, so that it regains its pristine purity, and spreading it among non-believers. Their madrasas are different from those of other sects in that they are well organized, and in a limited way teach modern subjects. Their pass-outs are also better equipped to cope up with the modern world. Nonetheless, they are equally fundamentalist and manage to strengthen a separate Islamic identity in their students.[56]

Even greater difference exists between madrasas belonging to Sunni sects and those which are established by Shi'as and have a Shi'a-specific *nisab*. Shi'a understanding of Islam is very different from that of Sunnis, so that even the most liberal of Sunnis and Shi'as are not ready to try to understand each other's philosophy. We will have an occasion to discuss the Shi'a version of Islam in the next chapter.

Fiqh is equally important for Shi'as, but their schools of *fiqh* are different from those of the Sunnis, and they teach their own jurisprudence and laws. Though Shi'as acknowledge all authenticated *hadiths* recognized by Sunnis, the emphasis and relative priority of various *hadiths* are different. Even greater difference lies in Shi'as' use of Persian as the medium of instruction. Unlike Sunni madrasas, recourse to Urdu or any mother tongue is minimum. Even the Quran is taught in earlier stages through Persian. Arabic is introduced later, and then taught thoroughly. English and Hindi are also taught in many Shi'a madrasas which are spread throughout India. However, Shi'as are a minority among Muslims in India and as a result Shi'a madrasas are fewer than those of Sunni, and are estimated to be only a few hundred.[57]

A more basic difference lies between most madrasas which are autonomous, deciding everything about their curriculum from syllabus to years of study required, and all other details, such as introduction of modern subjects (*asri uloom*) and providing opportunity for games, etc., and those lesser number of madrasas which are affiliated to various State Madrasa Education Boards. The West Bengal Madrasa Examination Board was the first to be set up in 1948. After that Bihar and then Orissa, Madhya Pradesh and Assam constituted their Madrasa Education Boards. Madrasas affiliated to these Boards get some nominal financial aid and, in turn, agree to teach the syllabus prescribed by the Board.

In Assam and Madhya Pradesh the syllabus of modern subjects taught in the madrasas is the same as that taught in other schools, with two additional periods allotted for religious education. Detailed religious subjects are introduced at a later stage. In Bihar and some other states the syllabus is an attempted synthesis of modern and religious. It consists of usual modern subjects as Hindi, English, mathematics, social sciences and natural sciences, as well as all subjects of Deobandi syllabus, including Arabic grammar, *hadiths*, *fiqh*, *usool-e-fiqh* and so on. We will have an occasion to discuss the syllabuses of different Madrasa Boards in the next chapter. It is not certain whether the students of madrasas affiliated to State Boards are able to master such a vast material.

It is clear that madrasas affiliated to these Boards do teach modern subjects, some in elementary forms, others in a more detailed manner. These madrasas are to be sharply distinguished from the traditional madrasas which teach only Islamic subjects. Even though the education imparted in them is misnamed *dini*, their syllabus largely consists of the so-called rational sciences (*duniyavi uloom*). However, the worldly knowledge imparted in them, being several hundred years old, is highly outdated and irrelevant to modern times.[58] Some writers have given the syllabus of madrasas affiliated to State Boards which includes modern subjects, but give the impression that they are telling us about the syllabus of common madrasas.[59]

From the 1980s onwards various governments at the centre have been insisting on the modernization of traditional madrasas. This has become a big issue and can be tackled only when we keep the above distinctions between various madrasas in view.

NOTES

1. Quran XCVI: 1-5; *Meaning of the Glorious Koran*, Text and Explanatory Translation by Marmaduke Pikhtall, Delhi: World Islamic Publications, 1978.
2. Cf. similar verses: 'Thus do we expound the revelation for people who reflect.' Ibid., X.24, also ibid., XXX.28.
3 See ibid., LV.2 ff.
4 The source of this saying is not clear. Probably it is taken from *Ibn Ma'za*, a relatively less important *hadith*.
5. See Asma Afsaruddin, 'Muslim Views on Education: Parameters, Purview, and Possibilities', in *Journal of Catholic Legal Studies*, vol. 44, 2005, pp. 143 ff.
6. See ibid., pp. 153 ff.
7. Quran LV.2 ff.
8. See Maulana Saiyyid Manazir Hasan Gilani, *Hindustan Main Musalmano ka Nizam-e-Taleem aur Tarbiyat* (Urdu), Delhi: Jama Masjid, 1966, vol. I , pp. 77 ff., 109 ff, 144 ff., 182 ff., 209 ff., 305 ff., 377 ff. He is all praise for the earlier Madrasa system and contends that copying out books is much better than printing.
9. See ibid., pp. 7 ff., 109 ff., 144 ff. Also see Darul Uloom, Deoband's website: http//www.darululoom-deoband.com/english syst_of_ edu/index.htm, 'The Sysem of Education'.
10. Gilani strongly criticizes the emphasis on rational sciences under the influence of Mir Fathullah Shirazi, as it distracts the intellect, while Islam demands total faith and obedience to the Quran. See op. cit., vol. I, pp. 179 ff.
11. See Iqtidar Husain Siddiqui, 'Madrasa Education in Medieval India', in S.M. Azizuddin Husain (ed.), *Madrasa Education in India: Eleventh to Twenty First Century*, New Delhi: Kanishka, 2005, pp. 12–13.
12. Though it may or may not be so in the earlier period, we have definite documentary evidence that in India the 'lower class' Muslims (those converted from Hinduism) were looked down upon by both the court and the academics. See S.M. Azizuddin Husain, 'Introduction', and 'Mir Fathullah Shirazi's Contribution for the Revision of the Syllabi of Indian Madrasas During Akbar's Reign', in ibid., pp. 3 and 25. In both the articles he quotes Barani as strongly opposing 'the promotion of low born', or giving them education.
13. As we have no documentary evidence as to the Islamic *nisab* in the early stages, and as we know there have not been any revo-

lutionary changes in the madrasa system of education, it is best
to rely on a generalized but very good and comprehensive description of the same by Muhammad Akhlaq Ahmad, *Traditional
Education Among Muslims*, Delhi: R.K. Publishing Corporation,
1985, pp. 45 ff. We would have occasion to discuss the various
nisabs of Islamic sects in the next chapter.

14. See Gilani, op. cit., vol. I, pp. 391 ff.; vol. II, pp. 3ff., 88ff.
15. For a detailed account of the relation between the missionaries
    and the then government, see D.E. Smith, *India as a Secular
    State*, Princeton: Princeton University Press, 1963, pp. 72 ff.
16. See Kuldeep Kaur, *Madrasa Education in India: A Study of its
    Past and Present*, Chandigarh: Centre for Research in Rural and
    Industrial Development, 1990, pp. 177 ff. for a good account of
    historical developments in this context.
17. See Farhat Hasan, 'Madaris and the Challenges of Modernity
    in Colonial India', in Jan Peter Hartung and Helmut Reifeld
    (ed.), *Islamic Education, Diversity, and National Identity: Dini
    Madaris Post 9/11*, New Delhi: Sage, 2006, pp. 59–61.
18. See M. Mujeeb, *The Indian Muslims*, Delhi: Munshiram
    Manoharlal, 1995, pp. 277 ff. Also see Dilip Hiro, *Islamic Fun-
    damentalism*, London: Paladin, 1989, pp. 39, 271.
19. See Gilani, op. cit., vol. II, pp. 74 ff., 80 ff. The entire philosophy
    and programme of action of Jamaat-e-Islami and Tablighi Jamaat
    are based on this ideology.
20. For a brief but relevant description of madrasas that were started
    one after another in the nineteenth and early twentieth centuries,
    see Muhammad Akhlaq Ahmad, op. cit., pp. 22 ff.
21. See Darul-Uloom, Deoband website for details of the Madrasa's
    goals and approach http//www.darululoom-deoband.com/english/
    'The Universal Religious Call and Educational Movement of
    Darul Uloom'.
22. 'The aim of acquisition of knowledge in the Islamic system is not
    merely to satisfy an intellectual curiosity but to train rational
    and righteous individuals for the moral and physical good of
    their families, their people and for the entire mankind. The Is-
    lamic system of education strikes a balance between the need for
    individual excellence and the requirements of the society. . . .
    Finally Islamic education system is based on the whole hearted
    acceptance of the revelation or *Wahi* as a guide of all knowledge
    and conduct.' Manzoor Ahmad, *Islamic Education: Redefini-
    tion of Aims and Methodology*, New Delhi: Qazi Publishers and
    Distributors, 1990, p. 6.

If Shoyeb Ansari's study is to be believed, students of madrasas insisted that 'Only that knowledge is worthy that brings the students closer to God and Prophet.' They were divided as to whether madrasa education should be used for earning one's livelihood or not, but they were certain that professional education imparted along with the Islamic one would 'spoil the madrasas as well as the very purpose of their existence'. See Shoyeb Ansari, *Education in Dini Madaris: An Opinion Survey of Curriculum, Method of Teaching and Evaluation in Dini Madaris*, New Delhi: Institute of Objective Studies, 1997, pp. 94. ff.

23. Gilani contends that even in early times students took education with the sole purpose of getting prestigious jobs (Of course, he disapproves it!) See Gilani, op. cit., vol. I, pp. 285–6, 289–90, etc.

24. It was just a matter of popular practice that the *madaris* came to be called *dini madaris*. Otherwise, they could have been simply called madrasas while the institutions of modern education: schools. That would have been sufficient to distinguish the two systems of education.

25. See B.R. Nanda, *Gandhi: Pan-Islamism, Imperialism and Nationalism*, Bombay: Oxford University Press, 1989, pp. 51–5; also Rajmohan Gandhi, *Understanding the Muslim Mind*, New Delhi: Penguin, 1990, pp. 32 ff.

26. See M. Mujeeb, op. cit., p. 451; Rajmohan Gandhi, op. cit., pp. 31–5.

27. Quoted by Mohd. Arshad, 'Tradition of Madrasa Education', in Akhtarul Wasey (ed.), *Madrasas in India: Trying to be Relevant*, New Delhi: Global India Publications, 2005, p. 30.

28. See ibid., p. 31.

29. See ibid., pp. 31–2.

30. See Usha Sanyal, 'Ahle Sunnat Madrasas: The Madrasa Manzar-e-Islam, Bareilly, and Jamia Ashrafiyya, Mubarakpur', in the *Proceedings of International Workshop on Islamic Learning in South Asia*, May 2005, Erfurt, Germany, organized by Jamal Malik; Unpublished. Some of the articles have been later published in an edited version in Jamal Malik (ed.), *Madrasas in South Asia: Teaching Terror?*, London: Routledge, 2008. But I have relied on an unpublished version. I have personally met the Sadar Maulana of a postgraduate level Barelvi madrasa and he asserted word by word what I have written here in brief.

31. See the *Wikipedia, Free Encyclopedia* site for an introductory description of Tablighi Jamaat http//www.icna.org/tm/great

movement3.htm and http.www.en.wikipedia.org/wiki/Tablighi Jamaat. Also see Shail Mayaram, 'Rethinking Meo-identity: Cultural Faultline, Syncretism, Hybridity or Liminality?', and Muhammad Talib, 'The Tablighis in the Making of Muslim Identity', in Mushirul Hasan (ed.), *Islam Communities and the Nation: Muslim Identities in South Asia,* New Delhi: Manohar, 1998, pp. 283 ff. and 307 ff.

32. See Yoginder Sikand, 'Arya Shuddhi and Muslim Tabligh: Muslim Reaction to Arya Proselytization (1923–30)' taken from the internet. Therein he describes in detail the Tablighi goal of converting non-Muslims and quotes several earlier leaders of the movement. However, in the present literature found on Tablighi movement the main concern is the 'reform' of Islam as practised by the masses.

33. See B.R. Nanda, op. cit., pp. 228 ff.

34. See Hamza Alvi, 'Ironies of History: Contradictions in the Khilafat Movement', in *Islam, Communities and the Nation: Muslim Identities in the South Asia,* pp. 25 ff.

35. Quoted by Rajmohan Gandhi, op. cit., pp. 24, 66.

36. Quoted in B.R. Nanda, op. cit., pp. 109–10.

37. Quoted in ibid., p. 114.

38. 'The khilafatists envisioned a renascent Islamic world, in which all Muslim people were united—"the supernatural sangathan of Muslims in five continents"—built around the *khalifa* and supporting each other through that institution.' Mushirul Hasan, *Islam in the Subcontinent: Muslims in a Plural Society,* New Delhi: Manohar, 2002, p. 160.

39. Mushirul Hasan argues with documentation how the Khilafat leaders were fully aware of the apparent conflict, and declared that there is none, that is, nationalism and pan-Islamism can go very well together. Ibid., pp. 96 ff.

40. Quoted in ibid., p. 162.

41. Ibid., p. 372.

42. See Gilani, op. cit., vol. I, pp. 385 ff. He waxes eloquent about how modern education is the cause of *barbadi* (near destruction) of Muslim youth. It also destroys the thinking capacity of learners.

43. 'The key purpose of Darul-Uloom was to fail the attempts made by Lord Macaulay's education system and to produce a bunch of gallant Ulama who not only can perform the duty of saving religion in its true form but also can deliver it to the succeeding generations.' Mufti Shafi Usmani, quoted in Muhamadullah Khalili Qasmi, *Madrasa Education: Its Strength and Weakness,* Mumbai:

Markazul Ma'arif Education & Research Centre, 2005, p. 41.
Qasmi himself is a strong supporter of madrasa education. So
are Manzoor Ahmad and a lot of other Muslim intellectuals
and writers.

44. Manzoor Ahmad, op. cit., p. 32.
45. 'Deeni Talimi Council through its 20,000 independent and self-
supporting maktabs (primary schools) all over the state has played
a great role in inculcating and promoting Islamic ethos among
the Muslim children and in making them retaining firmly their
religious identity.' Qasmi, op. cit., p. 95, also pp. 94–6.
Also see Kuldeep Kaur, op. cit., pp. 203–7.
46. See Kuldeep Kaur, op. cit., pp. 205, 208–9.
47. Muhammad Akhtar Siddiqui, 'Development and Trends in Madrasa
Education', in A.W.B. Qadri, Riaz Shakir Khan, Muhammad
Akhtar Siddiqui (eds.), *Education and Muslims in India Since
Independence*, New Delhi: Institute of Objective Studies, 1998,
p. 74, also p. 75.
48. See Qamar Uddin, *Hindustan ki Dini Darsagahein: Kul Hind
Survey*, New Delhi: Hamdard Education Society, 1996, p. 302.
49. Manzoor Ahmad, op. cit., p. 17.
50. Ibid., p. 51.
51. See J.M. Khan, *Education among Muslims*, Jaipur: Classic Publishing House, 1993, pp. 64 ff., 164 ff.; and the article of Irfan
Habib, 'Familiar Discourse in an Unfamiliar World: Conflict,
Protest and Democratization in a Tahriki Madrasa of North
India', in the unpublished *Proceedings of the International Workshop on Islamic Learning in South Asia*, Erfurt, May 2005. The
author gives an excellent description of the ambience of Jamaat-
e-Islami's madrasas. But the article has strict instructions: 'Work
in progress not for citation'.
52. See notes 1, 2 and 3 of chapter 2 supra.
53. See Deoband's website http://www.darululoom-deoband.com/
english/sys_of_edu/index.htm
54. See Ahle-Hadees website http://www.ahlehadees.org/index.
'about us'.
55. See Ahle-Sunnat website http://www.jamaateahlesunnat.net . and
www.ahlesunnat.org .
56. See Jamaat-e-Islami website http://www.jamaateislamihind.
org/index . 'Ideology of Jamaat-e-Islami Hind' and 'Overview of
Programme'.
57. For information on the Shi'a sect see http://www.en.wikipedia.
org/wiki/Shi'a_Islam; also al Islam.org.com and the website of

a prominent Shi'a madrasa—Jamia Ahle Bait in New Delhi—ahle-bait 2002.com

58. Even conservative writers who strongly advocate the madrasa system of education admit this point. See Qamar Uddin, op. cit., pp. 97, 109, 129.
59. See Anita Julka, Neerja Shukla and Md. T.A. Rahi, *Existing Curriculum in Madrasas: A Study*, undertaken by the Department of Education of Groups with Special Needs (published by NCERT for limited circulation).

4

Madrasa Nisabs: An Effort to Understand Them and a Critique

1. MADRASA *NISABS*

1.1. MADRASA CURRICULUM AND SYLLABUS: APOLOGETIC ASSERTIONS

The aim of this study, to repeat, is not to explain the intricacies of Islamic textbooks, far less critically evaluate them. Nor is it to tell the *ulama* what to teach in their madrasas. Given that all Indian children have the constitutional right of getting minimum education up to the secondary level at least, present work's focus is on the early classes of madrasas, which would be roughly equivalent to the secondary level of modern schools. In this context it attempts to understand whether the madrasas teach subjects which can be called modern and which would enable their students to successfully cope with the challenges of modern society.

To understand any system of education we must know two things about it—first, the goal or purpose of that education; and second, its content or syllabus (*nisab*). We have discussed in brief the goals of Islamic education in our very first chapter, as well as in chapter 3. In this chapter we will glance at the syllabuses of different types of madrasas, briefly discussed in the previous chapter. As mentioned earlier, several writers claim that madrasa education is not only the sole avenue of education for Muslim children but also that it is contributing significantly in fulfilling the national goal of universal education. These writers exhort that more Muslim children come to the madrasas to study.[1]

These writers also claim that madrasa products are natural leaders and guides (*rahnuma*) of Muslims. As a result whatever is being taught becomes both important and influential for the entire Muslim community. According to one such ideologue: 'Doesn't the Islamic Society need Ulama who can guide it in religious field, educate Muslim children, defend Islam and devote their life to safeguard Muslims' future?'[2]

We, therefore, need to understand Madrasa syllabuses. The advocates of madrasa education and a large number of other Muslim ideologues, except a few hard core secularists, praise madrasas and their teaching programme as providing the highest kind of knowledge. Significantly, the advocates of madrasa system of education alternate between two conceptions of Islam and Islamic education—First, Islam is a religion and madrasas are meant for imparting religious knowledge. Second, since Islam is a whole way of life and doesn't distinguish between the worldly and secular, Islamic education includes both religious and secular subjects. Muhammadullah Khalili Qasmi says that 'Madrasas teach secular education more than religious education.' As an example of 'secular' education he includes 'Arabic Grammar, Syntax, Arabic language, Arabic Literature, Logic, History, *Balaghat* (Elocution), Philosophy, *Kalam* (Scholasticism), Geography, Metaphysics, Arithmetic, Biography, Anthropology, Civics, Rhetortic, Philology, Calligraphy, English, etc.'[3] He does not tell us that history and geography are of Muslim countries; that the sciences taught in the madrasas are of the period before Western Renaissance and Scientific Revolution; and that Arabic which seems to be the centre of the above list may be secular, but is totally irrelevant for the secular life of a Muslim whose mother tongue is not Arabic. Qasmi, at the same time, is a great proponent of the view that madrasas are meant to give religious education and produce *ulama* who are experts in Islamic 'sciences' which, according to him, are 17 in number.[4]

Qasmi is not alone when he talks in this way; almost all advocates of madrasa system of education talk in this manner. According to them, whether you consider madrasa system as imparting religious education (*dini taleem*) alone, or as giving knowledge of a comprehensive Islamic way of life, madrasas are doing a splendid job. There is no basic difference in Islam be-

tween what are called religious concerns and the life in the world—
din and *duniya*—as both are determined by the Quran and *sunna*.
However, when the secular world, i.e. opportunities in high
government jobs and secular education, were appropriated by
the English-educated Indians, the madrasas found that their
graduates were not successful in procuring government jobs. In
addition, the patronage of the feudal lords also diminished with
the diminishing of their power. Madrasas now accepted their
role as spiritual guides only. They thus appropriated the Western
duality of the sacred and the profane as signifying their own
philosophy, even though such a distinction was unknown in the
history of Islamic thought and education.[5]

Thus, we are told that Islam clearly distinguishes between religious and worldly concerns and madrasas address themselves
to the former alone. We are also told its opposite, that Islam is
a total guide to entire human life and that madrasa education
deals with all aspects of religious and secular life.

If our information, received directly from the two major
madrasas on their respective syllabuses, is any indication, the
tall claims about their 'modern' syllabus are not entirely true.[6]
Such writings and talks are misleading; and it is high time
that the facts came out without any embellishments, as also without being distorted by any bias for or against the madrasa
syllabuses or the values and attitudes they embody.

Madrasas are welcome to function as 'educational institutions
to preserve Islamic religion and culture', guaranteed in the
Indian Constitution. But if madrasas claim to be educational
institutions for a majority of Indian Muslim children, as ordinary citizens of India, we have a right to know as to what is
being taught in madrasas.

Our interest is in *all* Indian children getting modern education
up to not only secondary (as is mandatory in the government
efforts under Sarva Shiksha Abhiyan), but up to high school. It
is to enable them to become respectable, equal and empowered
citizens of the plural (however inefficient), secular, democratic
state and to earn their living in a satisfactory manner. We will
take a look at the madrasa system of education in view of the
prime question—as to how much the education provided in
madrasas is relevant for today's society, that is, how far does it

enable students for the above two tasks. We are also justifiably interested in trying to know about the madrasas' curriculum in order to be able to assess the frequently made claim that madrasas are contributing substantially to the national goal of universal education. As asserted earlier, we are not interested in the 'higher' Islamic education; not because it is not worthwhile but because very few students go in for it, and they remain the epitomes of Islamic identity and conservative values, which the Muslims have a right to be.

The biggest problem that comes in the way of a study of madrasa syllabus is that not only are most madrasas autonomous, there are also vast differences among them. As discussed in the last chapter, there are several bases on which madrasas can be classified. First, the term 'madrasa' is used indiscriminately for (a) maktab, (b) madrasa proper, and (c) jamia. We have described their differences in the previous chapter, but will briefly repeat them here.

Maktabs are mosque schools which give elementary knowledge to neighbourhood Muslim children. Mostly one *maulavi* teaches all children belonging to different age groups. Their basic goal is to teach their children fundamental Islamic beliefs, the correct way of performing *namaz*, and its related rituals like *wuzu* (washing hands, face and mouth in the prescribed way). Along with these, they teach Urdu and Arabic alphabets, perhaps a little Hindi and arithmetic, but not always.

Then there are madrasas proper which give regular Islamic knowledge. They generally start with Arabi *auwal* (first) and may continue up to any level. Many finish after Arabi *som* (third) or *chaharrum* (fourth) class. Some teach up to Arabi *hashtum* (eighth) class. Before joining Arabi *auwal* students generally spend one year in a preparatory (*aidadi*) class. (In larger madrasas like Deoband and Nadwa there is another preparatory class in between.) The students get the degree of *Alimiyat* after finishing Arabi *hashtum*. Importantly, *Alimiyat* is recognized as equivalent to B.A. by Aligarh Muslim University but as equivalent to intermediate (10+2) by Jamia Millia Islamia, Delhi and Lucknow University. (Most other universities do not recognize these degrees.) We will take it as equivalent to class 12, though we are fully aware of the high level of Islamic knowledge that is imparted in later years of this course. *Alimiyat* is followed by *Fazilat*, equivalent to B.A. or M.A. according to each one's standpoint. *Fazilat* consists of two years' specialization in any of several subjects offered. Bigger madrasas also offer research courses in Arabic literature and other Islamic subjects.

Now, specialization and research should be the prerogative of universities (*jamias*). But there are no specific Muslim universities in continuation with madrasas. (AMU and Jamia Millia cannot be taken as exclusively Muslim universities in this sense as they teach all subjects.) A large number of madrasas call themselves *jamias*, like Jamiat-al-Falah at Azamgarh, while the names of two distinguished and *jamia*-level madrasas of the North— Darul-Uloom, Deoband and Darul-Uloom Nadwatul Ulama, Lucknow—suggest that the term 'Darul Uloom' is equivalent to the English term 'University'.

In this division the greatest problem remains that there is no specific institution for primary education. Of the bigger madrasas, both Deoband and Nadwa have got full-fledged primary sections where students are taught subjects such as history, geography, and Islamic ethics in Urdu medium. They have regular textbooks, writing is encouraged, and written examinations are conducted.[6] Madrasas run by Jamaat-e Islami Hind have a primary section in which most modern subjects are taught. Such madrasas are definitely contributing towards both literacy and even universal more or less 'modern' education. But such 'enlightened' madrasas are mostly to be found in metropolitan cities, and not in villages or small towns.

Madrasas proper start with Arabi *auwal* but before that there is a preparatory class in the bigger madrasas devoted exclusively to learning of Arabic language. It is also assumed that maktab education, if it also includes a minimum of modern subjects like languages and arithmetic, is sufficient by way of primary education for the masses. If it is so, then it is an extremely unsatisfactory state, especially for those who discontinue their education after the primary classes. Most maktabs, with a few exceptions in metropolitan cities, do not teach much. And a minimum knowledge of the 3 Rs (reading, writing and arithmetic) is something which is almost as essential for living as the fulfilment of biological needs. Actually, even that is not sufficient. If we accept literacy as merely the capacity to read, then at least 40 per cent Muslim women in villages are literate, as they can read the Holy Quran in Arabic, of course, without understanding a word of it. While maktabs teach very little, except recognizing the Arabic and Urdu alphabets and a little arithmetic, madrasas mostly do not have a primary section. Besides, they teach in Arabic which is not the mother tongue of anyone in India. Thus the madrasa system of education does not seem to be contributing much by way of spreading literacy in the true sense of the word, at least not as well as is claimed by the advocates of madrasas.

A very important basis of understanding and classifying *madari*s is the differences in *maslaks* or sects. The greatest difference is between the Shi'a and Sunni sects. Significantly, the two sects not only follow the same religious texts, that is the Quran and authentic *hadiths*, they generally also follow the Dars-i-Nizami syllabus. And yet, the approaches and emphases in the syllabuses of the two sects are very different. The same is true for other sub-sects of Sunnis, briefly referred to in the previous chapter. They all follow the same texts and syllabus, yet there are marked differences in their attitudes and views regarding various issues. Understanding these differences is essential to understand in some detail the madrasa syllabus.

1.2. THE SUNNI ISLAM AND ITS SUB-SECTS

The majority of Muslims call themselves Sunnis or the followers of *sunna*. The latter word means practice or custom in Arabic but came to mean, according to the *Encyclopedia of Religion*, 'The exemplary, imitable and normative words, deeds and silent approvals and disapprovals of the Prophet.' Thus, the Prophet Muhammad is believed to be at once the vehicle of Allah's 'revelation', as well as an exemplar, or the source of Islamic *sunna* called *Sunnat-al-Nabi*. Gradually, reports of Muhammad's sayings and deeds, as narrated by his Companions or by those who heard from them, started spreading and became the authentic source of Islamic *shari'a* or way of life. Sunnis came to mean the people who followed the *sunna* of the Prophet.

The range covered by the *Sunnat-al-Nabi* was as broad as [to cover . . .] food and eating manners, clothing and jewelry, hygiene and grooming, social behaviour, forms of greeting, and etiquette, as well as weightier religious, political and economic matters. Consequently the sunnah of the prophet and the early community came to play a major role in the development of the Islamic legal system (shari'ah) and systemic discussion about God.[7]

While most Muslims regard the *sunna* as having more or less the same authority as the Quran (though the latter is theoretically above and prior to all other sources of law), some scholars assert that the *sunna* or any other legislation in the name of *shari'a* can have only a secondary authority, subordinate to the Quran. Its worth lies only inasmuch as it 'expounds specific aspects of the general principles of the Quran'.[8]

However, not all stories could be equally authoritative, as they were compiled long after the death of Prophet Muhammad. The *hadiths* in which the *sunna* of the Prophet was preserved were actually written down by people who had heard the report from some person who, in turn, heard it from still another person. Thus thousands of the *hadiths* came to be prevalent. The great Islamic scholar al Shafi'i (eighth and early ninth centuries) systematically sorted out the authentic stories from the spurious ones. The standard chosen was that the *hadith* must be traceable to the Prophet himself; the chain of narrators and their proof was called *isnad*. There gradually emerged six collections of these narrations, known as *hadiths—Bukhari Sharief, Muslim Sharief, Daud Sharief, Nasa'e Sharief, Tirmizi Sharief,* and *Mishkat Sharief.* There is a seventh equally quoted one, called *Ibn Ma'za.*

Since this literature is very vast, madrasas do not teach all the *hadiths.* They differ in terms of which *hadith,* or rather which portion of a *hadith,* is being taught. Al Shafi'i further asserted four hierarchical sources of Islamic *shari'a* or way of life: the Quran, *sunna, ijma,* and *qiyas.* Of course, the Quran remained as the supreme source of all laws and norms but it could be supplemented by the *sunna* of the Prophet. When neither of these could provide guidance, the Islamic community could come together and decide on some practical issue; their consensus or *ijma* could be a third source of Islamic *shari'a.* Finally, in exceptional cases, Muslims could use analogy (*qiyas*) from similar cases found in these three sources and decide a course of action.[9]

From the very beginning the emphasis in Islam has been on laws to guide all aspects of Muslim life. Gradually four schools of Sunni *fiqh* developed, those of Malik, Hanifa, Hanbal and Shafi'i. Obviously, since all these schools were separate and often gave conflicting judgements on the same issue, while all along claiming that they were following the texts, reasoning and human bias must have got a role to play. Equally obviously, the principle of *ijtihad* or reasoning based on the religious texts was allowed and was at work. But gradually there was ever greater emphasis on *taqlid* or unconditional, unquestioning obedience to the written word. It was thought that there was no further need for rational interpretation, and all that the following generations had to do was blindly follow either one of the four schools of *fiqh*. This was expressed by saying that the gates of *ijtihad* were closed by the end of tenth century.

Among the Sunnis, there are several schools or sects (*maslaks*) which have their own syllabuses and madrasas. The most important one, of course, is the Darul Uloom, Deoband which is not only a madrasa but is also an entire system of philosophy, way of life and conceptual framework. Some call it the Deobandi tradition. Majority of madrasas in the subcontinent follow the Deobandi *nisab* and its approach to both religion and the world. Actually, there is no dividing line between the two in the Deobandi approach.

Though Nadwat-al-Ulama, Lucknow has a prestige and following of its own, it should strictly be included in the Deobandi madrasas. Both follow the Dars-i-Nizami of Aurangzeb's time with certain changes, most of which were included at the outset by their respective founders in the mid-nineteenth century. Ever since, as we shall see, there have hardly been any changes in their curriculum except some cosmetic changes in the form of substitution of one book by another with the same content.

Deobandi movement or approach was born as a reaction to the popular Islamic practices commonly associated with the Barelvi school of Islam. The latter not only deny that they sanction those practices but also refuse to be called Barelvi. Instead, they prefer the name Ahle-Sunnat. Though the main religious texts are the same, their religious philosophy, with much greater emphasis on the person of the Prophet Muhammad, is very different from that of Deobandi Islam. They also have a large number of madrasas which follow their approach and syllabus.

Then there are madrasas of Ahle-Hadith *maslak*. They argue that since there are so many *ahadis* (*hadiths*), following anyone, or following any one interpretation of *fiqh* is wrong. Hence, they teach their students all *hadiths* and all schools of *fiqh*, though in brief. But they emphasize that the Quran and *hadiths* are the only sources of Islamic *shari'a*. The Jamia Salafiyya of Varanasi represents this philosophy.

Madrasas established and run by Jamat-e-Islami Hind are another class of madrasas. Their ideology is more or less the same as that of Ahle-Hadith, with a greater emphasis on the evangelical duties of the *ulama*. In addition they also teach modern subjects, along with the traditional ones.

1.3. SHI'A SECT OF ISLAM

Shi'as form an independent sect of Islam. They are in a minority in India, and literature on them is difficult to come by. Shiism means *Shi'at Ali*, the Partisans of Ali Ibn Talib, the cousin and son-in-law of Prophet Muhammad. Shi'as affirm direct affiliation of their sect to the Prophet and Ali, and also that early *Imams* should have been the direct descendants of the Prophet or Messenger of God. For them the direct descendants of *Hazarat* Ali in some way participated in the special near divine status of *Nabi* (Messenger of God) Muhammad. Since in the period following the demise of the Prophet these very persons who should have been selected as the *Khalifa* or *Imam* were persecuted, Shi'as, having emotionally identified themselves with Ali and his sons Hasan and Hussain and their 'martyrdom', have never been able to reconcile with the Sunnis, the main sect of Islam. Most Shi'as believe in the first eleven *Imams*, and a twelfth *Imam* who remained invisible. Abu Jafar Tusi (eleventh century) was the most important theologian who systematized the sect of Twelve *Imams*. He also established the first Shi'a madrasa.

The followers of this sect are called the Twelver Shi'as (*Ithna Ashariyah*) or *Imamiyah*. They wait for the coming of *Qa'im* (the Riser) or *Mehdi* who would truly establish the rule of Islam in the world. They also believe that the early Imams would intercede on behalf of their followers before Allah on the Last Day of Judgement. In the absence of a divinely inspired *Imam* or one who is a direct descendant of the line of the Prophet and Ali, Shi'as believe that they must always have a living *Imam* for guiding them and interpreting for them the *sunna* and *shari'a*. Therefore, they should elect an *Imam* who would rightly interpret *shari'a* and other religious matters to them. After the death of an *Imam*, his teaching are no more authoritative for this subsect of Shi'as. Therefore they must elect another *Imam*, also called *Mujtahid*, or *Usuliyun*.[10]

But there are other Shi'ites who have rejected the need for a living *Imam* and believe that the Islamic laws can be interpreted with the help of the Holy Quran, the *hadiths* of Prophet Muhammad, as well as the early *Imams*. The followers of this sub-sect of Sh'ia Islam are called *Akhbari*. The principle of *ijtihad*, or the individual right and capacity to interpret religious precepts and *shari'a*, is accepted by both groups of Shi'as. In India Shi'as are a minority among Muslims, and mostly live in north India and Andhra Pradesh.[11]

2. SOME IMPORTANT ISLAMIC SECTS AND THEIR MADRASA *NISABS*

2.1. DARUL ULOOM, DEOBAND

The greatest madrasa of the subcontinent was founded in 1866, and its chief founders were Maulana Muhammad Nanautawi and Mualana Rasheed Ahmad Gangohi. These *maulanas* and their friends were strongly convinced of the need to impart right Islamic knowledge to young Muslim boys and decided to establish similar institutions throughout India. That is how, soon after establishing the Deoband madrasa, another one called the Mazahar-e-Uloom was established in Saharanpur, very near Deoband and on the same lines.

As we have seen in the last chapter, the English, having consolidated their hold over India, substituted Persian with English as the official language. With the removal of Persian and Urdu as the official languages, the role of madrasas as preparatory institutions for future state officials ceased. Boys of feudal classes used to come to the madrasas mostly as a means of ensuring future state posts and court honours. When that lure faded, madrasas changed from places of *dars* where every kind of knowledge or teaching was imparted to *dini madaris*, places where *dini* or religious knowledge was imparted.

Traditionally, there is no distinction between religious and worldly knowledge in Islam because both the Holy Quran and *shari'a* give mandatory rules for both. Now the distinction between the religious and the worldly was per force accepted by the *ulama*. Through the ensuing period it has conditioned their psyche so much that they now boast of the other-worldly values of Islam and that the *dini* knowledge is not obtained for worldly gains.

Though the Quranic law and its associated subjects were no more required in everyday life as the English had developed their own purportedly common laws, they remained central to the syllabus of Deoband, or the *dars-i-nizami* as adopted by it. The maulanas of Deoband were very keen about the need to impart knowledge of 'pure' Islam to their students. On the one hand, they were afraid that the boys of 'upper' classes (*ashraf*) would be led astray by the influence of English education and culture. On the other hand, inasmuch as they became conscious of the 'lower' classes (*ajlaf*) for the first time, they observed that what the latter practised as Islam was very deviant from the 'pure' Islam as they understood and practised it. Thus 'purifying' the Islam of the masses and teaching them 'true' Islam through their madrasas became the core concern of Deobandi *ulama*.

The emphasis on *din* (religion proper) was bolstered by Shah Walliullah's Wahhabi movement. As we have seen in the last chapter, Shah was emphatically in favour of purifying Islam of all its accretions that had entered it during long centuries of contact with the local populace of India. He also advocated a central place for the Quran and *hadiths* (*ahadis* in Arabic) in the madrasa curriculum. So far, the so-called rational sciences (*ma'qulat*), as Arabic grammar, rhetoric, logic, philosophy, astronomy, as well as *fiqh* (Islamic jurisprudence), had formed the syllabus of madrasas or centres of higher learning. The Quran and *sirat* (the Prophet's biography) formed no part of this syllabus and *hadiths* and *tafsir* (Quranic commentaries) were given quite a secondary place. Shah Walliullah had argued strongly to make *hadiths* and other religious subjects central to Islamic education.[12] At first these subjects remained neglected in the syllabus of Deoband, but gradually the teachers of Deoband who were also the pioneers of what later came to be known as Deobandi Islam, started paying heed to these two advices of Shah Walliullah. They designated a whole year (*Arabi hashtum*) to the study of all the *hadiths* (ten in all, though generally the first six are regarded as more authentic).

The Deobandi curriculum and the general approach it upholds embody the first proposition of Shah that only the 'true' or 'pure' Islam should be followed, that is the Islam which is cleansed of all external influences. Deobandis not only disapprove the popular Muslim practice of visiting, bowing and praying before the *mazars* of sufi saints and others, but also discourage social customs and practices, such as singing, distributing sweets and other forms of festivities associated with occasions of birth, marriage and so on. The practice of visiting *mazars* and other social customs have been shared by Hindus and Muslims alike and have formed bridges between the two religious communities. The nineteenth-century movement for cleansing Islam had a very negative impact on the shared spaces between different sections of the Indian populace.

Deobandis have had close contact with Tablighi movement of Maulana Muhammad Ilyasi (early twentieth century). Without going into the details, Tablighi movement has a threefold thrust: The need to purify Islam; the assertion that all Muslims, irrespective of caste, class or even national boundaries, form a single Islamic brotherhood (*millat*); and the duty of all Muslims to give *da'wa* (invitation) to all non-Muslims to join the *millat*, that is, convert to Islam. The term *da'wa* is also used in the context of calling the Muslim masses, who were mostly lower caste Hindus converted to Islam, to practice 'pure' Islam.[13] *Da'wa* (invitation) still forms an integral part of Deobandi Islam. In fact, not just writers on madrasas, but responses of their students to the questions posed to them affirm that one of the most important goals of madrasa education is to prepare its students for *da'wa*.[14] One section of *ulama*, probably a minority, says that converting others to Islam is no longer the goal of Muslims in a plural society. *Da'wa* is rather addressed to the Muslim masses

to practice 'pure' Islam instead of the one they have been practising so far, and which largely consists of visiting and praying
at the *mazars* of saints.[15] However, even though the *ulama* and
Jamaat activists may adjust to the needs of a plural society and
may not insist on their right to convert others to Islam, they, like
Christian missionaries, are convinced of the finality and totality
of Islam as the complete religion for *all* persons in all circumstances.

In short, Deobandi madrasas and their syllabus (as we shall
see) stand for the advocacy of:

1. 'Pure' Islam freed of all its accretions.
2. An austere way of life that shuns festivities.
3. Unconditional superiority of this Islam to all other religions
   and ways.
4. The claim that the Quran, supported by *hadiths*, gives the
   right direction for *all* eventualities of life.
5. One Muslim *millat* that transcends all social and even geographical boundaries.
6. A greater emphasis on separate Muslim identity which would
   be the same globally.[16]

For the fulfilment of the above purposes the Deobandis had
to develop a *nisab* which represented 'pure' Islam and the concept of one Muslim *millat*. It does not appear that they made
any particular efforts to do that, and accepted that the existing
syllabus of madrasas fulfilled all their needs. At first, the Dars-i-
Nizami was adopted almost as such. Then at some stage *ahadis*
(*hadiths*) were added as an independent and full-fledged subject
of study, which was a right step. However, they have continued
to teach all the medieval subjects which were taught during the
time of Muslim rulers. Now, most of these subjects are not required as madrasas are no longer the training grounds for state
officials. In modern times these subjects are not required for any
other field of life excepting the assertion of a separate Muslim
identity through a rigorous reaffirmation of Muslim Personal
Laws. Let us take a brief look at the Deoband *nisab*.[17]

Deoband has a primary (*iftadai*) section. In the *atfal* (children) class itself both Arabic and Urdu alphabets (*qaida*) are
taught, as also numbers and their writing. In addition, funda-

mental beliefs of Islam, the first and second *suras* and the *Kalma* are also taught. From the first class itself serious studies start which include arithmetic and writing Urdu. Rest is Islamic education, including *nazira* (reading) of the thirtieth *para* of the Quran, memorization of a few *suras*, practice of Islamic rituals and *diniyat* (religious study) which teaches *Talimul Islam*—a good Urdu book. In second year, the emphasis remains on *dini* subjects; though Hindi and elementary geography are added. In the third year alongside elementary geography and Hindi, *Tarikh-e-Islam* (vol. 1), and Persian (Farsi) are added. The fourth year syllabus includes Persian grammar and literature, as well as Urdu literature, Hindi, elementary English, arithmetic, and elementary science. *Dini taleem*, consisting of *Tarikh-e-Islam* (History of Islam) and memorization of the Quran continues. The fifth year course is a repeat of the fourth year. While geography taught is that of India, history is only that of Muslim empires (advanced volumes of *Tarikh-e-Islam* are taught).

Inasmuch as this *nisab* includes Urdu reading and writing, Hindi, arithmetic, and even local geography and some science, it is welcome, though the emphasis on Persian language, which starts from the third year of primary school, is not understandable. Having completed the primary course, a student has to spend one year in what is called a preparatory class (*aidadia*).

After completing six years of study, a student enters the main Arabic course of the madrasa. In the first year, called Arabi or *sale auwal*, the subjects taught are *sirat* (biography of the Prophet), *nahw* and *sarf* (Arabic grammar consisting of conjugation and syntax), Arabic literature, *mantiq* (logic), *tajweed* (correct manner of pronouncing the words of the Quran), and correct writing (*khushnavisi*). In the second year (*sale dom*) the same subjects are repeated, *fiqh* (Islamic jurisprudence) being an addition.

The third year (*sale som*) includes the study of *hadiths*, *tafsir* (Quranic exegesis or commentary) and *akhlaq* (Islamic beliefs), all of which are *dini* subjects and rightly form part of a *dini* madrasa. There is also a subject called External or Self-study (*muta'laa*). The subject assigned is history (*tarikh*) of the period of Khilafat-e-Rashida.

The fourth year (*sale chaharrum*) has in addition to jurisprudence, *usool-e-Fiqh* (principles of jurisprudence) and *balaghat* (rhetoric). History is a part of the syllabus, but only that of the

Umayyad and Abbasid periods, as also of Turkey. 'Modern science', a proud part of the syllabus, consists of geography of the Arab peninsula and other Islamic countries. Students who successfully complete the Arabi *chaharrum* are awarded the *Sanawi* (secondary) certificate.

If we include five years of primary education, plus one *Aftal* or children's class and one year of preparatory class, which generally most bigger madrasas have before admitting the students to the Arabi classes, a boy/girl has spent about 10–11 years in a Deobandi madrasa (assuming it has a primary section). So this can be roughly said to be equivalent to tenth class of 'modern' schooling. But madrasa students are awarded the *Sanawia* or Secondary school certificate after the fourth class of Arabic syllabus. This leaves four more years of study till Arabi *hashtum* (eighth class), which is claimed to be equivalent to B.A. degree of other universities. The course content is very heavy. Since we are mainly interested in universal education up to high school we would not study the syllabus of higher classes.

There is a separate department to train the *maulavis* in the right way of issuing *fatwas*. A person who undergoes this course is called a Mufti. Most major madrasas train *maulavis* and issue *fatwas* on various issues, ranging from the correct manner of doing *wuzu* to the correct manner of sexual cohabitation. The *fatwas* issued by Deobandi authorities are thousands in number, and their collections are regularly published. Generally *fatwas* are given when so requested by individual Muslims, but the Muftis can issue *fatwas* on their own too. Often the issues on which *fatwas* are sought and given are very petty, though sometimes they have overwhelming implications, as in the case of Imrana who was raped by her father-in-law and then declared by Deobandi *alims* to be the mother of her husband! Various liberal Muslim writers have opined that these *fatwas* are just opinions of *alims* and are not binding.

2.1.1. *Some Critical Comments*

However, the hold of the clerics on Muslim masses is very strong, and the fact that some persons seek *fatwas* means that they intend to follow them. Generally if a *fatwa* is issued by a respectable institution like Deoband, it asserts a great psychological pressure on the Muslim psyche, as a result of which it becomes near impossible for someone to choose a course of action which would be seen by his/her community to be against the dictates of the *fatwa*. Since these *fatwas* are always issued according to some previous real or imagined precedence in Islamic *shari'a*, and most of those incidents or pronouncements had occurred in very different historical and cultural circumstances, these *fatwas* in fact force a medieval attitude among the masses, and most of them obstruct or negate the minimum demands of justice (as in the case of Imrana), which is said to be a basic value in Islam.

Madrasa students are overburdened by the number of languages they have to study—Arabic, Persian, Urdu, Hindi, English. The load is especially high in the elementary classes. Persian is regarded as important because some religious literature of Islam is written in the language. In fact, only Islamic mysticism (*tasawwuf*) is in Persian, which the Deobandis generally reject. Importantly, when Shah Walliullah translated the Holy Quran into Persian (with a mistaken view that through it more people would be able to understand the Quran), the *maulanas* opposed this move strongly. Since Arabic is the language of the Quran and majority of the *hadiths*, it is the sacred language of Muslims, not Persian (Farsi), and therefore Persian need not be taught to young children. Someone has argued that the knowledge of Persian is essential for learning Urdu. It is entirely wrong. The Urdu that is used in everyday life is not the Urdu loaded with Arabic and Persian words and phrases that *maulanas* and Muslim elite want to force on the Muslim masses, just as Sanskritized Hindi is not the language that is understood and used in everyday life, or even in most of literature. Even if Farsi words form an integral part of literary Urdu, they could be explained while teaching Urdu literature. No child, coming from an underprivileged family with no tradition of education (it is an acknowledged fact), can ever learn all theses languages. In fact, no child can do that. If all these languages are forced upon elementary class children, other subjects would suffer. Since the memorization of the Quran, and *diniyat* or other religious subjects cannot be neglected, what gets sacrificed is the minimum of arithmetic, science and Indian geography, as well as Indian history, Hindi or regional language and English. The point we are making is that such a heavy curriculum cannot be taught, unless it is at the cost of some modern subjects to the preference of traditional ones.

Actually, very few madrasas have a primary section. Since it is not common for children having finished their primary classes in some institution of 'modern' knowledge to enroll for madrasa education, the net result is that most children coming to madrasas have had their early education in some village maktab and have no knowledge of modern subjects.

The syllabus of madrasas mostly includes only the history of Islam and the geography of Muslim empires, especially that of Saudi Arabia. Our greatest objection to this syllabus is the confining of history to Islamic history. The history of the Prophet and his times may be essential to explain the 'revelation' of the Quran. The history of the first four *Khalifas* till Hazrat Ali might be needed to explain the differences between Shi'a and Sunni sects, or the development of *hadith* literature. But why should every Muslim child of India study the history of the Umayyad and Abbasid dynasties, the wars they fought and the expansion of their empires, rather than the history of India where he/she lives and whose society and culture sustain him/her?

In the fourth year madrasa students are taught the history of Indian Muslim kings. Teaching history of India starting from the middle ages seems to be a deliberate distortion of history and gives just one message to the Indian Muslim children—that even though they live in India, they do not belong to India, or are different from other countrymen who trace their history to ancient times.

This impression is further confirmed by the fact that the geography being taught is that of the Arab Peninsula and other Islamic countries. It is argued that this is important to understand the Holy Quran and the various places mentioned therein. If so, the briefest geography of the Arab peninsula might be taught along with the history or story of the Prophet's life. But the Prophet's biography is taught in the first year of the Arabic course, while geography of Arab and other Islamic countries is taught in the fourth year; and so would not be of any help to students of first year in understanding the biography of the Prophet. India's geography is taught in the elementary course;

and it is impossible that such small children would be able to grasp and remember the details that might be taught in one period in an entire year.

Exclusively teaching the history and geography of Islamic countries to Indian children is meant to emphasize the 'unity of the Muslim *umma* throughout the globe, or in other words pan-Islamism. True, the original ideologues of pan-Islamism joined Gandhi's freedom movement while they were fighting for the retention of Khilafat, and took care to express their loyalty to the nation's freedom. But while they could combine such diverse loyalties, young impressionable minds of madrasa students may very well accept this as a given fact that they mainly belong to the global Muslim *umma*, and are Indians only in a secondary sense. How can the history of wars fought by kings who happened to be Muslim inspire them to be better Muslims? How can an average Indian youth, coming probably from a poor family, get emotionally connected to the wars fought by Muslim kings for the expansion of their empires in foreign lands? Obviously he is being asked to identify himself with the Muslim *umma* the world over. To the extent the *maulanas* are successful in making their students emotionally and intellectually attached to Muslim empires of bygone eras in foreign lands they succeed in making their students feel that they are Muslims first and Indians afterwards.

2.2. Darul Uloom Nadwatul-Ulama, Lucknow

Nadwa, as it is popularly called, is an independent, well-recognized and respected Jamia-level madrasa, not very different from Deobandi madrasas and their approach. As is well known, the founders of Nadwatul-Ulama aimed at creating a synthesis of the two systems of education—the one being established and advocated by Sir Sayyid Ahmad Khan's Aligarhi movement and the Deobandi movement or approach, that is modern Western education and the traditional Islamic syllabus and approach of the founders of Deoband. Actually, the MAO College and later the Aligarh Muslim University were not totally westernized, they had a place for religious teaching and no place for women—both under pressure from the *maulanas* (though now girls are admitted in the Aligarh University). And yet the latter had felt threatened by it. At the same time, some *maulanas* felt the need of Western education also, though they were determined that it must not weaken the Islamic moorings of the syllabus of the new institution. They tried to establish an institution which combined the best of both systems of education—English and the traditional Islamic.[18]

Nadwatul-Ulama, Lucknow was established in 1898 with the combined efforts of Maulana Muhammad Ali Mungeri and Allama Shibli Noumani. Later on Maulana Sayyid Hasan Ali Nadwi became closely associated with Nadwa. However, the urge for 'reform' in the madrasa system became stagnant immediately after the establishment of Nadwa. Shibli Noumani resigned from the post of the Rector of Nadwa and established another madrasa in Azamgarh to carry out his dream of synthesizing the two systems.

Below is given the syllabus or *Nisab-e-Taleem*, directly procured from Nadwa.[19] Its entire course is divided into five groups—*Iftadai* (elementary, 5 years); *Sanawi* (secondary, 5 years); *Aiatadiya* (preparatory class for higher study, 1 year); *Darzat-e-Aliya* (higher secondary or B.A., according to different perspectives, 2 years); *Darzat-e-Fazilat* (M.A., i.e. specialization in any of the various subjects offered, 2 years). There is also *Darja-e-Aftal* (children's class). In all it takes 16–17 years to master the full course. Of course, there are separate classes for *Hifz* (memorization of the Quran). Boys from outside and those who have completed the *Iftadai* or the *Hifz* course are all expected to do one year preparatory course before joining *Arabi Auwal*, the proper madrasa *talim* (education).

Nadwa runs separate courses for training teachers (*Darja-e-Tarbiyat Muallimeen*) and training for Islamic preaching with a view to converting others (*da'wa*). There is also the *Darjat Khususi* which is a four-year course of Islamic education for those boys who come from outside this tradition. They can get the degree of *Alimiyat* after studying for one more year.

Nadwa's *nisab* seems to be more sensible and proportionate than that of Deoband, at least up to sixth or seventh class. As in Deoband, the syllabus for elementary classes is very comprehensive, including religious and modern subjects. Not only are children taught reading and writing in both Arabic and Urdu, they also have mathematics, elementary science, along with memor-ization of specific verses of the Holy Quran, as also other subjects included in Islami *din aur tarbiyat* (ethical manners) course. They also have local and Indian geography and Hindi (from class three), as well as P.T. and gardening. English starts from the fourth class and continues up to later classes. In fifth class they study *Islami tarikh* (Guided Caliphate period). This syllabus keeps *Islami din* and *akhlaq* (beliefs) at the centre and yet teaches all modern subjects, at least up to a certain stage. The load on the children must be heavy, but since purely Islamic subjects are taught in an elementary manner in the earlier classes it does not seem to be too heavy. Till the fifth class English is elementary and Persian is not included. The books for *diniyat* and *tarbiyat* (in Urdu) seem to be sensible and neither too heavy, nor regressive.

In Arabi *auwal* (*Al Ula al Sanawia* or class 6) in addition to *tajwid* and Arabic, *diniyat* and *tarbiyat majmun* (religious and ethical subjects) are taught in Urdu. Urdu is also taught sepa-rately; as also English, Hindi and elementary science (UP Board), or some social science, mostly geography (Asia) are taught. In Arabi *dom* (second year or class 7) Persian language is added to Arabic grammar and literature, Urdu, English, elementary science, or social science (geography), as also Islami *tarikh* (history) which starts with the coming of Muslims and ends with Bahadur Shah Zafar.

After class seven, there is a preparatory class for those coming from the mainstream. Its syllabus is more or less the same as above but with greater emphasis on Arabic grammar (both *sarf* and *nahw*). Such a preparatory class is held again after class eight or Arabi *som* (third year), mostly for those who have passed the *Hifz* course, and are ignorant of all *dini* subjects.

Thus, the students have to learn in addition to English, elemen-tary science, or social science (geography of Arab peninsula) and history. The latter has two parts—history of Muslim civilization (mostly that of Muslim empires), and *Hindustan ki Kahani* (from the coming of the British to Independence). From Arabi *som* (class three or eighth year of madrasa education) the entire emphasis and content of madrasa syllabus change to include almost all the standard subjects of Dars-i-Nizami.

In Arabi *chaharrum* (Arabi fourth or ninth class), *sirat* (biography of the Prophet), *insha* (Arabi composition), and *fiqh* (Islamic jurisprudence) are added, with special emphasis on Arabi grammar. In Arabi *panjum* (Arabi class five or class ten), *hadith* is added but is perhaps elementary, as only one book (*Tahzubul Ikhlaq*) is prescribed. However, in *fiqh* the entire *Kuduri* has to be studied. There is also *Tarikh al Islami* (Islamic history: Caliphate and Umayyad periods), as also self-study (stories of the Companions of the Prophet Muhammad).

We will not concern ourselves with the next three classes as we are interested only in education which is necessary for spending life as a respectable member of society, which is up to the eighth or at best the tenth class. Significantly, while in Deoband, Arabi class eight is dedicated to the study of various *hadiths*, Nadwa seems to put far less stress on them. *Sunna* (the sayings and acts of Prophet Muhammad, as narrated in various *hadiths*) is the second most important source of Islamic *shari'a*. And yet the Nadwa course of *shari'a* (*al Ula Aliya*) lays much less emphasis on the *hadiths*. In both Deoband and Nadwa, *aqeeda* (or basic Islamic beliefs) is taught as a subject in Arabi sixth class. One major difference is that Nadwa teaches the fundamentals of Islam to its primary class students in greater detail than does Deoband.

2.2.1. *Some Critical Comments*

That Nadwa teaches modern history, howsoever briefly, is an appreciable inclusion in contrast to the exclusive emphasis on the history of Muslim empires outside India taught in other madrasas. Other modern subjects are taught in this Madrasa but only until Arabi *som* or class eight which is better than not teaching modern subject at all.

If one were to suggest, it would have been far better if Islamic beliefs were taught in place of *fiqh* in the earlier classes. Should not Islamic beliefs be more basic for a true Islamic life than *fiqh*? Keeping *aqeeda* for later years also does not make sense as very few boys complete their studies, and would not get any opportunity for knowing basic Islamic beliefs. If *aqeeda* were given priority to Islamic *fiqh* in earlier classes, it is likely that madrasa-educated youth would not be so much obsessed with *fiqh* and would be more interested in understanding and practising *Islami din* and *akhlaq* (manners and morality) which can possibly be learnt better from the Holy Quran rather than from *fiqh*. However, the study of the Quran finds no place in the syllabuses of either Deoband or Nadwa. Some *paras* (set of certain *suras*) of the Quran are memorized by the children in their elementary classes; and the boys studying for *Hifz* would have to memorize the whole Quran along with proper pronunciation (*tajweed*). But most children memorize the Quran without understanding the meaning of a single word.

In *Hifz* madrasa the *maulavis* proudly proclaim that learning the meaning of the Quran would hamper the efforts to memorize the text. The Quran is, of course, taught through *tafsirs* but these *tafsirs* are written in an archaic and difficult style with elaborate commentaries and footnotes, which are further commented upon in other commentaries. So instead of simplifying the meaning of the Quran, the *tafsirs* make it even more difficult to understand the text. Instead of spending so much time trying to teach the complex language of these *tafsirs*, which any way do not fulfil their purpose of explaining the Quran, would it not be better if the students spent their time and energies in learning something modern and more useful?

However, our chief objection to present madrasa *nisab* is teaching Indian children history of empires of foreign Muslim kings instead of the country in which they are born and live. What is its religious significance?

Muslim writers proudly declare that Muslim clerics took an active part in the first freedom movement, and consequently suffered more than Hindus at the hands of the victorious British.[20] For those Muslims fighting and dying for India's freedom, India was their homeland; so how is it that the history of Umayyad and Abbasid empires is taught to the Indian youth and not that of India and its freedom struggle in which their forefathers took part?

The answer that *Hindustan ki Kahani* is also taught is highly unsatisfactory for two reasons. Beginning the story of India with the coming of Muslims is a distortion of history, as the story of India started more than two millenniums before the coming of

Muslims. The lives of Muslims could not have been possible had they not closely interacted with the local people. Also, it is high time that the Muslims realize that they are not 'foreigners', and India is their *watan* (place of their birth, motherland). While most Muslims are converts from Hindus, a few of them might have foreign blood in them. But that does not make them 'foreigners'; they have been living in India for almost a millennium now.[21] Our personal observation says that Indian Muslims are very different from Muslims of other countries. Except for some *maulanas* and lower middle class fundamentalists, Indian Muslims are much more liberal and secular and genuinely believe in religious tolerance.[22] They share with their non-Muslim compatriots a vast storehouse of common culture, social norms, family structure, values, as well as language(s), music, painting, and day-to-day practices.[23]

Now, when Muslim children are told that India was not worth talking about till the coming of Muslims, it in some way implies that not only did the Muslims bring knowledge, culture and true religion to Indians, they, as Muslims, are still the bearers of that knowledge, culture and religion. Later when the madrasa students come into contact with those other Indians, who are often in a better state educationally, socially and economically, it creates a piquant situation. The entire madrasa education is meant to instill a sense of immense superiority in their students as followers of the greatest religion and bearers of the greatest culture. However, when in real life they are confronted with people who are more educated and successful in life, and no less cultured, they are confused and suffer from an inferiority complex.

A second reason why such a truncated history is not right is that it makes its teachers and students alienated from the society and polity they inhabit. Nationalism is basically a feeling of togetherness, of sharing not only the present but also the past and future. Common history gives roots and emotional stability to a people. If the Muslim youth are not taught that common history, they cannot be attached to their fellow countrymen in a bond of solidarity. Since they are mainly taught the history of Muslim *umma* which, in fact, is the history of Muslim empires, they are continuously reminded of the 'fact' that they are Muslims first, an integral part of transnational Muslim brotherhood, and Indian afterwards. This is a falsehood. If we once glance around us we would find Muslim countries at war with each other; and the same was true in history too. The Ottoman Empire was not built fighting and defeating the infidels but by defeating and annexing other Muslim countries. In medieval India more than half the battles were waged between Muslim kingdoms, and their armies and even chieftains were indiscriminately chosen from either community.

Thirdly, if at all some Indian history is taught, so little time is given for it that it can but be taught very cursorily. The same holds true for the history as presented by the Hindu fundamentalists. They deliberately undermine or even try to skip the contribution of Muslims to Indian culture, especially the great heights to which India reached during the Mughal empire. Such truncated history of either group cannot lead to national integration.

The same is true of geography. Indian geography is taught in the primary section of both Deoband and Nadwa. But it is not known how much the young students can absorb, given the load of *dini* subjects. More importantly, very few madrasas have a fully functioning primary section. They take it for granted that the learning in maktabs is sufficient for a child and generally start with a preparatory class in which the main stress is on learning Arabic language. Thus most Muslim boys and girls studying in madrasas do not have even an elementary knowledge of India's geography or history.

In the later years, madrasa students are only taught geography of Arabia, and still later in some madrasas that of other Muslim countries. In Nadwa, there is some provision for teaching of world geography in Arabi *dom*. But how much of it is understood by young minds of that class in one period is anyone's guess. We are told that the geography of Arab peninsula, is necessary to understand the Holy Quran, as it mentions various places in Arabia. But the Quran itself is hardly ever taught in the madrasas with a view to making the students truly comprehend the text. If at all, small footnotes explaining the places should be sufficient to make them understand the context. And, of course, there is no need of, or justification for, teaching them the geography of other Muslim countries.

The entire syllabus of Deoband is dedicated to purely Islamic subjects of Arabic literature, grammar, *mantiq* (logic), Persian, and so on. There is no significant difference in the Nadwa *nisab* either. They retain most of the subjects of the primary section till Arabi *som* (Arabi class 3 or class 8). But from Arabi *chahrrum* (Arabi class 4 or class 9) the syllabus of Nadwa is almost indistinguishable from that of Deoband, though English language is continued.

According to Deobandi *nisab*, Arabi *sale chahrrum* is equivalent to eighth class of 'modern' schools, and the boys are awarded the *Sanawi* certificate after completing four years of Arabi classes. The remaining four years should make it up to higher secondary or 10+2 of 'modern' schools. This certificate of *Aliya* is recognized by Jamia Millia and Lucknow University as such, even though the Aligarh Muslim University acknowledges it as equivalent to B.A. In the Nadwa system there is a sudden break after Arabi *panjum* (class 5) which is called *Darja Dahum* (class 10). After that they start the Aliya course (*al Ula 'Aliya*) which starts with Arabi *shashtum* (class 6). The remaining three years do not add up to the 10+2 stage.

Nadwa's inclusion of *iftadai* (elementary) science, or social science, is welcome, but is insufficient. However, both the subjects are required at least until class 8, preferably till class 10 to make children rational and knowledgeable. We can take it for granted that most students would prefer *samaji uloom* (social science) to physical science, thus remaining ignorant of both the knowledge of, and attitudes associated with, modern sciences such as physics, mathematics and biology.

Equally important, students who have not studied in the primary section of Nadwa but in some maktab, and a majority of the students would be such, would be totally ignorant of even a minimum knowledge of science and mathematics. In fact, the Nadwa syllabus assumes that a majority of boys would come in from outside, either from maktabs/madrasas in other places, or from *Hifz* classes in which no other subject is ever taught. That is why they have two separate classes called *aidadiya* or preparatory class at different stages of their course. Along with their emphasis on the teaching of Arabic, they also teach elementary science, mathematics and English in these preparatory classes.

2.3. AHLE-SUNNAT

Another important sect (*maslak*) of Sunni Islam is Ahle-Sunnat, popularly known as the Barelvi sect. The general impression of Muslim and non-Muslim masses is that the Barelvis are most liberal sect, as they allow popular practices of Muslims, such as visiting and praying at the *mazars* of Sufi saints, singing and dancing on the occasions of annual *Urs*, wherein most prayers are directed to Nabi Muhammad rather than Allah. As we shall see, the *maulavis* and *maulanas* of Ahle-Sunnat wa Jamaat do direct their major attention and faith to Muhammad rather than Allah. At the same time they vehemently reject the accusation that they approve worshipping at the *mazars*. However, the conception of the masses to this effect continues and that is why Barelvi madrasas are more popular in villages.

Ahle-Sunnat or the Barelvi movement began in the 1880s under the leadership of Maulana Ahmad Riza Khan Barelvi. He was a follower of the Hanafi school of Sunnis, as also affiliated with the Qadri order of Sufis. The central tenet of Riza Khan and his followers is love for the Prophet Muhammad and faith in his immense supernatural powers. They even regard themselves as the true Sunnis, meaning that other schools of Sunni Islam are not authentic. For the Barelvis Prophet Muhammad was not an ordinary mortal. Since other *maslaks* believe him to be such, they are not true Muslims; in fact, they are *kafirs*. They link Nabi Muhammad with *Nur* (God's glory); tell us passionately that he could see what is beyond the wall, or what the future holds (*ilm-e-ghair*). Since other schools of Islam deny this, they are *kafirs* (non-believers).[24]

I personally met the Nazim of a higher postgraduate level madrasa of Ahle-Sunnat in old Delhi. He talked passionately of the great powers of the Prophet Muhammad and the falsification of this truth by other schools of Islam. He said their madrasas teach the same syllabus (Dars-i-Nizami), and that there is no difference between the Barelvi and Deobandi *nisabs*;

and Islam and its *nisab* are one and the same for all. Yet the Barelvi madrasa does not accept students of madrasas belonging to some other *maslak*, including Deoband. The reason for this rejection is that they are not Muslims! The difference between the Barelvis and others is that between Islam and *kufr* (non-belief).

The Nazim explained that though the *nisab* in the madrasas of different *maslaks* is the same, their beliefs (*aqaid*) are different. Thus, despite identical syllabi, the interpretations are so different that there are no meeting points. He gave examples of such differences. For instance, the Ahle-Hadiths say that the *namaz* should be read while rolling your head and body but the Ahle-Sunnat prescribe quiet reading. Some say that all the people should join in reading the *namaz*, while others say only the *Imam* or the person heading the *namaz* should read, others should be silent. The Nazim did not answer the comment that these are not big differences.

He declared that the Barelvis do not support the practice of bowing before *mazars*, but added that they do not stop the ignorant (*zahils*) people from doing so. He also said that they do not approve of women visiting *mazars* but let them do so. He also passionately contested the nomenclature of 'Barelvis', and asked to be called simply as Muslims or Sunnis.

I have met a large number of *maulavis*, *maulanas* and *muftis* in and around Delhi. Many of them seem quite liberal, though there are some dogmatic ones also. But I have not confronted any one who was so passionate and dogmatic that he had no time even to listen to any questions put to him. May be it was his individual nature but the main tenets of the faith, as declared by him, are definitely such that they could lead to fanaticism.

The greatest difference between the views of Ahle-Sunnat and those of other sects of Sunni Islam lies in their relative beliefs regarding the character and role of the Prophet. According to Ahle-Sunnat, the Prophet could see what is beyond the wall, or what is going to happen in future, and on the Last Day of Judgement (*Qayamat*). The Nazim of the Ahle-Sunnat madrasa condemned other schools as they do not believe in the Prophet's *ilm-e-ghayb* (knowledge of the unknown/unseen). He further added that Muhammad would do *shafa'at* (advocacy) on the Day of Judgement before Allah, as to whom to send to Hell and whom to Heaven. Even non-Muslims would have to beseech him to advocate their case before God. And it is definite that God would agree to his *shafa'at*, and punish or reward accordingly. Muhammad is expected to advocate only the case of his own followers. The Nazim contended that all this is written in the *Bukhari Sharief*.[25]

In fact, the Nazim of the Ahle-Sunnat Madrasa was reflecting the attitude of the founder of the sect Ahmad Riza Khan Barelvi. The latter spent his entire time writing over one thousand *fatwas* against rival sects of Islam, and left the organization and management of the madrasas of his sect to his followers.

There are two major madrasas of this *maslak*. The first to be established was Manzar-e-Islam at Bareilly in 1904. The madrasa is now not so prominent, though the Sufi *khanqah* established by Muhammad Riza is very popular. Another madrasa was established in Mubarakpur, Azamgarh, with the name Jamia Ashrafiyya. In fact, the small town of Gorakhpur has the distinction of having large madrasas of almost every sect of Islam. Though Jamia Ashrafiyya follows the Deobandi syllabus, its division of classes is somewhat different. It devotes the first six years to teaching *hifz* (memorization) of the Quran and *tajweed* (correct pronunciation thereof). After the completion of this course, students have to study another eight years to get the degree of *Alimiyat*. Since children doing *hifz* are not taught any other subject, obviously the students of this madrasa would not have learnt any other subject except memorization of the Quran without understanding its meaning. The subjects taught later are those of Dars-i-Nizami, and according to our sources it consists of around 40 subjects![26] The emphasis is on Arabic grammar, though history and geography of Muslim kingdoms are also taught. In the absence of more detailed information, we can only guess that even the minimum 'modern' subjects taught in Deoband and Nadwa are not included in Ashrafiyya syllabus.

2.3.1. *Some Critical Comments*

If we go by the assertions of the *maulanas* and spokespersons of Ahle-Sunnat sect, we would find them most fanatic. But the ordinary *maulanas* of this sect calling the faithful for prayer, would not be so. In villages common folk indulge in practices like praying at *mazars* and requesting for *taweez* (talisman) from *maulanas* for alleviating ailments. Both in villages and city gatherings all songs of worship—*natain* and *qawwalis*—are addressed to the Prophet Muhammad. All these practices are thoroughly condemned by other sects of Islam, while tolerated at least by the lower rung of *maulanas* of this sect.

As to their syllabus, the Ahle-Sunnat proudly declare that they teach Dars-i-Nizami. Obviously by this they mean the Dars in its original form, without including even the *hadiths* or other religious subjects which were neglected in the original, and later on gradually included in the syllabuses of madrasas of other sects. There is no possibility, therefore, of inclusion of modern subjects.

2.4. AHLE-HADITH (HADEES)

The followers of Ahle-Hadith sect call themselves Partisans or followers of the Prophet's Traditions. Though a very important sect of Islam the *New Encyclopaedia of Islam* gives a very brief description of this sect. The Ahle-Hadith is generally confused or juxtaposed with the Wahhabi movement or the Salafiyya approach, while they are definitely different from the Wahhabi movement of Saudi Arabia or earlier Egypt. Varanasi's Salafiyya madrasa is perhaps their biggest madrasa. Some information about their basic beliefs, goals and programme is available on their 'official' Urdu website. They have a big well organized madrasa with various classes and sections. They also have a modern girls' school and a regular girls' madrasa, all in Sanabil near Okhla, Delhi. When I visited the main madrasa they were most open about sharing their syllabus (in Arabic), and explained to me various basic tenets of their faith. But I could not visit their girls' madrasa entry to which was restricted.[27]

The Ahle-Hadith are opposed to: (a) excessive emphasis on

the detailed controversies over jurisprudence (*fiqh*) which has led to the division of Sunni Muslims into Hanafi, Hanbalis, and so on, and (b) extensive use of personal opinion and reasoning in matters of religion. However, the opposition to personal reasoning is limited to purely religious matters, and is encouraged in worldly or secular matters. But due to the lack of clear distinction between the religious and the worldly in Islam, the traditionalists' support for reasoning does not go very far.

Their main contention is that they are not bound to blind obedience (*taqlid*) to any of the four Imams of the *fiqh* schools. Instead, they turn to the two main sources of Islam—the Holy Quran and the *sunna* or the example of Muhammad, as recorded in the authentic traditions of the Prophet. They disregard the opinions of the founders of the four schools of *fiqh* if they find them in conflict with the traditions (*hadiths*) which are accepted as authentic because they have been reported by the Companions or the direct descendants of the Prophet.

The Ahle-Hadith attempt to go back to the first principles and to restore the religion to its original simplicity and purity of faith and practice. They affirm that Islamic faith is centered around the belief in *Tawhid* or the Unity of Allah and the denial of any supernatural powers to any of His creatures. (This brings them in direct conflict with the followers of Ahle-Sunnat.) Taking Islam back to its pristine purity means cleansing it of all its later innovations (*bid'a*) and additions, which creeped in due to the influence of the local faith or Hinduism. They are especially against the popular customs of saint worship or visiting and praying at the *mazars* of Sufi saints.

The four basic tenets of Ahle-Hadith may be said to be: (a) their opposition to the innovations or later additions in Muslim practices, called *bid'a*, especially in the Indian subcontinent; (b) their insistence on going back to the pristine glory of Islam of the times of the Prophet Muhammad and his Companions; (c) their opposition to the almost absolute authority of the founders of Islamic jurisprudence, and (d) their insistence on total reliance on the Holy Quran and the *hadiths*; While the Ahle-Hadith are mostly in harmony with most Sunni schools with reference to their first concern regarding the need to 'purify' Islam, they differ from them in their third and fourth contentions. That is, the other Sunni sects not only insist on blindly following medieval *fiqh* schools, they also seem not to give the Quran and *hadiths* the central place as given in Ahle-Hadith. Except in Deoband, *hadiths* are not taught in detail in other madrasas of India. What is rather curious, they are not taught in detail even in Ahle-Hadith madrasas.

Ahle-Hadith further do not give the same importance to Quranic exegesis or *tafsir*, and instead encourage direct reading of the holy text by individual Muslims. If so, they seem to be saying the same thing as Maulana Gilani that the Quran should be studied directly without the help of detailed complicated *tafsirs*. Direct reliance on the Quran and the *sunna* means the individual Muslim can understand and follow his/her own understanding of the two, though in actual practice this may not be happening. According to the Ahle-Hadith official website, the sect, as represented through Markazi Jamiat Ahle-Hadith, has the following goals or objectives:

(i) To motivate Muslims to adhere to pristine monotheism- (*Tawheed*) and follow the *Sunna* (precepts and practices of Allah's messenger).

(ii) To regenerate Muslim society by putting an end to innovations and un-Islamic customs (practices), and to persuade them to shun blind following.

(iii) To train and educate Muslims in all spheres of life in such a way that they become models of Islamic teachings.

(iv) To convey the message of Islam to non-Muslims in a positive and reasonable way, and to cooperate with them in the field of knowledge and welfare. The Ahle-Hadith further claim that their approach of rejecting the divisions of various schools of *fiqh*, if followed by others, would unify the entire Muslim *umma*.[28]

In this they are not very different from the Deobandis and the Tablighi Jamaat. And yet surprisingly they are equally vehemently critical of these latter sects also.[29] The former two have been working together to 'emancipate' the Muslim masses from not only the popular practices but also the common language, dresses and other social customs that they share with their local non-Muslim neighbours. Therefore, there is no basic difference between Ahle-Hadith and other Sunni schools, except Ahle-Sunnat. However, the refusal of the former to blindly follow any of the various schools of *fiqh* is not only unique to them, but brings them in direct conflict with all other Sunni sects which, for reasons best known to them, give central importance to Islamic jurisprudence in their religious education.

It is apparently a rational and liberal approach, but the followers of Ahle-Hadith sect are not known to be as liberal. They passionately, even aggressively, oppose the versions of Islam which are not in conformity with their own. The origins of their doctrine are to be found in the teachings and writings of Muhammad Abduh and Rashid Rida of Arabia. In their enthusiasm for 'purifying' Islam they are also influenced by the Arabian Wahhabi movement, and are often called so by their opponents. Of course, they reject this nomenclature. They are also related to the Salafiyya movement which idealizes and insists on following the Islam of 'pious forefathers (*al salaf al salih*)' and the movement for *islah* (reform).[29] Unfortunately, as practised in Saudi Arabia and some other Arab countries, this call for following the ways of 'pious forefathers' has led to an extreme form of regressive Islam which seeks to imitate the ways of seventh-century Arab society. There are unconfirmed reports that the Ahle-Hadith organization receives funds from Saudi Arabia. If true, it may result in this sect becoming more regressive and fanatic.

Ahle-Hadith's main madrasa, called Jamia Salafiyya, is in Varanasi. It was not possible to procure its syllabus, but the syllabus from its equally large madrasa in Delhi, called Jamia Islamia at Sanabil, has been given here.[30] It has a primary section, though this does not seem to be integral to its system. The *nisab* of madrasa proper starts with a preparatory (*aidadia*) class, a form of bridge course for all students who are expected to have studied in Urdu medium schools or maktabs. Children from common maktabs are also apparently accepted. This preparatory class teaches Arabic, Persian, Urdu, Hindi, English, and arithmetic, as also recitation and memorization of some portions of the Holy Quran with proper *tajweed* (manner of pronunciation and recitation).

In Arabi *auwal*, *aqeeda* (Islamic beliefs), Persian and elementary science are added. In Arabi *dom*, Arabic grammar and composition and *sirat* (biography of the Prophet) are added to the above subjects while Persian is removed. The same subjects continue in Arabi *som* and *chaharrum* classes. Islamic history is studied from class 3. In class 4, *hadith*, *usool-e-hadith*, *balaghat* (rhetoric) and *fiqh* are added. In Arabi *panjum* (roughly equivalent of class 10 of common schools) Indian history replaces Hindi.

2.4.1. *Some Critical Comments*

This syllabus of Ahle-Hadith madrasas, is more sensible than that of Deoband for several reasons. First, it contains most modern subjects, though Indian history and geography are not sufficiently covered, but at least they are taught, as are science and mathematics. There is no either/or system whereby a student can take either a subject from the science group, or a subject from social sciences.

Second, Ahle-Hadith has *aqeeda* (*aqa'id*, pl.) or fundamental Islamic beliefs from the beginning and the subject continues for several years, which makes much greater sense than the introduction of *aqeeda* in later years, as is the practice in Deoband. Third, it introduces Islamic jurisprudence (*fiqh*) in Arabi *chaharrum* (about class 9 of normal school), whereas in the Deobandi *nisab* it is taught from earlier classes. Surprisingly, though Ahle-Hadith puts the greatest stress on *hadiths*, they are introduced in Arabi class 4 only. Even in the higher classes the study of authentic *hadiths* in detail, which is done in the last (Arabi *hashtum*) year of study in Deoband, is not included.

But as against Deoband and Nadwa, Ahle-Hadith's last class has a separate subject of propagation (*da'wa*). Actually, *da'wa* is one of the major goals of all Islamic schools. Numerous works on the madrasa system by Muslim scholars have given a prominent place to training the students for *da'wa*. They even give the call to conversion as the second most important goal of Islamic education.[31] What is even more serious from a secularist, pluralist point of view is that madrasa students are enthusiastic about training for *da'wa* (as reported by Shoyeb Ansari). They even demand that there should be more books for teaching the art of *da'wa*.[32] If our future citizens come out of madrasas with the conviction that their second most important goal in life is 'calling others to convert to Islam', it would put them on a course of confrontation with other religious communities.

The two main Semitic religions believe in their own religion being the highest, or revealing the final truth about God and human salvation. Particularly, Christianity has always affirmed that the only hope for humankind to get salvation from their sins is to take refuge in Christ, the Son of God who died at the Cross to atone for the sins of humanity. Significantly it were the Christians in the Constituent Assembly debates who emphasized most a constitutional right to convert others. Islam also asserts that the Prophet Muhammad was the last one, or the Seal of Prophets; that Islam is the most perfect religion providing guidance to all humankind in every field of life, as it is based on a direct 'revelation' of God. Therefore it is but natural that Muslims should call upon all people to join the privileged Muslim *umma*.[33] Without questioning their respective faiths, it is to be acknowledged here that such assertions may not be conducive to harmonious relations in a plural society.

2.5. JAMAAT-I-ISLAMI HIND

Jamaat is a very important and influential organization. It has established madrasas throughout India, though largely in north India. Its main madrasa is Jamiat-al Falah in Balariaganj, Azamgarh. The founder and ideologue of the Jamaat was the well-known Maulana Abul Ala Maududi. Maududi dreamt of the overall hegemony of Islam. He asserted that the goal of Islam is best secured in an Islamic state, but where this is not possible, Islam must be made the determining factor in the lives of all Muslims. The propagation of Islam among the non-Muslims is an integral part of the Jamaat ideology.[34] The Jamaat affirms the supremacy of *shari'a*, and seeks total Islamization of Muslims in India. That means denouncing all customary practices of Muslim masses which are not based directly on the Islamic *shari'a*. In this aim Jamaat's programme becomes one with the Tablighi movement of the twentieth century. It is somewhat different from the Ahle-Hadith version of Islam. In the former it is the *shari'a* that is the determining factor of the lives of Muslims, in the latter, at least at the ideological level, it is the Quran and *sunna*. Curiously, in spite of no basic differences between the views of Jamaat-i-Islami, Deobandi and other related world-views, Jamaat ideologues spend considerable time and energy in refuting and even condemning Deobandi and other related approaches.

There is a difference in the ambience of Jamaat madrasas compared to those òf other sects. As is well known, in almost all madrasas education is totally free. Boarding and lodging, as well as other sundry expenditures needed for fulfilling both the physical and educational needs of madrasa students, are borne by the madrasa authorities. The authorities, in turn, depend on *zakat* (obligatory donations) from Muslims. *Maulanas* and *maulavis* are paid very low salaries due to the financial crunch. Two results follow from this—first, madrasas attract boys and girls from very poor Muslim families; second, low salaries fail to attract well-educated and able teachers, thus bringing down the standard of madrasa education.

On the other hand, madrasas established by Jamaat charge a certain amount of fee and also expect students to bear their sundry expenses, which are borne in other madrasas by the management. As a result, they attract boys and girls (of course, the two have separate madrasas) from the middle class. While in most madrasas students come from villages, and that too from illiterate families, students of Jamaat are generally offsprings of petty businessmen or a section of middle class, and their parents themselves are mostly madrasa educated. Since the boarding and lodging fee eases the Jamaat finances, they can hire better qualified teachers and therefore the standard of education provided in them is generally better than in normal madrasas. Jamaat further seeks to involve the parents in Jamaat movement, thus strengthening the drive for the spread of their particular brand of Islam throughout India. In fact, Jamaat-e-Islami Hind has grown into a formidable movement which not only tries to wean Muslims away from their ambivalent regional identities which have so far bound them to the society around them, but also emphasizes a separate Muslim identity which sometimes even undermines national identity and interests.

Jamaat has tried hard to get its certificates recognized by other

Indian universities. Not only the Muslim universities of Aligarh, Hamdard, Jamia Millia, and Maulana Azad University at Hyderabad, but also Lucknow University and the newly established University of Poorvanchal recognize their certificates. As a result, their students are able to see beyond their madrasas, and often have the ambition to join some mainstream university after completing the *Alimiyat* course.[35]

The curriculum of *Jamiat-ul-Falah*, the prime institute of Jamaat, consists of 16 years and is divided into three stages: primary (*Iftadai*, five years); secondary (*Sanawi*, three years), higher (*Auliya*, eight years), leading to the degree of *Fazilat* which is regarded as equivalent to M.A. In the first year of the primary section, fundamental beliefs of Islam, manner of *namaz*, Urdu alphabets and basic arithmetic are taught. In the second year, memorization and reading of some Quranic verses, *dini taleem*, arithmetic, elementary Hindi and English are taught. 'General knowledge' and geography are added from the third year. In the secondary stage these subjects continue, with elementary science, history and Persian being added.

Significantly, Arabic classes start after the secondary level. After this the main emphasis shifts to the learning of Arabic language, though Urdu, Hindi and English also continue to be taught. Elementary political science and elementary economics are also part of the curriculum. In the brief syllabus that is upon the internet there is relatively less emphasis on the study of *hadiths*, *tafsir*, *fiqh* and other Islamic subjects.[36]

2.5.1. *Some Critical Comments*

To want its students to join mainstream educational institutions is, of course, a very welcome approach. It is at the same time a curious situation. On the one hand, the Jamaat not only tries to improve its standard of traditional education, but also encourages its boys, girls, to go in for modern education. On the other hand, Jamaat's ideological position is some sort of 'Islamism', that is, a movement aimed at total Islamization of the Muslim community. While its emphasis on recognition by other universities and its encouragement to its students to join regular universities suggest a desire to remain in the mainstream, its emphasis on Islamization of entire life and attitudes of all Muslims naturally heightens their separate identity, and to that extent takes them away from the mainstream society and polity. We must reaffirm here that whenever we talk of 'mainstream' Indian life, we are not talking the language of Hindutva. 'Mainstream' here means the composite, pluralist culture of our nation which is seeking, however unsuccessfully, to establish a just, secular and democratic society.[37] In such a society, though plural communities are welcome to develop their individual cultures to enrich the cultural mosaic of the country, undue stress on separate identities, coupled with an equal stress on the right for *da'wa*, is bound to create schisms.

Teaching of Arabic at a later stage, lesser emphasis on *fiqh* and even *tafsir* and *sirat*, inclusion of Hindi, English and other elementary modern subjects in their syllabus, suggest that Jamaat followers are trying to strike a balance between their central faith in the immense superiority of Islam, the need to Islamize the Muslim masses and the mission of calling others (*da'wa*) to the 'true' faith, on the one hand and the need to adapt their students to modern times through 'modern' subjects, on the other. However, since we do not know the content of the history, geography and political science taught in their madrasas, we cannot assess these 'modern' subjects.

Jamaat's insistence on a separate Muslim identity, not only for its students but for all those parents and others, who can be approached by its *ulama* and ideologues is having an undesirable effect on the spontaneous harmonious relations between the country's two major religious communities.

2.6. SHI'A MADRASAS

Since most Muslim rulers were Sunnis, Shi'a madrasas could be established only in eighteenth century when Shi'a rule was established in Awadh. Madrasa-yi-Nazimiyya was established in Lucknow in 1890. The admission therein is restricted to the followers of Twelver branch of Shi'as. Among other important Shi'a madrasas is Sultan-al-Madaris, also in Lucknow, and Madrasa-yi-Jawwadiya in Banaras. A special madrasa—Madrasat-al Wa'izin—has been established in western Uttar Pradesh to train madrasa pass-outs in missionary work. While the syllabus of their higher courses is traditional and consists of all those subjects which constitute Dars-i-Nizami, they have introduced 'modern' subjects up to the secondary level. Many of these madrasas are affiliated to Arabi Farsi Board of UP, and get government grant. The Madrasa-yi-Nazimiyya's *Aliya* or secondary course consists of six years of primary (*Tahtaniyya*) and three years of secondary (*Fawqaniyya*) schooling, which can be roughly equivalent to the class 8 of common schools.

In the primary section, apart from the Quran and *diniyat*, arithmetic, geography of the province, general science, basic Hindi Urdu and elementary English are taught. The *Fawqaniyya* classes continue with mathematics (in Urdu), world geography, Hindi and English; *fiqh* (Islamic jurisprudence), *mantiq* (logic), Arabi *sarf* and *nahw* (grammar) and *adab* (literature) constituting the traditional subjects. Importantly, each of the above subjects has two prescribed books—one in Arabic and another in Persian. Literature, grammar and even logic and jurisprudence are taught in both the languages.[38]

2.6.1. *Some Critical Comments*

Persian is the medium of instruction in all Shi'a madrasas as it is Arabic in Sunni madrasas. Of course, the explaining is in Urdu. The emphasis on Persian seems be due to their close emotional links with Iran. A senior maulana of a big Shi'a madrasa—Jamia Ahle Bait in Okhla, Delhi—told me that even the Quran is taught in Persian! It seems taking things too far. Since the students have to learn Arabic, as most of the *hadiths* and other texts of Islam are in that language, they teach the same subject in both languages. However, learning the same subjects in two different languages must be confusing for the students, and would definitely increase their workload.

Equally significantly, there are not many truly *dini* (religious) subjects in this syllabus, except *fiqh* (which does not seem to be a religious subject as such). Even in the two years of Maulavi course (Arabic medium) *uloom-al-hadith, ilm-al tafsir* and *balaghat* and *hikma* (philosophy) are added, instead of any original *hadith* or *tafsir*. Any objective person would admit that rhetoric, logic and old-fashioned philosophy are no help in religion or *din.*

3. MADRASAS AFFILIATED TO MADRASA BOARDS OR STATE BOARDS

Such madrasas form an entirely different category as they introduce modern subjects in their syllabus and accordingly reduce the content of standard Islamic subjects. But they cannot all be grouped into one category. Some Madrasa Boards keep their Islamic subjects more or less intact and include modern subjects in brief. Other Madrasa Boards are directly affiliated to State Boards, and incorporate all modern subjects of those Boards. They not only teach all modern subjects, but also considerably reduce the *dini* content of their syllabus. Bihar, Uttar Pradesh, Madhya Pradesh, Rajasthan, Orissa, Bengal, Assam and Andhra Pradesh have got Madrasa Boards to which some of the madrasas of their respective states are affiliated.

Sometimes, sweeping generalizations are made to the effect that all modern subjects are taught in government-aided madrasas or those affiliated with Madrasa Boards.[39] They are dangerous in the sense that they give a false assurance that all is well with these madrasas.

3.1. ARABI AND FARSI BOARD OF UP

Below is given the *Nisab-e-Taleem* of Arabi and Farsi Board, Uttar Pradesh, as given by Ghulam Yahya Anjum.[40] It recognizes Dars-i-Nizami as the standard *nisab*, but includes modern subjects up to the higher secondary level. The Board and its *nisab* are meant for both Sunnis and Shi'as. Except a few religious subjects, all others are the same in the two courses. The total course is five years for primary and nine years after that, the completion of which is supposed to be equivalent to M.A. or even M.Phil. The curriculum is divided into several stages: *Tahtaniya* or primary up to class 5; *Fawqania* or secondary up to class 8. *Aliya* or *Maulavi* up to class 10; *Alim* up to 10+2 level. The syllabus includes education up to *Kamil* and *Fazil*, which does not interest us here.

As is the case with every madrasa course, earlier education is not given much importance. Our source, Anjum first gives the detailed course only for *Darjat-e-Aliya* or *Maulavi* level which is for two years and includes *diniyat*, Arabi *adab* (literature), Farsi *adab*, Urdu *adab*, general Hindi and *riyazi* (mathematics), or home science. There is only one paper for optional subjects in which category a student can choose either *ma'qulat* (traditional rational science), e.g. *mantiq* or logic, or *samaji uloom* (social science), or General English, or science. In next higher course of *Alim* (up to class 12) subjects are more or less the same though typing is added.

Diniyat covers traditional subjects, though they are relatively easy than those in Dars-i-Nizami. In the *Munshi* and *Maulavi* courses which are equivalent to class 10, the Board has separate *diniyat* for Sunnis and Shi'as. The syllabus includes translation of the Quran, *tajweed* (manner of pronunciation), *hadith*, *sirat-e-nabi* (biography of the Prophet), *fiqh*, *usool-e-fiqh* (principles of jurisprudence), *mantiq* (logic), as well as Arabi, Farsi (Persian), Urdu and all the other subjects mentioned above.[41] In Arabi or Farsi literature, the syllabus prescribes prose, poetry and history of literature, as also *funoon-e-adab* (art of literature) and *insha* (composition). Students of Arabi get the degree of *Maulavi*, while that of Farsi get that of *Munshi*.

Significantly while mathematics is meant for boys, home science (*uloom-e-khanadari*) is meant for girls. The syllabus for both social and natural sciences is sensible, and mostly uses NCERT books in Urdu. Social science in earlier classes refers to the Constitution of India and elementary Indian history beginining from the ancient times. In the higher classes, history of medieval India alone is taught in detail.

Most important, a student has to take only one of these modern subjects, or he/she may opt only for *mantiq* and not take any modern subject.

3.1.1. *Some Critical Comments*

Offering students the option of taking one of the several subjects is wrong, at least until the *Fauqania* (class 8) stage. Both social and natural sciences, as well as mathematics should be taught to all students, preferably until the class 10, or at least up the class 8. Otherwise a person knowing one of the social sciences, or physics or chemistry remains ignorant of the other equally important dimensions of knowledge.

Also these two groups of social and natural sciences go hand-in-hand. A child cannot understand physics or chemistry alone, or history or geography alone without having some knowledge of its sister subjects. The content of these subjects as given in the above syllabus is fine, despite the emphasis on medieval India in higher classes of the *Aliya* course. But this *nisab* also gives the option of *ma'qulat*, which means if a student opts for this traditional subject, he/she would be left totally ignorant of any modern subject. Actually the option of taking any one of modern subjects or one of the traditional sciences makes the whole exercise of inclusion of modern subjects meaningless. This is one aspect of the syllabus which should be taken care of immediately.

3.2. State Madrasa Education Board of Assam

The syllabus of this Board is much more comprehensive, and includes all the subjects present in the State Board of Education, Assam, as well as Islamic subjects with reduced content.[42] As usual, it starts after primary classes and consists of pre-Senior section of three years; *Dakhil* or senior section of three years; intermediate section of two years, followed by two years for *Fa'dil al M'arif* degree, thus making ten years in all.

The pre-senior section, which is equivalent of class 7 of common schools (in Assam the primary schools are only up to class 4), has English, mathematics, general science, social studies, Hindi and some vocational course. Importantly, its course content is that of the State Board, and the books used are those prescribed by the State Board. In addition, it has *diniyat* which consists of the Quran, elementary *fiqh* and *aqaid* (fundamental beliefs), Arabic language consisting of elementary grammar and composition, as well as Assamese or Bengali (course according to State Board) and elementary Urdu.

In its senior section, the same subjects continue. In *diniyat* we have the Quran and elementary *fiqh*. Arabic grammar is taught in some relative detail, as well as prose and poetry. Urdu is also taught to an advanced stage. While there are no optional subjects in the junior classes, senior section offers the option of history of Islam or Persian. In the senior class 4 (approximately class 11 of modern school) *usool-e-fiqh* (principles of jurisprudence) is added in *diniyat* and in the next class elementary *balaghat* (rhetoric) is added.

However, even modern subjects continue in senior classes, though their course content is sensibly reduced in proportion to the increase in *dini* subjects.

3.3. MADHYA PRADESH MADRASA BOARD

As in Assam, Bengal, Bihar and Madhya Pradesh Madrasa Boards function in close relation to the respective State Boards. They have all the subjects of State Boards plus *diniyat* (religious subjects) and Arabic. The general approach is more or less the same as that of Assam Madrasa Board described above. As another example, we give here the syllabus of Madrasa Board of Madhya Pradesh which is directly affiliated to MP State Board of Education.[43]

Significantly the MP Madrasa Board has a primary section. Its syllabus includes mathematics, Hindi, Urdu, English, general knowledge and EVS or environmental studies. In addition, Arabic language and *diniyat* are taught. The same subjects continue at the upper primary level, with EVS being replaced by social science and general science, and Arabic being added. Some madrasas dedicate a period for moral education, while all of them have a games period, though the teaching time is limited to about four hours. Generally, the time given for *diniyat* and Arabic is 45 minutes (one period), while that for modern subjects is three hours.[44]

The Board makes bold claims as to the number of madrasas registered with it which are teaching modern subjects, calling it 'mainstreaming' of madrasa education. It also talks of the aid given to a large number of madrasas and distribution of free textbooks and so on. Most of these 'reforms' or additions of modern subjects are made under SSA. But these claims are yet to be proved at the ground level. The syllabus is very boldly conceived, but its successful implementation has many hurdles which we will look at in chapter 8.

3.4. Some Critical Comments on 'Modernized' Madrasas

The syllabuses of the Assam and MP Boards are worthy to consider for two reasons. First, they include both social science and general science, as well as mathematics, thus making the madrasa students at par with those in common schools. Second, they considerably reduce the load or content of traditional subjects, and give up the so-called *ma'qulat* or rational subjects which have nothing to do with the preservation of Islam and Muslim culture. Of course, the load would still be much more on madrasa students than on those in common schools. Especially, the number of languages that madrasa students are expected to master is very large, especially in the Assam Board, and could hardly be successfully handled by them.

Equally important, there seems to be no additional teachers for modern subjects in the madrasas affiliated to these Boards. Even the regular teachers are not given any monetary incentive to learn and teach modern subjects. There also seems to be no effort to increase the timings of the madrasas with the result that children are unable to even cope with the heavy syllabus, forget mastering it. For example, Madhya Pradesh students attend madrasas for 3½ hours which was the timing even earlier.

So far there has not been any effort to assess the extent to which madrasa students are able to master the modern subjects. The Madhya Pradesh Board has proposed to give regular examinations, but whether this proposal has materialized or not is not known. There is also no proper supervision of how the modern subjects are being taught.

4. CONCLUDING REMARKS

An important dimension of the whole issue of Madrasa *nisabs* is that *maslaki* (sectarian) differences are given undue importance. Two results follow—madrasa teachers are constantly engaged in theological disputes and writing tracts demolishing (*radd*) the beliefs and practices of other *maslaks* or sects. Real religious issues are rarely touched upon in these controversies, and petty peripheral issues are given all the attention. The author has a personal experience of the attitude of condemnation towards other sects and the way peripheral issues get highlighted. For example, the Principal of a senior madrasa of Ahle-Sunnat in Old Delhi condemned all other sects of Islam with such passion. He in fact declared that they were not even Muslims! Immense energy is wasted in these constant inter-*maslak* arguments and conflicts, energy which can be better utilized elsewhere. Also, these controversial practices can hardly be called religious, and students unnecessarily get involved in these disputes.

Bigger madrasas like Deoband and Nadwa have regular student debates in which fanatic adherence to one's *maslak* is encouraged. As it is, rhetoric (*balaghat*) is an integral part of madrasa curriculum. The more passionate and rhetorical a student is in these debates the more appreciation he earns. The result of continuous brain-washing is that the students sincerely believe that the understanding of Islam by their *maslak* is the only true one, that they are somehow a victim of the followers of other *maslaks*, thus creating an atmosphere of conflict within Islam.[45]

The author has witnessed one such talk in an Ahle-Hadith madrasa in Delhi, and the delivery and passion of the young speaker were almost mesmerizing. Naturally when the pass-outs of these madrasas enter real life they can sway the masses to their own point of view regardless of the merits of whatever they are asserting. There is a regular website of the Ahle-Hadith sect condemning other sects, mentioned earlier.[46] Other Islamic sects must also be boasting of similar sites. This is rather dangerous both for the students who are being turned into fanatics and for the society where these students will brainwash the masses. The practice of emphasizing inter-*maslak* differences so passionately, as if that is all Islam is about, diverts both the teachers and students from true religion and the practical problems of daily life.

There is too much emphasis on blind following of the written word (*taqlid*). Questioning of the prescribed books is never tolerated. In fact, the entire emphasis and culture of madrasas is based on blind obedience to both the book and the teacher. This *taqlid* is not only emphasized in matters of faith but also in matters of dress and behaviour. *Shari'a* and *fiqh* have thus become central to Islamic education, giving the impression to non-Muslims and to the students that Islam is all about them. To quote M. Mujeeb,

Orthodoxy maintained the identity of Muslim community by condemning the unbelievers in the inherited theological phrases, but demanded from the Muslims little beyond conformity at the lowest religious and ethical level.[47]

And,

The power of the orthodox official *ulama* lay in their being able to assert what was true belief and correct practice, and to insist on precision in both these spheres of religious life. They concentrated on *taqlid*, on believing and saying and doing exactly what had been believed and said and done by the rightly guided orthodox *'ulama* of the previous generations.[48]

Mostly students just memorize what is being told to them or from a few prescribed books. Smaller madrasas have very little writing work, whereas bigger madrasas hold written examinations. Students are brainwashed such that they never deviate from the orthodox position, nor do they dare do so. The responses of students, as reported by Shoyeb Ansari referred to earlier, are so orthodox, even retrograde, that it is shocking to read them. There is very little chance that these students would think anew of present-day issues and the demands of the times, being so convinced of the absolute correctness of the orthodox position. Quoting medieval texts in the context of present-day problems is taken as a sign of *ulama's* learnedness and is much respected and even followed. This is not desirable either for the Muslim community or for the society at large.

As no outside reading material is allowed in most madrasas, the students remain cocooned in the four walls of the madrasas, or rather in the make-believe world of medieval Arab culture. They are cut-off from outside world, except perhaps when they go home. Meanwhile they have imbibed such negative attitudes towards the outside world, especially towards anything modern, that they function as a regressive pull for the entire Muslim society, excepting the middle and upper classes. Even having a dialogue with them is difficult because of their rigid or closed mindset. When a *maulana* said that outsiders have no right to tell madrasa teachers what to teach, he was right. Our interest in madrasa *nisab* and the mindset it creates is not because we want to question the right of minorities to establish their own institutions to preserve their religion and culture. Rather it is because we are rightly concerned about the influence of madrasa education on Muslim society. The *alims* and pass-outs of madrasas, not only look very different in their dress, language and manners from the common people, but are regarded by the generally illiterate Muslims as symbols of the ideal Islamic way of life. The madrasa pass-outs thus also exert a regressive influence on the people around them.

With the exception of Ahle-Sunnat, all sects of Sunni Islam are insistent on the need to 'purify' the Islam as practised by the Muslim masses. (We not know much about Shi'as, but obviously they too must be equally eager to 'purify' Islam according to their conception thereof.) It means cleansing it of all customary practices, religious as well as worldly, which might have had their origin in the non-Muslim or the Sufi culture as understood in India, or which are seen as opposed to *shari'a*. These practices include not only visiting and praying at *mazars* of Sufi saints but also many innocent social and family practices which are shared with other religious communities. Even the use of regional dress and language is frowned upon. Significantly, these are the very customs, practices and even values which secularists have been hailing as symbols of India's synthetic culture.

In this goal of 'purifying' popular Islam, and Islamizing the masses, the Quran and the *hadiths*, which should have been the core of any Muslim religious education, are made secondary. Instead *shari'a,* as it is being interpreted by a certain *alim* in a given situation, and *fiqh* (jurisprudence) have become the core of modern 'Islamism'. In earlier times *fiqh* was the core of the syllabus of madrasas, or Islamic education, as it aimed at training future *qazis, muftis* and other government officials who were expected to govern according to Muslim laws. Earlier, as well as in modern period, the truly *dini* subjects like the Quran and *hadiths* find much less space (except in the Arabi *hashtum* of Deoband) than *fiqh* in various Madrasa *nisabs*.

Would it not be far better that our *maulanas* and those who decide the madrasa syllabus face the fact that a greater part of the *fiqh* has become irrelevant due to the changed circumstances? With the exception of Personal Laws all other laws applied in our administration and courts are religion-neutral, secular and common. The *shari'a* criminal law was abolished and substituted by the common Indian Penal Code in 1860–1 by the British. Even several aspects of the so-called Personal Laws of Muslims are determined by the Shariat Act, 1937 passed by the British, which the Muslims accepted without any protest. As to the rest of *shari'a*, we have to accept that a large part thereof is specific to the then culture and times, and it is not desirable to be emphasized and enforced in today's world.[49] This refers specifically to the dress and other everyday details. *Tablighi* activists and their related organizations emphasize the need to Islamize Muslims' dress, food habits and even language. These are the things which create togetherness among the people of a particular region. It is difficult to see any integral connection between dress, language and other locality-specific minor details regarding the behaviour pattern of a group of Muslims and the religion of Islam.

Mushir-Ul-Haq has very sensibly explained the phenomena. According to him, the secularists are not able to assess the average Muslim's attachment to his/her religious identity. Further, in Islam, religion is not merely faith but *shari'a* too, and the latter covers every aspect of human life.[50] As our discussion above has indicated, Islam lays much more emphasis on *shari'a* which includes petty details of religious rituals (as to the position of hands in different stages of *namaz*), as well as detailed rules regarding the daily transactions of life. Interestingly, these detailed rules are not written down anywhere, they are determined by the understanding/interpretation of *shari'a* by choosing one *hadith* or the other and applying it to the given situation. *Maulanas* and *muftis* mostly determine the *shari'a* through the institution of *fatwa*. Bigger seminaries such as Deoband and Nadwa have regular departments to issue such *fatwas*. The latter in fact defines

the *shari'a* for the masses. The *shari'a* that is sought to be enforced upon the masses is more concerned with petty issues of
common dress, language and a few innocent customs, such as
singing of songs or distribution of sweets on joyful occasions.
We, however, wonder as to where this *shari'a*-based identity
was hidden until now as many of the Hindus and Muslims in
the past were practically indistinguishable from one another, even
though the 'reformist' movements were started long back. Obviously, this 'Muslim identity' has been deliberately created by the
ulama belonging to various reformist, revivalist organizations.[51]
   The fact is that the emphasis is more on asserting the external
identity of Muslims which keeps them apart as a unified community separate from the rest of the populace. Naturally external details more than inner faith are seen as conducive in
establishing and proclaiming that separate identity. It is so because faith never separates, nor does it ever create friction, while
over emphasis on the separate identity of Muslims in apparently
external matters is likely to create division among neighbours.

My parents'-in-law's house in Lucknow was in a lower middle
class colony, and a large number of relatively poorer Muslim
families lived near our house. They respected my parents-in-
law no end, and the latter were equally affectionate towards
them. On the occasion of my brother-in-law's marriage, as
is the custom in both communities, all the neighbouring
Muslim ladies, along with the Hindu ones, sang songs to the
accompaniment of the *dholak*, at the end of which we distributed sweets. It was really a joyous occasion in which I was
struck by the fact that not only were the songs common to
both communities, there was no feeling of discrimination between the neighbours.

   No one is questioning the separate religious identity of Muslims, but secularists, including me, have been arguing all through
that religion alone must not determine the 'entire identity' of a
large section of the populace which has been historically diversified on the one hand, and generally integrated with its neighbours
on the other. Over-emphasis on the separate identity of Muslims, rejecting all the regional, linguistic and other differences

amongst them, is bound to adversely affect the integration of Muslims—at least of those who come under the influence of such propaganda—with the wider society. How is it that the Muslim ideologues insist on a separate and implied monolithic identity of Muslims but on the other, are busy themselves in countering and even abusing other sects of Islam?

Finally the goal of *da'wa* has been recognized by our Constitution. But too much direct or indirect emphasis on the same would affect the young minds of madrasa students. When they come out in the wider society and assert that their religion is the highest and final and that others would be better off if they converted to their religion, it is bound to create conflict in a multi-religious society like India. Mostly Muslims do believe and act towards others in an attitude of sincere religious tolerance. In fact, there are grounds to assert that Muslims are more tolerant of other religious faiths than vice versa.[52]

Certain liberal *maulanas*, like Maulana Wahiduddin contend that in the present context *da'wa* does not mean trying to convert others but only calling upon one's co-religionists to follow the pure form of Islam.[53] However, the duty and right to convert others has been an integral part of the belief system of Semitic religions. Our Constitution too gives this right to minorities. My only concern is that proselytizing or *da'wa* involves, first, the claim that their religion alone is the only true religion; and second, that the religion followed by others is false and even evil (*kufr*). Such an approach creates conflict in a multi-religious society.

Mushir-Ul-Haq has given a very clear account of how Muslims are so absolutely convinced of the ultimate and final nature of their religion that though they can tolerate others with goodwill, they cannot give them 'equal respect'—the popular Indian conception of a secular approach—as that would amount to a lack of absolute commitment to their own religion.[54] We admit that sincere religious commitment or faith, call it *ihsan*, requires a firm belief in the 'truth' of one's religion, and it would be difficult for a person committed to his/her religion to affirm that all religions are equally true, and as such deserve equal respect. But we are not sure whether this faith in one's religion also requires the equally firm belief in the 'falsehood' of other religions, without which belief perhaps the 'duty' of converting others would not follow.

We agree with Mahatma Gandhi who believed that one can accept the truths or insights of other religions as well as give them equal respect without giving up commitment to one's own faith.[55] At the same time, two things must be remembered here.

First, in spite of the insistence on the duty of *da'wa* by *ulama* and the *tabalighi* ideology, they hardly have been aggressively assertive about their desire to convert others. Second, getting converted to the faith of one's choice is a constitutional right which we are not contesting. Our only submission is that desire and efforts to convert others to one's faith in a multi-religious society creates avoidable problems.

Moreover, the unconditional conviction of the final and absolute truth of one's religion creates an arrogant attitude among the *ulama* with whom it is very difficult to enter into any kind of dialogue. Even though such a conviction is required for profound faith, do we have men and women around us who are really so intensely and profoundly absorbed in their faith or *din*? Such a faith characterized the Sufi saints (and Hindu *bhakta* or devotee saints) of the medieval period. However, they did not find any conflict among themselves.[56] Unfortunately present-day Islam has rejected Sufism. The conflict between *shari'a* and Sufi *tariqa* was present even then. But while the Sufis took care not to undermine *shari'a* their emphasis on inner faith must have resulted in a softening of the externalism of *shari'a* and introduction of greater emphasis on inner faith. Even if the contemporary *ulama* are not ready to give Sufi saints their due, they should give heed to Rabi'a bin Ismail al 'Adwaiya, who flourished in the early second century Hizri. She rejected most male-determined customs (*shari'a*) and was revered by the great Muslim scholars of that time for her intense piety.[57]

The approaches both to Islamic education and to outside society that are encouraged in madrasas do not seem very promising for a modern plural society. They train their students' minds not only to blindly follow the teachings of their religion but also the customs and practices of the then society (from seventh to tenth century) of the Arab world and nurture an attitude that regards them (medieval society's customs) as the panacea for all problems. They know nothing about the world around them. Neither are they capable of entering into a dialogue with any one from the wider society, nor are they capable of successfully confronting the present complex society. It follows that even though they are regarded as the guides of the Muslim masses, they are far less capable of guiding their fellow religionists in a way so that they need not remain 'backward' and alienated from the rest of society.

NOTES

1. Manzoor Ahmad, *Islamic Education: Redefinition of Aims and Methodology*, New Delhi: Qazi Publishers and Distributors, 1990, p. 32; also see ibid., pp. 4 and following. Cf. Muhamadullah Khalili Qasmi, *Madrasa Education: Its Strength and Weakness*, Mumbai: Markazul Ma'arif Education and Research Centre, 2005, pp. 41 ff., 94 ff., 101 ff., Qamr Uddin, *Hindustan ki Dini Darsgahein: Kul Hind Survey*, New Delhi: Hamdard Education Society, 1996, p. 302.

2. Mufti Taqi Usmani, quoted in Qasmi, op. cit., pp. 151–2.

3. Ibid., pp. 101–2.

4. Ibid., pp. 147 ff. Cf. 'Darul Uloom at Deoband introduced computer application in 1994. Apart from computer, other technical courses have also been given due place in the curriculum of the seminary [. . . It teaches] modern disciplines like Modern Indian History, Islamic History, Civics, Geography, General sciences including some information in Zoology, Botany, principles of health care, some chapters of Indian Constitution, principles of economics, philosophical theories, life history of modern philosophers and computer application.' Amir Ullah Khan, Muhammad Sadiq and Zafar H. Anjum, 'To kill the Mockingbird: Madrasah System in India: Past, Present, and Future', at website http//www.chowk.com/article/6216. 5 August, 2003.

5. See Farhat Hasan, '*Madaris* and the Challenge of Modernity in Colonial India', in Jan-Peter Hartung and Helmut Reifield (eds.), *Islamic Education, Diversity, and National Identity: Dini Madaris in India Post 9/11*, New Delhi: Sage, 2006, pp. 58 ff.

6. See *Nisab-e-Talim: Darjat-e-Arabia wa Urdu, Diniyat wa Farsi-Nisab*, Deoband: Darul Uloom, Deoband (Urdu); and *Nisab-e-Talim, Darul Uloom Nadwatul Ulama* (Urdu), Lucknow: Nadwatul Ulama.

7. See the article on *Sunnah* in *The Encyclopedia of Religion*, ed. Mircea Eliade, New York: Macmillan, vol. 14, pp. 149 ff.

8. See Mahmud Shaltout, 'Islamic Beliefs and Code of Laws', in Kenneth W. Morgan (ed.), *Islam the Straight Path*, Delhi: Motilal Banarsidass, 1987, pp. 135, and 134 ff.

9. *The Encyclopaedia of Islam, New Edition*, ed. C.E. Basworth, E. van Donzel, B. Lewis and Ch. Pellat, Leiden: E.J. Brill, 1978, vol. IV, p. 151.

10. The above account is based on the article by Wilfred Madelung, 'Shiism: An Overview', in the *Encyclopedia of Religion*, vol. 13, pp. 242 ff; and Syed Nazmul Raza Rizvi, 'Shi'a Madaris of Avadh: Historical Development and Present Situation', in *Islamic Education, Diversity, and National Identity: Dini Madaris in India Post 9/11*, pp. 104 ff.

11. See Rizvi, op. cit., p. 106; and *The Encyclopedia of Religion*, vol. 13, pp. 242 ff.

12. See M. Mujeeb, *The Indian Muslims*, Delhi: Munshiram Manoharlal, 1995, pp. 277–82; Dilip Hiro, *Islamic Fundamentalism*, Great Britain: Paladin, 1989, pp. 39, 41, 271.

13. See Deoband English website http/www/darululoom_deoband. com/English/aboutdarululoom/edumovement.htm

14. See Shoyeb Ansari, *Education in Dini Madaris: An Opinion Survey of Curriculum Method of Teaching and Evaluation in Dini Madaris*, New Delhi: Institute of Objective Studies, 1997, pp. 53, 97.

15. This view was expressed by Maulana Wahiduddin Khan in a personal recorded interview. Actually the Tablighi Jamaat activists mostly approach the already converted Muslims, and do not much try to convert others afresh. However, the latter remains the ideal goal of various Islamic sects.

16. See the Deoband website http/www/Darululoom_deoband.com/ English/aboutdarululoom/preaching_services.htm ; and Arshad Alam, 'Understanding Deoband Locally: Interrogating Madrasat diya-al-Uloom', in *Islamic Education, Diversity, and National Identity*, pp. 175 ff.

17. The following account is entirely based on *Nisab-e-Talim* of Deoband, directly procured from the Darul Uloom, Deoband. The Urdu-Arabic specialist teacher Ahmad Farid helped me to understand it.

18. See Mohd. Arshad, 'Tradition of Madrasa Education', in Akhtarul Wasey (ed.), *Madrasas in India: Trying to be Relevant*, New Delhi: Global Media Publications, 2005, pp. 26 ff.; Jan-Peter Hartung,

'The Nadwat al-'Ulama': Chief Patron of Madrasa Education in India and Turntable to the Arab World', in *Islamic Education, Diversity, and National Identity*, pp. 195 ff.

19. *Nisab-e-Talim*. (*Primary, Secondary, Preparatory and Special classes*) (Urdu), Darul Uloom Nadwatul Ulama procured from the Darul Uloom.

20. See Deoband website 'Darul-Uloom in the Fight for Freedom'.

21. Some Muslims belonging to the *ashraf* (elite) class who claim to be the descendants of Muslims of 'foreign' origin, as Afghans, or those of Middle-East countries, and having an educated, economically secure lifestyle, often try to distance themselves from the common folk, even indicating that the latter are lower, uncultured and having degenerate (i.e. Hindu) customs and habits. We have encountered them personally.

22. See a wonderful comparative study by Peter B. Mayer, 'Tombs and Dark Houses: Ideology, Intellectuals and Proletarians in the Study of Contemporary Islam', in Imtiaz Ahmad (ed.), *Modernization and Social Change Among Muslims in India*, New Delhi: Manohar, 1983, pp. 1 ff., especially 17 ff. and 29 ff.

23. Jawaharlal Nehru, Bipan Chandra, S. Abid Husain, Mushirul Hasan and many more secularists emphatically believe in our composite culture; so does the author.

24. See the articles of Usha Sanyal, 'Ahl-e-Sunnat Madrasas: The Manzare-Islam, Bareilly, and Jamia Ashraffiyya, Mubarakpur', and Arshad Alam, 'Making Maslaks: Constructing Identity in a Barelwi Madrasa', in the unpublished collection of papers presented at the International Worship: Islamic Learning in South Asia, held at Erfurt, Germany, May 2005. (Some articles presented at the Conference were later published in the volume *Madrasas in South Asia: Teaching Terror?*, ed. Jamal Malik, Contemporary South Asia Series, New York: Routledge 2008. But the volume leaves out several papers and adds new ones. Therefore I prefer the original collection of papers).

25. From a recorded personal interview with the Nazim of Ahle-Sunnat Madrasa, Jamia Hazarat Nizamuddin Aulia, Zakir Nagar Estate, Old Delhi.

26. See the article by Usha Sanyal, op. cit.

27. The following account is based on an extensive interview with the Nazim of the Junior Section of Ahle-Hadees madrasa—Jamia Islamia, Sanabil, Okhla. This madrasa is run by a big organization, called Islamic Awakening Centre near Jamia Nagar. It teaches up to *Fazil* level. It also has a Primary section which, as

usual, is run independently and is also not given much importance. It also runs two girls' schools—the first is a madrasa proper
to which entry of outsiders is almost prohibited; second is a regular school in which all subjects are taught. We visited only its
junior section up to Arabi *Som* (class 3). They gave us their
detailed syllabus, 'Curriculum for 'Alia and. U'lya classes' in
Arabic (which I got translated by my Arabi scholar teacher).

28 See Ahle-Hadees official website http//www.ahlehadees.org.;
and Wikipedia, the free Encyclopedia, at en.wikipedia.org/wiki/
Ahle_ Hadith. Also see the brief account of Ahl-e-Hadith in *The
Encyclopedia of Islam*, ed. H.A.R. Gibb et al., New Edition,
London, Leiden: E.J. Brill, 1960, vol. 1, pp. 259–60.

29. See the detailed article on Salafiyya in *The Encyclopaedia of
Islam*, ed. C.E. Bosworth et al., New Edition, Leiden: E.J. Brill,
1995, vol. VIII, pp. 900 ff.

30. Based on the *Nisab* of the entire Ahle-Hadees madrasa, subdivided into several separate madrasas under one umbrella organization. See note 27 supra.

31. Even one of the most apologetic writers on Islam, Yoginder Sikand,
while putting all blame for the orthodox Muslim goal of proselytizing on the temporary Shuddhi movement by Arya Samaj in
1920s, quotes extensively from various *ulama* of Tablighi Jamaat,
how their final aim is the conversion of not only all Hindus but
also the entire world to Islam. See 'Arya Shuddhi and Muslim
Tabligh: Muslim Reaction to Arya Proselytisation (1923–30)',
at ysikand@islaminterfaith.org., April 2004. (It seems to have
been published later in an anthology, *Religious Conversion in
Islam: Motivation and Meaning*, ed. Rubena Robinson and
Sathia-nathan Clark, New Delhi: Oxford University Press, 2003.)

32. See Shoyeb Ansari, *Education in Dini Madaris: An Opinion
Survey*, pp. 53–5.

33. 'It also follows that if Muhammad is the seal of the Apostles, the
Quran is the final scripture. The Quran [. . .] states the basic
beliefs and basic principles of worship and of human dealings,
and the ideal of morality.' Mahmud Shaltout, 'Islamic Beliefs
and Code of Laws', in Kenneth W. Morgan, *Islam the Straight
Path*, Delhi: Motilal Banarsidass, 1982, p. 107.

34. 'Muslims inhabiting this land [. . .] should consider their duty to
the country to present through words and deeds those principles
and values which being universally true and beneficial they consider
as imperative for the building of a healthy and righteous society.
These principles and values [. . .] have been the common heri-

tage of all mankind. They are really good [. . . nothing] should
be allowed to stand in the way of their adoption.[. . .]
Islam as a social order has greater claim to unprejudiced consideration.'
'Ideology of Jamaat-e-Islami-Hind', at their website: jamaate-islamihind.org/newwebsite/index. Also see 'Overview of Programme' on the the same site.

35. Some of the above has been taken from an unpublished paper by Irfan Ahmad of University of Amsterdam presented at the Erfurt Workshop on Islamic Learning, cited earlier. He has strictly written at the top of each page 'Not for citation. Work in Progress.'

36. Syllabus of Jamiat-al-Falah, *Nisab-i-Talim Jamiat ul-Falah*: Balariaganj: Jamiat ul-Falah, 2001.

37 I acknowledge that the concept of 'mainstream' is problematic. It has become even more so after the aggressive campaign by the supporters of Hindutva who aim to establish what they term as Hindu *Rashtra* in which Rama and Shivaji would be the only heroes, and so on. In such circumstances the talk of 'mainstream' is likely to be misunderstood. However, I do not agree with those secularist academics who assert that India is constituted of several 'nationalities' or independent cultures. Life and society are very complex affairs indeed, and they consist of a large number of strands or dimensions. For a person or group, whether based on religion, language, economic or political formation, one aspect of her/its life may be more important, but there are always other aspects of her/its life which integrate her it with the wider society. There is a real need to stress those aspects of society and national culture which we share with other such groups. See author, *Secularism in India: A Reappraisal*, New Delhi: Har Anand, 1995, pp. 229 ff., 247 ff.

38. The above fully depends on the article of Syed Nazmul Raza Rizvi, 'Shi'a Madaris of Awadh: Historical Development and Present Situation', in *Islamic Education, Diversity, and National Identity*, pp. 104 ff. The syllabus of Shi'a madrasas is also borrowed from the Appendix to the article of Rizvi, ibid., pp. 121 ff.

39. *Existing Curriculum in Madrasas: A Study* by Anita Julka, Neerja Shukla, Md. T.A. Rahi, New Delhi: NCERT, is a glaring example of such confusion. First, the title suggests as if the writers are telling us of the general curriculum of madrasas. Not even in the Preface is it acknowledged that they are talking of 'modernized' madrasas. Later on the syllabuses of a few State Boards are given, without recognizing that even they cannot be

put under one umbrella title of 'Existing Curriculum of Madrasas'. Other apologetic writers have given their own and even more misleading versions of the comprehensive, secular syllabuses of madrasas. See Khalili Qasmi, op. cit., pp. 101–2.

40. See *Nisab-e-Taleem (bra-e-darajat-e-'aliya) Imtihanat: Arabi wa Farsi, Uttar Pradesh Board*, Ghulam Yahya Anjum, New Delhi: Jamia Hamdard, 2000 (Urdu).

41. Ibid., pp. 35 ff., 44 ff.

42. *State Madrasa Education Board: Reorganized Senior and Title Madrasa Curriculum, Courses & Syllabi, 1992*, Guwahati: State Madrasa Education Board, Department of Education, Government of Assam. Recently some changes have been made in the madrasa curriculum to further integrate the two courses.

43. *Syllabus of Madhya Pradesh Madrasa Board*, a Government of Madhya Pradesh publication, signed by the Chairman of MP Madrasa Board, Prof. Muhammad Haleem Khan.

44. Timetable procured directly from some 'modernized' madrasas of Madhya Pradesh.

45. See Arshad Alam, 'Making Maslaks: Constructing Identity in a Barelvi Madrasa', in *The Proceedings of International Workshop*.

46. 'Mission to save Islam'@http//www.geocities.com/nur_ul_islam.

47. M. Mujeeb, *The Indian Muslims*, p. 79.

48. Ibid., pp. 238–9.

49. We shall have occasion to discuss not only the Islamic *shari'a* and *fiqh* but also different conceptions of the same through the centuries in chapter 5.

50. See Mushir-Ul-Haq, *Islam in Secular India*, Simla: Institute of Advanced Study, 1972, pp. 3 ff., 15 ff., 19 ff.

51. As I have briefly pointed out earlier, Indian secularists, such as Jawaharlal Nehru, S. Abid Hussain, Bipan Chandra, Mushirul Hasan, Imtiaz Ahmad and others, including the present author, have found enough ground-level evidence for their thesis that the two major religious communities of Hindus and Muslims share a lot in their culture, customs, values, family structure, art, especially music, language and even sometimes religion. Just to quote one sentence from Bipan Chandra: 'It is necessary in this respect to distinguish between religion as an ideology or a belief system and the ideology of religious identity which is communalism.' *Communalism in Modern India*, New Delhi: Vikas, 1989, p. 159.

52. See Peter B. Mayer, 'Tombs and Dark Houses: Ideology, Intel-

lectuals and Proletarians in the Study of Contemporary Islam', in Imtiaz Ahmad (ed.), *Modernization and Social Change among Muslims in India*, New Delhi: Manohar, 1983, pp. 1 ff. Mayer argues that the differences between the two major groups and their emotional responses are determined by the regional circumstances and politics. See also several articles by Qamar Hasan, Talmeez Fatima, N. Husnain and Muhammad Ghufran, in N. Husnain (ed.), *Social, Psychological Dimensions of Muslims*, New Delhi: Institute of Objective Studies, 1998, pp. 1 ff., 61 ff., 91 ff., etc. All of them argue that not only the Muslim youth are not more alienated from their society than their Hindu counterparts, the emotional responses of both communities are very similar in similar circumstances.

53. Based on my personal, recorded talks with Maulana Wahiduddin Khan.
54. See *Islam in Secular India*, pp. 16 ff.
55. M.V. Desai, ed., *Gandhi Reader for 1988*, New Delhi: Namedia Foundation, pp. 2, 18, 31, 35. Mahatma, like many other Indian thinkers and saints, believed that there can well be several paths to the Goal (God), and therefore there is no reason for mutual conflict.
56. See the monumental work of S.A.A. Rizvi, *A History of Sufism in India* (2 vols.), New Delhi: Munshiram Manoharlal, especially vol. 1, chapter 1 on Early Sufism and chapter 2 on The Chishtis, also vol. 2, chapters 2, 5 and 8.
57. See ibid., vol. 1, pp. 30 ff.

5

Islam, Shari'a, *Women and Their Education*

1. ISLAM AS A RELIGION AND A WAY OF LIFE

The nature of Islam and the place of *shari'a* in it should have been the first topic to discuss in our effort to critically review madrasa education. But the way the study developed, we could not take up the central concepts which we are attempting now.

Most of us who try to understand Islam often start with the Western conception of 'religion' as concerning man's relationship with God based on some 'Divine revelation', and consisting of a definite creed and certain rituals. On this basis, Islam can truly be said to be a religion (in contrast to most religions of Indian origin which would not fit this definition easily). However Islam is much more than a religion, it is an entire way of life. Ideally the way of life of Muslims is thoroughly determined by the Quran and the *shari'a*, which together constitute both the Islamic way of life and Islam itself. That is to say, Islam is not merely a religion (*din*) concerned with man's relations with God but something which is equally concerned with his/her relations with fellow human beings, especially fellow Muslims, and governs all aspects of his/her life, both interpersonal and personal.

1.1. THE MEANING OF ISLAM

Different meanings are assigned to the word 'Islam'—'to become integrated'; 'to be at peace with oneself'; and 'to submit to God'.[1] According to the *Encyclopaedia of Islam*, while the word 'Muslim' (one who submits to God) occurs frequently in the Quran, the word 'Islam' occurs only eight times. The Encyclopaedia goes on to explain that the word 'Islam' means both 'surrender to God' (an inner action) and 'profession of Islam', or adherence to the message of the Prophet.[2] Ameer Ali, an Islamic scholar of the early twentieth century, explains:

Salam in its primary sense means to be tranquil, at rest, to have done one's duty, to be at perfect peace, [. . . and] in its secondary sense, to surrender oneself to Him with whom peace is made [. . .]. The word (Islam) does not imply, as is commonly supposed, absolute submission to God's will, but means on the contrary, *striving after righteousness.*[3]

The two meanings of the word 'Islam'—'being at peace with oneself' and 'surrender to God' seem to be quite different. Though affirmation of the twin beliefs in the absolute oneness of God and Muhammad being His Messenger (*Nabi*), that is *Kalama*, is integral to Islam, Islam as a religion seems to give greater importance to human will and practice. What is more, actions are to be understood in the social context. Sometimes, scholars make a distinction between Islam and *ima'n*. The two terms are integrally related; but while Islam is a 'religion' practised in a 'religious community', owing its allegiance to the Prophet, *ima'n* means adherence to or inner dimension of faith.[4] According to the *hadith* of al Bukhari, the Prophet explained the term Islam as, 'Islam is to adore God without associating anything with Him, to observe the ritual prayer (*sala't*), to pay *zakat*, to fast during the month of Ramadan.' It is also to feed the hungry and to give the greeting of peace to one and all.[5] This seems the best and most comprehensive definition of Islam.

The emphasis everywhere is on the communal sharing of the faith. That is why theology is less important in Islam than *shari'a* and *fiqh* (both connoting law regulating human beings' interpersonal behaviour). The *Encyclopaedia of Islam* elaborates:

Any one who describes himself as a Muslim means to affirm thereby not so much his care for the practice and personal observances (although certainly not neglecting these matters) as for adherence to a community of those who acknowledge the *Kur'an* and Muhammad.[6]

Overtime, admission to the community became the most preferred aspect, and that admission depended upon one's (outward) adherence to the commands of the texts. Islam prescribes that the prayer (*namaz*) must also be accompanied by a determined set of (unchangeable) rituals. And these rituals and prayers must be performed, except under exceptional circumstances, in the company of fellow Muslims. Islam is a strongly world- and life-affirming religion (to borrow the famous phrase of Albert Schweitzer). And that means that in Islam religion is less a matter of profound religious piety (*ima'n*), which also is acknowledged to be necessary, but more a matter of living a righteous life among one's co-religionists. The Quran repeatedly asks believers to be compassionate to the needy, and *zakat* (compulsory donation of a certain determined portion of one's income) is one of the five famous pillars of Islam.[7] It means that Islam is as much a religion which defines human beings' relationship to God, as also one that emphasizes their mutual relationship. Also, even though the rituals compulsory for the recitation of *namaz* have not been prescribed in the Quran, they have become more important to the Muslims. Of course, from the very beginning it was stressed that the compulsory rituals associated with *namaz* have to be performed along with one's co-religionists, thus underlying the communitarian nature of religion.

1.2. THE TWO SOURCES OF ISLAM:
THE QURAN AND *SUNNA*

While inner faith cannot be regulated or determined by textual commands, external conduct can be controlled by them. Hence almost from the beginning Islam gives greater importance to external conduct being in consonance with the commands of the Holy Quran, Prophet's *sunna* and *shari'a*.

The Quran, of course, is the most important source or foundation of Islam. It is unanimously accepted as 'Divine Revelation' which is divine, true and authentic verbatim. At the same time, Islam as we have seen, is not a matter of inner faith only, but also a matter of adhering to the commands of religion. Islam claims to be both the perfect and final religion, as also the total guide to human life.

But when early Muslim scholars set about formulating those commands, the do's and don'ts, which could guide Muslims in all places and times through all eventualities of life, they found that such comprehensive guidelines were not available in the holy Text. The Quranic injunctions actually are mostly in the form of normative guidelines and do not provide details. For example, *sala't* or *namaz* is the second most important pillar of Islam, first being the assertion of faith. But the Quran does not give any details regarding how to perform the *sala't*. As we have seen, outward rituals gradually became more important in Islam, as they could be transmitted to different people, or insisted upon more easily than inner faith. With the expansion of the Muslim empire new situations were arising for which the early Muslims did not find any clear answer in the holy Quran.

Since Islam is supposed to govern and regulate the entire life of Muslims, the Quran alone was often found to be insufficient. Hence from the early times, it was supplemented by the Prophet's *sunna*. Whenever any social or legal (there were hardly any reference to moral dilemmas) problem arose, the *ulama* came up with a *hadith* describing how the Prophet Muhammad behaved or refrained from doing any thing in a similar situation, and that *hadith* had to be followed unquestioningly.

Thus, in addition to the Quran, *sunna* became the second most important source of Islam, or the second authority to regulate the conduct of Muslims. The word *sunna* means 'a well-trodden path' or customary norms of conduct. In Islam it took the meaning of cannons or norms for conduct derived from the exemplary, imitative, normative words, deeds and silent approvals or disapprovals of the Prophet himself, and in a secondary sense from the teaching of his immediate followers, known as Companions. The *sunna* was, in turn, based on *hadiths* or reports of Prophet Muhammad's sayings and acts, as recorded, not by his Companions but by their followers of the next generation or even the third and fourth generation. As recorded in the *hadiths* the *Sunna al Nabi* (the traditions or norms of the Prophet) superseded all previous *sunnas* (customary laws and practices). Prophet Muhammad was thus accorded the twin distinctions of being the vehicle of final 'revelation' of Allah, and also the supreme exemplar of the final laws of conduct (*sunna*).[8]

The Prophet Muhammad's position in Islam is both very important and unique. He is generally declared a human being like all of us who was chosen by Allah to be the receptacle of His 'revelation'. This equation of the Prophet to ordinary human beings has been challenged by certain theologians and sects such as Ibn al Arabi and the present Ahle-Sunnat sect of Islam. However, according to every sect of Islam, every word of God's 'revelation' to the Prophet, as recorded in the Holy Quran, is true, even if the latter was compiled after his death.

As Islam expanded its frontiers, Muslims met or were confronted with new people who had their own customary set of norms and a different culture. Also kings and empires changed, and the new kings and dynasties had different priorities and cultural values. Even though they had accepted Islam, their culture and way of life were not yet determined by Islam. The differences between the cultures and priorities of two early Muslim empires—the Umayyads and the Abbasids—are a case in point. If objectively viewed, not only the kings, princes and their courtiers but all the rich men of the society lived by standards that were entirely un-Islamic.[9] Yet as Muslims they were expected to abide by Islamic laws.

As Muslims settled down in new lands, new cases and eventualities arose for their rulers and judges (*qazis*) for which they had no precedence either in the Quran or the existing *hadiths*. Therefore new *hadiths* came up which were at once supposed to provide solutions to the unfamiliar problems and issues, and also claimed to be authoritative, being derived from sources that could be traced back to the Prophet himself. These 'reports' of his deeds, sayings, and often silent approvals or disapprovals are taken to be the compulsory model on which all Muslims are expected to mould their conduct.

Thus, the corpus of *hadiths* grew in size and number to thousands. The earlier followers of Prophet Muhammad took their responsibility seriously and preserved the *Sunnat al Nabi* by first listening to it from the Companions of the Prophet, memorizing it and later on writing it down. The later *hadiths* were not the reports of the Companions. The only requirement for being accepted as authenticated was that the writer heard it from someone who, in turn, heard it from some person who, in his turn, heard it from still another person till the line could be traced either to Prophet Muhammad himself, or to his Companions.

These *hadiths* (pl. *ahadis*) were at first oral traditions and later came to be written down. The persons who finally narrated or recorded these *hadiths* were often removed from the time of Prophet Muhammad and his Companions by as much as two centuries. A greater part of the *hadith* collections we possess today were written down in the beginning of the Abbasid period. When *hadiths* continued to proliferate, scholars started questioning their veracity, as they often gave contradictory judgements on the same issues or supported different views on controversial matters. Scholars had to decide which *hadiths* were to be taken as authentic reports and which had been invented for various political and sometimes theological purposes. In the eighth century the great scholar, al Shafai'i sought to develop rules which could help sort out authentic *hadiths* from the spurious ones. For this purpose various techniques were employed, and a whole science called 'Principles of Hadith' (*Usool-e-Hadith*) was developed laying down the meticulous criteria for judging the reliability of a *hadith*, particularly that of the transmitters of them. Meticulous care was taken to judge both the character of the narrator and the correctness of the chain of transmitters leading to the last narrator. The list of persons through whom a particular *hadith* was transmitted was called an *isnad*. The text was known as *matn*.[10]

These *hadiths* are essential supplements to the Holy Quran, clarifying its various issues or commands. They are the most important sources of *sunna*, the basis of the *shari'a*, variously translated as the Muslim way of life, or the Islamic law. Muslims are expected to learn the way of life of the Prophet Muhammad and his Companions, and to imitate them in their lives unquestioningly. The Islamic *fiqh* or jurisprudence is also expected to be based on the *sunna* of the Prophet. Even the authors of the *tafsirs* or commentaries on the Quran were expected to possess the knowledge of *sunna*. Believers argue that many Quranic instructions are vague and impossible to follow without the guidance of the *sunna*, as recorded in the *hadiths*.

Shafai'i also developed the four sources of the Islamic law— the Quran, *sunna*, *qiyas* (analogical reasoning based on the first two sources), and *ijma* (consensus of the *umma*, or the learned), their authority being in a strict hierarchical order.[11]

The *sunna*, as recorded in these *hadiths*, came to cover every aspect of a Muslim's life, including food, eating, manners, clothing and jewellery (especially for women), hygiene, social behaviour, forms of greeting, as well as religious, political and economic matters.[12] All through the emphasis was on practice and the need to blindly imitate the practices of the Prophet and his Companions (*taqlid*). That is the way of the orthodox, and it was required in order to keep the varying peoples and cultures together after the unprecedented expansion of Islam. M. Mujeeb gives a comprehensive definition of the orthodoxy 'as the principle and system of maintaining uniformity in belief and practice by determining what is true or desirable, by discouraging deviation, and applying appropriate social and legal sanctions to enforce conformity'.[13]

The uniformity was gradually achieved by insisting on *taqlid* and refusal for any rational argument or attempt to reinterpret the first two sources of Islamic law. A famous *hadith* describes Muhammad as encouraging one's rational judgement, of course, in accordance with the Islamic texts.[14] Till about the tenth or eleventh century, the use of reason was quite common in everyday affairs and even in theological matters. That is how two very different schools of theology developed—those of the Mu'tazilites and the A'sharites. But the *ulama* soon came to see rational thinking as dangerous and so all further reasoning in any matter, whether theological or practical, was declared illegitimate, by announcing that the gates of *ijtihad* or rational thinking were closed henceforward.[15]

2. THE TWO CONCEPTS OF *SHARI'A*

2.1. THE MEANING OF *SHARI'A*

A very important question remains as to the exact meaning and status of *shari'a*. While some scholars translate the word *shari'a* as Islamic law, others understand it as meaning the 'Islamic way of life'. We have to understand not only the meaning of the term but also its place in Islam, or rather in the lives of Muslims. M. Mujeeb defines *shari'a* as 'The Islamic way of life, comprehending beliefs, ritual practices, public and personal law, and being stretched even to include dress, personal appearance and rules of behaviour in social intercourse.'[16]

The term *shari‘a* is used only once in the Quran, suggesting the Divine command—'We have set you on a *shari‘a* or command, so follow it.' (XLV.18) At another place the word *shar‘a* is used to denote way or path—'To each we have appointed a *shar‘a* and a *minhadi*.' (V.48) The *hadiths* also don't use the word *shari‘a* commonly. It occurs once in Ibn Hanbal—'The community shall remain on the *shari‘a* provided. . . . ' Even the great scholar who finalized the *hadiths*—al Shafai'i—hardly uses the words *shari‘a* or *shar‘*. According to Western scholars, even in Muslim literature the term has a general connotation and does not signify jurists' law or *fiqh*.[17] However, gradually the term *shari‘a* began to be used as denoting the Divine command.

And yet, with the exception of *Kalama* or assertion of faith in the fundamental creed of Islam which is unanimously accepted and followed, it is *shari‘a* which has been most influential in the lives of Muslim masses. *Namaz* is accepted as important, but very few Muslims, busy in earning their daily bread, can afford to attend *namaz* five times a day. The same is true for *haj*; those who can afford, go several times, others do not. *Zakat* also is not strictly adhered to. *Roza* is very well respected, but is mainly followed by the middle class. The poor cannot work hard on an empty stomach and keep a few *rozas* only. The English educated upper middle class mostly do not follow these commands regularly.

However, *shari‘a* is one thing which seems to regulate a majority of Muslims' life in all its aspects, not so much the lives of upper-class Muslims, but definitely of those residing either in villages or in city ghettos. Till the late nineteenth and mid-twentieth centuries, a large number of Muslims shared their neighbourhood culture and often followed customary laws. Then, as we have seen in the chapter on the History of Madrasa Education, the *ulama* started paying attention to them and ever since have spent most of their energies in 'reforming' the ways of Muslim masses. Since no one can dictate inner faith, the main emphasis has been on outward dress, conduct and customs. As we have seen earlier, there are regular organizations, such as the Tablighi Jamaat, which devote all their energies in weaning the Muslims from local culture and milieu. Their goal is 'the reawakening of faith and reaffirmation of religio-cultural identity of South Asian Muslims'.[18]

In Muslim-dominated city localities (*mohallas*) madrasa-educated youth work constantly to 'reform' the ways and customs of the masses.[19] They insist that the people do not celebrate the occasions of birth of a child or marriage with songs or distribution of sweets. The net result is that Islamic *shari'a* becomes the most important, perhaps the only thing important, in the lives of Muslims who come under the influence of these 'reformers'.

The 'reformers' ask the people to follow their diktats saying it is the word of the *shari'a*. This *shari'a* is not written down anywhere and is said to be based on the *hadiths*. But the *hadiths* themselves comprise a huge corpus, and to believe that anyone who is declaring a certain course of conduct as right and another as wrong and punishable has read and understood all these *hadiths* written in archaic Arabic language is a little difficult.

Generally the local or caste panchayat with the help of the local *maulavis* decides which conduct is according to the *shari'a* and which is not. It is the elders, and naturally the more conservative persons of the caste group, who decide what is the law relevant to that given case. Once someone is declared guilty, it is they who decide the punishment, which may be monetary, or the order to ostracize that person or family, or some more fundamental life devastating decision.[20] Hence the need of understanding the exact meaning and extension of *shari'a*.

2.2. THE ORTHODOX VERSION OF *SHARI'A*

The orthodox define the term *shari'a* as Islamic law. Law is something definite, written down and tangible, but *shari'a* does not seem to be so. Also, unlike law, *shari'a* can be interpreted in different ways by different persons, according to their personal biases and social conditioning. Though socially and morally powerful, it is not enforceable by law.

The orthodox version of *shari'a* has four elements: first, *shari'a* means Islamic law; second, it is derived from and based on the Holy Quran and the Prophet's *sunna* as recorded in the *hadiths*; third, *shari'a* is 'divine'; and fourth, therefore it is universally applicable and binding for all humankind, above all for Muslims.

This is the old doctrine of *taqlid* (blind following of the written word), except here there does not seem to be any written word. In order to understand Islam as it is practised globally in the present-day world we must know both the exact connotation of the term *shari'a,* and why it is absolutely binding. If it is 'divine', how can it be so? As far as we have understood, *shari'a* is that unwritten system of law which is considered inviolable because it is based on the Holy Quran as well as the *sunna* of the Prophet, the latter being accepted as a necessary supplement of the 'Divine revelation' in the Quran. Accepting that, the question arises whether being based on 'Divine revelation' can be the same as being 'divine'. Moreover, *shari'a* is not only based on the Holy Quran but also on the *sunna* or *hadiths.* Are these also to be considered 'divine' then? This question we would have to take up in our next section.

I sincerely wanted to understand the connotation and place of *shari'a* in Islam. There is a regular Institution devoted to *Shari'a* in Delhi. But I did not have the courage to put my apparently heretic queries before the orthodox *ulama.* So I chose the two most liberal *maulanas* in Delhi—Maulana Wahiduddin Khan and Dr. Mufti M. Mukarram Ahmad, Shahi Imam of the Fatehpuri Masjid in old Delhi.[21]

Maulana Wahiduddin Khan is a kind person, well respected for his emphasis on and efforts for communal harmony and avocation of religious toleration. He is also strongly in favour of modern education for Muslim children. However, when asked the meaning and 'divinity' of *shari'a,* and whether it had to be followed in all circumstances, his answer was that *shari'a* is Islamic law based on the Holy Quran and *hadiths;* and *shari'a* and *fiqh* (law) are one and the same. *Shari'a* is definitely 'divine' like the Quran, though it is not immutable, and it means that it has to be followed by every Muslim unconditionally. About the Imrana case he simply said that the *maulanas* who gave the judgement were ignorant fools.

Though I could not follow Maulana Wahiduddin's detailed explanation about the 'divinity' of *shari'a,* he insisted that *shari'a* is 'divine' and it must be followed unquestioningly.

The Shahi Imam Mufti Mukarram Ahmad is like an oasis in

the desert of fundamentalist Islam. (The madrasa attached to the mosque embodies such an Islam.) He believes in religious tolerance, modern education for Muslim children and is highly critical of casually established madrasas which he calls 'teaching shops'. But when asked the above questions he too asserted categorically the *shari'a* is 'divine' and must be followed.

2.3. Some Critical Observations

A few questions come to our mind for which we could not find answers in the approach of the two respected maulanas. First, the criminal law aspect of *shari'a* is almost universally abrogated, except in Saudi Arabia. It was replaced by modern Western laws during the British period in India in the 1860s. Rest of the Muslim nations have also obviously realized that the laws of *shari'a* in criminal cases are too cruel and discordant with the spirit of modern times. If *shari'a* were 'divine' and hence applicable for all times, then there should have been no question of the need to abrogate the criminal law aspect of *shari'a*.

Second, how can *shari'a* be declared 'divine', as it is based not just on the 'divine revelation' in the Holy Quran but more on *hadiths* which, since they are the narrations of ordinary people, who depended entirely on the narrations or reports of earlier generations who, in turn, depended on a still previous group of narrators, and therefore which cannot be held as 'divine'.

We will come later to the issue of *hadiths* and their role in explaining the Quran. Here let us reiterate that if liberal Muslim *maulanas* believe *shari'a* to be 'divine', then we would have to accept it as such. We can also take it for granted that not only the *maulanas* mentioned above, but most others would also be believing in the divinity of *shari'a*. If they were ever doubtful about the inviolability of the *shari'a*, they would not be passing thousands of judgements (*fatwas*) everyday on every possible issue.

Third, it is also to be remembered that *shari'a* as such is not written down. On each occasion it has to be derived from someone *hadith* or the other. The understanding and application of *shari'a* on practical issues depends entirely on how profound the knowledge of the interpreter of all the *hadiths* is, his personal biases, as no one can be absolutely objective about values and norms, and his capacity to understand the issue at hand in its entire social context (as in the case of Imrana or Mukhtaran Mai of Pakistan).

Fourth, it is not only the case of an Imrana or Mukhtaran Mai; there are thousands of other similar cases in which unjust pronouncements are being made by the *maulanas*, most of whom discriminate against women in the name of *shari'a*. Now, if all these cases are acknowledged as misinterpretation of *shari'a* by *maulanas* who were ignorant or not knowledgeable, then how can we decide which judgement or interpretation of *shari'a* is correct and which is not?

Sometimes it is said that *fatwas* are the opinions of the concerned *mufti*, and not necessarily binding. But the fact is that once they are pronounced, no Muslim belonging to economically and educationally backward classes, or even belonging to lower middle classes, all of whom live in Muslim majority areas, dares to go against them. Excepting a very small educated minority, most Muslims are in awe about *shari'a* and *fatwas* and try to obey it, even in cases where it is against all their emotional needs and instincts. Thus the 'divinity' of *shari'a* is implicitly believed by a majority of Muslims.

2.4. POSITION OF WOMEN IN ISLAM

It is commonly argued that Islam is not only a comprehensive religion, meant to guide humanity in all aspects of life, it is also a liberal religion; and especially the status of women in Islam is highest among all world religions. Asghar Ali Engineer has written extensively in support of this argument. True, the Quran prohibits female infanticide and gives a certain share of parental property to women—two facts that are cited to argue that Islam improved the lot of women in Arabia which was far worse in pre-Islamic days. The argument is valid only because the Arabia of that time was populated by different tribes with different norms and customs, some of whom might have been quite uncivilized.

It is asserted that during and immediately after the Prophet's life, women could pray in mosques, presumably separately from males, and even become *Imams*. Ayesha and some other women acted as Imams to their extended family which included both men and women. It is also argued that Islam gives its women so much freedom that a bride's consent is necessary for the validation of the marriage process. It is, however, conveniently forgotten that such a consent is not required at the time of unilateral divorce by the males, leaving the wife and children literally on the street.

At the same time, it is true that the frequently quoted Quranic verses present an egalitarian vision of all men and women as being the creation of God. The text often addresses men and women together: 'For Muslim men and women.' Let us quote a few verses of the Holy text.

Men who resign themselves to Allah and the women who resign themselves, and the believing men and the believing women [...] for them Allah has prepared a rich recompense. (Quran XXXIII: 35)

They have rights similar to those against them in a just manner. (II. 228).

And who does good deeds, whether male or female, and he or she is a believer, those shall enter the garden. (IV.124)

Allah has promised the believing men or believing women [shall dwell in the gardens], and best of all is Allah's pleasure that is the grand achievement. (IX.71–2)

As we have been saying all through, life, culture and religion are complex phenomena and any one-sided account of them can never do justice either to the complexity of the phenomena, or to its profound relationships with other aspects of life. Arabia of the Prophet Muhammad's time was inhabited by various warring tribes which had different social structures, norms, as well as attitudes towards women. While in some tribes the status of women was much lower, in others it was better. Islam, therefore, definitely improved the lot of the women in most tribes but this cannot be generalized to cover the entire region.

3. SHARI'A: AN ARGUMENT FOR
CULTURAL RELATIVITY

Before starting the discussion let us clarify a few points. First, as we argued earlier, it is difficult to accept the 'divinity' of *shari'a* for various reasons. But the approach of Muslim orthodoxy regarding the need for blind following of the *shari'a*, or its absolute authenticity, seems to be based on this assumption of its 'divinity'. The authenticity of *shari'a* is based on the fact that it, in turn, is based on the Holy Quran and *Sunnat al Nabi*, the records of the approvals and disapprovals of the Prophet of certain forms of conduct, as given in the *hadiths*. How can we assume the 'divinity' of *shari'a* unless we take for granted the 'divinity' of its important source, that is, the *hadiths*?

Second, these *hadiths* themselves were not the direct reports of the conduct or approvals or disapprovals of the *Nabi*. In fact, the writers of the *hadiths* were removed by several generations from the Prophet. They are thus reports of the reports of earlier reports. That during transmission from one generation to another, no element of personal or cultural bias would have creeped in is difficult to believe. As everyday experience testifies, there are probably no two persons whose description of a given event would perfectly match. And here we are dealing with *hadiths* whose narrators were removed from the Prophet Muhammad by several generations, so that there was a chain of narrators between the Prophet Muhammad and his Companions and the person who put it down in writing. No one can ever be sure that no subjective bias entered at any stage of passing down of some occurrence relating to the Prophet. This raises the question of the authenticity and reliability of the *hadiths* themselves. There is a strong argument for the possibility of cultural conditioning of the narrators of *hadiths*, to which we shall return presently.

Third, cases of misinterpretation of *shari'a* and *hadiths* have been acknowledged by learned *ulama* as wrong, based on ignorant interpretation of *hadiths*. This opens the possibility of such misinterpretation in other cases. Misinterpretations are possible because *shari'a* is nowhere written down, and the number of *hadiths* being very large and their social contexts being very different from present-day circumstances, there are innumerable opportunities for the *maulanas* to pick and choose the *hadith* they want to apply in a given case.

Fourth, how can anyone be sure that the *hadith* that is being quoted in some decision regarding *shari'a* is really authentic? True, by the time of al Shafai'i (ninth century) all authentic *hadiths* had been finalized, by meticulous application of certain criteria.[22] Actually there is a detailed discipline called *Usool-e Hadith* which teaches the methods of proper understanding of a given *hadith*. Still, inasmuch as different schools of Islamic *fiqh* differ from each other, while claiming that they are based on the same *hadiths*, the unconditional authority of these *hadiths* does not appeal to reason.

Fifth, not only the Muslims, even post-modernist thinkers strongly oppose any attempt at critical evaluation or even an attempt to understand other cultures which have developed in entirely different conceptual frameworks. The latter believe that these conceptual frameworks, which are integral to and formative of their respective cultures, do not overlap, and a person working from within a particular cultural framework cannot understand the beliefs, practices, much less norms and values developed in another culture with a very different cultural framework.[23] Leaving here the post-modernists whom I have criticized in detail elsewhere,[24] I still agree that as an 'outsider' to the faith, I have no right to question the beliefs and practices of Muslims.

The only thing that we are trying to say here is that since these *hadith* narrations have been written down several generations after Prophet Muhammad and his Companions, the possibility of cultural and personal bias entering into them at any stage of their being handed down from one generation to another cannot be ruled out. And that means *shari'a*, founded on the Quran as well as the various *hadiths*, cannot be called either 'divine' as the Holy Quran, or inviolable. Given the possibility of their being culturally conditioned, they reflect the conditions and needs of the then times and cannot be upheld as eternally valid and binding on Muslims of all ages and climes.

3.1. ASGHAR ALI ENGINEER: ARGUMENT FOR REINTERPRETATION
       OF *SHARI'A* IN THE PRESENT CONTEXT

Engineer points out various practices in Muslim society which treat women in a humiliating manner—denial of voting rights, right to education, employment outside homes, and so on. He observes that women are punished for rape instead of men, simply because they cannot produce four witnesses. They can be thrown out of their homes simply by the utterance of the word

talaq three times by the husband.[25] But to declare that these prohibitions and practices are according to *shariʻa* is wrong. Even if
right, says Engineer:

The blanket assumption that *shariʻah* is divine and hence unchangeable has to be contested. This is the popular view in the Muslim
world. [...] such a view is misplaced. *Shariʻah* law is a men's interpretation of divine injunctions and it took several centuries to evolve.
The law makers faced new problems and new situations and provided for it through analogical reasoning (*qiyas*) and consensus (*ijma*)
among ulama for those problems for which they did not find any
answers in divine sources. This is the reason why there are differences in various schools of law (*madhahib*) like Hanafi, Shafaʼi
Maliki, Hanbali, Zaʼffari, Ismaiʼli, Zaidi, Zahiri and so on. [...]
Some used one Hadith, while others rejected it in favour of the other.
Or some used one Quranic injunction and some Hadith giving it interpretation, while others used different interpretation using some other
Hadith.[26]

Elsewhere he says the same thing:

In Islam it is the common belief that *shariʻah* is divine and hence
immutable. [...] It is important to note that *shariʻah,* though undoubtedly based on the Holy Quran, is a human endeavor to understand the Divine will. It is an approach to rather than the divine will
itself.[27]

Engineer further points out that:

There is a big gap between scriptural, i.e. the Quranic pronouncements and *shariʻah* formulations. While the Quranic pronouncements
are purely transcendental in spirit, the *shariʻah* formulations have
been influenced by human situation, as well as human thinking in all
related issues.[28]

He adds that women were in a subordinate situation in the
then patriarchal societies, and this situation came to be reflected in
the *shariʻa* laws. The transcendental spirit of the Holy Quran
was forgotten in order to legitimize the practical situation in
those societies.[29] He further opines that as *shariʻa* is after all a
human approach to the Divine will, it is not uniform but has
several variants. Referring to the various schools of law in Islam,
he explains that this could happen only by some thinkers choos-

ing one *hadith*, while others rejecting it in favour of another. Even among the *hadiths* some are acknowledged as weak, while some are admitted to be of doubtful origin, or outright forgeries.[30] Engineer rightly contends that the conception of *ijma* (consensus) is similarly controversial. Whose *ijma* are we talking about: that of the *ulama* or of the entire community? The truth of the matter is that the *ulama*, let alone the entire community, have never agreed or developed a consensus on any issue. In some matters one *Imam* is more liberal, in others another *Imam* is more favourable towards women. Thus except the Quran, the remaining three sources of *shari'a* are human and hence controversial. Even regarding the Prophet's pronouncements, as recorded in the *hadiths*, there is the question whether they should be considered 'divine' or human.

Among the Shi'as also, there is vast difference between the various schools of *fiqh* (jurisprudence). Shi'as give great importance to the *Imams*; but the juridical pronouncements of these *Imams* differ from one another, often even in matters of principle. Engineer concludes that had *shari'a* been divine and hence immutable like the Quran, it could not have had so many differing interpretations.[31] The fact of the matter, as argued earlier, is that the human intervention, inevitable in the narration and recording of the *shari'a*, necessarily brings in the conditioning influence of age and culture (that of the Abbasid period) in the interpretation of the Quran and *sunna*. Therefore,

The Shari'ah, being based on human interpretation of divine word, can and does admit change; what was thought to be just in respect of women's rights in medieval ages, is no longer so. The idea of justice always changes with changing consciousness and what is just in one age may not necessarily be just in another.[32]

Here Engineer goes into the details of the *hadiths*. He reminds us that at one time there were 6,00,000 *hadiths*. Out of them Imam Bukhari accepted 4,000 and rejected the others as spurious. This indicates people were producing so-called *hadiths* to serve their own limited interests. Imam Abu Hanifa accepted only 17 *hadiths* as authentic, but while developing his own Hanafi school of *fiqh* he used many more. 'Unfortunately', says Engineer, 'many of these Hadiths went into juridical formulations in general, and about women in particular,' even though they might well not have been authentic. He contends that the Prophet had strictly prohibited the compilation of his sayings because he knew that such distortions would naturally creep in. Even the first Caliph Abu Bakr, it is said, did not allow such a compilation.[33] Engineer concludes that,

The *hadith* literature [. . .] cannot be considered as a highly reliable source of Islamic legislation. But the Islamic *juris corpus* is as much based on the problematic *hadith* literature as on the holy Quran. Still the Ulama project it as unquestionable, divine and hence immutable. They refuse to admit any change even though sweeping changes are taking place in the social, cultural, economic and political circumstances. The doctrine of *taqlid* (mechanical imitation) is emphasized by the contemporary Muslim jurists in the world of Islam. They maintain that rethinking about the formulations of the great Imams is not permissible. In fact these formulations are treated as divine.[34]

Even the Holy Quran presents some problems. To quote Engineer again,

The Quran, which is unanimously held to be divine by all Muslims, contains many pronouncements which are directly related to the then Arab social structure. These pronouncements also reflect social norms or social problems as they existed then. These pronouncements cannot be of universal application in other societies and cultures.[35]

After giving examples of verses in the Quran which are no longer applicable, like the injunction to treat slaves kindly, Engineer concludes that 'such verses in the Quran should be treated as contextual, i.e. revealed in the context of that society and are no more valid as social practices have changed'.[36] He bemoans the fact that madrasas continue teaching the formulations of Islam and *shari'a* that were developed over a thousand years ago: 'They have frozen their minds in the classical age of Islam. What was temporal has become permanent, and what is permanent is just brushed aside as of no consequence.'[37]

Having reiterated his faith in the Quran being a 'Divine revelation', Engineer contends that the Quranic verses should be divided into normative, meant for all times and cultures, and contextual which were revealed in special circumstances peculiar to those times. He opines that we have to go by Quranic values rather than certain verses relating to concrete historical conditions then prevailing. According to him, 'Any legislation which ignores these fundamental values could be anything but Islamic.'[38] Thus, Engineer has correctly elaborated upon the one basic fact that there is conflict or tension between the Islamic first principles or ethical vision and the *shari'a*. From the above, Engineer reaches a rather radical conclusion: 'The Quran must be re-read and reinterpreted in today's context as the classical jurists read and interpreted it in their own context.'[39]

However, not many would agree to this suggestion of Engineer, as the Holy Quran is unanimously regarded as the immutable Word of God. It is regarded as eternal, not a single word of which can be questioned. Engineer himself, writing elsewhere, while arguing for some other reforms, has often repeated the official position that Quran being the Word of God cannot be questioned.

3.2. LEILA AHMED: INFLUENCE OF MEDIEVAL CULTURE ON *SHARI'A*

In an excellent study Leila Ahmed has argued how the women of Arab tribes, especially those of the Jahilia, were relatively independent and active in community activity, including even warfare and religion. Some tribes even followed the matriarchal system and polyandry. Women could contract their own marriage, and divorce their husbands. However, 'Their autonomy and participation were curtailed with the establishment of Islam, its institution of patrilineal, patriarchal marriage as solely legitimate and social transformation that ensued.'[40] She gives the example of Khadija, the first wife of Muhammad, who was a rich widow from the Jahilia tribe and stipulated at the time of marriage that Muhammad could not take another wife. Ahmed contrasts the lot of Ayesha to that of Khadija. Born to Muslim parents Ayesha was given away in marriage to the Prophet when she was only nine or ten.[41] Of course, she became very prominent during and after Prophet Muhammad's demise.

During his lifetime and even afterwards the Prophet's wives

were well respected. After his death they, especially Ayesha, were consulted and even regarded as authoritative sources in the process of the collection of *hadiths*. Ayesha addressed the warriors, though from behind a veil, and even took part in war. Ahmed attributes this to the fact that it was a transitional period. After this period, women's condition and place in the society constantly deteriorated.[42]

She adds that in contrast to Khadija's independence, autonomy of women and monogamy were absent from Muhammad's life once Khadija died. Further, the male prerogative of polygamy and unilateral divorce were thereafter to become standard features of Islamic marriage. Ahmed repeatedly argues that Islam transformed the condition of women relatively from independent members of society to one of subordination to males. 'Implicit in this new order', she says, 'was the male right to control the women and to interdict their interactions with other men.'[43] She further contends that marriage as sanctioned and practised by Muhammad included polygamy and the marriage of girls nine or ten years old. It also included the male right to divorce at will, as well as the right of men to have sexual relations with slave women captured in war.[44]

The Prophet himself prescribed *purdah* (veil) for his wives, which was perhaps dictated by the circumstances (since the Prophet was constantly thronged by his followers, most of whom lived in the same mosque premises where Muhammad's living quarters were). During Prophet Muhammad's life the Quranic verses enjoining seclusion applied mostly to his wives. Gradually, the practice of seclusion of women and the necessity of total *purdah* were adopted by his followers, may be in an effort to gain recognition as true believers of Islam.

The problem here is that exponents of different views, like Leila Ahmed and others, selectively refer to and quote from the mass of data available. This cannot help in understanding the complex reality of any culture or religion. While the apologetic writers on Islam declare that Islam gives the highest position to women, and that Islam improved the lot of women in the then Arabia, they choose to forget many historical facts that the Arabia of that time was divided into various warring tribes with very different cultures, as well as many more *shari'a* pronouncements. Leila Ahmed concentrates on the data available on Jahilia women who seem to have been much more free and independent than the women of other tribes; and she comes to the conclusion that Islam undermined the status of women, which may equally be a one-sided version of Islam.

Having argued that Islam did undermine the status of women in society, Ahmed at the same time recognizes that these practices were against the ethical vision or ideal of the Quran. She quotes Quranic verses which treat Muslim men and women at par and admits that Prophet Muhammad did have an egalitarian vision of the society in which rich and poor, men and women were to be treated equally.[45] She also reminds us that the restriction put on women's attire in the Quran (24: 31–32) had a simple rule—to guard their private parts and to have a scarf on their bosoms—but later these normative suggestions were translated into the mandatory *burqa* and the seclusion of women. What Ahmed is driving at is that all these distortions entered Islam later, but present-day Muslims regard them as true Islam.

Ahmed observes that some sects arose in the early centuries of Islam which emphasized Islam's ethical teachings as fundamental, and regarded the Prophet's practices and regulations as having been made in the then social context. Many 'revelations' in the Quran have come at specific points of time in response to specific historical or contextual situations. These can hardly be considered as meant for all times to come. Orthodox Islam, on the contrary, has given far greater importance to these practices and regulations than to the central message and values of the Quran, while laying down or elaborating Islamic law. So Ahmed avers:

There appear, therefore, two distinct voices within Islam, and two competing understanding of gender, one expected in the pragmatic regulations of the society [. . .] the other in the articulation of ethical vision.[46]

With the expansion of Islam over the entire Middle East, the values and social norms of these other cultures also influenced the Muslim thinking. In some of these cultures the conditions of women was far worse than in pre-Islamic Arabia. Their perceptions and attitudes, especially towards women, must have influenced Muslim law-givers.

The military victories brought wealth and above all a large number of slaves, both men and women. The social position of a person was often decided by the number of slaves, as well as wives and concubines he possessed! Ahmed presents a vivid picture of the high society after the death of the Prophet, especially during the Abbasid period.[47] There was a thriving market for the sale of slave women. Men preferred having concubines instead of wives; the latter had some rights, while slave women could be treated callously. Gradually, argues Ahmed, women came to be perceived as objects of sexual gratification, and distinction between concubine, women for sexual use and an object or possession blurred.[48]

During the early Abbasid period the *hadiths* were being collected and sometimes edited or even written down entirely. To imagine that the writers or collectors of these *hadiths* remained untouched by the then cultural attitudes would be naïve indeed. Islamic *shari'a* which is supposedly based upon or constructed by the *sunna* of the Prophet and his Companions, was also indirectly being constituted by those collectors of *hadiths* who could not but have been conditioned by the attitudes and values of the times.

Ahmed argues that, the 'Quranic precepts consist mainly of general propositions chiefly of an ethical nature, rather than specific legalistic formulations.'[49] However, Islamic law is a result of culture-based reinterpretation of the Quranic precepts:

The weight Abbasid society gave to the androcentric teachings over the ethical teachings in Islam in matters concerning relations between the sexes was the outcome of collective interpretative acts reflecting the mores and attitudes of the society.[50]

Here Leila Ahmed is saying clearly what Engineer has said in a general way, that Islamic law or *shari'a* is the result of interpretation of the Quranic verses in the light or context of the then society, that is, the role of the interpretative act in the collection and writing down of *hadiths* is reasonably certain. If so, the *shari'a*, which is based more on the *hadiths* than on the Quran, can hardly be called 'divine'. Ahmed contends:

The religion's emphasis on equality and equal justice to which women
were entitled has left little trace on the law developed in the Abbasid
age. [. . .] Had the ethical voice of Islam been heard, I here suggest,
it would have significantly tempered the extreme androcentric bias
of the law, and we might today have a far more humane and egalitarian law regarding women.[51]

3.3. NAILA MINAI: STATUS OF WOMEN IN ISLAM

Like Ahmed, another woman author Naila Minai gives serious
thought to the gradual deterioration of women's status in the
society under Islam. There is some difference between the approaches of the two authors. Ahmed acknowledges the ethical
vision in the Quran which gives equal status to men and women,
but equally points out to those passages of the Quran which
lend themselves to an androcentric view of women. Minai puts
greater stress on the former and argues that Prophet Muhammad was constantly concerned about the poor and the destitute.
She contends that a considerable number of passages of the Holy
Quran are devoted to women's economic rights both in marriage and in their paternal family.[52]

While Ahmed believes that the seeds of male superiority and
androcentric approach to women were sown during the Prophet's
time itself, Minai believes that Prophet Muhammad and the
Quran were most liberal about women. Muhammad put restraints
on his wives due to their special circumstances; he did not prescribe *purdah* for the rest of Muslim women. Instead the Quran
clearly states:

Say to the believing women that they should lower their gaze and
guard their modesty; that they should not display their beauty and
ornaments except what must ordinarily appear thereof; that they should
draw their veils over their bosoms. . . . (XXIV.31)

But like Ahmed, Minai goes on to point out that this ethical
vision was hardly heeded by the law-givers and rulers. Rather,
keeping their womenfolk in seclusion became a symbol of one's
social status. Women were gradually turned into mere sex objects. With the conquest of foreign lands an ever larger number
of women slaves were available as sex objects. *Harems* were over-
crowded. Women even became dispensable.[53]

Minai independently says the same thing as Ahmed, that as time elapsed after the passing away of the Prophet, the condition of women deteriorated. This was especially true in the upper classes where women came to be perceived as nothing more than mere sex objects. According to Minai, even though the Quran sanctioned certain practices which were detrimental to the welfare of women, such as polygamy and unilateral *talaq* (divorce), its conception and attitude towards women were much more positive than what later Islam came to represent. The marked change that came in Islam with time can only be understood as a result of cultural conditioning.

Both Ahmed and Minai contend how ethical vision of the Quran was soon forgotten by the rulers, the feudal elite, and the *maulanas*. The famous theologian, al Ghazali (eleventh–twelfth centuries), asserted: 'A woman should not leave her spindle, or her private apartment, nor look down the street from her terrace.'[54]

When we quote the above authors approvingly, we are not advocating post-modernist cultural relativism, but the simple fact of life that no human being, far less a group, can remain totally untouched and uninfluenced by the people and culture which circumstances or their own victories bring them into contact with. That is why the narrators of *hadiths*, who mostly belonged to the Abbasid period and must have tasted the wealth and other pleasures that the rich enjoyed during that time, could not have remained totally untouched by the ways and norms of that era. And degradation of women's position was an integral part of the culture and norms of that period.

Let us leave aside the ordinary mortals who were the narrators of these *hadiths*, even the greatest saints and prophets have not remained uninfluenced by the culture and values of their times. Thus Jesus believed himself to be the Messiah because the Jews of his times were waiting for one. Similarly, Gandhi supported the abominable traditional Hindu belief that everyone must do one's hereditary duty, howsoever unpleasant it may be. And finally, Prophet Muhammad accepted the institution of slavery in his Islamic society wherein everyone was supposed to be equal. (Of course, he recommended gentle treatment of slaves.) Thus to think that *hadiths* represent the spirit of the Holy Quran, or even the approvals or disapprovals of Prophet Muhammad, without the slightest distortion due to lapse of considerable time, as also due to the fact that many of the *hadiths* were written in Syria and Iran and not in Arabia, whose authors were naturally not so familiar with Arab culture and norms of the Prophet's time, seems to be either naïve or purely dogmatic.

Interestingly, the gates of *ijtihad* or individual judgement on the basis of holy texts were supposedly closed in tenth–eleventh centuries. But some Sufi saints and thinkers had started questioning this line of approach as far back as the thirteenth century. Sheikh Sharafuddin Maneri expressed a revolutionary thought which could be relevant even now: 'Handling traditions is an extremely difficult task. Seven centuries have elapsed during which the traditions have come down to us. [. . .] Who knows perhaps somebody, in order to bolster his opinion, might have said, "The Prophet said such and such".' Maneri gave a test to judge whether a tradition is authentic or spurious. If the tradition or commentary on the Quran starts by asserting that whosoever will read this chapter would get all his wishes fulfilled, then that tradition is false! If someone still believed in the said tradition, he said, let him try out; not a single wish would have been fulfilled![55] Here is a rational approach to traditions (*ahadis*) which no one in the present time dares apply.

4. *FIQH*

In Islam *shari'a* and *fiqh* are mostly indistinguishable. Though *shari'a*, being unwritten, is not even a direct subject of study in madrasas, yet the two are integrally related. Generally it is believed that *shari'a* is 'divine', while *fiqh* is a human construction. But as we have discussed above, the conception of *shari'a* as 'divine' is problematic. Every discussion of *shari'a* at some stage or the other gets merged into that of *fiqh*, and the latter is not considered 'divine'. Somehow *fiqh* is central to Islam as theology is central to Christianity. Does it suggest that outward adherence to the written word, both in religious (*dini*) and worldly (*duniyavi*) matters (*taqlid*) is more important in Islam than inner faith (*ihsan*)?

The importance of *shari'a* and *fiqh* can be gauged by the fact that though early Sufi saints excelled in their inner faith and love of God, they were either denounced or relegated to the backstage by the orthodox as they often undermined *shari'a* in their pronouncements and practices, and contrasted *tariqa* (Sufi way) from *shari'a*. And yet almost all of them took care to adhere to the basic laws of *shari'a*. Thus Baba Farid remained lost in his remembrance of God (*dhikr*), but got up to perform *namaz* five times a day. And yet, they were seen as not sufficiently 'Islamic' and hence their lack of importance in orthodox Islam.

Fiqh is Islamic jurisprudence. It refers to the science of law extracted from detailed Islamic sources, or jurisprudence. While there are cases where the Quran gives a clearly defined and concrete answer on how to deal with different issues, on others it gives only general prohibitions and injunctions, whose details have to be worked out. Generally these details were worked out with the help of the *sunna*, constituted of Prophet's acts, sayings and approbations or disapprobations (often silent ones), as recorded in the *hadiths*. The historian Ibn Khaldum describes *fiqh* as: 'knowledge of the rules of God which concerns the actions of persons who are bound to obey the law respecting what is required (*wajib*), forbidden (*haram*), recommended (*manzoor*), disapproved (*makrooh*), or merely optional (*mubah*).[56]

This may suggest that since *fiqh* describes God's laws that cannot be disobeyed, it is as sacred or 'divine' as *shari'a*. But generally it is regarded as a product of human interpretation of divine commands, and therefore not 'divine'. If so, why is it inviolable in the sense that every Muslim must obey the laws of *fiqh*? However, Muslim jurists (*fuqaha*) do not always agree in their interpretation of the Quran and the *sunna*. These differences of opinion have resulted in the establishment of various schools of *fiqh* (*mazahib*)—Hanabali, Ma'liki, Shafai'i and Hanafi among the Sunnis; Za'fari, Zaidi and Za'hiri among the Shi'as. But there can well be various issues in which the two sources do not provide any guidance; in such cases early jurists took recourse to reasoning by analogy (*qiyas*) and consensus (*ijma*) of the community or among the *ulama*.

According to Asghar Ali Engineer, Leila Ahmed, Noel J. Coulson and other critical thinkers, the Quranic precepts generally consist of broad principles, mainly of ethical nature. These precepts, being rather general, raise many practical and legalistic problems. On the contrary, the specific content of the laws, supposedly derived from the Quran, is based on deliberate selection of verses to suit the jurists' own values and norms. Moreover, the ethical injunctions of the Quran were declared as mere directions which were not mandatory, and their following was left to the conscience of the individual.[57]

For example, judges have differed among themselves in similar cases. While Quranic permission to take up to four wives was taken seriously, its accompanying advice that they should be treated equally was neglected. In a case of divorce while one judge declared that the Quranic injunction 'to make a fair provision' for a divorced wife was mandatory, another judge declared it to be only a suggestion. In view of the above, Ahmed concludes,

The growth of this legal and administrative corpus of rulings was haphazard, the materials and sources it drew on heterogeneous, and the Quranic elements within it were largely submerged.[58]

As Noel J. Coulson has pointed out,

The great bulk of the law had originated in customary practice and in scholars' reasoning [. . . the development of] classical theory was the culmination of a process of growth extending over two centuries.[59]

Coulson and Doreen Hinchcliffe opine that,

A considerable step—a process of juristic development extending over more than two centuries—separates the Quran from the classical formulations of Islamic law. [. . .] The modicum of Quranic rulings were naturally observed, but outside this the tendency was to interpret the Quranic provisions in the light of prevailing standards.[60]

However, traditional Islamic belief came to hold that the law as articulated in this literature was operative from the beginning. While Islamic law is a result of gradual historical growth, says Coulson, the Islamic orthodoxy sees it 'as a process of scholastic endeavour completely independent of historical or sociological influences'.[61]

Though in the early centuries of Islam *maulanas* and jurists had occasionally used analogical reasoning and even their own interpretative judgement, in the tenth century they declared the body of already existing laws as final. The duty of all the following jurists was to imitate their predecessors and never to reinterpret the law according to changed circumstances of the times. The gates of *ijtihad* (reasoning according to scriptures) were declared to be closed henceforward. 'The law that had evolved,' says Ahmed, 'over the first Islamic centuries was considered as the complete and infallible expression of the divine law.'[62] It was done in spite of the fact, as argued above, that the Islamic law was the result of different interpretations of the Quran and especially of the *hadiths* in the context of the then culture of the Abbasid period. 'That its central texts embody acts of interpretation,' says Ahmed, 'is precisely what the orthodoxy is most concerned to conceal and erase from the consciousness of Muslims.'[63]

In case secular, liberal writers are considered heretic, and hence carrying no weight, let me refer to the views of Ameer Ali, the most respectable ideologue of Islam and a nationalist leader of early twentieth century. His book *The Spirit of Islam* has been one of the most authentic works on Islam in modern times. He argues that the Prophet was the greatest upholder of the sovereignty of reason. He could never have presumed that the revelations that were vouchsafed to him 'by the passing necessities of a semi-civilized people should become immutable to the end of the world's [. . .].'[64] He refers to the famous *hadith* about Mua'z, the governor of Yemen, who was praised by Prophet Muhammad when he said that in the case he did not find any precedence in the Quran or *sunna*, he would exercise his own judgement. Ameer Ali goes on to assert that:

The present stagnation of the Musalman communities is principally due to the notion which has fixed itself on the minds of Moslems, that the right to the exercise of private judgment ceased with the early legists. [. . .] No account is taken of the altered circumstances in which Moslems are now placed; the conclusion at which these learned jurists arrived several centuries ago are held to be equally applicable to the present day. [. . .] The Prophet had consecrated reason as the highest and noblest function of the human intellect. Our schoolmen and their servile followers have made its exercise a sin and a crime.[65]

All decisions by the *ulama* are taken on the basis of some *hadith* or the other, the Holy Quran is rarely cited. Then there is the issue whether the *hadith* being quoted is really authentic. We have seen above that al Shafa'i and other *ulama* had decided about the authenticity of certain *hadiths* by the tenth century, after which they have not been questioned. We also saw that Sheikh Sharafuddin Maneri questioned this blind faith in the *hadiths* in the fourteenth century itself.[66]

Islamic law generally covers actions that are recommended, not-recommended and prohibited. Islamic *shari'a* and law (*fiqh*) cover and determine the entire life of Muslims, from the details of inter-personal relationships to intimate personal matters. Generally the laws are classified as under: (a) theological, (b) marital disputes, (c) criminal matters, (d) financial dealings, and (e) military matters. There are elaborate laws relating to religion which include citing of the moon; the major sin of abandoning the prayer; forcibly taking the place of someone who was ahead of you; rulings regarding wiping the shoes; the detail of *wuzu* (obligatory purification prior to the *namaz*); things which invalidate *wuzu*; whether women can touch, read or recite the Quran in the state of impurity; laws for pre-dawn meal before fast in the month of Ramzan and for breaking the fast after sundown; prayer in congregation; on placing the hands in the correct position; on the raising of the hands up to a definite height during the prayer, and whether reading *Sura Fa'tiha* is compulsory, and so on.[67]

What we are driving at is that in everyday Islam, *taqlid* or blind following of the written word has gradually supplanted inner faith and piety. When minute details of rituals are given such a great importance in religious (*dini*) matters, such as the level to which the hands must be raised during *namaz*, religion is reduced to mechanical performance of rituals and blind following of the law, as understood by the more conservative *maulavis*.

Shari'a based on the Quran and *hadiths* governs and controls every aspect of human life, particularly family relations. When some complex issue arises it is decided by blindly following some arbitrarily chosen *hadith*, without the slightest consideration for either the changed times and culture, or the special circumstances of the case.

5. THE INSTITUTION OF *FATWA*

In the early centuries of Islam, a distinction was made between *qazis* or judges and *muftis*. The *qazis* decided disputes in interpersonal matters like family disputes (marriage, divorce and inheritance) and thefts, mostly in courts. (For some reason murder has not been taken as seriously as theft.) Then there were *mufits* who were learned in Islamic law and gave their judgement or *fatwas* on matters relating to the *shari'a* which ranged form the details of *ib'adat* (works of worship) to matters of interpersonal relationship (*ma'mla't*), and to such ordinary matters of etiquette as the proper manner of eating and even sexual relationship between the husband and wife. Perhaps the most frequent matters on which *fatwas* were and are issued relate to marriage and divorce.

Generally *fatwas* are issued only if someone queries about some matter. The *mufti* gives his decision according to his knowledge and understanding of various *hadiths* and *shari'a*. Nowadays there are regular post-graduation courses on the right manner of issuing *fatwas*. There are also regular departments to receive requests and issue *fatwas*. In Deoband alone thousands of *fatwas* are issued every year. They are later collected and published. These *fatwas* also become a basis of future *fiqh* formulations.

But, these courses do not provide any understanding of modern conditions and values. Far worse, the *muftis* do not consider the special circumstances of the case in point, and simply refer to some ancient *hadith* of the seventh century and apply it in the twenty-first century (as we saw in the Imrana case).

Equally important, both *shari'a* and *fatwas* deal with every aspect of life. They often deal with either rituals relating to the *namaz*, or the exact manner of breaking of the fast, and the correct manner of doing *wuzu* (washing hands and mouth prior to saying the *namaz*). There are controversies relating to whether the congregation should repeat the words of the Quran, being read by the *Imam* or keep silent and the level to which one should raise one's hands, or the angle to which one should bend while doing *sazda*. Sometimes even pettier issues are put forward for guidance, such as if some fine particles of food are left in the mouth, would the *namaz* done in such a condition be valid.

Even the details of proper sexual relationship with the wife have been dealt with. The issues relating to *talaq* are perhaps the most frequent topics of *fatwas*.

Sometimes weightier socio-political issues are also tackled by the *fatwas*. In late eighteenth century, several *fatwas* were issued to the effect that since Hindustan was *Darul-Harb* (an abode of enemy), being ruled by the British, Muslims should migrate to Afghanistan; some of them even did so and tried to establish a Muslim kingdom there. But they failed and many of them returned. During the freedom struggle and the Khilafat movements, *fatwas* were not only issued, they were sought by national leaders to launch a united movement against the British. It may seem that these *fatwas* were nationalist in their intention, but they also strengthened the role and hold of the *ulama* over the Muslim masses.[68]

Now, in the twenty-first century, when the *ulama* decree that a Muslim woman (Imrana) raped by her father-in-law has become the latter's wife and the mother of her husband, even if she has several children by the latter; or when they declare that a gang-raped woman on the behest of the elders of the community (Mukhtaran Mai) is the guilty party; and the masses accept their judgement, it simply means a march back to the seventh-century Arabia. The above cases saw a huge public outcry. But apart from making Mukhtaran Mai famous, nothing could be achieved in her case; in the case of Imrana, her natural and legal relations with her husband could never be restored. Later the senior Deoband clerics issued a clarification saying that they did not know the particulars of the case. If so, why did they issue the *fatwa* at all? The *Nazim* of Deoband later declared that in future they would not issue *fatwas* in such cases. We do not know what exactly this promise means. What does seem clear is that the authoritative hold of these *maulanas* and *muftis* shows no sign of decreasing. That means that the Muslim masses are so dependent on these *muftis* and the half-literate village *maulanas* that they can never dare take any decision about their personal lives without consulting them first. If they fear that their contemplated step, such as providing their daughters higher secular education, or allowing their womenfolk to go out to work, or go out without the *burqa* or veil, goes against the *shari'a*, then they would never dare take that step. It is to be noted further that most of these *fatwas* go against the interests or even the basic dignity of women, as most *maulanas* are extremely conservative.

Another interesting category consists of *fatwas* which the *ulama* and *maulanas* are continuously issuing against their rival sects within Islam. An example of this are the thousands of *fatwas* issued by Muhammad Riza Khan, one of the chief founders of Ahle-Sunnat sect of Islam, against all the rival sects. Similarly, the *maulanas* of Ahle-Hadith sect are continuously issuing *fatwas* against rival sects. Interestingly, each of these sects declares itself as the real Sunni Islam, while rejecting the others as not even being Muslims. The result is that all the energies and thinking of these *muftis* and *maulanas* are exhausted in these petty matters and no time or energy is left either for truly religious matters or for social issues of the Muslims.

6. *SHARI'A* AND WOMEN

It may be rightly asked here as to what the above discussion has to do with women. The fact, however, is that we could not selectively access the *fiqh* material exclusively dealing with women. Examples of *shari'a—fiqh* dealing with prayer and other petty daily matters have been given in order to point out how rituals and blind following (*taqlid*) are supposed to be the essence of man's relations with God. Naturally, it would be more so in worldly or interpersonal matters, especially concerning women.

We have discussed Leila Ahmed's views, who says the conditions and social status of women was better in pre-Islamic Arabia and Islam put greater restraint on them. But such a version is one-sided, her views being chiefly based on the Jahilia tribe. There were other tribes; and the wide prevalence of female infanticide goes against her version of a liberal pre-Islamic Arab society. However, the truth of the matter lies somewhere between Ahmed's contention and certain apologetic Muslim writers declaring that Islam gives the highest place to women, or that Islam improved the lot of women.

On the other hand, there seems to be some truth in Leila Ahmed's contention that pre-Islamic women mingled freely with males and took part in social and religious activities. Islam seems to have put a stop to these freedoms. First, of course, is the compulsion of the veil and seclusion which widely narrows down the field of activity for women. It is pointed out that the Quran does not prescribe *burqa*, but only to cover one's body fully. But we are here talking of *shari'a* and not the Quran alone, and according to the *shari'a*, the veil is the prescribed thing. In Saudi Arabia, present-day Iran, Afghanistan and even north-west Pakistan, there are restrictions even on unescorted women going out of their homes; or their working in public places; or even getting educated, at least in common colleges, all in the name of Islamic *shari'a*. Some of these restrictions have been modified but without any perceptible change in the social condition of women.

Worst of all is the marital status of women. It is repeatedly claimed that the consent of the girl is taken before her marriage. But first, that consent is mostly obtained under family and societal pressure; and second, the sanction for polygamy makes a mockery of that consent. In the middle ages, men could divorce their wives and marry new ones to stick to the mandatory number of four wives.[69] Of course, the practice of polygamy has been drastically reduced in most Islamic countries now. But it is very clearly allowed in the Quran and the *sunna*. And no one can ever say that polygamy is conducive to a better status of women in the society.

Moreover, while a girl's consent is supposedly taken before marriage, no such consent is required while divorcing her. Again, Prophet Muhammad put some restraints or laid guidelines for giving *talaq* to one's wife. But these restrictions were soon disregarded. Above all, *talaq* remained and still remains the prerogative of man alone. There is also the issue of triple *talaq* which has been allowed in the *sunna*. The Muslim Personal Law Board has refused to derecognize it. Everyday, there is someone or the other who pronounces *talaq* three times in anger or under the influence of alcohol but feels repentant immediately afterwards. But once uttered, the *talaq* is final and cannot be reversed unless the wife marries somebody else, and somehow gets divorced from the latter. Whatever the earlier sensitivities, present-day conscience is very uncomfortable with the provision of triple *talaq*, and the *shari'a* remedy of marrying another man and getting divorced to undo it.

Even in the case of ordinary *talaq*, the poor woman might have been married to the man for decades and having a number of children, but as a husband and father the man owes no obligation to his wife and children once he divorces her. All he is required is to give some maintenance during the *iddat* period of three months and for the youngest child till it is being breast fed. Afterwards she is supposed to return to her 'own people', that is, those whom she left behind decades back. The *dowr* (the money given or promised to the bride at the time of marriage) is supposed to take care of her and her children all through their lives. This *dowr* may be a few thousand, or a few hundred rupees given decades ago and can have no value at the time of divorce. Rajiv Gandhi got an Act enacted in order to appease the most conservative elements among Muslims, called 'The Protection of Muslim Women's Rights (on Divorce) Act'. According to it, since the divorced woman's ex-husband becomes a stranger (*paraya mard*) to her, she cannot approach him for maintenance; therefore she should either go to her parental home or seek help from the Wakf Boards.

Apart from the pathetic position in which the said Act puts a divorced woman along with her children, three other things strike us as odd. First, there are no Wakf Boards established for this specific purpose, and any way, the finances of these Wakf Boards are notoriously in a bad shape. Second, if a person with whom the woman has spent long years of her life is a stranger to her, how is it that the men managing the Wakf Boards are not strangers? Third, how is it, that the father has no responsibility towards his young children?

Islamic law expects that the children should be 'returned' to the father after they reach a certain age. This too is unjustified. First, how is the mother supposed to bring up the children to that age without help? Second, after taking care of them from inception to breast-feeding and later on till puberty, why is she expected to 'return' them to their father whose only contribution to their lives was in their conception?

This Act, enacted at the instance of *mullas* and *maulavis*, howsoever reprehensible its political motivation, expresses the position of Islamic *shari'a* and *fiqh* and its cruel neglect of the condition of women. It is true that the Quran repeatedly exhorts society to take care of widows and orphans, but that was because those were times of wars and widows must have been aplenty. The holy text also advises men to marry widows. Perhaps the sanction for polygamy was also inspired by the disproportion in the population of men and women at that time, and such advices were in favour of those women.

But all said, it still remains a fact that the Quran sanctions both polygamy and discontinuance of maintenance money after the three months of *iddat*. Much is made of the Quranic injunction to 'pay her maintenance at a reasonable scale' (II.241). At the same time it is admitted that the amount deemed to be 'reasonable' is left to the conscience of the husband. It is also said that a woman is free to remarry in Islam and her children get a home at their father's place.[70] Both assertions are against the facts of life, as well as the demands of justice. So, divorced women hardly ever get justice under *shari'a*.[71]

Interestingly, upward social mobility is sought to be achieved through the adoption of a severely traditional style of life. Womenfolk of the so-called lower castes do not observe *purdah*. But if any of these people want to earn social respectability, they start by making their womenfolk stop working outside their homes and observing *purdah*. An important indicator of social and economic empowerment of a people is the participation of its womenfolk in jobs outside their homes. Talking of *beradaris* in Old Delhi, Douglas E. Goodfriend contends that,

[B]eradaris are hierarchically ranked [. . .] according to a religiously informed value system. [. . .] Conservative social practices, such as strict maintenance of *purdah*, support for traditional Koranic and Arabic education for *beradari* children, mosque building and consistent observance of Muslim personal law are still highly regarded. Formal *beradari* associations still do formulate such rules to maintain or raise their collective status.[72]

Hasan Ali points out that a broad distinction exists in the lifestyles of ethnic groups with higher and lower status in the religio-social hierarchy. This distinction operates especially in relation to the observance of *purdah* and religious duties. The norms of *purdah* are strictly observed by womenfolk of Saiyyeds and Pathans. The practice of *purdah* enjoys such respectability that families, that are lower down in the religio-social hierarchy but have managed to earn economic well-being, withdraw their womenfolk from traditional occupations involving going out of their homes.[73] It means that the real burden of carrying out the commands of *shari'a* falls on the women. Or we may say that the real victims of this insistence on blind following of *shari'a* are women.

The Quranic and *shariat* prescriptions regarding women must be understood in the context of seventh-century Middle East, especially the Arab society. But unfortunately this cannot be done as both the Quran and *shari'a* are declared as 'divine'. We have questioned above the claim for the divinity of *shari'a*, but no one can ever question the belief that every word of the Holy Quran is a 'Divine revelation', or even more than that, eternal and uncreated. However, this makes the references to historical events, and also many other verses that were 'revealed' in response to certain specific situations, problematic.

We have referred to Asghar Ali Engineer's article in which he has contended that the Quran 'contains many pronouncements which are directly related to the then prevailing Arab social structure. These pronouncements also reflect the social norms or social problems as they existed then. These pronouncements cannot be of universal application in other societies and cultures.' He adds that 'such verses in the Quran should be treated as contextual, i.e. revealed in the context of that society and are no more valid as social practices have changed'.[74]

Engineer has suggested that the Quranic verses should be divided into two categories: contextual and normative. While contextual verses need not/cannot be obediently followed in modern times, normative verses should be universally mandatory. Engineer's favourite examples of normative verse are those *suras* which address men and women together, implying their equality before God. That is so; but if the rest of the Quran is also a 'revelation' of God, a reproduction of the eternal text, then we cannot agree with Engineer when he repeatedly asserts that the place of women in Islam is highest (among world religions). To return to his distinction between the contextual and normative verses, we do not know whether he would regard the verses of the Quran that deal with divorce, and which definitely do not give a fair deal to the divorced women, normative or contextual. The language of the verses suggests that they are expected to be normative, that is, to be universally followed.

Any way, perhaps very few Muslims, excepting a minority of liberal and secular ones, would agree to reject the 'contextual' verses as irrelevant to modern times. The reason is simple. Since the entire Quran is 'revealed' no verse of it could be considered as contextual and not applicable for modern times. And yet Engineer's suggestion is worth being considered by the *maulanas* who decide the fate of Muslim masses.

The Muslim understanding of the Quran is integrally related to whatever is known about Prophet Muhammad's views and conduct from the *sunna* as recorded in the *hadiths*. But as we have argued, even though the *hadiths* are regarded at par with the Quran by Muslims, they were recorded one or two centuries after passing away of the Prophet, and hence to regard them as exact or verbatim reports of Muhammad's life, conduct and opinions is not correct. The differences in various *hadiths* in different collections should have made the traditional Muslims conscious of this possibility. Moreover, Islamic *shari'a* and *fiqh* carry with them the load of centuries of interpretation, which could not but have been influenced by the culture and times in which the various commentators of *hadiths* and *tafsirs* (commentaries on the Quran) lived. Even though the gates of *ijtihad* (rational thinking on the texts) were supposedly closed in the tenth century, which itself is quite an arbitrary contention—commentaries on commentaries on *hadiths* and earlier *tafsirs* continued to be written. In madrasas the Quran is never taught directly but through *tafsirs* which, as we have seen earlier, carry many more commentaries. Thus Muslims' understanding of the Quran is itself conditioned by the various *hadiths* and equally by various complicated *tafsirs*. Hence the advisability of agreeing with Engineer's suggestion that the Quran must be reread in the present times' context.

7. EDUCATION OF WOMEN

7.1. GIRLS' EDUCATION—FROM MEDIEVAL TIMES TILL INDEPENDENCE

The Quran calls to both men and women to get knowledge. Quranic exhortations to this effect are generally addressed to all without any distinction. This is taken to mean that Islam encourages women's education. But if we care to read and understand the historical circumstances of those times, we would find that it was a world in which wars and violence were common place, and that made men naturally the dominant sex. Gradually, as we have seen above, the restrictions on women increased, and with the emphasis on seclusion of women, the education of common womenfolk was neglected.

From the earliest times free elementary education was imparted to all children in mosques. But generally it was confined to the reading of the Quran, learning to do *sala't* (*namaz*), as well as its prerequisite *wuzu* (ritual washing), and a little arithmetic. For most people education ended there. Only a few studied further, mostly under learned tutors at the latter's homes. But there was no place for women's education in this set-up. Daughters of rich houses perhaps studied at their homes in veil under tutors, as we have evidence of learned and gifted princesses and other ladies of the higher class.

When the first madrasas were established around the tenth century, there was no place for women in them. We do not have a record of a separate girls' madrasa in those days. Gradually those few women who had some education at home started teaching others, and thus women of upper classes gained some education. It is not that the relative neglect of women's education was peculiar to Islam; it was the same everywhere in the world in ancient and medieval periods.

The real spurt to women's education came with the reformist-revivalist movements in the late nineteenth century. Such movements, especially directed at the improvement in the lot of women and their education, first started in Hindu society. Gradually, Muslim reformists also felt the need of educating women. However, unlike the Hindu movements, the Muslim reformist movements were less concerned about women's education and more about revival of the original Islam of Prophet's time.

Tablighi movement started in the last decades of the nineteenth century and gradually became a strong mass movement. Its leaders concentrated on rural Muslims, especially those whom they perceived to be sharing a common culture and customs with their non-Muslim neighbours, which seemed to them to be un-Islamic.[75] Since they visited village communities regularly, and since they found that Muslim women were more responsible for practising what they declared un-Islamic practices and customs, they addressed both men and women. As the womenfolk could not be weaned from 'un-Islamic' customs unless they knew what 'true' Islam was, it became essential that they have some education so that they could read the Quran.

Maktabs continued to function throughout the middle ages, teaching students of both sexes to read the Quran (without understanding it), and imparting knowledge about other basic Islamic rituals related to performing the *namaz*. But higher studies were confined to boys.

In the late nineteenth century, as we have seen earlier, there were two highly significant movements in the field of Muslim education—the first was that of Sir Sayyid Ahmad Khan and the second of the Muslim clerics. Two biggest madrasas of India—those at Deoband and Nadwa—were established, followed immediately by the establishing of several other large madrasas. But nothing was done for the education of women at first.

It was only in the beginning of the twentieth century that some effort at the education of Muslim women was undertaken. In Uttar Pradesh Dini Talimi Council was established with the aim of establishing maktabs and *dini* madrasas throughout the state. It has been active ever since. Though it lays great emphasis on religious education, its syllabus includes modern subjects at the primary stage. As the maktabs established by the Council are better organized, and both boys and girls attend them, girls have benefited for the first time in getting some modicum of education, other than mechanically reading the Arabic Quran. Since girls could not study in boys' madrasas, the need was felt for separate girls' madrasas, which very gradually came into being.

It was argued by the supporters of women's education, such as Maulana Thanvi (who was otherwise quite conservative) that the neglect of women's education goes against the egalitarian message of Islam. However, the motivation for teaching the girls was still conservative. The reason given was that women and mothers are the backbone of the family, and women educated in Islamic knowledge and values are far more capable of bringing up families steeped in the Islamic way of life (*shari'a*) and values. They would also have better hygiene and health considerations, useful for bringing up a healthy family.[76]

Gail Minault has traced the independent efforts of two different groups of reformers to provide Muslim women both kinds of education—traditional and modern. Like the *maulanas,* English-educated middle-class Muslims were also eager to give their daughters and wives modern education. Here also the motivation was selfish—they wanted their womenfolk to be able to adjust to the modern society of Westerners and westernized Indians in which they themselves wanted to move.[77]

Some educated Muslim women, along with some liberal well wishers started women's magazines and organized Muslim women's conferences, such as the Anjuman-i-Khavatin-i-Islam. The latter, of course, were attended only by the higher class women of English-educated families. They passed resolutions against the *purdah* system, polygamy and certain kinds of unilateral divorces. Some organizations and individuals also established girls' schools, though all these changes took place very gradually. However, as Minault observes, these reformist efforts did not weaken the control of males over their womenfolk.[78]

7.2. MUSLIM GIRLS' EDUCATION TODAY

As we have seen in chapter 2, perhaps the greatest hindrance in women's education in the present times is the lack of separate schools for them. We found that since Muslims are scattered all over the country, therefore their demand for separate schools for girls would mean opening separate upper primary as also high schools in every nook and corner of India. This is a near impossible goal to be achieved in the near future. A far better option would be for conservative Muslims to allow their girls to study in common schools with separate seating arrangements, and a definite presence of lady teachers in sufficient numbers in every school.

The overall situation is improving. The Muslim masses now want to educate their girls as much as their boys. According to certain surveys, girls are studying far better and longer than boys.[79] At the same time the Muslims living in exclusive Muslim localities or *mohallas* are more conservative and avoid sending their girls to schools, preferring madrasas instead for their education. This happens in spite of the availability of neighbourhood girls' schools.[80] The reason, as we have seen in chapter 2, is the strong influence of the *ulama* and other conservative elders in these *mohallas*. Not only middle-class parents who definitely prefer modern education for their children, but even the economically poor folk, if left to themselves, are not averse to sending their children, including girls, to modern schools. But those who come under the influence of the *ulama* ignore modern education and send their children, especially girls, to madrasas. Thus parents' education and the area where they live, not their poverty, are the chief factors that decide whether daughters go to schools or to madrasas, or drop out from both.

Here too the influence of tradition comes into picture. Muslim girls are removed from schools as early marriage is very common among conservative Muslims. This practice of marrying off the daughters at an early age not only stops their education but also affects their health, as also their status in the family and society.[81]

7.3. Traditional Education for Muslim Girls

Since the *shari'a* emphasis on *purdah* or seclusion of women required that women be sent to separate madrasas, there was the urgent need for establishing such madrasas. But in view of the size of the country and the fact that Muslims live in every nook and corner of it, thousands of madrasas would be needed, clearly an impossible goal. In truth, we have a very small number of women's madrasas, obviously inadequate to give traditional education to all Muslim girls, especially those living in remote villages.

There is the question of approximately how many girls' madrasas are there in the country. At present we do not have any idea as to the number and location of girls' madrasas in India. Athar Afzal describes several girls' madrasas in the small city of Mau in western Uttar Pradesh but we have no idea of either their standard of teaching or their internal milieu. Even if it were true of Mau, hundreds of other cities and towns do not have separate girls' madrasas.

The existing girls' madrasas vary within themselves. The main difference is whether they are for day students, or provide boarding and lodging. We can also categorize them on the basis of the level up to which they teach. Generally they teach up to Arabi *som* (class 3), as in most boys' madrasas. Very few teach up to *Alim* and *Fazil* levels. Then, of course, the *maslak* (sect) to which they belong determines the framework and syllabus of the madrasa. There may be some which teach modern subjects also up to a certain level, but most do not. There is an important difference between madrasas that owe allegiance to the Deobandi tradition and those which are established by the Jamaat-e-Islami. The latter aim at a more broad-based education and include modern subjects in their syllabus, while Deobandi madrasas do not.

There are some entirely separate kind of madrasas which are in fact Urdu-medium schools which also teach basic religious education. Most of these are affiliated to one State Madrasa Board or the other.

Perhaps the most common factor in all these madrasas is that the girls are kept in strict discipline (read restraints). They observe *purdah* and are nor allowed to go out of the premises of the madrasa. If they have to go out at all, they must be in *burqa* and escorted by some male approved by the madrasa authorities. The education imparted in these madrasas lacks two things—knowledge of and contact with the society around them and self-confidence to deal with practical situations of everyday life. Girls educated in madrasas perhaps have even less self-confidence than their uneducated Muslim neighbours. This is because they are denied any contact with the outside world.

Most madrasas provide boarding, for the simple reason that there are only a few such institutions, and Muslim population is spread throughout this vast subcontinent. At the same time, the girls of the particular place where the madrasa is situated would also come to the madrasas. Within the confines of the madrasa, they must observe strict rules of *purdah*. They are not allowed to listen to the radio or see TV, or take part in the celebrations of their non-Muslim neighbours.

Girls from remote villages hardly come to madrasas, as rural Muslim families do not feel the need to teach their girls beyond the maktab stage. This is true not only of Muslims, most Indian families except those living in metropolitan cities are unwilling to send their girls to distant places for gaining education.

A few accounts are available of larger madrasas in cities. Delhi has several girls' madrasas. A relatively large one in Sanabil, near Okhla is run by the Ahle-Hadith society called Islamic Awakening Centre. Though one can freely access the large boys' madrasa, entry to the girls' madrasa is restricted. One has to formally apply to the chairman of the society. We tried several times over the phone but could not get permission.

However, a young foreign lady, Mareike Jule Winkelmann succeeded by her sheer perseverance to get admittance to a girls' madrasa. Her account of *Madrastul Niswan* (Girls' Madrasa) gives the most comprehensive, objective and sympathetic glimpse of the inner atmosphere of a girls' madrasa.[82] The madrasa's real name is Madrasa Jami'at-ul-Banat, and it is situated near Nizam-uddin Auliya's *Mazar* in a Muslim-majority area. Other well-known madrasas are Jamiat-us Salihat at Rampur, western UP, Jamiat-al Salihat at Malegoan in Maharashtra, and Jamiat-al Falah at Azamgarh. While the earlier mentioned madrasas follow the Deobandi syllabus, the last, a Jamaat-e-Islami madrasa has almost 3,000 girls enrolled, and also teaches some modern subjects.

The rules of strict segregation or *purdah,* however, are the same everywhere. The discipline, of course, is strict. Since generally, at least in India, girls are more hard working than the boys, both the general atmosphere and the standard of education in girls' madrasas are much better than those of boys. While the madrasas at Malegaon, Rampur and Azamgarh give education up to *Alimiyat* and *Fazilat*, most madrasas teach up to the secondary level only, as is the case with most boys' madrasas. Almost all girls' madrasas teach Dars-i-Nizami, but in view of the fact that women are not allowed to become *muftis* and *maulavis*, the *fiqh* (Islamic jurisprudence) course is much reduced for the girls.

As mentioned above, a girls' madrasa, a branch of the Jamiat-al-Falah at Azamgarh (Balariaganj), is a madrasa run by the Jamaat-e-Islami, and teaches the latter's syllabus. Its syllabus, as given by Qamr Uddin, is being given here.[83] It has all the standard subjects—Arabi grammar (*nahw*), syntax (*sarf*), composition (*insha'*), memorization of selected *suras* of the Quran and *tajweed* (correct pronunciation and manner of reciting the Quran) from Arabi *auwal* (class 1 of Secondary school) onwards. In addition there is home science and English. From Arabi *som* (class 3) *fiqh, hadiths* and *usool-e-hadith* (principles of understanding hadith) are added. From the next class *usool-e-fiqh* and *usool-e-tafsir* are also added. There is no substantial difference in this course and that of Dars-i-Nizami. Possibly, the courses are shortened. Home science and English are included and they continue even in senior classes. Interestingly, the degree of *Alima* (usually regarded as equal to class 12) is given after only five years of Arabi classes. Even if we add five years of primary classes, which are hardly ever up to the mark, this makes it equivalent to class 10 only. The explanation given is that this is done in view of the limitation of girls' capacities!

7.4. A FIRSTHAND ACCOUNT OF A GIRLS' MADRASA

The best glimpse into a girls' madrasa, its teaching and general milieu comes from the wonderfully sincere account of Winkelmann who spent more than a year within the madrasa. She tells us that the girls were between the ages of twelve and seventeen years. At first she found it difficult to establish rapport with them but later on they became very friendly. Teachers, especially the Principal was very helpful, and the former talked freely with her. Winkelmann also tells how these girls never sat idle, studied laboriously, observed strict *purdah*, and could not go out of the four walls of the madrasa, except when their guardians came to take them home for holidays. She further narrates how optimum piety was encouraged in every respect.[84] The madrasa is affiliated to the Tablighi Jamaat and the latter's ideology has a deep impact upon the teachers and girls. The author tells us about the views of the founder of the madrasa: 'to improve the personal life of the students with the aim of increasing religious consciousness' among them.[85]

Winkelmann observes that neither the teachers nor the students were familiar with the alternative type of education, and therefore nurtured negative stereotypes of the latter. More importantly, they were not familiar with the world outside of their madrasas, and were hardly capable of coping with any eventuality of life, even less than other illiterate women of the neighbourhood.[86] However, the Principal acknowledged that common education for girls till the age of *purdah* is good (largely confined to primary education).[87]

The Madrasat-al-Banat has nursery and primary sections also. Winkelmann has given the syllabus of both primary and secondary classes as Appendix. But there are discepancies in her account, therefore we are only giving the general account of the syllabus given by her in the main text of her work.

The curriculum of the madrasa consists of five years. It is preceded by primary education. The first or preparatory year consists of memorization of some portions of the Quran, learning *tajaweed* or the correct manner of reciting the Quran, learning other Islamic fundamentals and rituals. In addition students also learn *fiqh* and Islam's history, as well as Arabic and Urdu languages. The second year introduces *hadiths* and *tafsir*, which continue in the third and fourth year. The fifth year's course is like that of the Arabi *hashtum* (class 8 which is equivalent to class 12 of regular school) of Deoband, and includes all the *hadiths* and one or two *tafsirs*. For girls there is also a prescribed book, *Fazail-e-Amah* whose daily reading is compulsory. The emphasis seems more on discipline and nurturing of piety than on academic knowledge.[88] The author tells us that though the syllabus includes science, mathematics, Hindi and English, in actual practice no other subject apart from English was being taught.[89]

As in most madrasas, Thursdays were fixed for discussion and *taqrir* (rhetorical speeches). The madrasa's emphasis was on 'calling to faith' (*da'wa*), and speeches were largely centred round it. Many of the speeches were in Arabic, but were translated in Urdu for everybody to understand. Often neighbouring women also came to hear these speeches. Sometimes the girls were sent, along with teachers and male escorts, to neighbouring Muslim areas on their mission of calling everyone to faith, which mainly means telling them of the 'true' Islam (as understood by the Tablighis). Winkelmann says that even though they were always in *burqa*, the girls enjoyed these outings.[90] The restriction on radio and TV was easy to follow for residential students, as they could not access them in the madrasa. But the girls coming from neighbouring areas also had strict instructions not to go in for these un-Islamic indulgences. They were not allowed even to wear minimum jewellery or colourful clothes.

The founder of the madrasa spoke to the author in favour of women's education, even though by it he did not mean modern education. He also told her that *shari'a* allows the women to work outside their homes, provided they wear *burqa* and work in a gender segregated environment![91] The madrasa had only female teachers except one male to teach *hadiths*. When the time for his class came, the girls in *burqa* went to an upper storey much prior to his time. There they waited for him. And the teacher delivered his sermon from the ground floor which reached the girls through microphones![92] Of course, there is no question of any communication between the teacher and students, or getting queries cleared in such a scenario.

Winkelmann gives a vivid and interesting account of how the students tried to convert her to the only 'true religion—Islam'. Not only did they pursue her to that effect, they used an amusing, practical and ingenious approach to trick her into admitting that she had actually got converted to Islam![93] This happened because *da'wa* or calling others to Islam is the core element of the ideology of the Tablighi movement whose patrons were founders of the madrasa. The episode expresses not only the piety and religiosity inculcated in the students but also the fact that their talents are hardly used, far less encouraged, in the strict confines of a girls' madrasa.

The author observes that not only were the madrasa teachers and girls completely out of touch with the outside world, they were also protected from the religion and practices of the nearby *mazar* of Hazarat Nizamuddin Auliya, a great Sufi saint. It is because the Jamaat is against such practices as bowing before the *mazar*, or singing *qawwalis* and *nats* praising Nabi Muhammad and the saint. They were trained to live a life of austerity, not wear any ornaments or good clothes. They were also taught to show contempt for simple pleasures of ordinary life, as singing on the occasion of marriage which is so common in Indian society, or seeing TV. As the author observes, the students had totally 'internalized the world-view of the founder's community'.[94]

There are three fundamental weaknesses of this system of madrasa education for girls. The first two are common to both girls' and boys' madrasas. First, most madrasas proper start with Arabi *auwal* (first), while some have one year's preparatory class. But no one knows what happens before the beginning of madrasa education, that is, what is the child's level of knowledge. Since modern subjects are not taught in most Arabi madrasas, it is assumed that children have completed five years of primary education in which modern subjects are taught. But if children have studied in maktabs, as most of those who come to madrasas for higher studies do, they would not have studied any modern subject, excepting Arabic and Urdu alphabets, elementary arithmetic, and only in some cases some Hindi and English. Because of this presumption, and Muslim leaders' giving lesser importance to maktabs and their syllabus, Muslim children studying in madrasas remain forever ignorant of not only modern knowledge but also the conditions and demands of modern society. Of course, this is not true of the very big madrasas which have primary sections, but they are very few. And even then, they do not encourage extracurricular reading.

The second weakness has been mentioned several times in the present study. It is that most subjects taught in these madrasas date back almost a full millennium. Both the level of knowledge and the conditions of the world around us have been totally transformed since then. But madrasa students, both boys and girls, are still being taught the same subjects through the same books.

The third weakness relates especially to girls' madrasas. They are forced to live in a segregated atmosphere. Their lives are not only extremely austere and bereft of all fun, by studying in the madrasa they lose all contact with the outside world, and become even less capable of handling real life situations in the wider society. The knowledge acquired can at best be by rote, and whatever positive influence such a knowledge has would be due to the impact of the general atmosphere of the madrasa and its strict discipline. The rest is the result of a kind of brain washing in which the subject starts by assuming that whatever is being taught is the final truth about everything. Such a knowledge does not lead either to the blooming forth of the individual's personality, or to her being better integrated with the society.

Thus emphasis on, or even enforcement of, regressive *shari'a* rules and norms and madrasa education of girls feed on each other; and the lifestyle of those who are influenced by either the madrasa values and ambience, or the *maulavis* and *imams* of their local mosque continues to be extra conservative and resistant to change with time.

NOTES

1. See E. van Donzel, W.P. Heinrichs and G. Lacomte, eds., *The Encyclopaedia of Islam*, New Edition, Leiden: E.J. Brill, vol. IV, 1978, p. 171; Mircea Eliade, ed., *The Encyclopedia of Religion*, New York: Macmillan Publishing Company, vol. 7, p. 303.
2. *The Encyclopaedia of Islam*, op. cit., p. 171.
3. *The Spirit of Islam: A History of the Evolution and Ideals of Islam with a Life of the Prophet*, Delhi: Low Price Publications, 1990, pp. 137-8.
4. *The Encyclopaedia of Islam*, op. cit., p. 172.
5. Ibid., pp. 172 ff.
6. Ibid., p. 173.
7. Quran LXXXVI. 8-9; XCI. 18, 20. See also Ameer Ali, op. cit., pp. 152 ff.
8. *The Encyclopedia of Religion*, op. cit., pp. 309-10, 149-50.
9. See Leila Ahmed, *Women and Gender in Islam: Historical Roots of a Modern Debate*, New Haven: Yale University Press, 1995, pp. 81 ff.
10. *The Encyclopedia of Religion*, op. cit., pp. 309 ff. See also Leila Ahmed, op. cit., pp. 88 ff.
11. Ibid., vol. 14, p. 151.
12. Ibid., p. 150.
13. M. Mujeeb, *The Indian Muslims*, Delhi: Munshiram Manoharlal, 1995, p. 57.
14. This *hadith* is found both in *Timrizi* and *Mishkat*. See Ameer Ali, op. cit., p. 183.
15. 'After the formulation of four schools of thought, i.e. Hanafi, Shafai, Maliki and Hanbali, the gates if *ijtihad* (efforts for interpretation) were closed with the exception of Jafari. This was contrary even to the founders of the schools. None of them ever claimed finality which the later generations assigned to them. The doctrine of *taqlid* (faithful adherence) was emphasized. This attitude in part was due to the fear of rationalism and analytical thought.' Abdul Qadir Badauni, quoted in S.M. Azizuddin Husain, 'Introduction', in Husain, *Madrasa Eduation in India: Eleventh to Twenty-First Century*, New Delhi: Kanishka, 2005, p. 3; also see *The Encyclopedia of Religion*, op. cit., vol. 14, p. 152; Mujeeb, op. cit., p. 57.
16. Mujeeb, op. cit., p. 57.
17. See *The Encyclopedia of Islam*, vol. IX, 1997, op. cit., pp. 321-2; also 'Sharia' *Wikipedia, the free Encyclopedia*, at the website http://en.wikipedia.org/wiki/sharia.

18. See the 'Tablighi Jamaat' in Wikipedia, at the website: en.wikipedia. org/wiki/Tablighti_Jamaat; and 'Great Movements of the Twentieth Century', no. 3, 'The Jamaat', by Mumtaz Ahmad, at the website http//www.icna.org/tm/greatmovements.htm.
19. See Dougles E. Goodfriend, 'Changing Concepts of Caste and Status among Old Delhi Muslims', in Imtiaz Ahmad (ed.), *Modernization and Social Change Among Muslims in India*, New Delhi: Manohar, 1983, pp. 119 ff.
20. Examples are Imrana, Mukhtaran Mai and the relatively recent case of a woman ordered to be gang raped as a revenge to her family by the village panchayat, the latter two in Pakistan. The court, acting according to *shari'a*, ordered her to be punished by 100 lashes plus imprisonment while leaving her rapists untouched. (The former was changed due to international pressure.) There have been other cases of women being flogged for their alleged adultery while the males have been left untouched, all in the name of Islamic *shari'a*, in various parts of Pakistan. Based on Newspaper reports.
21. The following interviews are carefully recorded with simultaneous extensive notes by me.
22. See *Encyclopedia of Religion*, vol. 14, 'Sunnah', pp. 150 ff.
23. See the articles of Lucius Oulaw, 'Lifeworlds, Modernity and Philosophical Praxis', and Richard J. Bernstein, 'Incommensurability and Otherness Revisited', in Eliot Deutsch (ed.), *Culture and Modernity: East-West Philosophical Perspectives*, Delhi: Motilal Banarsidass, 1994, pp. 21 ff., 88 ff., etc. There is a large corpus of literature on this theory in the Continent.
24. See the author, *Ethical Relativism and Universalism*, Delhi: Motilal Banarsidass, 2001, chapters 3 & 4, pp. 75 ff., 123 ff.
25. See Asghar Ali Engineer 'Shari'ah, Women and Traditional Society', *Islam and Modern Age Series*, August 2005.
26. Ibid.
27. 'Islam, Women and Gender Justice', in Asghar Ali Engineer (ed.), *Islam, Women and Gender Justice*, New Delhi: Gyan Publishing House, 2001, pp. 24–5.
28. Ibid., p. 25.
29. Ibid., pp 25–6.
30. Ibid., p. 26.
31. Ibid., p. 27.
32. Ibid., p. 27.
33. Ibid., p. 28.
34. Ibid., p. 33.

35. Ibid., p. 28.
36. Ibid., p. 29.
37. Ibid., p. 37. Cf. 'My point is that in modern times one has to bear in mind the rights of women. One cannot simply quote a ruling given more than a thousand years ago to decide a case in twenty-first century (here the case of Imrana).' 'Shria'h, Women and Traditional Society', op. cit.
38. Engineer, *Islam, Women and Gender Justice*, p. 35.
39. Ibid., p. 37.
40. Leila Ahmed, *Women and Gender in Islam: Historical Roots of a Modern Debate*, pp. 42 ff.
41. See ibid., pp. 47 ff.
42. See ibid., pp. 60 ff., 72 ff., 79 ff., etc.
43. See ibid., p. 62.
44. See ibid., p. 62.
45. See ibid., pp. 64 ff.
46. Ibid., pp. 65–6.
47. See ibid., pp. 79 ff.
48. See ibid., pp. 85 and 83 ff.
49. Ibid., p. 88.
50. Ibid., p. 87.
51. Ibid., p. 88.
52. See Naila Minai, *Women in Islam: Tradition and Transition in the Middle-East*, London: John Murray, 1981, pp. 9 ff.
53. See ibid., pp. 26 ff.
54. Quoted in ibid., p. 25.
55. Quoted in Iqtidar Husain Siddiqui, 'Madrasa Education in Medieval India', in S.M. Azizuddin Husain (ed.), *Madrasa Education in India: Eleventh to Twenty-First Century*, p. 19.
56. See *Wikipedia*, at http//en.wikipedia.org./wiki/main_page-Fiqh, and ibid, at Ibn_Khaldum
57. See Ahmed, op. cit., pp. 88–9.
58. Ibid., p. 89.
59. Coulson quoted in ibid., p. 90.
60. Coulson and Doreen Hinchcliffe, quoted in ibid., pp. 91–2.
61. Coulson quoted in ibid., p. 90.
62. Ibid., p. 90.
63. Ibid., p. 94.
64. Ameer Ali, *The Spirit of Islam*, p. 182.
65. Ibid., pp. 183–4.
66. See note 55 supra.
67. Based on *Fiqh-us-sunnah*. . .Website presenting true Islam, peace-

ful, tolerant, rational. . . 'at www.allahuakbar.net/fiqh/index. htm and 'Fiqh' *Wikipedia, the free Encyclopedia* at http://en. wikipedia.org/wiki.fiqh

68. See Hamza Ali, 'Ironies of History: Contradictions of the Khilafat Movement', in Mushirul Hasan (ed.), *Islam, Communities and the Nation: Muslim Identities in the South Asia*, New Delhi: Manohar, 1998, pp. 25 ff.

69. Ayesha's brother-in-law left one thousand concubines, Caliph Ali acquired nine wives after the death of Fatima; and his son married and divorced one hundred women. Leila Ahmed, op. cit., p. 80. (This is based on Ahmed's account; I am not sure of the historical facts.)

70. See Naila Minai, op. cit., pp. 10–14.

71. For a realistic description of the pitiable conditions of divorced women in India see 'Muslim Women in the Indian Subcontinent', in Mariam Allana (ed.), *Muslim Women and Islamic Tradition: Studies in Modernisation*, New Delhi: Kanishka, 2000, pp. 40 ff.

72. See Goodfriend, 'Changing Concepts of Caste and Status among Old Delhi Muslims', in *Modernization and Social Change Among Muslims in India*, p. 129.

73. See Hasan Ali, 'Elements of Caste among the Muslims in a District in South Bihar', in Imtiaz Ahmad (ed.), *Caste and Social Stratification Among Muslims in India*, New Delhi: Manohar, 1978, p. 27.

74. See notes 35 and 36 supra.

75. See the Wikipedia, free Encyclopedia site for an introductory description of Tablighi Jamaat at http//www.icna.org/tm/great movement3.htm./ also http.www.en.wikipedia.org/wiki/Tablighi Jamaat. Also see Shail Mayaram, 'Rethinking Meo-identity: Cultural Faultline, Syncretism, Hybridity or Liminality?', and Muhammad Talib, 'The Tablighis in the Making of Muslim Identity', in Mushirul Hasan (ed.), *Islam, Communities and the Nation: Muslim Identities in South Asia,* New Delhi: Manohar, 1998, pp. 283 ff. and 307 ff.

76. For an excellent study of the gradual start of Muslim girls' education see Gail Minault, *Secluded Scholars: Women's Education and Muslim Social Reform in Colonial India*, New Delhi: Oxford University Press, 1998, pp. 61 ff.; also see Patricia Jeffery, Roger Jeffery, and Craig Jeffrey, 'The First Madrasa: Learned *Mawlwis* and the Educated Mother', in Jan-Peter Hartung and Helmut Reifeld (eds.), *Islamic Education, Diversity and National*

Identity: Dini Madaris in India Post 9/11, New Delhi: Sage, 2006, pp. 227 ff.

77. See Gail Minault, op. cit., pp. 215 ff.
78. See ibid., pp. 267 ff., especially, p. 307.
79. See Zoya Hasan and Ritu Menon, *Educating Muslim Girls: A Comparison of Five Indian Cities*, New Delhi: Women Unlimited, 2005, pp. 50–1.
80. See ibid., pp. 71 ff.
81. 'As soon as a daughter reached 9 or 10 years of age, the mother's biggest worry was marrying her off.' 'Muslim Women in the Indian Sub-continent', in Mariam Allana, ed., op. cit., p. 53, also see ibid, pp. 49 ff.
82. *From Behind the Curtain: A Study of a Girls' Madrasa in India*, Amsterdam University Press, 2005. Winkelmann stayed in the madrasa, taught the girls English language, and gives in the book an excellent first-hand account of its general milieu based on personal experience.
83. *Hindustan ki Dini Darsgahein: Kul Hind Survey* (Urdu), New Delhi: Hamdard Education Society, pp. 352 ff.
84. See Winkelmann, op. cit., pp. 50 ff.
85. See ibid., pp. 46 ff.
86. See ibid., pp. 26–7, 48 ff.
87. See ibid., p. 27.
88. See ibid., pp. 67 ff.
89. See ibid., pp. 47–8.
90. See ibid., pp. 46, 56–7.
91. See ibid., pp. 46, 64 ff.
92. See ibid., p. 72.
93. See ibid., pp. 42–3.
94. Ibid., pp. 54 ff., 79 ff., 85 ff.

6

Madrasa 'Reforms' (I): Reforms from Within

1. SOME INTRODUCTORY OBSERVATIONS

1.1. MUSLIM 'BACKWARDNESS' AND MADRASA EDUCATION

We have been hesitant to take up the subject of 'Madrasa reforms' which has been discussed and analysed threadbare by three groups—the government, the 'secular' intellectuals and the traditional Muslim ideologues. Could we possibly add anything worthwhile to the same by further discussion? At the same time, it is the most important subject, especially in the context of the ever increasing number of madrasas and the determining influence of *ulama* on the masses. Even after reading Muslim writers' passionate defence of Madrasa system for several years, we are still convinced of our starting point that all or at least most of Indian children must study in common modern schools, because studying in separate educational institutions leads to the formation of separate identities, as a result of which people remain Hindus or Muslims or Sikhs, rather than Indians.

It can be questioned here that educational institutions are not the only factors in the formation of identities; the role of larger society and the fact whether it provides a rightful place to the 'minorities' are equally important. I fully agree with this assertion, and acknowledge that in the last few decades there have been developments which have tended to harden separate religious identities. However, two things cannot be denied: first, that madrasas do stress on a universal Muslim *umma*, and thereby emphasize pan-Islamic identity, indirectly undermining the Indian identity of their students. Second, the minds of children and adolescents are impressionable and what they learn and absorb in their early years remains with them all through their lives. While a large number of middle-class intellectuals come out strongly in favour of madrasa education, almost all of them send their own children to English medium schools who generally become successful in the civic society. At the same time they lament the poor educational, social and economic status of Muslims, as well as the near absence of Muslims in higher government and other jobs.

The Sachar Committee Report has documented the ground realities which were already known to all of us. We have discussed the Report and its findings in chapter 2. Without doubt a majority of the Muslims are both educationally and economically backward. But instead of indulging in blame game, would it not be better that together we find out the complex causes for the unfortunate state of affairs and also their possible remedies.

One of the government's immediate responses to the Sachar Committee Report was its reassertion of a better implementation of the 'revised' Scheme for the 'modernization' of madrasas. This seems to imply that if Muslims are to be educated and brought out of their pitiable socio-economic and educational backwardness, that goal can be achieved only through madrasas. Even if Muslim clerics and some intellectuals agree with this presumption, it is an entirely wrong one. However, it is still true at the ground level that a large number of Muslim children, especially in the villages where the condition of government schools is still worse, go to maktabs and madrasas for their education. Does madrasa education, or even its half-hearted 'modernization', provide an answer or solution to Muslims' overall backwardness? We will try to search some answers for this crucial question in this and the following chapters. The present chapter deals with the issue of 'reforms' from within as it were, while in the next chapter we would try to deal with the vexatious issue of introduction of modern subjects in madrasas, mostly on the initiative of the government.

Assuming the educational and economic backwardness of a large number of Muslims, we need to try to find the reasons of this backwardness. In chapter 2 we tried to understand and analyse the socio-economic and psychological reasons for a large number of Muslims opting to reject modern school education for their children. There we found, that apart from poverty, the influence of family conditions, *beradari*, emotional closeness to madrasa *maulavis* and the somewhat alien ambience of modern schools make the Muslim parents opt for madrasa education for their children. There are other objections to modern education as it exists in contemporary India, which has also been taken up in the aforementioned chapter, and some of which we will return to in the last chapter. When all is said, we can still sincerely assert that regular education is the panacea of most of the problems of the majority of Muslims. This is, of course, not denied by anyone. The question is—which type of education do the Muslim children need and which institutions could provide them that education?

Could it be that Muslims are not finding government or even private jobs for the simple reason that a majority of them do not have sufficient educational qualifications? The possibility of discrimination against them, which is often cited as the reason for the almost insignificant presence of Muslims in high paid jobs or even institutions of higher learning, would come only after the applicants are found qualified in their education and capabilities which, in turn presupposes modern education.

Syed Abul Hashim Rizvi repeats the argument most frequently cited for Muslims' preference for madrasas for their children's education; that is, madrasas are doing a wonderful job of providing free education to a large number of Muslim children, as often they are the only option available for their education. Rizvi adds, that 'A vast majority of Muslim students acquire their school education either in *madaris* or in Muslim managed secular schools (usually in Urdu medium).' The author admits that while the teaching of modern subjects is non-existent in madrasas, it is provided in a very poor manner in the minority managed schools.[1] Given the absence, or poor quality, of modern education being provided in these institutions, it is no surprise that the Muslim youth find themselves inferior to those educated in modern schools when facing the challenges and requirements of twenty-first century.

As Imtiaz Ahmad observes, it is the middle class that most puts a premium on education, and Muslims do not have a middle class, largely because almost the entire Muslim middle class migrated to Pakistan at the time of Partition, leaving mostly peasants, artisans and other poor Muslims here. Thereafter a proper middle class could not be developed among them probably because of a lack of enlightened leadership. Economically there are a sufficient number of well-off Muslim families but they do not have the typical attitudes and values of a modern middle class, and therefore do not value modern education as the earlier middle-class Muslims did.

A contributing factor is the fact that a large number of relatively underprivileged Muslims live in ghettos. The majority community's aggressive stance towards them may or may not be responsible for this preference of Muslims to live together in congested localities. May be they are scared of Hindus (which I do not believe to be the case in most areas of our country); may be, they have a minority complex which leads them to assert their Muslim identity more, and which is best preserved by living in exclusively Muslim colonies. In these colonies the *ulama*, as well as other fundamentalist and even communalist leaders, have a determinative say. Muslim women hardly ever venture out; men go out for work but then return to their ghettos, and constantly gather together under the influence of these regressive leaders. A separate Muslim identity is constantly being created, strengthened and preserved. No one is allowed to act in a way which is perceived as against *shari'a*.

More Muslim women are taking to *purdah* (veil); and more Muslims are being encouraged to dress and behave in a traditional manner. Many conservative and obscurantist customs and practices are being adopted by the masses in an effort to achieve social mobility, a process which in the Hindu context is called *Sanskritization* and in the Muslim context may be called *Islamization*. An important part of this religious-social mobility is outward religiosity which includes regular *namaz* at the local mosque, *roza* (fast) during the month of Ramzan, and so on. An integral part of this effort at Islamization is the education of their children. Though modern education is not generally frowned upon and the use of modern technology for economic gains is very welcome, the overall *mahaul* (atmosphere) is such that madrasas are preferred for the education of their children. One or two madrasas (not only maktabs) are always available in these Muslim localities. Boys may go to these madrasas, or they may go to nearby government or private schools. Girls are definitely sent to maktabs/madrasas, as they are not to be sent 'outside' after puberty.[2]

Let us remember here that it is not the fate of Muslim children alone but of all Indian children whose parents cannot afford high fee of private schools. The only difference between these two groups of children is that while poor children from other religious communities still go to government schools and get a modicum of 'modern' education, a considerable number of Muslim children in that economic category are sent to madrasas and are deprived of any 'modern' knowledge. Thus the underprivileged children of other religious communities remain in the mainstream of the society and are conscious of the opportunities and other aspects of modern life, even though they are not successful in competing with private school pass-outs among urban youth, while Muslim children, either going to madrasas or even going to modern schools but living in ghettos, are deprived of this contact with modern society.

A CASE FOR MADRASA SYSTEM OF EDUCATION

Almost every writer on madrasa education praises madrasas, asserting rhetorically that madrasas are doing a splendid job giving education to Muslim children who have no other alternative, an education leading to the full development of the students' personality. Most writers, such as Manzoor Ahmad and Shoyeb Ansari, justify the system remaining within the Islamic framework. They point out how significant the contribution of madrasas is towards the state goal of universalization of education; how madrasas not only provide education but also boarding and lodging; how poor Muslim parents have no other option but to send their children to madrasas; and how they save thousands of Muslim children from vagrancy. Such apologetic writings defending the madrasa system of education is found in Urdu magazines and books as well as English language writings. The few years of NDA government's Hindutva-inspired policies gave a fillip to such writings. Manzoor Ahmad, an enthusiastic supporter of madrasa education, asserts:

At present there are more than 30,000 such non-governmental educational institutions, spread all over the Indian Union. This is the largest people's endeavor, on absolutely voluntary basis, in the field of education in history anywhere in the world. These madaris do not accept government aid for fear of dilution of their character and charter. Their contribution towards mass literacy, theological education and maintenance and deepening of Islamic identity has been incalculable and invaluable.[3]

Ahmad further opines that, 'For various reasons, however, there has been stagnation in the development of these madaris, more so after 1947.'[4] This is a strange assertion, as all other writers assert that the concerted efforts of the *ulama* have led to even more madrasas being established throughout India post-Independence.[5] It is a well-acknowledged fact that there has been a spurt in this activity since the 1980s. Such statements as Ahmad's express a sense of being wronged in post-Independence India and strengthen the divide between different communities. Ahmad is also a great protagonist of community-specific education and believes that the unity and integrity of worldwide *umma* can be preserved only through such an education. He advocates:

[A]n integrated and unified system of education bridging the gulf between the two systems in order to ensure the preservation of *our* civilization and culture, and access to the opportunities of an industrializing society [. . .] in order to turn out well-educated young men with Islamic conscience and *worthy heirs of the great Muslim civilization of the first millennium* (italics added).[6]

Ahmad constantly refers to 'our society', 'our culture', 'our people'; this 'our' consciously excludes the rest of Indian populace. He goes on to discuss how 'our people' need knowledge of modern sciences, and since they are against Islamic values, an all-out effort must be made to unify Islamic values with the knowledge of modern sciences. His work is full of such statements as 'one of the goals of modern Islamic education is the technological advancement of *Muslim societies*'; 'Therefore the study of social sciences also will have to be reorganized in order to serve the *Millat*'. Such an education system 'will decide the quality of life for *our people* in future. It will equip them to build a vibrant and dynamic *society for their children*. . .' (italics added).[7]

Most apologetic writers have a sensible argument, the gist of which is that the madrasas are doing the job they are meant to do, that is producing experts in Islamic learning, and therefore there is no need for their so-called modernization, or even reform in their curriculum. Muhammadullah Khalili Qasami quotes Mufti Taqi Usmani with great approval:

The question is, if the madrasas have focused all their attention on Islamic Sciences, and they produce no doctor, no scientist, no economist, so why people create havoc. Are the Islamic sciences, such as Tafseer, Hadith, Fiqh, Kalam and others, not too valuable to be taught in special institutions and produce Ulama specialized in these sciences?[8]

Qasmi agrees: 'The madrasas aim at producing Ulama who are masters in Quran, hadith and concerning sciences which are about 17 in number.'[9] Qasmi is clearly against the 'modernization' of madrasas. If it is undertaken by the government, it would rob the traditional autonomy of the madrasas and undermine the very purpose for which they exist, that is, teaching Islamic sciences. Farhat Hasan rightly points out that 'when we attack the *madaris* for ignoring modern education, we overlook the fact that their prime objective was to provide religious education and lessons in moral purification'. He traces the history of madrasas during the colonial period and contends that the sacred-secular dichotomy was foreign to Islam, but with the role of providers of secular knowledge for future state officials being taken away from them, and due to the confrontation with the Western civilization, these *madaris* started to perceive themselves as the preservers of Islamic religion and culture.[10] With their self-perception changed thus, they transformed themselves into *dini madaris*, and that is their goal now.

However, in their enthusiasm to extol madrasa education, writers such as Qasmi further claim that madrasas teach every possible subject under the sun—both traditional and modern. In fact, Qasmi declares that madrasas teach secular subjects more than religious ones! Among these secular subjects he counts Arabic grammar, Arabic language and literature (Greek), logic, history, geography, rhetoric, and so on.[11] Of course, he does not tell us that the history and geography are of Muslim countries alone.

The consensus on this subject seems to be that the purpose of madrasa education is to teach students detailed Islamic subjects, so that they become experts in the same, capable of leading the rest of the Muslim populace on the Islamic way of life. They also assert that the curriculum of madrasa education as it exists now, obviously from long centuries, is perfectly suited for that purpose. At most, minor changes in books or portions of books that are to be taught can be brought about.

1.3. SOME CRITICAL OBSERVATIONS

The question we need to ask is, can the education being imparted in madrasas be a substitute for the modern education we are talking about? That is, can a syllabus that was framed several centuries ago prepare students to successfully face the challenges of modern times? Can the secular subjects these writers talk about as being taught in madrasas be of any relevance in today's times?

We have pointed out from time to time how the two assertions, that the poor Muslim children have no alternative but to study in madrasas; and that madrasas are contributing in a big manner to the national goal of universal education, are not exactly true. We have answered in detail the first contention about Muslim children not having any avenues of eduation in chapter 2. There are government schools in most Muslim neighbourhoods, though we agree with the criticism that they provide poor quality education, and have very poor infrastructure. In this situation, it is the duty of entire nation to see that conditions in primary and secondary government schools are considerably improved. We shall return to this issue again in our concluding chapter. However sending Muslim children to madrasas is not a solution of this problem.

It is also noteworthy that not only government schools but even most madrasas provide relatively poor quality eduation. Madrasas being mostly autonomous, there is no check on the quality of education provided in them, as well as their infrastructure, such as a proper building, toilet, drinking water, and at least a black board. Mohammad Shoyeb Ansari is a conservative writer, who has done a survey of various issues related to madrasa education among madrasa students. Even he admits that there is generally a poor 'educational climate' in madrasas, and adds that 'These things develop inferiority complex among students and when they go back to the society after long segregated life of madrasa, it becomes difficult for them to adjust with their new surroundings.'[12] His conclusions, supposedly based on the ambivalent responses of students, include: Texts and bookish knowledge are overemphasized. Teachers come often unprepared and even lose temper if asked for some clarification. Extra curricular activities are not encouraged. If correct, his survey projects students as even more conservative than the *ulama*. However, he does not change his basic approach regarding the most important issue of the need to change the centuries' old madrasa *nisab* which has become quite irrelevant for modern times, but which he does not think needs any substantial changes.[13]

The argument that madrasas are doing a good job of producing *'ulama* who are experts in Islamic sciences', may well be true. But here is the big question, if madrasas are expected to be the educational institutions of most Muslim children, as persons like Qamar Uddin hope,[14] then what would they all do in their later life? Faced with the criticism that madrasa pass-outs do not have many career options, it is sometimes argued that madrasa education is not meant for teaching the way to earning one's livelihood. This argument is debunked by several Muslim scholars and clerics, including the Shahi Imam of Fatehpuri Masjid, Mufti Mukkarram Ahmad. The latter contends that all students studying in madrasas hope to earn a living after passing out. If they do not get good jobs, they open their own madrasas (which the Imam Ahmad calls teaching shops).[15] A boy having spent 12–13 years studying in a madrasa naturally expects that he would be able to earn a living after that. Let us remember that till the coming of British, the goal of madrasa education was to produce *qazis* and *muftis* who would get government jobs thereafter. Children from higher social strata used to study in madrasas to qualify for these jobs. In fact, most of the Dars-i-Nizami was meant to train officers of the Mughal court, and hence contains a large number of the 'rational sciences', as well as very detailed *fiqh*.

Present-day madrasa pass-outs can at best expect jobs as *maulanas* in various madrasas to earn between Rs. 1,000 to

Rs. 2,500 (only in very big madrasas or Darul-Ulooms salaries are higher). Or they could be employed as *Qaries* (who recite the Holy Quran), *Imams* in *masjids*, or *ustads* in maktabs with even lower salaries. Failing all these, they could open their own autonomous madrasas and provide religious education of questionable standards.[16] Their chief interest becomes to perpetuate a mindset in which they remain dominant in Muslim society, and which they instil in the minds of the common people using the doctrine of *taqlid* as the very essence of Islam. Madrasa graduates, having such low-income jobs as a career alternative is only one side of the story. We have also to consider the less than desirable effects of the regressive mindset promoting blind following of the written word being instilled in the masses by the madrasa-educated *ulama*. As Mushir-Ul-Haq rightly observes, 'the *ulama* have undoubtedly considerable influence through the institution of madrasas and *fatwa* over Muslim public opinion'. He adds that 'As a result the Muslims have developed a religious attitude which makes them look backwards, away from the modern way of life.'[17]

The Muslim masses are religiously, emotionally and socially extremely dependent upon the madrasa-educated *ulama*. They believe in whatever the *ulama* tell them and dare not go against the latter's innumerable *fatwas*. They can 'modernize' or 'progress' only to the extent the *ulama* are 'modernized'. According to Mushir-Ul-Haq, the Muslims are more attached to their religion and religious identity than is usually realized by others. They unquestioningly rely on madrasa-educated *ulama* and their various *fatwas* for guidance in all matters. Our intellectuals have failed either to understand their profound attachment to their religion, or to convince them that secularism—and we would add modern education—are not against religion.[18]

It is high time that the defenders of madrasas acknowledge that madrasas are meant for those few boys who want to become religious specialists, but definitely not for the rest of Muslim children. Without undermining the Muslims' need for religious education, we must realize that in order to progress with the modern world, the majority of Muslim children, if not all, must get their education in mainstream schools. Our intention in trying to critique madrasa system of education is not to interfere in the rights or autonomy of minority institutions, rather to underline that they must be developed and even nurtured as institutions to preserve Islamic sciences and to train *muftis* and *ulama* as specialists in Islamic sciences. But they must not expect, nor should their well-wishers like the government, assume that most Muslim children would go to madrasas for their education.

Madrasa pass-outs also must not remain excessively conservative and even regressive in their views and approach, as their influence on the Muslim masses is tremendous. This leads us to the controversial issue of 'madrasa modernization'.

Before proceeding further let us take a cursory look at what madrasas teach to the future citizens of India. Let me quote Tariq Rahman, a Pakistani writer, about the syllabus of madrasas:

The Dars-i-Nizami has come to symbolize the stagnation and ossification of knowledge. It is taught through canonical texts which, however, are taught through commentaries (*sharh*); glosses or marginal notes (*hashiya*) and super commentaries (*taqarir*). There are commentaries upon commentaries explained by even more commentaries. For the South Asian students they no longer explain the original text, being themselves in Arabic. They have to be learned by heart which makes the students use only their memory and not their analytical powers. Indeed the assumption on which the Dars functions is that the past was a golden age in which all that was best has already been written. What remains to the modern age is merely to preserve it.[19]

Madrasa *nisab*, as well as the emphasis on memorization of given texts, and the general ambience of the madrasa system affirm the doctrine of *taqlid,* that is, blind obedience to the written word, which almost negates individual reason and even the dictates of conscience. Not only does the entire system go against the spirit of modern times, it even undermines the Prophet's own emphasis on reason. It would be pertinent to remember that as early as fourteenth century, the Sufi saint and thinker Sheikh Sharafuddin Maneri had complained how he was forced to learn several books on Arabic grammar, and how he wished that his teachers had made him learn the Quran in the same way, instead of those (apparently irrelevant) books.[20] Agha Khan (early twentieth century), admittedly no great authority on this subject and yet whose contribution to the education of Muslim children in the subcontinent is substantial, was extremely critical of the madrasa system of education and its style of 'parrot like' teaching.[21]

There is no doubt that madrasa students are generally better disciplined and more fastidious in their religious practices. But since the textbooks are in Arabic, students do not understand them, at least not fully. Since writing is not given much importance, they are not able to understand what they are being taught, far less articulate it. Several Muslim scholars have acknowledged that all the energies and intellect of the children are spent in deciphering and memorizing the Arabic texts; understanding the content of the text can hardly be undertaken if reading it requires so much effort. No wonder, not only the students but the teachers of most madrasas are hardly conversant with Arabic language, that is, cannot understand, write, or talk in it. True, the text is supposedly 'explained' in Urdu, but do the teachers themselves have mastery over the text to teach it? If not, how do they explain their content to their students?

Significantly, there is a substantial number of *ulama* and even madrasa students who favour that the Arabic texts be studied in the original; that there is no need for them to be explained in the mother tongue of the student. In modern times it is now well recognized that at least in the earlier stages education should be provided in the mother tongue. Moreover, it is to be remembered that the Arabic language used in madrasa textbooks is very difficult and tortuous. It is written in an archaic style which has to be learnt with the help of a very elaborate and difficult grammar, including etymology of word, conjugation and other details, as well as logic (*mantiq*), as it is well recognized that the language is so difficult that it cannot be understood without first mastering the old system of logic. The fact is that there is almost a total concentration on the teaching of Arabic language, and the material being taught becomes rather secondary.

Here the views of Ameer Ali, the great Islamic thinker and nationalist leader of early twentieth century, are worth considering. According to him, it is the inner spirit that is much more important than the words of prayer. Moreover, the words that are used in prayer can be in any language, the idea being that the worshipper understands them:

Divine words rendered into any language retain their divine character and devotions offered in any tongue are acceptable to God. The Prophet himself had allowed his foreign disciples to say their prayers in their own tongue. He had expressly permitted others to recite the Koran in their respective dialects; and declared that it was revealed in seven languages. [. . .]

[. . .] Imam Abu Hanifa considered the recitation of *namaz* and also of the *Khutba* or sermon lawful and valid in any language.[22]

Shah Walliullah, the great pioneer reformer of eighteenth century, himself translated the Holy Quran into the Persian, since it was supposedly the *lingua franca* of the then Muslims. Of course, his assumption regarding Persian language was wrong, but the principle still holds that not the language but the spirit and content of prayer are more important. That is why, his son translated the text into Urdu language.[23] But the Shah's stance was not welcomed by his contemporary *ulama*, nor is it accepted now. The result is that a major portion of the energy and time of the students is spent trying to learn archaic Arabic, the rhetorical language of the *tafsirs* through which the Quran is taught in madrasas. If the Quran is thought to be so sacred that it must be read only in the original, then at least the other texts can be translated into Urdu.

Moreover, the knowledge contained in Arabic books is mostly not relevant for everyday life. Most subjects being taught are medieval both in their content and approach. Since no outside literature is allowed in the premises and no questioning of the stated position of the *maslak* to which madrasa belongs is ever allowed—*taqlid* or blind following of the written word being the norm—such an education can hardly sharpen the human intellect or even sensitize the human conscience or heart. As such madrasa teaching is a far cry from our present-day conception of education. To quote Ameer Ali again:

The present-day stagnation of the Muslim community is principally due to the notion which has fixed itself on the minds of generality of Moslems that the right to the exercise of private judgment ceased with the early legists, that the exercise of it in modern times is sinful. [. . .]

No account is taken of the altered circumstances in which Moslems are now placed; the conclusion at which these learned legists arrived several centuries ago are held to be equally applicable to the present day. [...] The Prophet had consecrated reason to the highest and noblest function of the human intellect. Our schoolmen and their servile followers have made its exercise a sin and a crime.[24]

We have referred to Ameer Ali's views in an earlier chapter too. If a thinker in the difficult circumstances of a century ago could think in these terms, why cannot our present writers and ideologues realize the demands of changing times? The need is to acknowledge that both the madrasa system of education and its syllabus Dars-i-Nizami, developed during Aurangzeb's time, are not suitable and beneficial for modern children, at least in their present form.

In an interesting article Arshad Alam describes the rigorous routine of madrasas, where no other views but those of the particular sect (*maslak*) that the madrasa subscribes to is entertained. 'Control,' he says, 'is inbuilt in the madrasa pedagogy, often going to the extent of control over students' bodies.' He adds that the madrasa system forms what he calls the 'habitus' of the students; he explains the 'habitus' as including 'the person's beliefs and dispositions and prefigures everything that a person may choose to do'.[25]

Thus not only the madrasa *nisab* but also the general ambience of the madrasas determine the thinking of their students and of all those in the society who are directly influenced by their views and attitudes. In fact, reasoning and questioning or ever trying to interpret the classical texts is prohibited in the madrasas. Saiyid Naqi Husain Jafri agues that 'These retrograde measures were in total defiance of the Quran and the *ahadith*.' He goes on to point out how the Quran and the *ahadith* always encourage new knowledge. However, as early as the eleventh and early twelfth centuries Ghazali and other theologians of Abbasid period had denied any place for reasoning in the field of 'revelation'. Jafri contends: 'The spirit of free inquiry and empirical investigation had, to quite some extent, been replaced by literal interpretation [*taqlid*] and strict adherence to the doctrines within the Islamic fold.'[26] He describes the university system which offers both employability and financial ease as 'a reservoir of knowledge that fosters free inquiry, tolerance and better understanding of the world around us'. He adds that compared to the

products of the modern system of education, 'the madrasa graduates seem to be lagging behind and this often results in a siege
mentality and near total alienation from the society'.[27]

As we have seen above, the apologetic writers on madrasa
education sometimes emphasize the conception of a global Muslim *umma* in a manner that seems to undermine the Muslims'
Indian identity. When Manzoor Ahmad talks of 'our' culture
and 'our' society, we get worried whether he even remembers
that he lives in India which has her own proud history, in which
Muslims of the second millennium so willingly participated to
develop a rich composite culture. Also what would be the effect
of such blatant communal approach on those innocent minds
who read it? As he means by 'our people', 'our culture' and 'our
society' only Muslims, their culture and society, how does he
anticipate that Muslims can live and build 'a society for their
children' which is segregated from the rest of the society and
polity? Can they, or any other so-called community, survive by
separating itself from the rest of the nation and identify themselves with other peoples (who happen to be constantly fighting
each other in the world)? He seems to provide an answer:

> We have to recognize the existence of a community which, amidst a
> variety of nationalities and cultures [. . .] is aspiring for *fundamental
> solidarity of its people* despite transitory differences. The curriculum
> has to help the community in translating this aspiration into reality,
> and also help the Indian Muslim community in maintaining its
> fraternal ties with other components of the great *Ummah*.[28]

True, the original Islam did anticipate one Muslims *umma*,
but that was in the days when Islam had not spread worldwide.
The Khilafat of the Ottoman Empire that Indian Muslims fought
for during India's freedom struggle was developed by fighting
and vanquishing other Muslim nations. Now, international
rivalries and conflicts in the so-called Muslim world have increased further. However, some kind of pan-Islamism is built in
the very conception of madrasas in modern times. As we have
noted in chapter 3, madrasas underwent two drastic changes in
the colonial period: First, their field of activity and financial
support shifted from the upper class Muslims or feudal lords to
the masses, who they found, practised an Islam very different

from their own conception of the religion. Hence they set about 'reforming' popular Islam. Second, they felt threatened by the onslaught of English education and Western culture, and therefore set about emphasizing their separate unique identity and implied superiority. Jan-Peter Hartung argues how the main aim of the *ulama* was to preserve their Islamic identity both against the Western rulers, as also against the majority Hindus whose influence lingered in the religion of the Muslim masses. He suggests that the madrasas were established to preserve this Islamic identity. He further contends that this identity was perceived in terms of pan-Islamism; and to emphasize the latter the need to study Arabic language as the storehouse of all Islamic knowledge was stressed.[29]

Granting both the Muslims' attachment to their religion, and their sense of separate identity which has been the result of concerted efforts by various Islamic organizations, the rhetoric of Ahmad and others in favour of a unified *umma* and a unified system of education for all Muslim nations, irrespective of their national circumstances, is bound to mislead young minds, and that is dangerous.

The building of separate and segregated identities within a nation-society is definitely against national interests; but it is also equally against the interests of Muslims. No person can live in isolation. Other scholars have sensibly argued that emphasis on Islamic identity and loyalty and love for one's nation can easily coexist, as every person has several identities. We agree with the above suggestion. The problem comes when one identity becomes predominant, thereby overwhelming other identities of a person or group. Madrasas as they exist today are doing just this, that is, emphasizing the Islamic identity of Indian Muslims at the cost of their Indian identity. This is what happened during the Khilafat movement in which the *ulama* took an active part and constantly emphasized the masses' religious identity which supposedly connected them to the whole world of Muslims or *umma*. Otherwise there was no reason for Indian Muslims to organize the Khilafat movement.[30] The influence of this mindset led even the 'nationalist' *ulama* of the Jamiyat-e-Ulama-e-Hind assert:

It is true that in a country like India where innumerable religions are found, every citizen has to be friendly and considerate to others. But it is also true that this concept of *muttahadah qaumiyat* (common nationality), that the Muslims should give up their own *Islamic culture* and be absorbed in a culture which is not their own, is completely wrong. [. . .] *To them [Indian Muslims] religious freedom is more important than political emancipation.* (italics in the original quote)[31]

Elsewhere we have argued in detail against communal identities which are built on one single dimension of human life, that is, religion.[32] People follow different religions, but they also belong to different regions, speak different languages, and belong to different castes (in India this is true for both Hindus and Muslims).[33] Above all, they are divided on the basis of education, economic status and habitat (rural or urban). Can Manzoor Ahmad assert that Muslims of North and South India are the same, or that an English-educated Muslim industrialist or IAS officer is unified inextricably with those poor Muslims who live in villages and send their children to madrasas? Will the latter share the problems of *roti, kapada aur makan* (minimum necessities of life) and *bijli, sadak, pani* (electricity, road, water) with the educated and financially well-off Muslims; or with their neighbours? Moreover everyday life and economic transactions presuppose interdependence. True, religion is a much more fundamental dimension of the lives of Muslims, but so it is with Hindus. Left to themselves Indian people have wonderfully adjusted to each other, shared innumerable problems relating to their economic status, various customs, and joys and sorrows. Unfortunately, they are instigated to assert their separate identities by politicians, respective religious leaders and above all by their respective well-educated middle-class 'intellectuals'. To quote Manzoor Ahmad again: 'We should also devise a composite curriculum for the study of Islamic culture for our students who are divided in sub-cultural groups based on their pre-Islamic cultural legacies, traditions and historical background.'[34]

Ahmad clearly states that conversion to Islam nullifies all pre-Islamic legacies, that is, regional and cultural identities, customs, norms and values, and by implication even post-Islamic national identity, because in their post-Islamic life Muslims must identify themselves with the Muslims of the world and de-identity themselves from their immediate neighbours and facts of history.

Secularists have tried to understand this phenomenon in terms of Hindus' aggressive 'Hindutva' stance, Muslims' minority complex and insecurity. That may be so, but the exclusive emphasis on Islamic history, geography and culture (in other countries), as being taught in the madrasa syllabus, and the communalism of Muslim intellectuals cited above, would not help the Muslims in any way. If India's Muslim masses are told that they primarily belong to the worldwide *umma*, thus rejecting their identity as Indians, they would not become effective members of this worldwide *umma* for the simple reason that no such *umma* exists. They would thus be left incapable of becoming good Indian citizens either.

In this context, Maulana Gilani's work provides a welcome change. In his monumental work he often seems to suggest that India is a Muslim country and Hindus are expected to study a common syllabus, largely consisting of Islamic disciplines. We do not agree with this view. However, Gilani writes wholly in the Indian context and there is no suggestion in his work for the need of Muslims to identify themselves with the worldwide *umma*. In addition there is never any suggestion of extra-territorial loyalties for Muslims in his work.

Most *ulama* of madrasas are loyal citizens. They also support the idea of religious tolerance (even though their conception of tolerance may be different than the popular one) as it is in the interests of Muslims that the majority Hindus and the state do not interfere in their religion. What is needed is to remove the excessive emphasis on a single worldwide *umma*. Nothing in real life corresponds to this myth. National boundaries and region-specific cultures and needs dictate the approaches and actions of Muslims situated in different circumstances. Everywhere Muslim nations are fighting each other, and even killing their co-religionists, as in Sudan and Iraq, mostly for self-interest, sometimes in the name of religious differences, as in Iraq.

We have referred to the subtle distinction between the two terms *umma* and *millat* on the one hand, and *kaum* or nationality on the other, made by Maulana Husain Ahmad Madni in chapter 1. It is tempting to quote his views again:

Millat implies a *shar* (way) or *din* (religion), while the word *kaum* means a group of people living together, held together by a common bond. This bond may be a religion, or country or race. [. . .] The

Hindustani qaum comprises every inhabitant of India, whether he speaks Urdu or Bengali, whether his colour is dark or fair, whether he is a Hindu or a Muslim, a Parsi or a Sikh. Every Hindustani, regardless of these differences, is an Indian.[35]

Typically, Mushirul Hasan criticizes Islamic conservatism. According to him, the conservatives' basic aim has remained unchanged from the colonial period, and that is 'the preservation of cultural and religious identity within the defined Islamic framework. Its more tangible manifestation has been resistance to modern education, opposition to the composite and syncretic trends in Indian Islam, and the tendency to thwart reformist initiatives.' Hasan agrees with Nehru that 'the Indian society was at no stage structured around religious solidarities, or polarized along "communal" lines'.[36] In contemporary society, the real need is good quality modern education for most, if not all, Indian children, including Muslims and all others who are socially and economically backward.

We repeat that we do not question the Muslims' right to establish their own religious institutions, nor do we question the need of Islamic education for Muslim children. How the latter could be ensured for the Muslim children without depriving them of modern education is the greatest issue for which we, like others, are trying to find a solution.

2. MADRASA 'REFORMS'

2.1. MADRASA REFORMS VS. MADRASA MODERNIZATION

The issue of 'madrasa reforms' is a complex and multi-dimensional one, but unfortunately it is discussed in simplistic terms, especially in the media. Muslim clerics' and most intellectuals' response to suggestions for 'reform' is also mostly clothed in simplistic terms.

Actually 'reform' (*islah*) in the Islamic context means 'reforming' or 'purifying' the Islam as practised by the masses. Deoband Madrasa has taken a leading role in this effort. It is only in a secondary sense that we can talk of 'reform' of madrasa system. However, the issue of 'reform' of the madrasa system has also been talked about a great deal. Various Muslim clerics and intellectuals have written and conferences are regularly held on the issue of 'reform'. Their unanimous conclusion is always the same— that all is well with the madrasa system. The system has produced great scholars and even scientists in earlier days, and the madrasas are capable of doing so even now. Often some cosmetic changes are suggested, to which we shall return presently.

Most people writing on the madrasa system of education and its 'reform' are of the view that it is an almost perfect system and does not need any change. The oft-repeated argument in favour of a *status quo* in the syllabus and functioning of madrasas is that the latter are meant for imparting religious education and aim at making their students morally upright and true Muslims, and they are serving that purpose successfully.

Madrasa reforms can be rationally conceived without any reference to their 'modernization', that is the introduction of modern subjects in the madrasa *nisab*. The madrasa system of education is an independent system which has hardly any common points with the modern system of education or modern attitudes and approach to the world and life. It is another thing that the Arab pioneers of knowledge had a very different mindset while dealing with new fields of knowledge.

From the very beginning the *ulama* have been against modern education for various historical and psychological reasons. During the British rule, this opposition was symbolic of their opposition to the British and their perceived threat from Christianity and Western culture. In a perceptive article Farhat Hasan describes the madrasas' self-perception as symbolizing the greatness of Islam, and its culture as against the British and their culture.[37] Islam being a global religion, its conceptualization by Indian *ulama* was also that of a transnational 'religio-culture', resulting in the pan-Islamism of various *ulama* and Muslim ideologues of the second and third decades of the last century, as expressed in the Khilafat movement. This resulted in a deliberate attempt for 'Arabizing' of Islamic education and culture which, in turn, necessitated emphasis on learning the Arabic language in detail. Hence the persistent emphasis on centuries' old *nisab* and an inbuilt opposition to modern subjects being imparted in madrasas.[38]

The conservative section of the Muslim society felt threatened even by Sayyid Ahmad's advocating of English education. This opposition to modern education resulted in the establishing of various large madrasas, in spite of S. Ahmad's giving into the demand of religious education in MAO College; and the refusal to allow admission of girls in it. Various scholars have lamented the fact that S. Ahmad gave up his reformist, modernist stance in order to make his male co-religionists agree to receive modern education.[39] And yet the *ulama* perceived S. Ahmad as engaged in harming Islam and its values. This opposition to any thing new which is not there in the Holy Quran or *hadiths*, is inbuilt in Islam since the 'original' Islam is perceived to be the final truth not only as a religion but as the storehouse of all possible knowledge. That is why most *ulama* have been constantly against the introduction of modern subjects in madrasas, from the times of Maulana Asharaf Ali Thanwi, Maulana Muhammad Qasim Nanatauvi to Maualana Taqi Usmani. Thanwi, as others of his time, was against *duniyavi* (secular/modern) subjects being included in madrasa *nisab* as, according to him, it would destroy the religious character of madrasa education. The aim of madrasa education is not, said he, to prepare their students for earning a means of livelihood; rather it is 'to make their students totally concerned with the "hereafter" '.[40] Surprisingly, these *maulanas* did not realize, nor do they realize now, that the Dars-i Nizami, as it was conceived at that time, and is being taught even now in very changed circumstances, consists mostly of what Thanwi calls *duniyavi* or this-worldly subjects. Mushir-Ul-Haq sensibly observes:

Even a cursory glance on the Nizami syllabus shows that syllabus served to equip students with more secular knowledge than religious. That was necessary because [. . .] the education aimed basically not to produce 'religious preachers' and the ulama of our present type, but to produce potential government servants.[41]

This was so also because the original Islam does not make any distinction between religious and secular life and knowledge. That is why the early Arabs could make such tremendous advances in secular, scientific knowledge, as *ilm* (knowledge as such) was valued by the early Muslims. It was only after coming of the British when the *ulama* realized that their role as the educators and trainers of state officials was no longer required and they accepted the Western dichotomy between the religious and secular knowledge, and started calling themselves *dini madaris*.[42] But once they accepted this alien conceptualization of knowledge, they adhered to it fanatically. This dichotomy fitted into their general mental conceptual framework which emphasized the doctrine of *taqlid* (blind following of the written word) and the need to maintain the separate identity of Islamic way of life as they perceived it. And as late as the last decade of twentieth century *maulanas* and *alims* were adhering to this dichotomy, and resisting the introduction of modern subjects as foreign to the Islamic values.

We have personally visited many madrasas in and around Delhi, and found that with a few exceptions, most madrasas were not in favour of including modern subjects. Some have introduced some modern subjects, such as a big chain of masdrasas established by the Islamic Awakening Centre, at Okhla, New Delhi, named Jamia Islamia, Sanabil, affiliated to the Ahle-Hadees sect, and another chain of madrasas known as Madrasa Nusarat-ul-Islam, with many branches spread all over the city. But most others, such as a well-known Madrasa Ali'a Arabia at Fatehpuri, Old Delhi, Madrasa Jamia Arabia Nizamia, Old Delhi, and Jamia Hazrat Nizamuddin Aulia, a Barelvi madrasa in Old Delhi, were passionately against introduction of modern sciences, as they are supposedly against the beliefs of Islam.

We have also visited several maktabs and a few medium class madrasas which proudly told us how they also teach Hindi, English and arithmetic. At least in cities almost all maktabs are doing that, though there is no guarantee of their doing it efficiently.

Mufti Taqi Usmani explains why madrasas must not teach modern subjects, and why their *nisab* need not be 'reformed':

First, madrasas have been established for a particular purpose of producing Ulama having command over Islamic Sciences that require full time and attention. In today's complex life it is experienced that, after being engaged in technical field service of Islam remains only a pleasant dream that never comes true. Second, [. . .] doesn't Muslim society need Ulama who can guide it in religious field, educate Muslim children, defend Islam and devote their life to safeguard Muslims' future?[43]

Here a very comprehensive role is being envisioned for the *ulama*. They not only guide Muslims in the religious field, but also educate (presumably all) Muslim children and safeguard Muslims' future. Thus madrasas are expected not only to impart Islamic knowledge but also to prepare *ulama* who would be the guides and leaders of the entire Muslim community which, of course, is seen as a separate entity, different from the rest of society.

This has been the refrain of a majority of writers on the madrasa system, as well as the conclusion reached by various conferences called to discuss the issue of 'reform' in the madrasa system of education. In one such Conference held at Deoband in 1994, Maulana Marghub ur-Rahman, the Rector of Darul Uloom, argued that Islam had 'clearly divided' knowledge into two distinct categories: religious and worldly. 'The paths and destinations of these two branches of knowledge are totally different.' If someone seeks to travel on both paths together, that is, combine religious and worldly knowledge, he would be like a person trying to ride two boats simultaneously and would be neither a good Muslim, nor a well-educated modern man. Madrasas must remain 'purely religious', and if anyone wants modern education, they can go to modern schools. The Conference concluded that Islam being the perfect religion, and the perfect guide for the entire life, no other kind of education is needed. It also declared that madrasas are doing a splendid job in achieving the goal of imparting Islamic education to Muslim children, and preparing them for guiding and leading the Muslim community in every dimension of their lives. The Islamic *nisab* need not be changed, the only changes needed were concerning some books.[44] Most writers on madrasa education assert that modern subjects must not be introduced in madrasa studies, as any basic changes in the *nisab* of madrasas may undermine the basic objectives of madrasa education.[45]

Often the mere suggestion of reforms in the madrasa system infuriates the *maulanas*. In a personally recorded interview with the *maulanas* of a well-known madrasa in the heart of Delhi, I was told two things by two different *maulanas* of the madrasa. First, they do not believe in modern science and cannot include it in the madrasa syllabus as it says things which are opposed to what is written in the Holy Quran, every word of which is true. The second *alim* argued that madrasas do not need to include modern subjects; instead, colleges and universities need to incorporate religious education in their syllabus. When I put before him that several religions are practised in India and every school and college would have to keep several teachers to teach those religions, the *maulana* looked uncomfortable and said that there is no need to teach other religions; the teaching of Islam alone is sufficient as it is the only true religion and is all-encompassing.

SUGGESTIONS FOR REFORMS FROM WITHIN THE SYSTEM

Some other writers, like Qamar Uddin of Hamdard Education Society, remain ambivalent, talking of the need for reforms but not suggesting any. Qamar Uddin surveyed 576 madrasas only in order to do an All India Survey of madrasa system of education under the aegis of Hamdard Society. His Urdu work based on his Survey provides an interesting example of saying many things in favour of reforms and then asserting that no reforms are needed in the syllabus and basic structure of madrasa system of education. He talks at length about the ideal education being child-centred, leading to the development of the entire personality of the child, especially her intellect and reasoning power. He adds that madrasa education aims at the same![46] However, he acknowledges that madrasa pass-outs do not have many career options, especially because the number of madrasas is increasing. At places he even says that madrasa pass-outs are not proficient either in Arabic, Persian, or even in Urdu.[47] He acknowledges that the books in the madrasas are 300 years old and some of them need to be changed. (Actually most books are older, as at the time of Mulla Nizamuddin when the present Dars-i-Nizami was developed most of the books were already being taught.) He also admits that too many books are prescribed for several subjects and students are not able to handle this load.[48]

Qamar Uddin also admits that the old *mantiq* (logic) and *falsafa* (philosophy) that are taught in the madrasas are no longer in vogue and have nothing to do with the *dini taleem*, and therefore can be dropped from the syllabus. He further sensibly contends that teaching Persian is unnecessary, and it is better if the education is imparted through Urdu medium.[49]

Qamar Uddin, however, after casually suggesting these changes, goes on to say that changes in *nisab* are less important, as changes in the methodology of teaching and examination system are all that are needed by way of reform.[50] It is interesting to note that a large number of madrasas have already adopted the year-wise division of classes and regular examination system. None of these were part of the original system. In view of that Qamar Uddin's suggestions by way of reforms seem superfluous. Though advocating change in the methodology of teaching, Qamar Uddin makes no concrete suggestion, perhaps because the methodology of teaching is integrally related to the subject matter and the values it enshrines. (We do not agree with the view of Saiyyid Hamid, expressed in his Foreword to Qamar Uddin's book, that teaching methodology is irrespective of the nature of subject being taught.) If *taqlid*, or blind following of the written word without any questioning is the norm of madrasa education, then the methodology of teaching cannot be changed. How is someone supposed to give a reason for something which is to be blindly followed? Even more interesting is his claim in another article that most of the madrasas surveyed by him welcomed the idea of overall reforms, when he has made no such contention in his main work.[51]

Though Qamar Uddin has acknowledged two weaknesses of the madrasa *nisab*, regarding the large number of prescribed books, as also logic and philosophy being very old, his conception of 'modernization' of madrasas is a truncated one. He believes that for 'modernization' of madrasa *nisab, any one* of the several social sciences, and also *any one* of physical sciences may be taught in the madrasas on an *optional basis*.[52] This suggestion of incorporating *any one* subject each out of the two groups of modern sciences in madrasa *nisab* is repeated by several other writers on madrasa 'reforms'.[53] Equally important, other writers are not ready to drop even old *mantiq* and *falsafa* which are acknowledged as based on ancient Greek thought. They argue that the textbooks in *tafsir* (commentaries on the Quran) and *hadiths* are written in an archaic style which cannot be understood without earlier knowledge of (Greek) logic and (Greek) philosophy, therefore they must continue in the present *nisab* also.[54]

Unlike the above writers Maulana Sayyid Manazir Ahasan Gilani is a great advocate of integrating religious and 'secular' or 'modern' education in madrasa *nisab*.[55] While his conception of secular subjects is more enlightened than that of writers like Khalili Qasmi, it is still a confused one. Some of his suggestions are however sensible and worth considering. Though there is no documented evidence to this, Gilani claims that the *nisab* during the Sultanat period included *diniyat*, that is the Quran, *tajweed*, *hadiths*, *fiqh*, *usool-e-fiqh*, and very few *aqaliyat* (rational sciences) like *mantiq*, *falasafa*, *riyazi* and *kalam* (scholastics). He criticizes these latter subjects, which were so prominent in Dars-i-Nizami, as it was conceived at first, as mere argumentation which creates rifts and unnecessary new thoughts and doubts. Dars-i-Nizami has very little *dini* content and is just full of superfluous *ma'qulat*. According to Gilani, there are about 40–50 books on *ma'qulat*, each of them written in the same complicated intellectual style (*akaliyat* or *aqali fanoon*). As a result the purely *dini* subjects are neglected.[56] According to him, what the Prophet and his Companions have told should be accepted, and doubting or questioning these fundamental assertions is wrong.[57] He regards the *nisab* of pre-thirteenth-century madrasas or roughly the one prevalent during the Sultanat period as the ideal one. According to him, the need is not to develop a new *nisab* but to re-establish the earlier one.[58]

Gilani's own writing is convoluted, lengthy and often rhetorical. But his basic argument, that *ma'qulat* (rational sciences) taught in modern madrasas are not only irrelevant from a *dini* point of view, but also involve an avoidable waste of energy and time of madrasa children, deserves consideration. He strongly argues for a radical reduction of the *ma'qulat* books and even asserts that not all *hadiths* need be taught. He points out that both *hadiths* and *tafsirs* (commentaries) are taught through lengthy argumentative and complex guide books and footnotes, which miss out on the content of the text being studied, besides wasting time and energy.[59] He goes on to assert that the main purpose of *dini taleem* is to read and understand the Holy Quran. For that, direct reading along with its translation (in Urdu) is sufficient. After explaining the direct meaning of the Quranic verses, a student should be left to understand it and try to get near God through it by himself/herself.[60]

Gilani further suggests that in *dini* subjects, only *Jalalen* (*tafsir*), *Mishkat* and *Hidaya* (*hadiths*) and *Sharah Wa'qiya* (*fiqh*) should be taught. Madrasas should restore the old (*jadid*) *nisab*, thus keeping a few basic books in *dini taleem* and leaving out Persian and *ma'qulat*.[61] Further, though a Muslim boy must learn Arabic language and grammar (*sarf* and *nahw*), but that can be done through a simple book instead of the complicated and lengthy ones used at present. Also only that part of Arabic needed for religious education should be taught, the rest of the language should be made optional. Gilani also suggests that the religious texts should be translated into Urdu, while the Quran should be read in the original along with its translation in Urdu.[62] The time and energy thus saved should be devoted for teaching the 'language of the government' and those sciences and arts which are 'demanded nowadays by the government'. Maulana Gilani very reasonably argues that the present *nisab* has far too many 'rational' sciences which have outlived both their utility and relevance in modern times, and therefore should be removed from the madrasa curriculum. This would make way for teaching modern subjects. He further argues that in medieval times people learnt Farsi (Persian) and *ma'qulat* to secure government jobs; similarly modern Muslims can likewise learn the language and subjects 'demanded by the present-day government'.[63]

Gilani points out that 'hundreds of books' are being written on 'thousands of *masail* (issues)', and there are continuous arguments on such petty issues as where to keep one's hands during *namaz*, to what level should one raise one's hands, and so on. An apparently important problem for constant discussion is whether the Imam alone should read the *Sura-e-Fatiha* and the rest of the congregation say 'amen' at the end, or whether all should read it simultaneously. Such never-ending discussions consume much time and energy. Teachers talk for hours in favour of their respective *maslak* and lengthy, argumentative articles are published in the journals of some madrasas on these issues. In fact, there is a vast literature in defence of different *maslaks*. As a result no energy or time is left for other more important matters.[64]

However, Gilani goes on to say that there should be only one system of education, including both *dini* and *duniyavi* subjects, and this unified system should be followed by both Muslims and Hindus. At least till High School both Hindus and Muslims should study in the same madrasas or schools. This would have been an excellent suggestion if Gilani had not emphasized that the education should only be religion-centered and that the religion should only be Islam.[65]

He rhetorically talks about the evils of modern education, how it tells 'tales' and does not develop the intellect; and goes on to assert that all colleges must have these three fundamental books in *dini* subjects—*Jalalen*, *Hidaya* and *Mishkat*; and modern sciences could be optional.[66] He also criticizes the modern examination system, preferring the earlier informal way of examination.

Often Gilani's views swerve towards extreme conservatism. He criticizes Sufism, condemns Akbar's liberalism and objects to the 'rational' sciences as they create doubts and a questioning tendency in the students' minds. He also declares the efforts by modern Muslim scholars to reinterpret the meaning of the Quran as wrong, since Islam does not allow that freedom.[67]

But Gilani's suggestions that the *ma'qulat* or purely rational sciences of earlier times be reduced or even removed, religious education be imparted in a simple manner and the time made available by these changes should be devoted to the learning of modern subjects, especially English language, are very sensible. If madrasas want to introduce modern subjects, they must reduce the length and complexity of Dars-i-Nizami.

2.3. SOME CRITICAL COMMENTS ON THE ABOVE
CONCEPTIONS OF MADRASA 'REFORMS'

Modern disciplines cannot be taught or understood in isolation. What would a student understand about, say, chemistry without also knowing something about physics and mathematics? The same would be true for social sciences. History, geography and economics are interdependent and cannot be understood in isolation. Any scientific theory or assertion, even of the simplest kind, cannot be understood without some basic knowledge of other disciplines. How can a child or youth understand the history of any nation without having some knowledge of its relative position in the globe and its geographical spread, its resources, economic structure, and political ideology? The same is true of every other modern discipline. Such truncated teaching of modern subjects, as proposed by some writers, quoted above, does not make a person either knowledgeable or 'modern'. Even more significantly, the Arabi and Farsi Madrasa Board of Uttar Pradesh offers the *choice of any one modern subject* out of all modern subjects (including *samaji uloom* or social sciences, and natural sciences), in addition to elementary English, Hindi and elementary mathematics, in the name of 'modernization'.[68]

Writers on madrasas sweepingly say that their syllabus includes history and geography without bothering to tell us whose history and whose geography are being taught. The *nisabs* of Deoband and Nadwa clearly state that they teach Islamic history and geography of Muslim countries. At least, most traditional madrasas teach the same. Some other madrasas have introduced Indian history and geography which is a welcome step. But this innovation has yet to take its final shape. Moreover, even when introduced, Indian history almost always starts from the medieval period with the coming of foreign kings who happened to be Muslims, which, as we have said earlier, is a distortion of Indian history.

The fact is that the madrasa syllabus is too heavy, consisting of Arabic grammar, Arabic literature, Persian, *mantiq* (logic), *falsafa* (philosophy)—the last two greatly influenced by Greek thought—astronomy of Ptolemy, as well as *tafsir* (Quranic exegesis or commentaries on the Quran), *fiqh* (Islamic jurisprudence), *usool-e-fiqh* (principles of jurisprudence) and *hadiths* with several commentaries. As a result very few madrasas can include modern subjects. It is also to be remembered that there is relatively less *dini* content in the syllabus, while its so-called rational sciences (*ma'qulat*) are out of date and irrelevant in modern times. The Quran is not taught directly, only *tafsirs* are taught, and they are very complex texts. It is acknowledged even by pro-madrasa scholars that *tafsirs* are written in an old and complex or flowery style which cannot be understood without the knowledge of ancient logic. Besides, each commentary has several commentaries, which in turn, have other commentaries, with detailed footnotes. A youth who has not yet mastered Arabic language, spends all his energy deciphering the sentences of these *tafsirs*, and trying to memorize the same without understanding anything, least of all their context, i.e. the Quran.

Qamar Uddin, a very conservative writer, himself recognizes in his survey work that the Arabic language is too complex and archaic and beyond the reach of not only the students but also the *ulama*. He goes so far as to contend that most *ulama* of madrasas can hardly read Arabic and are equally poor in Urdu. Yet while claiming to argue for madrasa 'modernization', he asserts that students must be forced to speak only in Arabic in madrasas.[69] More honest and liberal writers assert that the heavy and complicated Arabic language of the prescribed *tafsirs* is a great strain on the intellect of the students. To quote Waris Mazahari:

They [madrasas] give too much stress to memorization, and too little to actual comprehension, critical questioning and debate. Also they focus on the learning of particular books rather than on actually understanding a particular subject. [. . .]

Since Arabic is not the mother tongue of the students, they often find it very difficult to understand the Arabic grammar books, and few of them are actually able to converse in it even after spending years in madrasas.[70]

It is for everyone to see that even madrasa teachers are barely conversant in Arabic language. The present method of learning a language is direct reading which is much less elaborate and easier. Here Maulana Gilani's suggestion that a simple book of grammar be used to teach Arabic instead of the present books which analyse every word, thus losing the content, is remarkable and worth considering. In fact, he suggests that the Arabic of the Holy Quran is easy to understand. Gilani is also a great advocate of directly approaching the Quran, and not through *tafsirs* which are elaborate and come with further commentaries and footnotes.[71]

Unfortunately, Gilani, after offering such wide ranging and almost revolutionary changes in the madrasa curriculum, asserts that the Quran does not give individual freedom of thought, and therefore no one should try to interpret the Quran anew.[72] This means that all the talk of education sharpening individual's intellect and reasoning power are nothing but blind imitation of Western thought without any attempt to relate it to madrasa education. Gilani further affirms that there should be one unified syllabus and same institutions for the education of *all*. This would have been a very welcome suggestion but for the fact that Gilani conceives education as centred round religion in which modern subjects can be taught optionally. He also affirms that the religion taught in these common educational institutions would be Islam and even prescribes three compulsory books for the same. Though non-Muslims would not agree to this, there is a certain naïve sincerity when Gilani asserts that Hindus and Muslims should unite together in a system of education that combines both kinds of disciplines. Further he does not recognize any conflict between religion (Islam) and secular (modern) knowledge.[73]

The saddest part of madrasa education is expressed in students' response to a questionnaire put by Shoyeb Ansari. If his reporting is to be believed, the students of madrasas exhibited an extremely conservative and regressive approach to the issue of introduction of modern subjects. While the students' views on matters regarding teaching method were divided, when it came to the curriculum (*nisab*), they came out to be even more conservative and narrow-minded than the usual *maulanas*. Most of them supported such negative and regressive suggestions as the need for prior 'Islamization' of modern subjects. They also opined that these subjects should be learnt in order to be better able to counter them.[74] A majority believed that technical education may be good, but it must not be taught during the years of Arabic education; and contradictory subjects should not be taught together.[75] Teaching of pure physical sciences is no use to the students of madrasas, while *mantiq*, *fiqh* and other traditional subjects are needed; only their books need to be changed![76] The students strongly favoured the encouragement of Arabic language.[77] Above all they asserted that only that course content is right which creates a motivation for preaching or proselytizing (*da'wa*). They even wanted more books for that purpose.[78]

If the above responses of students are correctly reported, and are in any way representative of the madrasa students' attitude towards knowledge, the answer to the issue of 'modernization' is already there—it is not possible!

The Indian Constitution has declared preaching one's religion to be a fundamental right. However, we should understand that you cannot invite others to your faith without first, declaring your faith to be the only true religion, and second, arguing how other religions are far inferior, or worse, a form of irreligion (*kufr*). Such an attitude is bound to create divisions and antagonism between religions. In one Seminar held at the Jamiat-ul Falah, Azamgarh, almost every speaker talked of India as a land of *kufr*, 'land of idolaters', and even 'land of enemies of one's religion (*barista*)', and called for their duty of *da'wa* to those people.[79] As far as our knowledge goes, such language was not common even during medieval India. This approach is not welcome in a multi-religious society as India's. Of course, it is wrong to downplay a religionist's faith in the 'truth' or even 'finality' of his/her faith, but the challenge of a pluralist democratic society is reconciling this inner commitment with not only tolerating others' faiths but also *respecting* them as the believers of the same God or fellow travellers in the search for Truth or God.

Certain liberal *maulanas*, such as Maulana Wahiduddin, assert that *da'wa* is not directed towards others, at least in the Indian context; rather it is addressed to the Muslim masses who are asked to give up their un-Islamic ways and adopt the true Islam as depicted by the Quran and the *sunna*.[80] This assertion is borne out by the fact that very few Muslims in present-day India have ever tried to convert Hindus. If at all, Christians have been more eager to convert others. But even the Christians have now reduced their ambition for conversions. At the same time, *da'wa* or inviting others to one's faith, is openly acknowledged by Jamaat-e-Islami Hind as one of the goals of the organization.[81]

Of course, Muslims in general express a strong faith in the secular state and in the idea of religious tolerance. Here we have to be more honest in spite of our secularist mindset. Mushir-Ul-Haq has rightly pointed out that secularists and others have not been able to fathom the intense attachment of Muslims to their religion. He adds that this attachment, though it admits of religious tolerance, cannot accept the ideal of equal respect to all religions. Even if they accept (with some reservations) that all paths (religions) lead to one God, they are still firmly convinced that the 'Straight path' leading to Him is one, and that is Islam. Convinced in this way, it is difficult for the *ulama* and average Muslims to accept that all religions are equally true.[82]

The Deobandi madrasas and Tablighi Jamaat activists have made all out efforts to 'reform' Islam as practised by the masses. This includes their efforts at nullifying the culture, including dress, language and social customs, which the two major religious communities have shared ever since the coming of Muslims. It was these latter shared spaces that had built bridges between the two communities across ages. We secularists, from Jawaharlal Nehru to Bipan Chandra, Mushirul Hasan, myself and a host of others have concentrated on and celebrated these shared spaces and the composite culture of India built on their basis.[83] Were we all living in an imaginary world? If not, then there is still hope of Muslims regaining their previous goodwill and harmony with the rest of society, though their conception of the immense superiority of their religion may come in the way.

Interestingly, the *ulama* are not only fanatically sure of the superiority and finality of Islam, they are equally fanatically convinced of the finality of their own version of the truth about Islam. This conviction results in madrasa teachers' and students' confrontation, not with non-Muslims but, with other Muslims who follow different interpretations of Islam. These different interpretations are called *maslaks* or sects, or even *mazahib* (religions). Generally there are no textbooks prescribed for that purpose, though there are plenty of pamphlets on the subject. Great emphasis is laid on drilling into the minds of students the superiority or truth of the *maslak* or religious denomination to which the madrasa belongs. It is necessarily accompanied by rhetoric aimed at condemning or declaring other *maslaks* as false (*radd*). Declaring other views as false (*radd*), or the views and practices of other *maslaks* as *bid'a* (harmful innovations) are important ingredients of madrasa education. Proving the above through argumentation and selective citing of *hadiths* or *tafsirs* is a respected art. Madrasa teachers stress on these things, while those who are capable write long treatises, tracts or articles on various petty subjects with the one aim of condemning other *maslaks*.[84] Rhetoric (*balaghat*) and flowery language (*ma'ni*) along with elaborate grammar have been the favourite subjects of madrasa curriculum. These arts were used in medieval ages to criticize Greek philosophy and the apparently heretic doctrine advocated by *Mutazzilas* (Dissenters). Now, these very arts of rhetoric and flowery and argumentative writing are used to criticize and condemn other schools or sects of Islam.

Several academics within the system have been arguing for the need for moderating the negative thrust in madrasas regarding inter-*maslak* rivalries. Waris Mazhari and Arshad Alam have strongly criticized the excessive emphasis on *maslaki* differences which are invariably focused on some dogmatic beliefs or petty issues of external rituals. Arshad Alam asserts the wasteful tendency of over-emphasis in the madrasa system on *maslaki* differences. In one of the documents of the Ahle-Sunnat madrasa, the term Sunni, which according to them, is identical with the follower of Ahle-Sunnat sect, is defined as: '[Sunni is] one who follows the path of al Hazarat. Sunni is one who believes in every word written by al Hazarat. At the same time Sunni is one who fights the Deobandis, Wahhabis, Shias, *ghair Muqallids* (Ahle-Hadith), etc.'[85]

Alam contends that madrasa teachers and students know nothing about other religions, especially Hinduism, just as Hindu pundits know nothing about Islam. Moreover, they are out of touch with the social reality which makes them misfits in the wider society. A knowledge of the wider society would not only help them in their day-to-day life, but also help them in understanding the Quran in a way more relevant for today's world.[86] The madrasa syllabus is well known to be book-centred. Generally there are no specific prescribed books extolling the truth of a particular *maslak* and condemning others. The same books of *tafsirs, hadiths* and grammar are prescribed in these madrasas. And yet their students are brain-washed to such an extent that half their energies are spent on condemning the views of other *maslaks*. Let us quote again Arshad Alam's observations: 'In most madrasas belonging to different denominations a strategy to learn to defend their own Islam, as well as to propagate what it considers as true Islam is institutionalized and considered a very important part of the overall madrasa pedagogy.'[87]

Almost all major madrasas are residential; Thursday evenings are reserved for religious debates. In Madrasa Ashrafia, Mubarakpur (UP) it is called *bazm*. Apparently, students manage their own debates, senior students supervising the rest. Such practices are meant for training students in the skills of oratory and boosting their self-confidence, in order to make them more rational, alert and quick witted. However, all the rhetoric in these debates is almost always directed towards describing the beliefs of their *maslak* in fanatic tones and condemning those of others. Alam describes in detail a *bazm* that he attended in Madrasa Ashrafia. Students were most forthcoming, emphatic and passionate while condemning not only the Deobandi madrasas but also the respected *maulanas* associated with it. Student after student repeated the central dogma of the Barelvis, that Muhammad Saheb was not an ordinary mortal, and those who say so commit a grave sin.[88] Alam further observes that the institution of debates is an integral part of every madrasa. Even though the prescribed books are the same, these Thursday sessions convince the students of the immense superiority of their sect's version of Islam. Students sharing the same *maslak* and views develop a unique identity which consists in a sense of being wronged by other sects and the final truth of their own version of Islam.[89] If the teachers and students are so convinced about the immense superiority of the Islam as conceived in their particular sect of Islam, they would have a similar or even stronger sense of superiority to other religions.

I have myself witnessed such a *taqrir* (speech or oratory) in the junior section of Ahle-Hadees madrasa in New Delhi. It was regular madrasa time and a regular class of *taqrir* (oratory) was taking place. I could make out that here was an example of excellent oratory though I could not understand the Urdu being spoken, as it was heavily laced with Arabic and Persian words. The speaker belonged to Arabi *Som* (class 3) and was about 16–17 years old. The boy was speaking of some war and the *shahadat* (martyrdom) of Muslims who died in it. More importantly, there was such dogmatic passion, confidence and even fanaticism in his loud voice and body language that it could move anyone. He could speak for a long time without any notes, which could only mean that the things he was talking about have been repeated indefinitely, so that he had appropriated them as his very own. He now had the capacity to move his listeners to his way of thinking. He was not the only boy; everyone present in the class was capable of giving such a speech and would have taken his turn after we came away.

Since madrasa students are rarely allowed to read outside material, such strong convictions drilled into young minds and the passion they create, unchecked by any other widening experience, could only lead to fanaticism. The passion that pours forth from adolescent Muslims during *bazm* or other similar sessions is an expression of such a fanaticism which is not a healthy frame of mind. When such youngsters delivers speeches after the *namaz* (*khutba*) they are capable of moving or hypnotizing the gullible masses.

Such fanaticism may also lead to susceptibility to wrong elements, appealing to them in the name of religion. It would also hamper the Muslims in getting integrated into the larger society as citizens of a plural democratic state. Negative goals and emphases in any movement or education are always counter-productive in the long run. If madrasa teachers devote a large part of their energy and time to inter-*maslaki* differences, naturally the purely *dini* (religious) subjects would be neglected.

3. 'MODERNIZATION' OF MADRASAS

3.1. INTRODUCTION OF MODERN SUBJECTS IN MADRASA SYLLABUS

There is a big difference between 'reforms' in madrasas, and 'modernization' of madrasas, though the two terms have often been used interchangeably in the contemporary debate on the issue. We have discussed the ideas of and proposals for 'reforms' in madrasas. 'Reforms' refer to changes from within the system brought about, in this case, by the *maulanas* and other intellectuals who are convinced of the immense superiority of the Islamic education. These persons contend that some minor changes may be brought, while taking care not to disturb the basic *dini* thrust of the madrasa education. We found that the majority of *ulama* and other writers on the subject are of the opinion that all is well with the madrasa education and no basic changes are required. At most the teaching methodology has to be improved and a few books have to be changed here and there.[84] With the exception of Maulana Gilani and a few liberal academics, all other writers contend that there is no need to make any basic changes in the *nisab* of madrasas. Unfortunately even Gilani proves to be quite conservative when he declares that the Quran gives no freedom of thought, and unnecessary reasoning only creates doubts and must be discouraged.[91]

When we talk of 'modernization' of madrasas, we mean something quite different. The idea of 'modernization', in fact, comes from outside the traditional system. Basically 'modernization' means three things: First, it implies inclusion of modern subjects like physical and social sciences, modern mathematics, and some of the modern languages like English and Hindi. Second, 'modernization' should mean an entire change of approach to knowledge and life, giving reason a prominent place in human judgement, and even refusing the role of any authority, religious or traditional, in the face of reason. Third, 'modernization' in the field of knowledge means an effort to understand new knowledge through reasoning, questioning, and then applying (or at least intending to apply) the knowledge to day-to-day problems.

As we have seen in chapter 1, Western thinkers acknowledge

that 'education is imparting something "worthwhile" to the children'.[92] However, we may differ as to what is 'worthwhile'. Moral values definitely enter in to our conception of worthwhile education. But while in Western thought morality is regarded as autonomous, that is, not dependent on religion or authority, religions, especially Islam, emphasize that morality is derived from religion (*din*) and cannot exist without being thus grounded in faith. As we have seen in chapter 1, Mahàtma Gandhi and Maulana Azad differed on this issue. While Gandhi asserted that only those beliefs and values which are common to all religions should be imparted to children in common schools, Azad insisted that specific religious instructions should also be given.[93] A majority of Muslim thinkers and of course all *ulama* insist on the need of religious education for all Muslim children, though they may differ regarding the extent or the level of religious education that needs to be given to every Muslim child. Some *maulanas* go to the extent of demanding that religious education (Islam?) must be imparted in modern schools and colleges. Maulana Gilani is one such writer; he even prescribes Islamic textbooks which should be compulsorily taught in colleges. He further says that instead of madrasas becoming modern, it is the modern schools and colleges that should be made religious.[94]

This brings us to our second point—that most madrasas are not really interested in 'modern' subjects. Starting with the assumption that early writers have written the last word on every possible subject under the sun, the madrasa teachers see no reason why they or their students should learn 'modern' subjects. Their basic argument is always the same—that what madrasas are teaching is worthwhile and adding new subjects would deter them from their chief purpose. Most writers on madrasa 'modernization' further assert that those who want to introduce modern subjects do not know the objective of *madaris,* which is to produce experts in Islamic sciences. They add that one can either be an engineer or an *alim,* but not both together. Alternatively some *maulanas* add that modern subjects, including modern languages, can be included in the madrasa syllabus, as a prior knowledge of them would help the *alims* to counter them better.

Greek philosophy, logic and astronomy of Ptolemy were included in madrasa curriculum during medieval times because they were at that time the most rational assertions in their respective fields. Gradually they became an integral part of madrasa *nisab*. Studying a subject with the sole motive to controvert it, as is sometimes suggested, is a negative purpose which does not enrich the learner, whereas all education is meant to enrich the mind of the learner.

Some scholars opine that instead of introducing modern subjects as a patch-work, it would be better to provide a separate course of religious education to those who are studying in modern colleges.[95] This is a good suggestion, but the basic idea here is that students of madrasas do not need to learn any modern subject.

Interestingly, it is often argued that the government must have some ulterior motive in wanting to introduce modern subjects in madrasas. This motive can only be to gain control of madrasas and deprive them of the autonomy they have enjoyed so far. Naturally, madrasas are not enthusiastic about the government scheme of 'modernization' of madrasas.[96]

There are some 'modernist' or 'secular' Indian Muslims who go beyond the regressive mindset of *alims* and *maulanas*. Two such persons are Waris Mazhari, the editor of an Urdu magazine published from Deoband, and Muhammad Aslam Parvaiz, editor of *Science*, the only Urdu daily on popular science in India. The two plead for the study of modern science and other subjects without going out of the Islamic framework in all their 'modernist' arguments. Mazhari writes:

The syllabus generally employed in the Indian madrasas is several centuries old. In many respects it is irrelevant, and is not able to meet the challenges of modern life. There is an urgent need to reform the syllabus, as well as the whole system of madrasa education. For this we need both to introduce the new subjects as well as new books for teaching old disciplines. [. . .] Take for example the case of the *Sharah-i-Aqai'd*, a treatise on theology (*kalam*) written some eight hundred years ago which continues to be taught in many Indian madrasas. It is written in an archaic style and is full of references to antiquated Greek philosophy that students today can hardly comprehend. Rather than providing the students with a firm understanding of the basic principle of Islamic theology, it deals with imaginary and hypothetical problems and verbal puzzles. So, it asks questions such as: 'Is there one sky or seven or nine? Can the sky be broken into parts?'[97]

He also advocates reforms in Islamic *fiqh*:

Fiqh must always evolve with the times, for as conditions change and new issues emerge, new *fiqhi* or jurisprudence responses must be articulated. This calls for the need to exercise *ijtihad* to examine matters afresh and to take into account new developments. Now in matters of faith and worship and other areas that are specially legislated in the Quran, there can be no *ijtihad*, for these are given for all time. But in large areas in the domain of social transaction one must be open to the possibilities of new interpretations. Unfortunately this is strongly discouraged in Indian madrasas.[98]

Mazhari also suggests that the study of the Quran through *tafsirs* (commentaries) written several centuries back does not make students truly familiar with the holy text. According to him:

Medieval Quranic commentators were, after all, human beings, and no matter how pious they may have been, they were certainly not infallible. [. . .] Many of the classical commentators used *tafsir* for polemical purposes. [. . .] Further, they were naturally also influenced in their thinking by their own social locations, by the general prevailing social environment, as well as by the then available stock of knowledge, and all this is reflected in the different *tafsirs* that have been written down the ages. So today, when social conditions have undergone such a radical transformation, and when the stock of human knowledge has increased manifold we need new interpretations of and commentaries on the Quran.[99]

The suggestions for 'reforms' in madrasas mooted by Aslam Parvaiz and Waris Mazhari are far-reaching, as also sensible. Typically, the suggestions for changes in madrasa syllabus are made within the Islamic framework, and should be acceptable even to the traditionalists. Mazhari is also concerned about the fact that most madrasas inculcate and promote extreme insularity and a lack of concern for the problems of others. Similarly, the Muslim press is concerned about the problems of Muslims alone, as a result of which they are cut-off from the rest of the population, and develop an imaginary sense of being persecuted. They are unable to adjust and mingle with other sections of the society, far less cooperate with them for common social goals. He adds that madrasa students must know what is going on around them. For this they must have access to newspapers and the visual media. But, 'there is a strictly observed ban on reading anything other than the literature supportive of the particular school of thought that each madrasa subscribes to'.[100] Mazhari observes that this could be because *maulanas* are afraid that if the Arabic books are changed or new ideas allowed then their own influence would diminish.

We agree with Mazhari's suggestions. If modern media, i.e. newspapers, radio and television, is allowed in madrasas, as also some modern literature, the extremely conservative and exclusive mindset that characterizes madrasa students would be corrected. He also suggests that madrasa students should learn Hindi and English, so that they can communicate better with others. This, of course, has been half-heartedly accepted by many other writers on the subject.

It is heartening to note that not only several Muslim intellectuals from the relatively traditional stream but also some *ulama* have now started to recognize that the books prescribed in the Dars-i-Nizami are too many and written in a very complicated style. In fact, these books, according to one such writer, are quite boring. It is also suggested by some scholars that the syllabus should be made lighter by including only one book each in *hadith* and *fiqh*.[101] Maulana Habib Rehan Nadwi admits that 12–13 years spent in madrasas do not result in much by way of accomplishment. He calls for wide ranging changes in the *nisab*, but gradually. He asserts that till the tenth or twelfth class modern subjects should also be taught, but adds that every Muslim child should be given *dini* education.[102]

Sadly, the number of such persons among the traditionalists is not very large. The views of the just quoted *ulama* were presented in a Seminar at Azamgarh (mentioned earlier) in which most speakers were not only against the inclusion of modern subjects in the madrasas, but even used abusive language against non-Muslims. It means that these suggestions for reform in the *nisab* stop half-way through and do not lead to modernization of the approach and attitude of the madrasa teachers and students.

The issue of introduction of all modern subjects in madrasas is an independent one. Sayyid Hamid, the greatest protagonist of 'madrasa modernization', conceives the inclusion of all modern subjects in the madrasa syllabus. We would return to his views in the next chapter.

3.2. SOME SUGGESTIONS FOR MADRASA 'REFORMS'

While acknowledging that 'outsiders' must not deem to either criticize or suggest any reforms in madrasas, we are still making some general suggestions. The emphasis on Arabic language as the medium of instruction consumes most of the energies of students, without making them experts in the language. More important, the Arabic texts in *tafsir* and even the original *hadiths* are written in a very difficult, archaic style, and it is admitted that the students must learn *mantiq*, without the knowledge of which they cannot understand those texts. The deliberately difficult, flowery language, and the apparently logical style were in fashion in middle ages as a means of showing off one's scholarly status. Does this desire to show off one's knowledge make the books written in that style necessarily worthwhile, or integral to Islamic knowledge? A related question is—does a person with a different mother tongue necessarily need to study Islamic subjects in Arabic? It is believed that the reading and memorization of the Quran Sharief brings *sabab* (merit), so one has to learn Arabic to read the Quran. Personally I think that at least Urdu translations must be provided along with the Arabic text.

Since Shi'as feel closer to Iran, they use Persian (Farsi), instead of Arabic, to teach Islam to their children. Far worse, as we have mentioned in chapter 4, each subject has two prescribed texts— one in Arabic and another in Persian, thus making the understanding of the subject all the more difficult. Waris Mazhari and some other liberal writers have argued for the replacement of present textbooks in *tafsir* and *fiqh* by more relevant modern ones.[103] And they should be in Urdu or any other regional mother tongue of the children. If the traditional *ulama* do not accept this change, at least all the classical books can be translated into Urdu, and if required in the regional languages.

It is true that certain words, phrases and concepts cannot be translated. That is why, not only the advocates of Arabic but those of Sanskrit also argue for the need of studying the ancient works in the original. The words and concepts that cannot be translated can be used as such in the translation, with a brief explanation in the footnotes in the language in which the work is being translated. Of course, those who want to specialize in a particular field of knowledge must read the original works and for that learn that language. We are here only talking of those large number of students who study in madrasas for getting 'education'.

If classical works, except perhaps the Quran (for which also translation can be provided along with the original text), are translated into Urdu and other Indian languages, the labour and time of the students would be halved. Moreover, they would be able to understand what they are reading; teachers would be able to do a much better job of teaching than they are able to do now. And the emphasis on rote learning, which has been the chief instrument of providing Islamic education in madrasas, would reduce or vanish altogether.

It is common knowledge that children doing *Hifz* (memorization of the Quran) are not told the meaning of the text. But even children of maktabs and madrasas are taught reading the Quran (*qirat*) with proper pronunciation (*tajweed*) but without the meaning. Very few madrasas translate the Quran so that children can understand it. It is also common knowledge that the number of women who can read the Quran fluently far exceeds the number of men, even though most of them do not understand it, nor are they expected to do so.

However, this was not the original intention of the Quran which was expected to be read and understood by every Muslim. It is clearly stated that God spoke to Prophet Muhammad in a particular dialect of Arabic so that all persons could understand the message of God.[104] Obviously it was assumed that Arabic was the language of the people among whom Islam first spread. But what happens when Arabic is not the language of a people, such as Indian Muslims? Then they are expected to learn Arabic, which they do, but for various reasons are not able to master fully. As a result they read the Holy Text without understanding 'God's message' fully. The original intention was that each Muslim would learn to read and understand 'God's message' directly, without the need for mediators. However, now Muslims must turn to the *ulama* who are supposed to understand the Quran and the *hadiths* and explain the norms and laws to the people.

Islam asserts that religion guides, even determines man's relations with God and with other human beings. Islamic *shari'a* or *fiqh* determines those relations. Does *fiqh,* which was developed in a relatively primitive society, have as much eternal verity as the Holy Quran? Is *shari'a* or *fiqh* as divine as the Quran? Most *maulanas* and *alims* regard *shari'a* as 'divine' and inviolable. We have argued in detail in chapter 5 how this claim is difficult to accept in view of the fact that most *hadiths* were compiled much after the passing away of the Prophet.[105] We find that the central place that is given to *shari'a* or *fiqh* results in the religion of Islam being reduced to some compulsory rituals and a very large number of antiquated laws and norms which all Muslims are expected, even forced, to blindly follow (*taqalid*). Another result of this domination of *fiqh,* instead of the faith and conviction of the heart, is that all freedom has been taken away from Muslims; they have become mere automations following the dos and don'ts of the *shari'a* or *fiqh* which were written more than eight centuries ago but which still keep the Muslims tied up to a very medieval regressive mindset. The third result of the great importance of *fiqh* is the excessive importance and authoritative role enjoyed by the madrasa-trained *ulama*. Since they alone are expected to know the intricacies of Islamic *fiqh,* they are consulted by the common people on every occasion, and their writ is the unquestionable law for the masses.

Lastly, except the bigger madrasas or those which are either 'modernized' or are administered by some liberal and sincere persons, the living and classroom conditions of most madrasas are not, to say the least, up to the mark. Classrooms are mostly small, without proper ventilation, and fans. Clean toilets and drinking water are often a luxury. Living quarters are equally insufficient in terms of minimum hygiene requirements. There are no play grounds in most madrasas, and no scope for or encouragement of physical activity. Above all, the students are completely cut-off from the outside world, not being allowed even to read other than a few 'approved' Urdu newspapers.[106] Girls, as we have seen in the previous chapter, are kept in total *purdah* and are cut-off from the realities of life.[107] We are repeating these well-known facts here because much is made of the fact that madrasas provide free education as well as free boarding and lodging; that but for them most Muslim children would remain illiterate and even become vagrant. This may be true; it may also be true that most madrasas are in a better condition than government schools. Yet the rosy picture that is painted for us is not true either.

As is acknowledged by some writers on the subject, the teaching method is largely a monologue-type lecture by the teacher, and mechanical repetition and memorization by the students, generally without understanding the subject. However, more important is the fact that the much repeated assertions that relations between madrasa teachers and pupils are very cordial, the former loving the latter as their sons, is perhaps not true. There are always exceptions and there are well-managed madrasas which employ good qualified teachers. Yet, corporal punishment is common; teachers get irritated if a student asks questions or seek clarifications (probably because they do not know the answer). Students, therefore keep quiet.[108] They are expected either to listen to the teacher passively, or mechanically read and memorize the Arabic texts without understanding them. In addition, they are deprived of any knowledge of any material other than what is prescribed in their syllabus. These two practices do not make for a meaningful, desirable education.

NOTES

1. See Syed Abul Hashim Rizvi, 'The Introduction of Natural Sciences in Madrasa Education', in Jan-Peter Hartung and Helmut Reifeld (eds.), *Islamic Education, Diversity, and National Identity: Dini Madaris in India Post 9/11*, New Delhi: Sage, 2006, pp. 289–90.
2. See Douglas E. Goodfriend, 'Changing Concepts of Caste and Status among Old Delhi Muslims', in Imtiaz Ahmad (ed.), *Modernization and Social Change Among Muslims in India*, New Delhi: Manohar, 1983, pp. 121 ff., especially 129 ff., 134 ff.

3. Manzoor Ahmad, *Islamic Education: Redefinition of Aims and Methodology*, New Delhi: Qazi Publishers 1990, pp. 32–3. Cf. Muhammadullah Khalili Qasmi, *Madrasa Education: Its Strength and Weakness*, Mumbai: Markazul Ma'arif Education and Research Centre, 2005, pp. 192 ff.

4. Ibid., p. 33.

5. 'The persistent efforts of the Ulama in the post-independence period to resuscitate madrasa education ultimately brought it back on the track, and ever since, it is steadily progressing and refurbishing.' See Mohammad Akhtar Siddiqui, 'Development and Trends in Madrasa Education', in A.W.B. Qadri, Riyaz Shakir Khan and Mohammad Akhtar Siddiqui (eds.), *Education and Muslims in India Since Independence*, New Delhi: Institute of Objective Studies, 1998, p. 74.

6. Manzoor Ahmad, op. cit., p. 16. A separate system of education, with separate syllabus combining both religious disciplines and modern sciences, in separate institutions, is a favourite theme of various Muslim intellectuals. Mohd. Sharief Khan has developed this theme in his two books—*Islamic Education*, 1986; and *Education, Religion and Modern Age*, 1990, both published by Ashish Publishing House, New Delhi.

7. Manzoor Ahmed, op. cit., pp. 23 ff. The entire short book is full of such views.

8. Mufti Taqi Usmani, quoted in Khalili Qasmi, op. cit., p. 151.

9. Ibid, pp. 150–1.

10. See Farhat Hasan, 'Madaris and the Challenges of Modernity in Colonial India', in *Islamic Education, Diversity, and National Identity*, p. 67.

11. Qasmi, op. cit., p. 101.

12. See Mohammad Shoyeb Ansari, 'Students' Perception of Teaching, Learning Process in Madrasas', in *Education and Muslims in India Since Independence*, p. 97, also see ibid., pp. 96 ff.

13. See Ansari, op. cit., pp. 99 ff., 104 ff.

14. Qamar Uddin, *Hindustan ki Dini Darsagahein: Kul Hind Survey* (Urdu), New Delhi: Hamdard Education Society, 1996, p. 302.

15. Quoted from a recorded interview with the Shahi Imam of Fatehpuri Masjid.

16. See Mushir-Ul-Haq, *Islam in Secular India*, Simla: Institute of Advanced Study, 1972, p. 29.

17. Ibid., p. 52.

18. 'The Muslim community in secular India is more concerned with its religious identity than is usually realized by others. Their

ever increasing interest in establishing religious schools for imparting religious education, their unquestioning reliance on
madrasah-educated 'ulama for religious guidance in almost every
matter through the institution of *fatwa* (authoritative religious
decrees) attest the community's strong attachment to its religion.'
Ibid., p. 3; also see ibid., pp. 51–2.

19. Tariq Rahman, 'Madrasas: Religion, Poverty and the Potential
for Violence in Pakistan', in the unpublished Proceedings of the
International Workshop on Islamic Learning in South Asia, 19–
21 May 2005, IBZ, Erfurt (Germany), paper no. 4.

20. Sharaf-ad-Din (Sharafuddin) Maneri quoted in Paul Jackson,
'Madrasa Education in Bihar', in *Islamic Education, Diversity
and National Identity*, p. 158.

21. 'There are, indeed, a certain number of old fashioned Maktabs
and Madrassahs which continue to give a parrot like teaching of
the Koran, but even in these places no attempt is made to improve the morals of the boys or to bring before them the eternal
truths of the faith. As a rule, prayers are but rarely repeated, and
when said not one per cent of the boys understands what they say
or why.' Agha Khan, quoted in Farhat Hasan, 'Madaris and the
Challenges of Modernity in Colonial India', in *Islamic Eduation,
Diversity and National Identity*, p. 57.

22. Syed Ameer Ali, *The Spirit of Islam: A History of the Evolution
and Ideals of Islam With a Life of the Prophet*, Delhi: Low Price
Publications, 1990, p. 186.

23. See M. Mujeeb, *The Indian Muslims*, New Delhi: Munshiram
Manoharlal, 1967, p. 277.

24. *The Spirit of Islam*, pp. 183–4, also see pp. 182 ff.

25. See Arshad Alam, 'Understanding Deoband Locally: Interrogating Madrasat Diya' al Ulum', in *Islamic Education, Diversity,
and National Identity*, pp. 192 ff.

26. Saiyid Naqi Hussain Jafri, 'A Modernist View of Madrasa Education in Late Mughal India', in *Islamic Education, Diversity and
National Identity*, pp. 44–5.

27. Ibid., p. 43.

28 Manzoor Ahmad, op. cit., p. 51.

29. See Jan-Peter Hartung, 'The Nadwat al 'ulama: Chief Patron of
Madrasa Education in India and a Turntable to the Arab World',
in *Islamic Education, Diversity, and National Identity*, pp. 140 ff.

30. See Mushir-Ul-Haq, op. cit., pp. 100 ff.; Hamza Ali, 'Ironies of
History: Contradictions in the Khilafat Movement', in Mushirul
Hasan (ed.), *Islam, Communities and the Nation: Muslim*

Identities in South Asia and Beyond, New Delhi: Manohar, 1998, pp. 25 ff.

31. Quoted in Mushir-Ul-Haq, *Muslim Politics in Modern India: 1857–1947*, Meerut: Meenakshi Prakashan, 1970, p. 128.

32. See author's *Secularism in India: A Reappraisal*, New Delhi: Har Anand, 1995, pp. 208 ff., 256 ff.; cf. Mushirul Hasan, *Islam in the Subcontinent: Muslims in a Plural Society*, New Delhi: Manohar, 2002, pp. 40 ff., 54 ff., 348 ff., etc.

33. See articles by Peter B. Mayer, John Eade and Douglas E. Goodfriend, in Imtiaz Ahmad (ed.), *Modernization and Social Change Among Muslims in India*, New Delhi: Manohar, 1983, pp. 1 ff., 58 ff., 119 ff. Both Imtiaz Ahmad and Mushirul Hasan emphasize internal diversity among Indian Muslims, thus indirectly creating space for a shared culture between various religious communities.

34. Manzoor Ahmad, op. cit., p. 57.

35. Maulana Hussain Ahmad Madni, quoted in *Islam in Secular India*, pp. 110–11. Actually the quoted text does not appear in Maulana Madni's speeches as such but summarizes his views correctly. See Maulana Hussain Ahmad Madni, *Composite Nationalism and Islam (Muttahida Qaumiyat aur Islam)*, tr. Mohammad Anwar Hussain, Hasan Imam, New Delhi: Manohar, 2005, pp. 55 ff., 103 ff.

36. Mushirul Hasan is probably the most vocal scholar after Nehru in asserting India's historical and cultural unity. See his *Islam, Communities and the Nation*, pp. 42 ff., 54 ff., 102 ff., 160 ff., etc.; and Bipan Chandra, *Communalism in Modern India*, New Delhi: Vikas, 1989, pp. 13 ff., 53, 86–7, 159 ff.; and author, op. cit., pp. 256 ff.

37. See Farhat Hasan, 'Madaris and the Challenge of Modernity in Colonial India', in *Islamic Education, Diversity and National Identity: Dini Madaris in India Post 9/11*, pp. 60 ff.

38. See Jan-Peter Hartung, 'Nadwat al 'ulama': Chief Patron of Madrasa Education in India and a Turntable to the Arab World', in *Islamic Education, Diversity and National Identity*, pp. 142 ff.

39. See M. Mujeeb, *The Indian Muslims*, pp. 448 ff.

40. Maulana Thanwi, quoted in Yoginder Sikand, 'The Indian Madaris and the Agenda of Reform', in *Islamic Education, Diversity, and National Identity*, p. 272.

41. See Mushir-Ul-Haq, *Islam in Secular India*, pp. 26–7.

42. See Farhat Hasan, 'Madaris and the Challenge of Modernity in Colonial India', op. cit., pp. 60–1.

43. Taqi Usmani, quoted in Khalili Qasmi, *Madrasa Education: Its Strength and Weakness,* p. 152.

44. Discussed in detail in *Hindustan ki Dini Darsagahein,* pp. 120 ff. Also quoted in Yoginder Sikand, 'The Indian Madaris and the Agenda of Reforms', in *Islamic Education, Diversity and National Identity,* p. 274.

45. Khalili Qasmi quotes various scholars as being opposed to 'modernization' of madrasas, or even the need for definite reforms. See op. cit., pp. 144 ff. Also see Maulana Abul Hasan Azmi, '*Daure Jadid ke Takaze aur Dini Madaris ka Nisab*', in a collection of articles presented at a Seminar on Madrasa Reforms titled *Mulk aur Millat ki Tameer aur Dini Madaris* (Urdu), held in Jamiatul Falah, Azamgarh, Azamgarh: Idara Ilmia, 1994, pp. 175 ff. The gist of other papers presented in the Seminar was similar. See ibid., pp. 182 ff., 188 ff. 191ff. They all agreed that there is no need to add modern subjects, as this is proposed only by those who do not know the purpose of madrasas. Some speakers contended that if modern subjects were to be taught, it must be done in a purely Islamic context. Several asserted the need of separate educational institutions for Muslim youth, if modern subjects are to be taught.

46. See Qamar Uddin, *Hindustan ki Dini Darsagahein,* pp. 96 ff., 105 ff., 136ff., 146 ff., 154–5.

47. See ibid., pp. 109 ff., 123 ff., 146 ff., 247 ff.

48. See ibid., pp. 97, 129–31, 154 ff.

49. See ibid., pp. 129 ff.

50. See ibid., pp. 129 ff., 139 ff., 141–2, 147, 177 ff., 181 ff.

51. Qamar Uddin, 'Re-orientation of Madrasa Education', in S.M. Azizuddin Husain (ed.), *Madrasa Education in India: Eleventh to Twenty First Century,* New Delhi: Kanishka, 2005, p. 137. In his main work based on survey of madrasas he does not give that impression.

52. See *Hindustan ki Dini Darsagahein,* pp. 129, 141–2.

53. See Shoyeb Ansari, *Education in Dini Madaris: An Opinion Survey of Curriculum, Method of Teaching and Evaluation in Dini Madaris,* New Delhi: Institute of Objective Studies, 1997, pp. 100–1.

54. See Khalili Qasmi, op. cit., pp. 114–15; also Maulana Abul Hasan Azami, in *Mulk aur Millat ki Tameer aur Dini Madaris,* pp. 175 ff.; Another maulana, Abdullah Madni also emphatically opposed introduction of modern subjects in Madrasa *nisab* in a paper of the same title, '*Daure Jadid ke Takaze aur Dini*

Madaris ka Nisab', in ibid., pp. 186 ff. He emphasized the unity of *umma*, and the need to teach modern subjects, if at all, in a purely Islamic context.

55. *Hindustan main Musalmanon ka Nizam-e-Taleem, wa Tarbiyat*, 2 vols. (Urdu), Delhi: Jama Masjid: Nadwatul-Musannifeen, 1966, vol. 1, pp. 145 ff., 179 ff.; vol. 2, pp. 216 ff.
56. Ibid., vol. 1, pp. 196. ff., 260 ff., 273 ff., 290 ff.; vol. 2., pp. 107 ff.
57. Ibid., vol. 1, pp. 199 ff., vol. 2, pp. 380 ff.
58. Ibid., vol. 1, pp. 328 ff., 377 ff.
59. Ibid., vol. 1, pp. 179 ff., 264 ff.
60. Ibid., vol. 1, pp. 315–16.
61. Ibid., vol. 1, pp. 318 ff., 323 ff., 327 ff. , 373 ff.; vol. 2, pp. 400–1.
62. Ibid., vol. 1, pp. 315–16.
63. Ibid., vol. 1, pp. 315 ff., 325 ff., 373 ff.; vol. 2, pp. 400–1.
64. Ibid., vol. 1, pp. 315–16.
65. Ibid., vol. 1, pp. 320 ff.
66. Ibid., vol. 1, pp. 323 ff., 373 ff.
67. Ibid., vol. 1, pp. 179 ff., 196 ff., 320 ff., 368 ff.; vol. 2., pp. 103 ff., 378 ff.
68. See *Nisab-e-Taleem (Bra-e-darjat-e-'alia) Imtihanat Arabi wa Farsi Board, Uttar Pradesh,* as given by Ghulam Yahya Anjum, New Delhi: Jamia Hamdard, 2000, pp. 35, 45, 66, 88–9.
69. See *Hindustan ki Dini Darsagahein*, pp. 109 ff., 123–4, 154–5, especially p. 302.
70. Waris Mazhari, 'Reforming Madrasa Curriculum', in Akhtarul Wasey (ed.), *Madrasas in India: Trying to be Relevant*, New Delhi: Global India Publication, 2005, p. 38, see also p. 37.
71. See notes 55 to 60 supra.
72. See notes 57, 67 supra.
73. See notes 63, 64, 65 supra.
74. See M. Shoyeb Ansari, *Education in Dini Madaris: An Opinion Survey*, pp. 101 ff.
75. Ibid., pp. 101–3.
76. Ibid., pp. 103–4.
77. Ibid., pp. 98, 108.
78. Ibid., pp. 97 ff., 105.
79. See articles by Maulana Mohd. Inayatullah Asad Subhani, Mohd. Ashraf Ahmad and Maulana Abdul Wahab Khalji, in *Mulk aur Millat ki Tameer aur Dini Madaris*, pp. 22 ff., 135 ff., 218 ff.
80. Based on my personal recorded talk with the Maulana.
81. 'Ideology of Jamaat-e-Islami Hind', on their website jamaat islamihind.org./new website/index.

82. Mushir-Ul-Haq explains that Muslims easily agree to 'tolerate' other religions, and even agree that may be all religions eventually lead to one God. But they firmly believe that the 'straight' path to God is only one, and that is Islam; therefore they cannot give equal respect to all religions as if all are as 'true' and 'final' way to God as Islam. See op. cit., pp. 3 ff., 11 ff., 16.

83. Jawaharlal Nehru in his *The Discovery of India* and many other works; Syed Abid Husain in his *Indian Culture* and other works; Humayun Kabir in his *The Indian Heritage* and other works; Bipan Chandra in his *Communalism in India*; *Essays on Indian Nationalism*, and other works; Mushirul Hasan in his *Islam in the Subcontinent: Muslims in a Plural Society* and other works; and a host of other thinkers, such as M. Mujeeb, S.A.A. Rizvi, Muzzaffar Alam and the author in her *Secularism in India* have argued with conviction that Hindus and Muslims did live in comparative harmony, sharing socio-cultural spaces for centuries. Even now they could well have been indistinguishable had there not been such a concerted effort to make them assert their separate identity in all spheres of life.

84. See Tariq Rahman, 'Madrasas, Religion, Poverty and the Potential for Violence in Pakistan'. Rahman describes inter-*maslaki* differences and the passionate advocacy of the same by the *maulanas*. It is generally said that the atmosphere of madrasas of the two countries is very different; while those in Pakistan encourage fanaticism and even terrorism, ours do no such thing. It is probably true; but Tariq Rahman's description of madrasas in Pakistan sounds as if it is that of Indian madrasas, suggesting that the general approach and ambience of madrasas across the subcontinent is more or less the same. The same article is published in an edited version with a different title 'Madrasas: The Potential for Violence in Pakistan?' in Jamal Malik (ed.), *Madrasas in South Asia: Teaching Terror?*, London: Routledge, 2008, pp. 61 ff. The emphasis on 'terror' seems to distort the entire discussion, especially as other papers are dealing with internal differences in Islam.

85. Quoted by Arshad Alam in 'Making Maslaks: Constructing Identity in a Barelwi Madrasa', in the Procedings of the International Workshop on Islamic Learning, op. cit., paper no. 3. The same is published in an edited version with a changed title, 'Making Muslims: Identity and Difference in Indian Madrasas', in *Madrasas in South Asia*, pp. 45 ff.

86. Ibid.

87. Waris Mazhari, 'Reforming Madrasa Curriculum', in *Madrasas in India: Trying to be Relevant*, pp. 46–7.

88. 'Understanding Deoband Locally: Interrogating Madrasat Diya' al-'Ulum', in *Islamic Education, Diversity and National Identity*, pp. 90 ff.

89. Ibid.

90. See Qamar Uddin, op. cit. pp. 38, 41.

91. See Gilani, op. cit., vol. 1, pp. 240 ff.; vol. 2, p. 382.

92. Western Philosophy of Education is discussed briefly in chapter 1, see notes 53–6.

93. 'We have left out the teaching of religions from the Wardha Scheme of Education because we are afraid that religions as they are taught and practised today lead to conflict rather than unity. But on the other hand, I hold that the truths that are common to all religions can and should be taught to all children.' Mahatma Gandhi, quoted in Muktishree Ghosh, *Concept of Secular Education in India*, New Delhi: D.K. Publishers, 1991, p. 104.

  Cf. 'If national education was devoid of this element [religious instructions] there would be no appreciation of moral values of moulding of character on human lines.' Maulana Azad, quoted in ibid., p. 124.

94. Gilani, believing in a uniform syllabus for all Indians, even prescribes certain Islamic textbooks for colleges. At another place he asserts that instead of madrasas becoming modern, schools and colleges should become 'religious', and demands that the latter should teach religion. See *Hindustan main Musalmanon ka Nizam-e-Taleem, wa Tarbiat*, vol. 1, pp. 327 ff.; vol. 2, pp. 216 ff., 409–10.

  Kuldeep Kaur describes various Muslim organizations, such as Dini Talimi Council, Uttar Pradesh, and Islamic conferences, such as All India Muslim Conference, 1972, demanding that the government should provide religious education in schools. See *Madrasa Education in India: A Study of its Past and Present*, Chandigarh: Twenty-First Century India Society, 1990, pp. 204 ff. Also see our personal discussion with the *maulana* of a leading madrasa in Delhi. He also made the demand that all schools and colleges must have *dini* education, and that *din* or religion can only be Islam.

95. See Maulana Md. Inayatullah Asad Subhani, '*Dini Madaris Apne Mutawaqqa Kirdar Kyun Nahin Ada Kar Sake*', and M. Sultan Ahmad Islahi, '*Hindustan ki Maujuda Talimee Tahreekat: Ek Jayaja*', in *Mulk aur Millat ki Tameer aur Dini Madaris*, pp. 22 ff., 33 ff. 182–3. Also see Khalili Qasmi, op. cit., p. 119.

96. See Qasmi, op. cit., pp. 146–7. Even a relatively secular person as Syed Shahbuddin contends that 'In India, there has been a systematic campaign to vilify the madrasahs as dens of ISI and shelters for the terrorists and militants over the last few years. Out of the distrust and suspicion, came the Government Scheme for the Modernization of Madrasa Education.' Quoted in the article, 'To Kill the Mocking Bird: Madarsah System: Past, Present and Future', available on the website http//www.chowk.com/article/6216, 5 August 2003.

A few years back I attended a Seminar on Madrasa Education Reforms at the Indian Social Institute, New Delhi. There Shahbuddin said that taking government aid for 'modernization' would be like a poison for madrasas. When I objected that it is like the system of apartheid, saying 'don't bother about 'minorities', let them live in whatever condition they are', he retorted that it would be far better than taking the help of the government.

97. Waris Mazhari, 'Reforming Madrasa Curriculum', op. cit., p. 37.
98. Ibid., p. 38.
99. Ibid., p. 39.
100. Ibid., pp. 44–6.
101. See M. Sultan Ahmad Islahi, '*Hindustan ki Maujuda Talimee Tahreekat ek Jayaja*', and Maulana Habib Rehan Nadwi, '*Dini aur Asari Idaron ke Mabain aur Bahmi Tallukat . . .*' in *Mulk aur Millat ki Tameer aur Dini Madaris*, pp. 148 ff., 278 ff., 303–4.
102. See Maulana Mohd. Asad Subhani's article, op. cit., pp. 23–4.
103. Waris Mazhari, op. cit., p. 39.
104. 'Thus We have revealed it, a decisive utterance in Arabic, so that you may understand.' Quran XII.37.
'We made this (scripture) easy in your tongue (O Mohammad) only that you may bear good tidings therewith.' Quran XIX.97.
105. See chapter 5, notes 27–52.
106. See Mohammad Shoyeb Ansari's article, 'Students' Perception of Teaching-Learning Process in Madrasas', op. cit., pp. 97 ff.
107. See chapter 5, notes 78–85.
108. See M. Shoyeb Ansari, *Education in Dini Madaris: An Opinion Survey*, pp. 78 ff.

7

Madrasa 'Reforms' (II): Schemes for 'Modernization of Madrasas'

1. 'MODERNIZATION OF MADRASAS': ISSUES INVOLVED

To recapitulate our discussion in the previous chapter, the two issues of madrasa 'reforms' and their 'modernization' may be related but are different and must not be confused. Barring a few liberals, most madrasa teachers and apologetic writers on the 'reforms' are of the view that madrasas are doing a fine job in giving a large number of Muslim children and youth wholesome education. If some writers admit some weaknesses in the madrasa *nisab*, their suggestions for 'reforms', in the sense of madrasas becoming more suitable for modern times (such as the need for prior 'Islamization' of modern subjects or the need to learn them in order to be better able to counter them) are against all our conceptions of 'modernization'.[1]

The concept of 'modernization' is quite different. It involves: (a) teaching of *all* modern natural sciences—physics, chemistry, biology and mathematics—up to secondary or high school stage; (b) teaching of *all* social sciences (history, geography, political science and economics) to the same stage; (c) teaching in the mother tongue—Urdu in the North (even though it is not the mother tongue of most Muslim children), and some regions of the South, and regional languages in the North-East and other states of the South; (d) teaching of Urdu, Hindi, English and regional languages (if required); (e) inculcating a spirit of enquiry and habit of reasoning among the students; (f) And curtailing the vast and difficult Dars-i-Nizami in order to allow time and space for modern subjects.

1.1. An Important Conceptualization of 'Modernization' of Madrasas

Sayyid Hamid is the most prominent advocate of, and active participant in, the efforts for 'modernization', hence the import-ance of his conceptualization of 'Modernization of Madrasas'. During my personal talks and correspondence with him, he has asserted the following:

(a) All Muslims need religious education.

(b) This religious education includes both the Quran and the *sunna*. However, he later elaborated on his views, affirming: 'What I stated was in the larger context of Islam, it did not relate to madrasas. Its sources are Quran and *sunnah*. But it does not follow that every Muslim student has to go through the entire *Hadis* literature. The curriculum necessarily has to be very selective.'[2]

(c) Sayyid Hamid is of the further opinion that modern sub-jects must be included in the madrasa syllabus. He goes on to contend that religious and secular education have always been integrated in the Muslim education. Therefore the inclusion of modern subjects should not be difficult.

(d) Teaching of social sciences or social studies is essential and even more important than that of physical sciences, as 'it is social sciences that would lead not only to modernization of attitude but also to a better understanding of the changes that have engulfed humanity in the wake of scientific and techno-logical development'.[3]

(e) In order to accommodate modern subjects old 'non-reli-gious' subjects may be removed from the madrasa *nisab*; and 'it is entirely possible, as experience has shown, to streamline and abridge the madrasa syllabus'.[4]

(f) He admits that 'There should be no excessive emphasis on Arabic and translations will do for most.' He then reasonably adds that for serious scholars learning Arabic would be necessary as translations do err.

(g) He rejects the theory of prior 'Islamization' of modern sciences, 'for knowledge by definition is indivisible' (perhaps he means universal).

(h) One or two years may be added to the course to facilitate students learning the two courses together.[5]

(i) If these changes are carried out, madrasa degrees should be acknowledged by universities.[6]

1.2. SOME CRITICAL OBSERVATIONS

We agree with most of Saiyid Hamid's suggestions, such as modern subjects should be included in madrasa curriculum; social sciences, more than natural sciences, are required to be taught with the aim of widening the outlook of madrasa students, and we may add, that of integrating them in the national mainstream. In order to accommodate modern subjects, madrasas need at least to remove old 'rational sciences' (*ma'qulat*) from their *nisab*. One or two years need to be added to the course to enable madrasa students to grasp this new course.

Sayyid Hamid is right about the need for lesser emphasis on Arabic language, especially its detailed grammar and syntax. Though he says that the course has to be shortened, and 'streamlined', no clear suggestion as to the process or criterion of shortening the madrasa syllabus is given by S. Hamid. Nor do we agree about his contention that 'experience has shown' that the syllabus 'can be abridged and streamlined'. We are not aware where this has happened successfully. We also feel that the categorical assertion that Muslim youth need to learn not only the Holy Quran but also *sunna* is too wide-ranging and constraining.

We do not agree with the suggestions of S. Hamid and others that once some modern subjects are included in madrasa syllabus, their certificates must be recognized by the universities. There are several reasons for this. Madrasa teachers are not well qualified and often teach even the traditiohal subjects incompetently. Their knowledge and capacity to teach modern subjects are even more doubtful. Regular examinations are not always held. Many students are known to be unable to express themselves even in Urdu, especially in writing.[7] How then can we take for granted the teachers' and studnets' capacity to master modern subjects?

Whatever we have said above is not intended either to under-mine Hamid's views and efforts, or to suggest that no 'modern-ization' is possible. It is just meant to be a 'reality check'. We welcome Hamid's contention that it is more important to teach social sciences than physical sciences, as the former alone can liberalize the mindset of madrasa-educated persons. We have been arguing all through that teaching selectively only the history of Muslim empires in far off lands and geography of Muslim coun-tries, as also the excessive emphasis on the concept of the 'unity of *umma*', encourage a sense of separate identity of Muslims.[8] These emphases appear to tell innocent young minds that by virtue of their belonging to the 'Muslim *umma*', they are Mus-lims first, and Indians afterwards. On the other hand, if Muslim children are taught the history, geography, and political science of India, they would be better able to see themselves as Indians, and would be better able to participate in the nation's main-stream.

However, a person also needs some elementary knowledge of physical sciences and arithmetic. They are equally required for the broadening of the viewpoint, encouraging the spirit of en-quiry, observation and search for rational explanations of things and occurrences (as diseases). Most Indians, deprived of any con-tact with modern scientific views and approach, tend to seek primitive solutions and cures for diseases and other phenomena which only increase their suffering. A scientific spirit would go a long way in developing their self-confidence and better equip them to deal with life and its challenges. Liberal Muslims insist that the Quran itself emphasizes observing nature which is the root of all science, and therefore there is no conflict between Islamic education and modern science.

2. GOVERNMENT'S SCHEMES OF 'MODERNIZATION OF MADRASAS' (MOM)

2.1. First MOM Scheme

The Government of India's original Scheme of Modernization of Madrasas was formulated in 1993–4. The objective of the Scheme was to encourage traditional educational institutions like maktabs and madrasas to introduce the teaching of science, maths, social studies, Hindi and English in order to bring the students into the mainstream education. The process of modernization was entirely voluntary. The Scheme covered: (a) 100 per cent assistance for appointment of qualified teachers; (b) assistance for book banks or libraries; (c) provision of science and maths kits, and so on.[9]

Hamdard Education Society was asked to evaluate the implementation of the Scheme. Out of approximately 800 madrasas in Uttar Pradesh that were included in the 'modernization' scheme, the evaluating team studied only 78 madrasas, out of which half were affiliated to the Arabi and Farsi Board (to be considered later) and functioned independently. The MOM Scheme covered three types of madrasas (in UP)—(a) madrasas affiliated to and assisted by the Arabi Farsi Board; (b) madrasas affiliated to but not assisted by that Board; and (c) madrasas not affiliated to that Board.[10]

Two major conclusions come out of the Scheme and its implementation. First, it is not clear whether the government aimed at the inclusion of *all* modern subjects, that is, natural sciences, maths, Hindi, English and social sciences; or whether the first four alone were expected to be included. The Report acknowledged that the 'modern' subjects taught in aided madrasas differ significantly. Some teach only science, some science and maths, some others science and English. Similarly while some madrasas have made the learning of modern subjects compulsory, in others it was optional.[11] It makes another significant discovery—that there were several madrasas which were receiving grants but which existed only on paper, while there were others which were recognized as recipients of grants but did not receive any![12] Unfortunately the Report does not give this fact the importance it deserves in the context of disbursement of various government grants.

According to the Report, the Scheme had both positive and negative points, which are as follows:

Strengths

(1) The Scheme has widened the knowledge and enhanced the confidence of students, and made them aware of modern developments. (2) Students have become inquisitive and are learning to think instead of merely memorizing. (3) Enrolment of the

pass-outs of madrasas in institutions of higher learning has become easier. (4) Generally, enrolment in madrasas has increased by 10 to 20 per cent. 'This seems to be due to the augmentation of market value (of these madrasa pass-outs).'

Weaknesses

(1) It usually takes one or two years for the salaries of teachers under this Scheme to reach the madrasas involved. (2) There is the same delay in releasing funds for science and math kits. (3) Teachers employed under this Scheme are untrained and have low educational qualifications. (4) One teacher alone cannot teach all the subjects, i.e. English, Hindi, maths and science, to all classes. (5) The madrasa hours have not been increased. As a result both religious and secular subjects do not get their due. (6) The Report further suggests that social sciences must also be taught.[13]

2.2. The Second MOM Scheme

One of the objections of Hamdard evaluation team, that one teacher alone is not sufficient, has already been taken care of by the Ministry of Human Resources in its Second Scheme of 'Modernization of Madrasas'. Present Scheme envisages that grant for several teachers (number unspecified) would be provided for teaching modern subjects. The second or new Scheme is named Central Sponsored Scheme for Providing Quality Education in Madrasas (SPQEM). It gives its objective as:

The National Policy on Education (NPE), has adopted the concept of a national system of education implying that up to a certain level all students, irrespective of caste, creed, location or sex, have access to education of comparable quality.[14]

It almost casually suggests that madrasas would get affiliated either to National Institution of Open School or the State Madrasa Boards. This Scheme is based on an earlier draft proposal, called Area Instensive and Madrasa Modernization Scheme, but does not include many things of that proposal. Especially significant is the draft's specific proposal that the Urdu textbooks would be prepared by National Council for Promotion of Urdu Language (NCPUL) and grant will be provided to the Council for the same. The finalized Scheme does not say anything about the textbooks; in fact, it does not address itself to the issue of the syllabus or contents of the various modern subjects which it expects would be taught in madrasas.

The entire emphasis of the finalized second Scheme for madrasa modernization is on grants. It tell us that 100 per cent financial assistance will be given for qualified teachers (number unspecified) for teaching science, mathematics, social studies, languages and computers at the rate of Rs. 6,000 per month for graduate teachers and Rs. 12,000 per month for post-graduate teachers. It would give one time assistance to purchase science kits and essential equipment up to Rs. 15,000. There will be one time grant for books up to Rs. 50,000 and each year Rs. 5,000 would be given in addition to this for books. There will be one time grant of Rs. 1,00,000 per lab, and annual grant of Rs. 5,000 in addition. There are other grants for miscellaneous expenses also.[15] Pending approval from the Cabinet, it is expected to be turned into a Bill and become fully operational. How much it would succeed is another matter.

This is too utopian a Scheme and is almost bound to fail. First, generous amounts are being promised, including a ridiculously high grant of Rs. 50,000 for the library with an additional Rs. 5,000 per year for the same, and Rs. 1,00,000 for setting up a science laboratory. It is a well-known fact that madrasas emphatically discourage outside reading.[16] Even in the unlikely case of some madrasas accepting the teaching of modern subjects, they would still want their students not to be too familiar with modern thought for fear that it would undermine their Islamic identity and approach, which is the main purpose of madrasa education. Equally important, madrasa students are not used to, probably not interested in, wide general reading. Nor do we think that an institution requires one lakh to set up a science lab for students up to secondary/senior secondary classes.

Here it would be well to remember that none of this is available to government schools where a majority of children go for their education. Most of the time, the latter do not even have a black board or other teaching aids, forget a library, or a science lab.

The Scheme has provision for several teachers (number unspecified) to teach modern subjects. This should be assessed in the context of the fact that most government schools do not have even two or three teachers at the primary level; even at the secondary level the number of teachers in village schools is mostly less than required.

The Scheme is deliberately vague on the criteria to decide which madrasas are to get these huge grants. The criteria generally given are that the madrasa should have a pukka building, should be established by a registered society, and be in existence for at least three years. This however does not tell us the most crucial details about the madrasas, such as number of students, teachers, the level to which Arabic education is given, and so on.

It also does not take into consideration very marked differences among madrasas due to the sectarian (*maslaki*) differences, as well other circumstances. For example, the general ambience of madrasas established by Jamaat-i-Islami is very different from those, say, belonging to the Ahle-Sunnat sect. The former madrasas welcome the introduction of modern subjects without undermining their strictly religious and communitarian character. But the latter, and most other madrasas, protect their students from being influenced by the outside world. Thus, inclusion of modern subjects would be difficult in most of them. In view of the immense variety of autonomous madrasas, we can never be sure to which extent modern subjects would be taught and modern spirit inculcated, as is proved by the Hamdard Society's Report cited above.

The number of students in madrasas varies from 10–12 boys/girls to almost 3,000 boys/girls. Similarly the infrastructure of various madrasas are different—some have huge buildings, while others function from ramshackle houses. A large number of madrasas teach only up to Arabi class 3. Bigger madrasas not only teach up to Arabi class 8 after which a student gets *Alimiyat* degree which is claimed to be equivalent to graduation. Some madrasas teach up to the degree of *Fazilat* which is supposed to be equivalent to M.A.; and provide opportunities for research in Islamic subjects. Therefore, prior enquiry and later supervision by the government are a must. In view of the Hamdard Society Report's finding that a relatively large number of madrasas which were receiving grants were on paper only, the people's money in such huge amounts cannot be easily given in the name of 'modernization'.

Surprisingly the Scheme also aims at teaching of modern languages, and gives a prominent place to Arabi and Farsi (Persian) among modern languages. We do not think a secular government has any business in promoting the teaching of these languages which are taught in madrasas in a purely religious context, and which are not Indian languages at all. Besides, these are being taught in great detail in madrasas without the assistance of the government. The government can at best provide assistance for the teaching of modern subjects, though even for that a balanced perspective would have to be taken considering the investment done and results obtained.

The Scheme's implementation demands too much paper work on the part of both the government and the madrasas. That the madrasas are reluctant to answer any queries about themselves is shown by the failure so far of all attempts to survey or contact them by any organization. There is a well-known unwillingness in persons connected with or working in madrasas for any writing work, including keeping regular accounts and other details. We are not talking here about the few bigger madrasas which would not accept government grant any way, nor about the very small ones which would not qualify for aid, but of the middle-range madrasas. Even Hamdard Education Society could not get responses from a large number of madrasas during Qamar Uddin's *Kul Hind Survey*, and again when it was asked to evaluate the government's modernization scheme. The paper work involved in, or expected from, madrasas in such schemes is tremendous, and not many madrasas would be able to successfully and regularly carry it out.

We have personally visited an excellent madrasa in Nabi Karim, Old Delhi, which is up to class 5, and teaches all religious and modern subjects to the best possible level. It has shortened and simplified the religious curriculum; has a wonderful Urdu prayer based on the Quran but universal in its appeal; and teaches the two groups of subjects in two shifts to the same group of children. I was so impressed by its performance, that I sent it a form and detailed brochure to help it receive government grant under the old scheme. Not getting any response, I repeatedly asked the madrasa head why he was not trying for the grant. His answer was that he wanted the grant but was unable to understand the form fully. I offered to fill it for them but still got no response. This proves how the complex government paper work required for receiving the grant is not possible for most madrasa officials.

On the other hand as everybody knows, red-tapism, excessive paper work and administrative hierarchy are the bane of all government schemes. There is continuous political interference, as a result of which even sincere government officers are not able to undertake fruitful work. Add to it the fact that most government officers and clerks are not sincere towards their work and are generally corrupt; and we have the recipe for failure. The other drawback is that there are too many agencies involved. The grant will be released by the central government but it will be implemented by the states. Correspondence between various offices would take up almost all the energies of the persons involved, and the real work would suffer. Most schemes of grants to NGOs by the government have been bogged down with delays in release of funds on the one hand and inadequate documentation as well as implementation of the project for which the grant is being given to them on the part of NGOs on the other.

Perhaps the greatest weakness of the Madrasa Modernization Scheme in its present form is that there is no provision for supervision and checking of the proper distribution and utilization of grants or the implementation of the proposed scheme. Widespread corruption wherever money, especially such huge grants are involved, is the rule in our public dealings; religion of the persons involved in the money transactions does not count. We have seen in the implementation of earlier Scheme, that in many cases madrasas existed only on paper but were receiving grants; while there were many madrasas listed as beneficiaries that never received the money.

Earlier the grants were petty and even then they did not reach their intended beneficiary. Here we are talking of 5,000 madrasas which the Government of India intends to 'modernize'. The possibility of misappropriation of funds in this scenario would be huge indeed.

There is no definite provision, even though casual mention is there, for supervision of madrasas which would receive these grants, whether they have utilized them for the purpose for which they were given. Equally important is regular check-up. Supervision to monitor whether madrasas are teaching all subjects, and utilizing the grant for the purpose for which it was given and guidance are further needed concerning the standard of teaching of modern subjects in these madrasas. Equally important would be supervision of the quality and level of teaching of modern subjects to the level of modern schools. As of now, there is no provision for any supervision.

The strict hierarchy in the madrasa administration is often a hurdle in government's dealings with these institutions. The members of the Managing Committee have total control on madrasas, and since they are otherwise engaged also, they do not bother to answer any queries. Above all, madrasas are autonomous, and furiously protective of their independence. Even in medieval times they did not accept state patronage. Though the state as well as the feudal sections of the society gave them large grants, they never interfered with the working of the madrasas. The government is seen as an 'outsider', and taking grants from it goes against the grain of madrasas. Moreover, with the government grant comes the rider that the madrasa authorities will have to provide annual account of the utilization of the grant and overall progress report to the government. The latter may also (though does not) periodically supervise or check the academic progress of students, as also the utilization of the grant. This is as it should be, but not what autonomous madrasas are used to. They are unwilling to sacrifice the independence which they have been enjoying ever since their founding.

The recent proposal to provide scholarships to economically deprived Muslim children/youth is a more sensible scheme. If carried out effectively it would go a long way in improving the social and educational backwardness of Muslims, rather than the same resources and efforts being directed to a complete 'modernization of madrasas'.

3. SOME OTHER PROBLEMS IN 'MADRASA MODERNIZATION'

3.1. OPPOSITION FROM THE CONSERVATIVE ELEMENTS TO INTRODUCTION OF MODERN SUBJECTS

As we have observed in the previous chapter, not only the madrasa teachers and *maulanas* and other Muslim ideologues but also students of madrasas and a majority of Muslim intellectuals and writers assert their opposition to the very idea of inclusion of modern subjects in the madrasa syllabus. All of them opine that such a change in the madrasa syllabus would undermine the main purpose of madrasa education, as also create confusion in the minds of the students.[17] This is so because they have interiorized the Western opposition of the religious and the secular, forgetting that such an opposition is against the spirit of Islam.[18] The basic argument is always the same that madasas are meant to teach the Islamic subjects and they are doing a splendid job in their role as teachers and guides of Muslims.[19] If some writers acknowledge that modern subjects should also be taught, they put so many pre-conditions for teaching them, such as the need for prior Islamization' of modern subjects,[20] that the entire idea of 'modernization' evaporates. Thus, the idea of inclusion of modern subjects in the madrasa syllabus is rejected even before it is even properly formulated.

A few things are to be remembered here. First, if some madrasas have introduced modern subjects, it is out of their own free choice and not under any government scheme. Second, they have stead-fastly refused to apply for government aid, as this would adversely affect their autonomy. Third, the inclusion of modern subjects has been mostly influenced by public demand. And fourth, there is no surety about the contents and standard of modern subjects being taught, as there never has been any supervision of their efforts by any institution outside the madrasa or its founding society. Madrasas founded by some well-organized societies, such as Jamaat-i-Islami, or the Islamic Awakening Centre, Delhi, have a better organized system and even syllabus. It is also to be noted that these organizations have shortened their Islamic syllabus considerably. Any way, the Dars-i-Nizami changes according to the sect of the madrasa. Most madrasas which have included modern subjects belong to the Ahle-Hadith sect. Even here there is no set pattern or framework for the 'shortening and streamlining' of the *Dars*, madrasas or rather sects deciding their own priorities. (For example, modern subjects included in the madrasas established by the Islamic Awakening Centre in Delhi have been included haphazardly.)

Repeatedly, *maulanas* and other advocates of madrasa education have expressed opposition to the idea of including modern subjects in the madrasa *nisab*, especially if the idea is mooted by the government. This opposition is so strong that even some rumour as to the possibility of government interference results in a wave of protest.[21] A curious argument is often put forward that there must be some 'design' in the government's proposal for 'modernization' of madrasas—that the government wants to 'control' them.[22] This oft-repeated argument is wide off the mark. It might have been partially true during the NDA rule, but not so otherwise. It is not that other political parties are sincerely concerned about the conditions of Muslims. But the pressure of various reports and surveys, last of them being the Sachar Committee Report, has left no alternatives for the government except to confront the problem of low level of literacy among Muslims and other problems which follow from this. The need for votes further prompts the political parties to 'do' something tangible for the amelioration of the conditions of Muslims. We fail to perceive any hidden 'design' in the government's initiative to 'modernize' madrasas, even though we do not agree fully with such efforts. Not much positive result can be achieved when there is so much suspicion of, and resistance towards, the government.

Conservative Muslims, both *ulama* and those who have come under their direct influence, express an attitude of suspicion and hostility towards everything modern, especially towards the government. The recent contentions regarding some madrasas harbouring terrorists, both by the media and certain government circles (which sometimes have some justification), have strengthened this sense of alienation not only from the government but also from any 'outsiders' among madrasa teachers and students.

> We sometimes faced this implicit hostility to 'outsiders' when we visited madrasas in and around Delhi. There was no open hostility or uncivil behaviour towards us; the officials only said that the times are bad, so they do not want to talk to 'outsiders'. Most of all, we were never allowed to talk to the students directly except in the presence of some madrasa teacher. Even then it was noticed that the students were hesitant in answering the questions. While we were welcomed in the boys' madrasa of Islamic Awakening Centre, in spite of being a woman, I was denied access to the girls' madrasa and was later asked to give a written application for permission, which I did not.

We do not know how the government officials can overcome the madrasas' resistance to any new thing, the hostility to and suspicion of the government, and the emphatic autonomy of the madrasas as centuries' old independent institutions, especially as the former function at an impersonal level and are generally insincere in their efforts.

3.2. Two Courses are too Heavy, and their Mindsets too Different to be Combined

Apart from the government's utopian, impractical intentions to 'modernize' madrasas which we have critically discussed above, there are two most important hurdles in any attempt to include all modern subjects in a madrasa curriculum. As we have pointed out earlier, each of the two curriculums in their original form are too heavy and can just not be combined without making it impossible for madrasa students to master either. Certain Madrasa Boards have tried to include all modern subjects and have been forced to drastically reduce the content of *dini* (religious) subjects.

S. Hamid and a few others who genuinely want to include modern subjects in the madrasa *nisab* have not fully faced the issue as to how the removal of two or three medieval 'rational sciences' would create space for 10 to 12 modern subjects. It is clear that they do not intend to reduce the rest of Dars-i-Nizami which itself is a very heavy syllabus, especially its excessive emphasis on the teaching of Arabic language in an archaic style of excessive emphasis on grammar which consumes a great part of students' time and energy. Then there are *tafsirs* with their commentaries, along with additional commentaries and more commentaries and guides; six *hadiths* (which are never read in full but still demand a lot of memorization); other subjects such as *sirat, fiqh* and *aqa'id*. Each of these subjects has a large number of books to be memorized. It has been repeatedly argued that these books cannot be understood without prior learning of detailed Arabic grammar and old logic (*mantiq*). *Mantiq* again has a very large number of books prescribed. Leave aside modern subjects, how a student is expected to master all the above subjects is a mystery. Thus, even if some 'rational sciences' are removed, though the *ulama* and other traditionalists do not agree with this suggestion, the remaining syllabus remains very heavy.

At the other end, the modern syllabus is equally heavy. There are three languages and some of their literature to be learnt, three sciences (physics, chemistry, and biology), four social sciences (history and geography of both India and a little of the world, civics or political science, and economics) and mathematics. In spite of the constant talk for the need of reducing the syllabus of modern schools, it has only been increased. Additional subjects (such as disaster management and computers) have been added. The comprehensiveness, extensiveness and often even the irrelevance of a large number of topics of modern syllabus constitute a serious problem which is not being faced by modern educationists.

How can madrasa students, coming often from underprivileged background and studying in institutions with a very different ambience, who have to study their own extremely difficult and extensive *Dars*, ever master all the modern subjects when even the students of modern schools who have to cope up with only one set of subjects, find it so difficult to master?

The proportion of both groups of subjects, in case modern subjects are included in madrasa syllabus, is a very important problem which has to be faced seriously. Therefore, if we have to include modern subjects in the madrasa curriculum, then they would have to be general and elementary. Alternatively, the original *dini* syllabus would have to be curtailed to a great extent.

Apart from the near impossible load of a combined Dars-i-Nizami and modern curriculum, there is another very important reason why the two cannot be brought together easily. The pre-suppositions, goals, values and above all the mental frameworks of the two syllabuses are entirely different and almost contradictory.

Ideally at least, modern education seeks to instil in the child an inquisitive spirit and a desire to understand for herself her surroundings, both natural and social. Above all, it encourages, or at least its theoretical goal is, the development of the habit of enquiry concerning the causes of any phenomena and not to accept any explanations or contentions simply on the basis of someone's authority. Again at the ideational level, if not in practice, students are expected to put a 'why' to every assertion made, and the theory being taught is expected to answer that 'why'. The same is true of social sciences. If some theory or some statistics or explanations of some phenomena are given, students are simultaneously explained the reasons for the particular contention.

Moreover, modern knowledge is never static, it is continuously being added to, questioned and corrected. Even the theory of Relativism of arguably the greatest scientist of twentieth century Einstein has been questioned and qualified. Scientific world is abuzz with continuous controversies and efforts to learn about natural phenomena in a more comprehensive and rationally justifiable manner. In social sciences the theories that were once held to be sacrosanct, as Marxism in social economics, Freudian theory in psychology, are no more acceptable, and so on. Students are encouraged to read on their own whatever interests them. (We are not trying here to idealize modern education as it is mostly conceived and imparted in contemporary Indian schools.)

Contrast the above to the madrasa syllabus and approach. Most, almost all, the books prescribed are about seven centuries or more old. Since then the world has moved forward, while madrasa education has remained static, fossilized as it were in the pre-Aurangzeb period, or rather at the stage at which it existed in tenth-eleventh centuries, when the gates of *ijtihad* were supposedly closed. Subjects being taught and their basic ideas are even older. In astronomy Ptolemy's theory is taught, and in chemistry (*chemia*) mostly alchemy is taught, as also ancient Greek logic and philosophy. Recently, there have been suggestions of doing away the latter two, i.e. Greek logic and philosophy, but no thought has been given to natural sciences as they are taught. The fact is that Islamic knowledge has been fossilized. As we have seen during the course of this study, Arabs were the pioneers of all knowledge, and their capitals were the centres of greatest academic progress in the entire world in the early centuries of Islam. However, as early as thirteenth century, Abdul Qadir Badauni observed:

After the formation of four schools of thought, i.e. Hanafi, Shafaii, Malaiki and Hanbali, the gates of *ijtihad* (efforts for interpretation) were closed with the exception of Jafari. This was contrary even to the attitude of the founders of the schools. None of them ever claimed the finality which the later generations assigned to them. The doctrine of *taqlid* (faithful adherence) was emphasized. This attitude was, in part, due to a fear of rationalism and analytical thought.[23]

What happened after that? Why were the gates of *ijtihad* closed? These are questions that puzzle us. But it is not for us to try to find an answer. As of now, madrasa knowledge is far removed from critical reasoning, progress and correction through new discoveries. The only task of madrasa teachers is to impart to their students what has been written a long time ago; and for students to memorize that by rote. Questioning is not allowed, and may even be punished. Not only is no outside reading permitted in traditional madrasas, even that of other schools of Islam is banned. Those who dare to violate the rule are punished, and may even be rusticated. No outside material is allowed inside madrasas, and students' minds are kept enclosed in the norms and perceptions of medieval times. The main concern of the *maulanas* is to teach their students the final 'truth' of the particular version of Islam as understood by that particular sect, and the way to defend 'their Islam' by attacking the rival sects.[24] They are not interested in the outside world, nor in the Quranic injunction of observing nature. There is no critical or rational approach to anything, either concerning their own texts or daily matters. Such restrictions make for closed minds, and closed minds cannot gain meaningful knowledge.

Here we are not comparatively evaluating the two systems and syllabuses of madrasas and modern schools, only looking at the extreme differences in the ambience (*mahaul*) of two types of educational institutions. While modern thinking in both natural sciences and social sciences stresses freedom of thought and believes in constant progress in knowledge, madrasa syllabus and approach believe and actively promote the idea that the knowledge that existed during tenth and eleventh centuries in the Islamic world was final, and no addition or revision of that can be conceived and ever allowed. Maulana Gilani, who expresses a relatively more open mind and suggests shortening of madrasa syllabus and so on, finally declares that the Quran does not permit questioning. He adds that persistent argumentation is harmful for both the mind and character.[25] There is thus constant effort to enforce *taqlid* or blind following of the written word.

This blind following is in fact implicit in Islamic faith that the Quran is the 'final revelation' of God to the humankind. This would have been alright but for the fact that several *suras* of the holy text were 'revealed' in the context of the seventh-century Arab society, and cannot be easily applied in the context of today's world, like the *suras* dealing with the treatment of slaves. The text also does not provide guidance for every eventuality of life. Therefore, Islamic experts have included *sunna* or the stories of the approvals and disapprovals of certain acts by the Prophet, as reported in various *hadiths*. There are various problems related to the *sunna* and *hadiths*, some of which we have discussed in chapter 5.[26] The greatest problem is that most orthodox *ulama* and *maulanas* believe the *sunna* to be divine, thus implying that there is no scope for disagreeing with whatever is reported in *hadiths*. Importantly, the emphasis on blind following of the written word makes it very difficult for a majority of Muslims who have come under the direct influence of *ulama* and other conservative elements, to adjust with modern times and its spirit of relative freedom. Mushir-Ul-Haq observes that a majority of *ulama* and the masses believe that religion is not only faith but *shari'a* also; and nothing is believed to be *ultra vires* of *shari'a*.[27]

As referred to in the last chapter, madrasa teachers frequently put in the objection that they cannot accept the findings of modern science as they go against what is written in the Holy Quran. They insist that every word of the Quran, being God's direct 'revelation', is true. Sometimes some concession is made regarding the introduction of modern subjects in the madrasa curriculum. However, several conditions are put, such as the prior 'Islamization' of modern sciences. Such preconditions make the synthesis of two kinds of knowledge a near impossibility. The two kinds of educational systems—Islamic and modern—are so different that it would be really difficult to teach them to the same students in the same madrasas. For example, how can one teach a student of madrasa to believe blindly in whatever the Islamic texts and teachers say, and understand with an open and questioning mind whatever is being taught in the modern syllabus? It would create confusion in the minds of students, as has been suggested by various writers on the subject.[28]

3.3. THE NEED FOR SHORTENING OF ONE OF THE TWO SYLLABUSES

The above discussion does not mean that we cannot introduce modern subjects in the madrasa curriculum, but only that we would have to be more realistic about the facts before venturing on any such enterprise. Actually, we must 'modernize' our madrasas both for the sake of the youth who study there and for the sake of the masses who come under their direct influence. But we would have to take into consideration the difficulties in teaching two such heavy syllabuses to the madrasa children. We have two alternatives to teach modern subjects in madrasas. The first alternative is to drastically shorten the madrasa syllabus, but no *maulana* would agree to that and no outside agency can venture on this exercise as this would be even more unaccept-able. Even if there is general agreement on the need to shorten the syllabus or translate Arabic books into Urdu (or any other local language), a near impossible possibility, the task would take decades of both academic and even semi-political efforts (to make the *maulanas* agree to the changes) before such a short-ened syllabus is ready. Till then, to introduce the full load of modern subjects on madrasa students, along with the traditional *nisab*, is to expect the impossible.

It is also to be noted that a drastic shortening of the madrasa syllabus would weaken the *dini* character of madrasas. Madrasas exist and function as minority institutions which give specialized training in purely Islamic subjects; and the traditional *maulanas* would not agree to any such drastic shortening of madrasa *nisab*. Even though S. Hamid suggests the 'shortening and streamlining of madrasa syllabus' but he has not seriously addressed this issue.

Another alternative is to drastically shorten the syllabus of modern subjects so that the books give only elementary or introductory knowledge of modern sciences, both physical and social, some mathematics, elementary Hindi and English. Such books have to be prepared afresh. Writing new books in modern subjects in Urdu or other regional languages would be much easier than trying to 'shorten and streamline' the madrasa syllabus which has the sanction of long centuries of tradition. Of course, extra care would have to be taken to ensure that the new books do not carry any traditional bias. Services of regular educationists and experts in different subjects would have to be enlisted. Such a shortened course could perhaps be adjusted in the madrasa schedule if some traditional 'rational sciences' are removed. It would find much better acceptance with *maulavis* and *maulanas* than any suggestion of shortening the madrasa *nisab*.

A shortened course of modern subjects would be able to give the madrasa students some idea of both what is happening in the world outside the four walls of madrasas and modern thought and values. An introduction to modern sciences would offer madrasa students some inspiration to use their intellect or reason in day-to-day life. An introductory knowledge of Indian history (from the beginning and not since the coming of Muslim kings) and geography, as well as some political science and economics would, as S. Hamid says, 'widen' their extremely narrow perspective. Some knowledge of basic maths would help them in everyday transactions, even as knowledge of Hindi and English would make them more confident in communicating with others outside madrasas. An elementary knowledge of modern subjects would both preserve the *dini* character of madrasa education and give their students the necessary knowledge to cope up with the modern world.

4. *NISABS* OF THE STATE MADRASA BOARDS INCLUDING MODERN SUBJECTS

4.1. INTRODUCTORY REMARKS

Uttar Pradesh, Bihar, Bengal, Orissa, Assam, Rajasthan, Madhya Pradesh and Andhra Pradesh have Madrasa Boards. We should remember in this context that:

(a) The affiliation of madrasas to the Madrasa Boards is entirely voluntary.

(b) The *nisabs* (syllabuses) of these Boards are carefully developed with a view to include and synthesize both the traditional and modern subjects.

(c) The nature, comprehensiveness and emphasis on different branches of knowledge differ from one Board to another. While the traditional subjects are kept almost intact in the Arabi and Farsi Madrasa Board of Uttar Pradesh, and a small amount of modern subjects are added to the former course, in almost all other State Madrasa Boards modern subjects form the chief or equal content of the syllabus, to which Arabic language and *diniyat* (religious education) are added. In some of the State Madrasa Boards, traditional subjects are gradually increased in the higher classes.

(d) These Madrasa Boards usually prescribe NCERT or State Board books for all modern subjects; and aim at teaching modern subjects to the same level as general schools.

(e) They also encourage their students to appear in the examinations of either the State Board of Education or the National Institute of Open School.

(f) Only nominal monetary help is being given for 'modernization' to the madrasas affiliated to these Boards; or their grants are too late in coming, so that the madrasas, already starved of funds, have to bear the additional expenses of teaching modern subjects.

(g) Madrasa *maulavis,* themselves being ignorant of both modern subjects and modern languages, find it hard to bear this extra burden, especially in the absence of any monetary incentive. This is the situation up till now; we do not know if the second scheme, which proposes huge sums to madrasas for 'modernization', would make any difference.

4.2. ARABI AND FARSI MADRASA BOARD OF UTTAR PRADESH

The *nisab* of Arabi and Farsi Madrasa Board of Uttar Pradesh, as given by Ghulam Yahya Anjum,[29] is quite different from those of other Boards. It is under the supervision of the Department of Welfare of Minorities. It gives the certificates of *Alim* (Higher Secondary), *Kamil* (B.A.) and *Fazil* (M.A.) which are recognized by various universities. Its curriculum prepared by Jamia Hamdard in 2001 is meant to fulfil the needs of both Shi'as and Sunnis.

As usual there is no emphasis on the course for *Tahtaniya* or primary classes (five years). It is followed by *Fauqani'a* or secondary course (three years), *Aliya* (high) classes for *Munshi/Maulavi* certificate (two years, which is supposedly equivalent of class 10); and two more years for *Alim* certificate (which is equivalent to Intermediate or 10+2). *Ulya* (higher) classes consist of three years of *Kamil* (equivalent to B.A.) and two years of *Fazil* (equivalent to M.A.). We have given this *nisab* in chapter 4.

This *nisab* seems to be 'secular' in the sense that traditional *dini* subjects are given less prominence, the main emphasis being on the Arabic and Persian (Farsi) languages and their literatures (*adab*). On the other hand, the option of one subject out of all modern subjects seems to be a mockery of the idea of inclusion of modern knowledge, especially when the student can also opt for *mantiq* (old logic). Perhaps its main aim is the teaching of Arabi and Farsi. The Board receives substantial grants from the state government. But as far as 'modernization' of madrasas is concerned, the Board's contribution is not worthwhile.

4.3. STATE MADRASA EDUCATION BOARD, ASSAM

We are including the State Madrasa Education Board, Assam because it is a lesser known and discussed one; and because the percentage of Muslim population there is quite large. The 'Syllabi' published by the Department of Education, Assam, affirms the following features of education in madrasas up to the secondary stage:[30]

(a) In spite of addition of modern subjects, the curriculum retains the same duration of years as before.

(b) The curriculum prescribes the full secondary school courses and syllabi prescribed by the Secondary Education Board of Assam as compulsory subjects.

(c) It does not adversely affect or minimize the teaching of any theological or allied subject in any form. Rather the new syllabus has reintroduced the once-dropped subjects of *mantiq*, *hikmat* and Persian.

(d) Its Arabic language and literature are comparable to any university course. It also has introductory computer science and Hindi.

(e) There is provision for two years' title courses in *hadiths*, *fiqh* and *fatwa*.

(f) Although several new things have been added, it does not overload the students.

(g) The curriculum does not involve extra expenditure.

(h) It ensures the availability of teachers, textbooks, science and other apparatus and teaching aids.

(i) The curriculum thus paves the way for recognition of its F.M. (*Fa'dil al M'a'rif*) or final examination as equivalent to that of B.A.

(j) The curriculum makes madrasa education more need based.

(k) It also paves the way for better employment possibilities through quality education and training.

In pre-senior and *Dakhil* sections, comprising six years (up to class 10), all modern subjects, i.e. English, social studies, general science and general mathematics are compulsory. The books prescribed for modern subjects are those of the State Education Board of Assam. The curriculum also includes all religious or theological subjects, including *fiqh, tafsir* and *hadith*, the main emphasis, as usual, being on teaching the Arabic language.[37] We have given the Assam Madrasa Board's syllabus in chapter 4.

The impressive syllabus apart, the question remains if this curriculum is practical? Can any student take up so much load? The peculiar thing is that in the very beginning the authors or framers of the syllabus have claimed that the teaching of all subjects of the two independent groups has neither needed the increase in the timings of madrasas, not to say anything about increasing one or two years, as suggested by S. Hamid; nor has it involved any extra load, either in terms of labour for students, or in terms of considerable extra expenses. The students have to learn Bengali or Assamese as their mother tongue which is very rightly the medium of instruction. In addition, they have to learn other languages: Assamese if they are studying through Bengali medium, Urdu since it is believed to be the language of Muslims in India, and Hindi and English. The teaching of Arabic starts almost from the beginning of madrasa education and is taught with traditional grammar. Persian is added later as an optional subject.

The claim that madrasa children are able to master all modern subjects plus some elementary-level religious subjects in addition to learning several languages is unbelievable. How can so many additional modern subjects and languages be taught without over-burdening the children and incurring additional expenditure? The question is obvious, especially when neither the years of study nor the hours of study have been increased. To compress more than double the madrasa course in the same time frame would be nothing short of a miracle.

Equally important, there is no proper provision for periodical supervision of the functioning and teaching of these madrasas. Moreover these madrasa students are expected to give regular examinations of the State Madrasa Education Board up to the secondary level or high school, after which the madrasas function as regular *dini* madrasas for a few more years. But so far no attempt has been made to assess the number and percentile of students who have successfully passed these common examinations in secular subjects. In the absence of any such data, the entire enterprise remains a question mark.

Even more important, there is nominal aid for the modernizing programme from the central agency of Sarva Shiksha Abhiyan. The aid is insufficient, especially in the context when huge amounts are being promised to individual madrasas without any system for effictive monitoring. In Assam there is a regular organization already in place which has a large number of registered madrasas affiliated to it. The aid can be given to the Madrasa Board to be properly distributed among its affiliated madrasas. Of course, monitory and academic supervision remains the key to the success of any such scheme.

4.4. STATE MADRASA BOARD OF MADHYA PRADESH

Madhya Pradesh is another state that has tried seriously to introduce modern subjects in madrasas. Its Rajya Shiksha Kendra (Department of Education) established a separate Madrasa Board early, but a proper scheme for modernization of madrasas by including modern subjects in their syllabus started only in 1998 under the aegis of the District Primary Education Project (DPEP). Here the state and madrasas together have established the State Madrasa Board and DPEP entered later as a funding authority. A Report of a Study of the government school system discusses various government initiatives in the field of primary and secondary education, including its Case Study 6 on 'Modernization of Madrasas (MOM) Programme in Madhya Pradesh'.[32] It tells us that the 'primary objective of the intervention was to mainstream these (madrasa) children into formal education by introducing a modern curriculum in madrasas'. It further asserts that according to this Scheme, 'While madrasas continue to provide religious education, they have also incorporated the formal state curriculum for transaction in Hindi, English, Urdu, Environmental Studies (EVS), Social Science, Mathematics and Science at the primary and upper primary levels.'[33]

The Rajya Shiksha Kendra spends some amount for teachers' training (two teachers per madrasa, for 20 days) and a grant of Rs. 2,000 per annum to prepare teaching aids, and a teachers' grant of Rs. 500 for two teachers to prepare teaching aids for better classroom transactions to every madrasa willing to joint the scheme. Free distribution of textbooks for modern subjects to all children is a crucial aspect of the Madhya Pradesh Education Department's initiative. While most textbooks are in Urdu, those for mathematics and science are in Hindi. Registration of madrasas for receiving aid for 'modernization' is voluntary. 'The main criterion for registration,' according to the Report, 'is that they should have out of school children receiving only religious education.'[34]

Subjects taught at the primary level are mathematics, English, Hindi, Urdu, general knowledge, and EVS. In the upper primary classes, the schedule and the duration of total teaching time and other activities, such as games, prayer, recess, are more or less the same, and the subjects also remain the same. Most madrasas add general science and social studies, and some craft (called creative work) to the above-mentioned subjects, though some do not. The duration of periods is increased to 40 minutes instead of 30 minutes at the primary level, while the total madrasa timing is increased by 15 to 30 minutes! Till upper primary level only *diniyat* and Arabic (alternate days) are taught as religious subjects.[35]

MP state government makes tall claims regarding the success of its Madrasa Modernization Programme:

(a) The government has 4,300 madrasas registered in the state (possibly both madrasas and maktabs are included).

(b) 2,200 madrasas are recognized for primary and middle examinations.

(c) There is provision for training in computers at 12 madrasas.

(d) Midday meal scheme is implemented in 500 madrasas.[36]

The casual manner in which the Madrasa Boards state their programme and schedule expresses a lack of clarity on the part of both the officials of the Education Department and those of the Madrasa Board about most crucial issues. To give just one example, 'They [madrasa students] are being taught modern subjects like mathematics, English, physics, chemistry, etc., according to the syllabi prescribed by the State Open School and the Madhya Pradesh Board of Secondary Education.'[37] It seems there is no definite policy regarding which Board of Education the madrasas would be affiliated to, and which subjects would be taught. In the absence of any clarity on such fundamental issues, to expect that 'modernization of madrasas' would be successful anywhere is just naïve optimism.

There is one difference: while in the Assam Madrasa Board, the comprehensiveness of traditional subjects is preserved, and the total periods allotted to religious or traditional subjects are much more than to modern subject, in the Madhya Pradesh Board, it is the other way round. The madrasa timings are 4 hours and 45 minutes, or even less, out of which three hours are reserved for modern subjects and only one period of about 40 minutes for Arabic/*Diniyat* everyday. Actually out of the 4 hours 45 minutes of madrasa timing, the total teaching time is generally only three hours. The rest is taken up by 15 minutes for prayer;

30 minutes for recess and 30 minutes for games. While many madrasas are for boys only, there are some in which boys and girls both study; and number of girls is about 60 per cent in these madrasas. Thus, madrasas affiliated to Madhya Pradesh Board try to teach all or most modern subjects plus only two subjects of *Diniyat* and Arabic. On the whole this seems to be a more balanced scheme than that of Assam Board which is trying to include all subjects, both traditional and modern.

4.5. SOME CRITICAL OBSERVATIONS ON MADRASA BOARDS

On the basis of the above Report on 'Modernization of Madrasas' in Madhya Pradesh, we can generalize, as the government's functioning and general problems in the implementation of such schemes where several agencies are involved are very similar everywhere in India. The Report frankly puts forward several weaknesses of the MOM Programme in the state under discussion. The following observations, though depending on the above Study for documentary proof, are meant to apply to all such government schemes:

(a) The most important weakness of the earlier MOM programme was that there was no proper grant, nor any initiative to madrasas for modernization. The Study reports that madrasa teachers complained that they did not get any (monetary) incentive to teach modern subjects. Why should they, having studied in traditional madrasas and imbued with their spirit, be interested in teaching, or even studying and understanding modern subjects?

Actually, the financial aid to madrasas for modernization so far is minimal, not only in Madhya Pradesh but also in Assam, the two states we have studied in this context, we can assume that with the sole exception of Arabi and Farsi Board of UP, the situation would be the same everywhere. This is important, as these madrasas have themselves taken the initiative to get registered with the Madrasa Board and have expressed willingness to include modern subjects in their curriculum. The Government of India's earlier MOM Scheme made a provision for the payment of salary and training of one teacher of modern subjects per madrasa, but even that does not seem to be forthcoming in the above two states. The annual grant of Rs. 2,000 for teaching aids and Rs. 500 for two teachers' teaching aids is hopelessly inadequate. In the case of Assam, we did not even come across any such grant.

(b) It is well known that even this pittance of aid does not reach madrasas at the beginning of the session but at the end. Meanwhile the madrasas have to arrange for whatever is required for teaching modern subjects. Importantly, no thought is given for redressing this basic financial problem in the new scheme which, when implemented, would spend huge sums for modernization of madrasas. The existing problems of implementation and execution of such over-ambitious schemes involving several offices and organizations would remain in the implementation of the new Scheme also.

(c) The training of teachers (obviously *maulavis* who have no knowledge of modern subjects) for 20 days is far from adequate. How can madrasa-educated *maulana*s be taught all the modern subjects, which they are expected to teach, in 20 days, especially when the mindset, approach and teaching methodology are so different in the two streams of knowledge? All writers on madrasa education stress the need for teachers' training, including the Hamdard Education Society's Report; but even more important is the knowledge of subjects which the *maulanas* are expected to teach.

(d) There is a provision for free distribution of textbooks of modern subjects to all madrasa children in the original MOM programme of MP. However, as the Study states, they do not often reach in time to be useful and equally often, instead of Urdu, madrasas receive Hindi-medium books. *Maulavis* who are supposed to teach modern subjects are often totally ignorant of, and sometimes prejudiced against, Hindi.

(e) The Hindi used in Madhya Pradesh Education Board's textbooks is too Sanskritized to be understood by ordinary students, not to say anything of madrasa *maulavis* and students. According to the MOM programme, while social studies is taught in Urdu, science and mathematics books are to be in Hindi. It is true that translating science terms into Indian languages creates a lot of problems. But the problem can be solved if the original English terms are given in a transcribed form in brackets, along with their Hindi or Urdu translations. This holds true for all Indian languages. However, to expect the *maulanas,* who do not know the basics of science, mathematics, and for that matter Hindi, to teach these subjects in chaste Hindi is unjustified. Hence the need to provide teachers who are knowledgeable in modern subjects and languages.

(f) The MOM scheme envisages regular supervision and assessment of 'modernization' in madrasas. The Report contends that this has not been very successful. While the government functionaries are perhaps rightly hesitant in inspecting the madrasas (which are generally emphatically protective of their independence), members of the Madrasa Board have also not done their duty.

This is unfortunate, as it is near impossible for state officials to deal directly with 4,000 madrasas (the state government's records claim this). Inspecting them for eligibility, giving appropriate grants to individual madrasas, and periodically inspecting their progress require a regular organization. In Madhya Pradesh such an organization, State Board of Madrasa Education, does exist. That should be strengthened and given the above responsibilities. The government's Education Department should have the responsibility of supervising the functioning of Madrasa Board.

The same holds true for Assam and all other Madrasa Boards. There is hardly any attempt to supervise and monitor the performance of madrasas regarding the teaching of modern subjects, far less the standard or level of grasping of the same by the students. The Hamdard Society's Evaluation Report found that there was deliberate mix-up as to which madrasas were receiving grants for 'modernization'.[38] This clearly shows a total absence of supervision, besides, of course, corruption in the distribution of grants.

(g) According to the above Report on Madhya Pradesh, the involvement of the Madrasa Board was minimal and insufficient: 'Madrasa functionaries felt that the Madrasa Board had been largely ineffective, whether it was to do with conducting primary and upper primary level examinations on time or issuing school leaving certificates.' Elsewhere also it observes that 'The involvement of members of Madrasa Board appeared to be nonexistent.'[39]

(h) MP and Assam Madrasa Boards make a further claim that there is no additional burden on the children even if they have to learn modern subjects along with the traditional ones. The timings of madrasas in the two states remain the same— 3½ hours for primary and 4½ hours for secondary level. It is a miracle that so many modern subjects and two traditional subjects (*Diniyat* and Arabi language) can be taught in such a short time. The books prescribed for modern subjects are those of the State Board, which would be comprehensive and difficult, especially for those who are brought up and studying in a traditional atmosphere.

Though the Assam Madrasa Board does not make such hyperbolic claims as the MP one does, its course content is even more comprehensive, and it also prescribes textbooks of the State Board for modern subjects. It also does not increase the number of years of study. Moreover, being more or less a non-Hindi speaking and being a bilingual state, madrasa students of Assam have to learn several additional languages. Obviously the load of studies would be very heavy on young minds.

(i) There is persistent confusion in all schemes aiming at modernization of madrasas, from the Hamdard Society's Evaluation Report to all government drafts on the subject and finally even in the above Study. They all give different subjects as being included in the scheme, sometimes citing Hindi, English, mathematics and social studies, sometimes excluding social studies and including science.[40]

(j) MP Madrasa Board expects madrasas to teach modern subjects only up to the secondary level, the idea being that most children being introduced to modern education would enter mainstream schools after that, and those who are genuinely interested in only traditional religious education would continue in madrasas. The government's scheme of 'modernization' also envisages the same. However, Saiyid Hamid is of the opinion that modern subjects must be taught up to high school. This would necessitate drastically reducing the number and contents of traditional subjects, which would not be justified, since madrasas are specifically meant to teach traditional (*dini*) subjects. Therefore, if we have to teach modern subjects to madrasa students, it would be sufficient if they are taught till the secondary level, after which they would be free to teach *dini* subjects. The Assam Madrasa Board continues teaching modern subjects at higher levels, though it does reduce their content while increasing the number and content of purely Islamic subjects.

(k) Madrasa certificates are recognized on paper, but when the madrasa children seek admission in modern schools, these certificates are not given much value. It may be due to the bias of school authorities, but it is equally possible that madrasa children having teachers knowing little about modern subjects may not have received good grounding in modern subjects; or it may also be that the students themselves, being forced to study two streams of knowledge in a very limited time, have not been able to understand modern subjects.

(l) Personally we are not enthusiastic about the MOM schemes for various reasons, which we have been recounting from time to time. However, if all modern subjects are to be introduced in madrasas and considerable grants given to individual, traditionally autonomous madrasas, then the only way to ensure that such utopian and often poorly worked out schemes are not a total failure is to restrict such efforts to madrasas which are already affiliated to some Madrasa Board. This would mean: First, the state agencies would be dealing with those madrasas which have already agreed to the idea of 'modernization'. This would make easier the task of selecting the correct madrasas to be thus brought into the scheme, giving them grants and above all supervising their performance. Second, the government would have an already existing organization through which grants can be channelled. And third, if the Madrasa Board officials accompany the government officials, the opposition to the latter would be far less.

We have noted above how the members of Madrasa Board of Madhya Pradish do not take their duties seriously. All such observations can be generalized. Something would have to be done in order to make the functionaries of these Boards more responsible towards their duties. The officials are often honorary members. If so, they should be given salaries. Once they are made agreeable, they should be given grants as per the number of madrasas affiliated to them. The number of madrasas that the

Board of MP declares as affiliated to it is apparently an inflated figure, or includes maktabs also. Enquiries will have to be done by the government officials, assisted by the Board members.

Once the number of madrasas affiliated to a given Madrasa Board is validated, all grants should be given to the Board, which would be given the additional responsibility of overseeing the utilization of those grants. This utilization would have to be double-checked by the government officials. We have seen earlier, madrasas affiliated to various Boards being starved of funds, even though they want to 'modernize'. There must be some proportion in the amount of grants made to madrasas and their accounts will have to be kept by the government officers.

Anyone having the slightest knowledge of ground realities, including the madrasas' unwillingness to engage in correspondence, their almost total autonomy, opposition to modern knowledge, and suspicion of and hostility towards the State, must realize that dealing with individual madrasas is next to impossible, especially for the government officials. Of course, it would not reduce the responsibility of the government for supervision of both madrasas and the Madrasa Boards, both in the context of the utilization of grants and the successful teaching of modern subjects. If some Madrasa Boards are not teaching modern subjects, or teaching them incompletely, such as the Arabi and Farsi Board of Uttar Pradesh, then the state grant must not be given to them under the Madrasa Modernization Scheme.

4.6. Jamea-tul-Hidaya: A Successful Combination of the Two Systems?

Jamea-tul-Hidaya, Jaipur, is frequently cited as an example of a successful combination of the two systems of education. The website of the Jamea gives its objectives as:

1. To change traditional education system of Islamic madrasas and introduce modern subjects in the curriculum without disturbing the main theological subjects, like *Tafseer*, *Hadith* and Islamic *Fiqh*.

2. To cover the gap between Islamic madrasas and modern schools.

3. To produce vocationally trained *ulama* furnished with language skills, Arabic, English and Urdu, with advance knowledge of science and mathematics.[41]

Its syllabus consists of Islamic subjects (probably some details are reduced), and one of the three technical courses—Computer trade, Electrical trade and Mechanical trade—up to diploma or higher secondary level. They include some science and mathematics in addition to Hindi and English.[42] Care is taken to maintain the primacy of theological subjects.

It is clear that the goal is to make madrasa pass-outs capable of earning their livelihood; therefore the emphasis on technical knowledge and not on modern theoretical knowledge. The 'modernized' syllabus, though it serves a laudable aim, does not give modern knowledge as we generally understand it.

5. MODERNIZATION OF MAKTABS: SOME CRITICAL REMARKS

Maktabs, as we know, mainly teach details of Islamic rituals, especially those that are needed for the correct performance of *namaz*, including the prior mandatory *wuzu*. In addition, they teach Arabic and Urdu alphabets and a little arithmetic. Some Quranic *a'yats* (long verses or passages) are also memorized. However, children who have completed their maktab education cannot even read, far less understand, the Holy Text. There are lakhs of maktabs spread all over India. Often the *Imam* of the *masjid* fulfils the task of teaching the children. The neighbourhood children between the ages of 4 and 12 years gather in the morning for approximately three hours, to be taught by the one *Imam* or *quari* (one who has learnt to recite the Quran).

There are some problems with the maktab system of education. There is no standardization and a child may or may not learn much in his/her years of study in maktabs. Since children of all ages are put together and taught by the same *maulana*, it is a haphazard arrangement for imparting any education. And yet, unfortunately maktab studies are considered equivalent to primary education by a majority of Muslims.

Nowadays a large number of maktabs, especially in large cities, have started introducing some modern subjects, especially Hindi/regional language, English, arithmetic, and sometimes even a little EVS at a very basic level. This is done in response to public demand, as well as with the assumption that a large percentage of these children would drop out after their maktab studies, while some of them would go to madrasas where no modern subjects are taught. Often the years spent in maktabs are regarded by common folk as equivalent to primary classes, with the result that simple Muslim parents are satisfied that their children have had both religious and secular education.

Some state governments have tried to encourage the teaching of modern subjects in maktabs. For example, in Assam, Bihar and Rajasthan there is a regular project for converting these innumerable maktabs into alternative centres of education. In these states the central government's organization, Sarva Shiksha Abhiyan financially supports and guides the transformation of maktabs into institutions for providing 'non-formal' education for those children who don't go to regular schools. Some modern subjects are introduced without even providing an extra teacher, and there is no supervision.

The idea of providing non-formal education in familiar surroundings to those who are still beyond the reach of, or can't afford, regular education, is an excellent idea, but is even more difficult to practically carry out than giving education to children in regular schools with definite curriculum and syllabus. Sometimes this 'modernized' maktab education is described as providing bridge courses so that a child who might have started his/her education late may join mainstream modern education.[43] However, both these schemes of non-formal education and bridge course through maktabs are still in their preliminary stage, and much needs to be done.

Since maktabs are spread all over the country, even in remote villages and in small bylanes of cities, and are autonomous, approaching them for introducing modern subjects would be difficult. If the scheme does not provide for a single additional teacher who could teach modern subjects, the effort is unlikely to bear any real fruits. Maktabs in fact are not suited for the teaching of various subjects of different types, though there are always exceptions. The maktabs established by Jamaat-i-Islami and Dini Talimi Council in Uttar Pradesh seek to combine the two kinds of education more or less successfully.

However, this is not true for a majority of maktabs. They run on charity, and are generally attached to mosques, and situated in congested places. Their main aim is the teaching of Islamic rituals; and in that framework, a half-hearted introduction of some modern subjects, that too without a well-organized scheme, would not help much. Moreover, as the Assam state document acknowledges, most maktabs do not have any infrastructure facilities, such as pukka building, toilets and drinking water. That means the government would have to spend on all these, as well as on at least one regular teacher. A regular school can function better as the centre for non-formal eduation if the same amount of money is spent on it.

Choosing maktabs for imparting non-formal education or imparting bridge courses cannot succeed because of the inherent limitations of the infrastructure and framework of maktabs. Equally important, such a move will give them legitimacy in secular life which is not welcome. It also does not solve the problem of rest of the non-Muslim children who are also out of school and deprived of any opportunity for even basic education. Backward areas need non-formal education as well as bridge courses, but with the aim of taking their children to the mainstream education. But maktabs cannot always serve that purpose.

Before trying to use maktabs for imparting modern knowledge, we must ask ourselves the purpose of maktabs. It is simply and definitely to impart minimum religious education to the masses. The first maktab is said to have been started by the Prophet Muhammad himself. The aim was to teach the Holy Quran. Possibly, some reading, writing and arithmetic would have been included. But at that time Arabic was both the language of the Quran and that of the masses (though other dialects and even languages were also being used). Therefore, studying the Quran could be carried out along with learning some reading and writing. Now the language of Muslims is different from that of the Quran. Therefore, gradually the maktabs have taken a clear-cut course of teaching young ones Arabic and Urdu alphabets, making them memorize some verses (*a'yats*) of the Quran; and above all, teaching them the important rituals of Islam. Usually the

imam of the *masjid* is also the teacher in the maktab affiliated
with it; thus maktabs are an integral part of religious life of the
Muslim masses. Therefore, it would be best to leave the maktabs
to carry out their traditional role, and not try to transform them
into pseudo-modern schools.

The worst result would be, as we have pointed out above, that
poor Muslim parents would think that now their children have
not only learnt the Islamic rituals and some fundamental *a'yats*
of the Holy Quran, but also 'modern' subjects, so there is no
need to send them to modern schools after that. Therefore teaching modern subjects in maktabs through half-hearted schemes in
the hope that thereby children would gain modern knowledge
and also make a transition to upper primary schools seems to be
impractical.

This is not meant to disparage either maktabs, or the possibility of giving modern education to Muslim children attending
maktabs. Rather it is to stress that maktabs must remain institutions of religious education and modern education must be had
in modern schools. We shall return to this subject again in the
final chapter.

6. CONCLUDING OBSERVATIONS

We have listed above various problems in the implementation
of the MOM programme, both which are concerned with the
functioning of madrasas and the government, and those more
important ones which relate to the academic difficulties of
combining two such heavy courses, as well as the radical differences in the approaches of the two educational systems.

However, this does not mean that we should not teach modern knowledge to the youth studying in madrasas; only we will
have to be more realistic when making proposals and schemes.
The greatest requirement for the successful implementation of
any scheme for 'modernization of madrasas' would be to drastically shorten the syllabus of modern subjects. Since the common textbooks are too detailed and advanced to be combined
with the madrasa syllabus, new textbooks would have to be
written in Urdu or other regional languages to give an introductory knowledge of modern subjects to madrasa students.

As a long-term project the advocates of 'modernization of madrasas', along with the educationists, should seriously prepare a concise course, covering all modern subjects, including elementary Hindi and English, which should not be more than one-third of the syllabus of regular schools, or even less, with the sole aim of familiarizing students with the world outside the four walls of madrasas, so that when they come out they do not feel alienated from it. If possible, this course should be made compulsory for all autonomous madrasas. We will have to be extra careful that the books thus produced do not either 'Islamize' modern knowledge, or bring in any other pro-Islam bias, especially in the syllabus of social studies. But the MOM scheme will have to wait until then, for which neither the government, in its mistaken notion that 'if we want to give modern knowledge to our Muslim children, we must 'modernize madrasas', nor the other advocates of MOM would agree. Therefore, if the MOM programme has to be functional immediately, then as a stop-gap arrangement the textbooks of Education Boards meant for at least three classes below the madrasa class must be used. But the real solution lies in preparing a fresh, easier course for madrasas.

Trying to convert maktabs into institutions of modern learning is neither practical, nor desirable. Maktabs cannot provide good modern knowledge (though there can always be exceptions), and expecting them to do so would be distracting them from their main purpose of providing basic religious knowledge. Maktabs should be allowed to perform their traditional function, though in an improved manner, while all maktab going children must go to modern schools for their secular, modern education. We shall return to maktab education in our final chapter.

NOTES

1. See Shoyeb Ansari, *Education in Dini Madaris: An Opinion Survey of Curriculum, Method of Teaching and Evaluaiton in Dini Madaris*, New Delhi: Institute of Objective Studies, 1997, pp. 100–1, 142.

2. Saiyyid Hamid in a personal letter in response to my queries, dated 10 September 2003.

3. Ibid., and another letter dated 2 April 2005.

4. His two letters dated 10 September 2003, and 27 February 2007.

5. His letter dated 27 February 2007.

6. S. Hamid's 'Foreword' to Qamar Uddin, *Hindustan ki Dini Darsgahein: Kul Hind Survey,* New Delhi: Hamdard Education Society, 1996.

7. See the long article of Amir Ullah Khan, Muhammad Saqib and Zafar H. Anjum, 'To Kill the Mocking Bird: Madrasah System in India: Past, Present and Future'. At the end of it they give an account of their visits to a few madrasas, and note that neither the teachers, nor the students 'carry any writing material. It is entirely oral education.' Available at the website http//www.chowk.com/article/6216, 5 August 2003.

8. 'We have to educate *our* young people about the fragmentation of the Ummah, the world over. That the unity of the Ummah in the face of challenges, both from the West and the East, is a prerequisite of *our survival as a free people. . . .* ' The author then goes on to describe '*our historical achievements*' and so on. (italics added) Manzoor Ahmad, *Islamic Education: Redefinition of Aims and Methodology,* New Delhi: Qazi Publishing House, 1990, pp. 17 ff.

9. The first Scheme of 'Modernization of Madrasas' (MOM), as given in the *Evaluation Report on Modernisation of Madrasa Education Scheme* (Uttar Pradesh), New Delhi: Hamdard Education Society, 2000, pp. 1–2.

10. Ibid., pp. 12 ff.

11. 'The Study has revealed that . . . out of the 78 madrasas surveyed, 22 have taken up Science only, 5 have taken up Science and Mathematics only, and only 35 have taken up Science, Mathematics, English and Hindi.' Ibid., p. 38. It also observes that 16 madrasas have kept the teaching of these subjects as optional. Ibid., p. 26.

12. Ibid., pp. 25, 39.

13. Ibid., p. 31.

14. The second Scheme, called 'Central Sponsored Scheme for Providing Quality Education to Madrasas' is recently posted at the website http: education.nic.in/secedu/scheme_SPQEM.pdf. Its draft proposal was with the government for a long time and gave attention to academic details which are missing from the latest proposal.

15. Ibid.

16. 'Your reading table is not a table of public library. This is a madrasa's table [. . .] No book is to be found in our shelves the reading of which makes a man disturbed for weeks. No book should be read which creates doubts against those cherished ideals which are the foundation stone of our madrasas.' Maulana Abul Hasan Ali Nadwi, quoted by Mushir-Ul-Haq, *Islam in Secular India*, Simla: Institute of Advanced Study, 1972, p. 41.

17. See the opening speech of the Rector of Darul Uloom, Deoband at the All India Madrasa Conference in 1994, where he emphatically rejects the idea of the introduction of modern subjects in madrasa *nisab*. Quoted in Qamar Uddin, *Hindustan ki Dini Darsagahein: Kul Hind Survey*, New Delhi: Hamdard Education Society, 1996, pp. 120 ff. Many other Muslim ideologues, such as Maulana Ashraf Ali Thanwi, Maulana Muhammad Qasim Nanatauvi, Mufti Taqi Usmani et al. have also strongly opposed modern subjects being taught in the madrasas. Even madrasa students, as reported by Shoyeb Ansari, opposed this proposal, saying that it would undermine the very purpose of madrasa studies, and confuse the minds of students. See chapter 6, notes 40, 43, 44, 45.

18. See Farhat Hasan, 'Madaris and the Challenge of Modernity in Colonial India', in Jan-Peter Hartung and Helmut Reifeld (eds.), *Islamic Education, Diversity and National Identity: Dini Madaris in India Post 9/11*, New Delhi: Sage, 2006, pp. 60 ff.

19. Maulana Thanwi, Maulana Taqi Usmani and a large number of other maulanas as well as intellectuals, including those educated in the mainstream institutions and even serving in them, affirm that madrasas are doing a wonderful job in theire own field, while praising madrasas sky high. See M. Khalili Qasmi, *Madarasa Education: Its Srength and Weakness*, Mumbai: Markazul Ma'arif Education and Research Centre, 2005, pp. 41 ff., 75 ff., 81 ff., 147 ff., 151 ff., etc.; and various papers presented in the All India Seminar at Jamiatul Falah, Azamgarh, in 1994, titled *Mulk aur Millat ki Tameer aur Dini Madaris*, Azamgarh: Idara Ilmia, 1994, discussed in detail in chapter 6, note 95. Almost every speaker, except one or two, passionately opposed the idea of introduction of modern subjects in madrasas.

20. 'Many basic assumptions of the natural sciences [. . .] are so framed as to be a menace to Islamic culture'. Manzoor Ahmad, op. cit., p. 22; also see ibid., pp. 16 ff., 19 ff., etc.

21. See Mareike Jule Winkelmann, 'Muslim Reaction to Post-9/11

Media Discourse on the Indian Madaris', in *Islamic Education, Diversity, and National Identity*, op. cit., p. 263. However, we do not think that the media discourse in India changed drastically after 9/11. India has had sufficient terrorist activities, but the media, excepting perhaps some Hindutva-based writings, has not shown any alarmist or anti-Muslim bias like in the West.

22. See chapter 6, note 96 regarding Syed Shahabuddin's strong opposition to, and even questioning of the motives of the government in its MOM programme.

23. Badauni quoted in the ' Introduction' by S.M. Azizuddin Husain in S.M.A. Husain (ed.), *Madrasa Education in India*, New Delhi: Kanishka, 2005, p. 3. However he does not tell the original source.

24. See Arshad Alam, 'Making Maslak: Constructing Identity in a Barelwi Madrasa', in the unpublished proceedings of the *International Workshop on Islamic Learning in South Asia*, Erfurt, Germany, 15–21 May 2005.

25. We have frequently quoted Maulana Manazir Ahsan Gilani, who in spite of being relatively liberal, has emphatically asserted that the Quran does not permit argumentation; and any way, 'rational sciences' or even too much reasoning which creates doubts is not good, and must be discouraged. See *Hindustan main Musalmanon ka Nizam-e-Talim wa Tarbiyat,* Delhi: Nadwatul Musannifin, 1955, vol. 1, pp. 179 ff., especially p. 199; 276 ff.; vol. 2, pp. 382–3, etc.

26. See chapter 5, notes 26–66 supra referring to the views of Asghar Ali Engineer, Leila Ahmad and Sharafuddin Maneri contesting the view of divinity and inviolability of *shari'a*.

27. *Islam in Secular India*, p. 17, also pp. 10 ff.

28. See Maulana Taqi Usmani, quoted by M. Khalili Qasmi, op. cit., p. 151, and notes 17, 19, 20 supra.

29. Ghulam Yahya Anjum, *Nisab-e-Taleem (bra-e-darjat-e-'aliya) Imtihanat: Arabi wa Farsi Uttar Pradesh Board,* New Delhi: Jamia Hamdard, 2000.

30. *State Madrasa Education Board: Reorganized Senior & Title Madrasa Curriculum, Courses and Syllabi,* Guwahati: Department of Education, Assam.

31. Ibid.

32. 'Strengthening the government school system: Lessons from promising practices', Report commissioned by the Department of Elementary Education, MHRD, GOI, and International Labour Organization, New Delhi. The study was done by Kameshwari Jandhyala and Vimla Ramchandran, New Delhi: Education Re-

source Unit, May 2006, unpublished but used for academic circulation. Case Study VI , 'Combining Deeni Taleem and Duniyavi Taleem: Madrasa Education in Madhya Pradesh', by Shobhita Rajgopal in the above study.

33. Ibid.
34. Ibid.
35. The time tables of various madrasas were directly procured from them. These time tables gave the details of subjects being taught, as also the period-wise division of various subjects in different classes.
36. The brochure of Madrasa Board, Department of Education, Government of Madhya Pradesh, published by the government. It gives the 'achievements' of the Madrasa Board, and syllabus in brief.
37. Ibid.
38. Hamdard Education Society's *Evaluation Report on Modernisation of Madrasa Scheme*, pp. 25–6, 29–30.
39. Combining *Dini Taleem* and *Duniyavi Taleem*: *Madrasa Eduation in Madhya Pradesh*, pp. 108 and 110.
40. See ibid., pp. 105 and 107 which give different lists of subjects as being included in 'modernization' scheme.
41. See Jamea-tul-Hidaya's website jameatulhidaya.org/main/aims objectives/htm.
42. Ibid., Syllabus of Jamea-tul-Hidaya, as given on the above website under the head 'Syllabus'.
43. See *Evaluation of Alternative Schooling through Maktabs in Assam: Darrang, Dhubri, Marigaon Districts*, Mussouri: National Society for Promotion of Development, Administration and Training, 1999, unpublished, used for circulation in academic studies, pp. 47 ff., 71 ff.

8

Concluding Remarks

---

1. SOME QUESTIONS AND ANSWERS

We started with two basic questions: first, why do a large number of Muslim children go to madrasas for their education rather than to modern schools; and second, can madrasa education be a substitute for modern education?

We have discussed the first question in detail in chapter 2. Without going into the details, let us recapitulate the salient points that emerged from the discussion: First, no one knows the number of children going to madrasas (apart from maktabs), but it is definitely more than the 3–4 per cent, estimated by the Sachar Committee Report. Whatever the number, it is substantial enough to be a national concern. Second, the reasons for a certain, relatively large, section of Muslim parents opting for madrasas instead of modern schools are many and complex.

The alleged non-availability of good government schools in the vicinity of Muslim majority areas, which is often cited as the main reason for Muslim children studying in madrasas, has been discussed in chapter 2 (section 3). There we tried to understand the ground realities regarding the access of Muslim children to modern schools and found that primary schools are available in most areas. However, the availability of upper primary schools is more varied and often inadequate.[1] Therefore, every effort must be made to open good primary and upper primary schools within the reach of human habitation in all areas, as it is the nation's duty to provide a minimum of good quality education to all its children, its future citizens. We have also argued that in areas where such schools are not available, it is the duty of *all concerned citizens of the area, and not of people of a particular community*, to bring this fact to the notice of concerned authorities and see to it that they establish and run proper schools there.

Another reason for a large section of Muslim parents opting for madrasa education is said to be poverty and relatively high cost of modern education even in government schools. The discussion on this issue (chapter 2, sections 1, 2 and 4) resulted in our acknowledging that even though government and government-aided schools do not charge any tuition fee, the sundry expenses, especially on uniforms and books, are substantial. The expense on education increases in the upper-primary schools; and a family's burden increases in proportion to the number of children going to schools.[2]

In contrast, no expenditure is involved in madrasa education, even though the assertion that the latter also provide food and lodging is not exactly true. The solution to this is that not only the tuition fee but no fee of any kind be charged from the students of government schools. Our argument has been that it is mostly only the under-privileged parents who send their children to government schools; therefore the waiver of fee, and free textbooks and uniforms should be provided to all students, not merely to children belonging to SCs and STs and girls.

However, as we have seen in chapter 2 (sections 2 and 5), economic considerations do not always determine the choice of institution for the education of a family's children. Several scholars have found after detailed study (though of only small areas) that various socio-psychological factors, including parents' education, family size, profession, and above all the influence of *beradari* or local *mohalla* panchayat, have a determinate say in this choice.[3] In the ultra-conservative ambience of Muslim majority areas (ghettos) the natural choice of educational institution becomes the madrasa. Madrasas, often situated within the Muslim areas, naturally form a part of the community, while the ambience of modern schools is said to appear alien to conservative Muslims. In contrast, Muslims living in mixed colonies mostly choose modern schools instead of madrasas, for the education of their children.

We have also discussed several other related issues earlier, regarding the general Hindu ambience of a large number of government schools, the Hindu bias found in certain textbooks of state boards and the need for Urdu medium schools/sections and textbooks (chapter 2, sections 5, 6 and 7). While acknowledging the validity of these contentions, we do believe that these problems can be easily sorted out with a little goodwill on both sides and necessary steps being taken by all concerned citizens and the State.

However, the real influencing factor in certain Muslims' choice of madrasas is their intense attachment to a separate Muslim identity. Madrasas are rightly perceived as symbols of Muslim identity, both religious and cultural.[4] Madrasas and their *maulavis*, in their turn, emphasize and perpetuate this identity. Unfortunately, this Muslim identity is conceived mostly in terms of the *shari'a*, representing the customs and norms of medieval Arab societies of seventh to tenth centuries.

Two other related reasons for Muslim masses not being enamoured by modern education are given by Imtiaz Ahmad. He rightly points out that modern education is cherished most by the middle class; and the middle class among Muslims migrated to Pakistan. And the masses—whether Muslim, Hindu or any other group—are too busy earning their daily bread and not attracted to the idea of acquiring modern education. The other reason for the masses' indifference to education is that education as merely an intellectual pursuit has no meaning or value for the masses. To quote Ahmad:

The large majority of the general masses in every society who have had no taste of the beneficial effects of education [. . .] are unlikely to be persuaded to go in for education for its own sake. Their response to education is likely to be dictated by more concrete considerations.[5]

He explains that since education requires not only monetary investment but also that of time and energy, even if education was made completely free, people may hesitate in committing their children to it. They would be ready only if education gives them something in return, that is, the capability to earn a livelihood in future. Education, Ahmad says, is therefore much more popular among the seekers of jobs, where their educational qualifications count.[6] We know from history that madrasas provided education which trained their students for higher state jobs as *qazis* and *muftis*. That is why, most.youth of upper classes took up madrasa education. He means exactly what Sachar Committee has said about the 'cost effectiveness' of education. Since children can be useful at home, or as petty wage earners, they would be spared for education by the family only if they learn something useful thereby.

Significantly, Mahatma Gandhi perceived this reality long ago. This was the basis of his Wardha Scheme, or the conceptualization of *Nayee Taleem* by Dr. Zakir Hussain, which recommended that the children remain attached to their everyday life while getting their education. It also aimed at teaching them some craft or agriculture along with their studies. Of course, the Wardha Scheme was not fully worked out and some of conceptions were not in sync with those of modern education, so it did not succeed.

2. THE CRITERION OF RELEVANCE FOR MODERN TIMES: MADRASAS *VS.* MODERN SCHOOLS

In chapter 1 (section 3) we tried to confront the question—what is 'modern education' and why do we give this alone the title of 'education'? In other words, madrasas also claim to be providing worthwhile education. In fact, the most important claim of the advocates of the madrasa system of education is that they are making a singular contribution to the state's goal of universal education. A large number of Muslim academics have argued that modern schools are beyond the reach of Muslim children, therefore most Muslim children study in maktabs and madrasas.[7] It is not just the conservative writers but even some of the liberal ones often assert that

their [*dini madaris'*] role in providing free education (although in a rather traditional way) with boarding and lodging facilities to the Muslim masses needs to be recognized. In general, *madaris* help youngsters from economically weak families to acquire at least some education and thus become disciplined and useful members of the society instead of becoming wayward. They have to be taken seriously as educational institutions, since they are educating a very large number of Muslims.[8]

If so, why do policy makers and other academics include children studying in madrasas among out-of-school children? All surveys which give the number and percentage of out-of-school children presume so, thereby implicitly asserting that the education being imparted in madrasas is not equivalent to modern education. Now, the question arises: what is so sacrosanct about 'modern education' that it should be made a criterion to judge all educational systems? Imtiaz Ahmad has often questioned the idea of modernity though he does not seem to give his own conception thereof explicitly. Jamal Malik regards the conceptions of 'modernity' and 'useful education' as products of colonialism which seek to transform the European Enlightenment tradition into a 'global ethic'. He also deplores the 'homogenizing and essentializing assumptions of secular modernity'.[9]

Modernity, as we have seen in chapter 1 (section 3) emphasizes: (i) the essential rationality of human persons; (ii) the autonomy of the individual in the sense that he/she cannot be made a means to the goals of other persons, and is free to judge and act according to her reason/conscience, (iii) dignity of the human person based on her humanity and rationality (Kant); (iv) the equality of all persons due to their rational nature; (v) implicit or explicit rejection of authority (J.S. Mill), and (vi) justice to all in terms of equity (Rawls).

There is certain truth in the contention regarding the homogenizing thrust of modernity. It is against this thrust that postmodernism arose in Europe, but the latter went to another extreme. Admittedly, there is a certain amount of homogenizing thrust in this conception of modernity, further enhanced by the present economic globalization. We also agree that our conception of modernity is influenced by the European culture which is often detrimental to national and sub-national or regional cultures. Nevertheless, the conception of modernity with an emphasis on rationality and autonomy of the individual person exclusively based on rational human nature is a worthwhile one. It refuses to subsume the individual into the community. However, modernity does not undermine the claims of 'others' or the community on the individual. Modern philosophers, from Kant to Rawls, have successfully harmonized the reciprocal claims of the individual and society. If so, then modern education is one which seeks to develop a 'modern', that is, a rational mind or personality. The modern system of education further encourages, or at least wants to encourage, a questioning attitude of mind. It gives, or seeks to give, knowledge or information which a young person can apply to day-to-day situations.[10]

If we accept the above conceptions of modernity and modern education, then madrasa system of education cannot be an equivalent of modern education. The aims of education in the two systems are so very different that it would be difficult to bring them under one umbrella of 'education'. The ideal aim of modern education is to make the receiver an independent rational person who can be a responsible citizen in her/his adult life. In a way, this is also the declared aim of the madrasa system of education. However, the two philosophies of education, modern and Islamic, and their conceptual frameworks are very different. The emphases in the two systems of education are equally different. Modern education aims at developing a rational person who can understand what is being taught to her and use that knowledge to cope independently and successfully with the problems of day-to-day life. On the other hand, the emphasis in the madrasa system of education is entirely on memorization of texts, blind and unquestioning following of the same and training, or rather conditioning, the mind to recognize no truth other than that given in the Quran and *sunna*, or rather the conception of them as understood by the particular sect.[11]

When Malik contrasts the rich variety and culture specificity of Islam to the homogeneous modernity, we cannot agree with him. His contention is perhaps both historically and practically true in the sense that as Islam spread to different regions and cultures, its followers continued to follow a large number of their old traditions along with their new religion. This is especially true for the Indian subcontinent.

Still the very conception of Islam as the 'final revelation' of God, 'the only straight path' and the total determining guide of Muslims' life cannot be presented as the opposite to 'homogeneity of modernity'.[12] The reformist-revivalist movements within Islam, ever since Shah Walliullah (eighteenth century) and later Tablighi and Deobandi movements have consistently emphasized a few points: first, the conception of 'pure' Islam which goes

back to early centuries of the introduction and developments of
Islam; second, the unity of *umma* which transcends all boundaries; and third, the need to follow the *shari'a,* the unwritten
law based on *sunna* or *hadiths.*

Saiyyid Abu Ala Hasan Maududi, an influential ideologue and
maulana of early twentieth century, passionately advocated and
actively promoted the conception of the pristine purity of Islam.
He asserted that whenever Islam has mingled or adjusted with
alien cultures, as with Hinduism, especially during Akbar's time,
it has not only lost its purity but has caused the decline of power
of Muslims. Similarly he argued that if Muslims learnt Western
sciences now, as in Sayyid Ahmad Khan's MAO College, they
would further destroy Islam, and called the MAO College as a
'slaughter house'. At other times, he said that if Western sciences
were at all learnt, they must be 'Islamized' first. Alternately,
Muslims should learn them in order to be able to condemn them.
He also emphasized that there is no place in Islam for a distinction between religion (*din*) and world (*duniya*). That is why
fiqh (Islamic jurisprudence) was central to Islam and Islamic
education in Maududi's scheme.[13] This meant Maududi and
Jamaat-e-Islami, founded by him, sought to control the entire
life and mind of Muslims.

The above is a very homogenizing conception of religion, more
than comparable to the notion of modernity. As against this
conception, Imtiaz Ahmad, Muzaffar Alam, Mushirul Hasan
and others emphasize the variety and sectarian differences within Islam. Granting the diversity of sects (*mazahib*) within Islam,
each sect claims to have transnational validity, as admitted even
by Malik. Above all, each sect, Barelwis and Deobandis alike, insist
on a blind following of the understanding of Islam of that sect.

In addition, character building or transforming a young man
into a true Muslim (*momin*), or a man of piety is perhaps the
most important goal of education in Islamic thought. It is true
that building the moral character should be one of the important goals of education, including the modern one. But a majority of Muslim ideologues regard religious education as the
foundation of moral training. As we have seen in chapter 1
(sections 2 and 3), even a relatively liberal thinker as Maulana
Azad insisted that religious education is a must for character

building. Many other writers and ideologues of Islamic education declare that moral character and religious education are integrally related and the former cannot be had without the latter.[14]

In Islam a person of moral character is one who strictly follows the dictates of *shari'a*. From al Ghazali, who has written extensively on education, to Saiyyid Maududi, majority of traditionalist thinkers have emphasized the need for blind following of the norms and laws of *shari'a*.[15]

Developing a rational, balanced personality of the child-youth is also regarded as the goal of both modern and madrasa systems of education. But the traditionalists' emphasis on *taqlid* (blind following of the written word) does not aim at developing a rational, independent mind. Madrasas create a mindset which is extremely traditionalist and anti-modern. The *maulanas* accept modern technology as it makes life easier but are not ready to accept any scientific knowledge which is the basis of modern technology.[16]

Much more serious is the fact that Muslim masses look up to the *maulanas* as role models and guides. They both mould themselves on the *maulanas* and obey their diktats, called *fatwas*. The *fatwas*, in turn, depend upon their half-understood knowledge of traditions (*hadees/hadiths*) collected between the eighth and tenth centuries. As we have seen earlier (in chapters 3 and 5), *hadiths* are only taught partially in most madrasas (except Deoband). Yet the *maulanas* give judgement on the problems and ways of twenty-first century on the basis of their extremely partial knowledge thereof, thus effectively nipping in the bud any tendency of Muslims to act independently, or according to the demands of the times. Sadly Muslim masses are only too willing to obey them.[17]

The above answers Jamal Malik's contention regarding the openness and flexibility of Islam as against the rigidity and homogeneity of modernity. Let us repeat the views of Ameer Ali, the great nationalist leader and Islamic thinker and reformer of early twentieth century:

But to suppose that the greatest Reformer the world has produced, the greatest upholder of the sovereignty of Reason, the man who proclaimed that the universe is governed by law and order [. . .] ever contemplated that even those injunctions which were called forth by

the passing necessities of a semi-civilized people should become immutable to the end of the world, is doing an injustice to the Prophet
of Islam.[18]

Following the same line of thinking, he further says:

The present stagnation of Muslim community is principally due to
the notion which has fixed itself in the minds of the generality of
Moslems, that the right to the exercise of private judgment ceased
with the early legists, that its exercise in modern times is sinful, and
that a Moslem [...] should abandon his judgment absolutely to the
interpretations of the men who lived in the ninth century, and could
have no conception of the necessities of the twentieth. [...] No account is taken of the circumstances in which Moslems are now placed;
the conclusions at which these legists arrived several centuries ago
are held to be equally applicable to the present day.[19]

The madrasa system of education does just that. It creates a
backward looking mindset which does not understand modern
times. In contrast, modern thought emphasizes the autonomy of
ethics and rejects the place of religion in a secular framework of
education. Modern thinkers, from Kant to Rawls, give the greatest importance to moral values and duties, but reject the idea
that morality is founded on, or derived from, religion.

The above is not meant to denigrate the madrasa system of
education for the purpose for which it exists, but just to bring
out the fundamental differences between the two systems of
thought and education. However, one criterion we can apply to
both, as both systems of education seem to acknowledge it as a
goal of education, and that is preparing their students for their
future life in society. Inasmuch as in Islam it also includes the
'life hereafter', the emphasis is changed. As far as preparing their
students for future life in modern society is concerned, modern
education fares much better than Islamic education. Interestingly, the madrasas, both in other Muslim countries and in
India, were doing just that—preparing their students for future
life as state officials.

As we have seen in chapter 3 (section 2), the role of madrasas
changed after the coming of the British, when madrasa pass-
outs were no longer required for government jobs. Madrasas
accepted the nomenclature *dini madaris*, i.e. not institutions where

education *per se* is imparted but as places where *dini* or religious education is imparted.[20] However, we also know that the Dars-i-Nizami, being taught in all but a few of the madrasas of the subcontinent, does not have much of *dini* content. It mostly consists of *fiqh*, *usool-e-fiqh*, *hadiths*, and so on, written in an archaic style of Arabic, necessitating the study of Arabic language with a very detailed and equally archaic grammar, as also *mantiq* (old Greek logic).

History taught in madrasas is of Muslim empires in foreign lands, and the geography is that of the Arab peninsula and even other Islamic countries. Sometimes Indian history is taught as an optional subject, but it starts with the coming of the Muslim kings and ends with the decline of Mughal empire. In the name of science *chemia* (chemistry as alchemy) and astronomy of Ptolemy are taught. Often madrasa students do not even know the modern way of writing numbers, or modern languages (except in Nadwa where English is regularly taught). Even Urdu as a language with a rich literature is not taught separately. The students of most madrasas are forbidden, or at least discouraged from, reading external material or learning the views of others, or anything of the outside world through the modern media. They are not equipped with any means of coping up with the modern world.[21] If preparing the pupils for their future life in society was one of the main goals of education, accepted by all writers on the madrasa system, then madrasa education does not do that.

Modern education as it is being imparted in schools in India has its own shortcomings. An exclusive emphasis on a half-understood notion of secularism often results in even ethical values and moral duties being neglected or even undermined in the syllabuses of modern schools, which does not follow from either the theory of autonomy of ethics, or that of secularism. Both theories acknowledge the worth of some kind of moral education or development of a sense of moral values and moral accountability towards other persons in civic life; they only say that religious education is not needed for the imparting of moral education. Somehow, our present school system fails to develop the moral character of its students. This is a problem which our educationists, sociologists and secular ideologues must address.

Giving education of different religions to different groups is not
the solution to the problem. It is also true that modern education does seek to develop a rational approach to life and its
problems. For the time being, we have to assume that modern
education is best suited to equip a person for dealing with today's
world. This closes our argument regarding the desirability of
modern education for *all* Indian children belonging to every religious community, and region.

3. THE DESIRABILITY OF MODERN EDUCATION AND 'MODERNIZATION OF MADRASAS'

Once we accept the desirability of modern education in modern
times, the equal desirability of 'modernization of madrasas' seems
to follow. We have discussed this issue in detail in chapters 6 and
7. To recapitulate in the briefest manner, not only the madrasa-
educated *ulama* and *maulanas*, but also a large number of
English-educated Muslim intellectuals praise the madrasas both
for contributing to the national goal of universal education and
as institutions which alone teach Islamic sciences which are
of immense worth.[22] They also often express opposition to the
idea of 'modernization'. It goes against their fundamental belief
that Islam is a complete guide to human life, and a final storehouse of all knowledge. As we know, Maududi emphasized the
pristine glory of Islam and rejected any idea of diluting this glory
by learning alien thought and sciences. Interestingly, while
Maududi perhaps correctly asserted that there is no distinction
between *din* and *duniya* in Islam, most contemporary *ulama*
have accepted the Western distinction between the two and
emphasize the *dini* character of madrasas. And yet both Maududi
and other *ulama* of the latter view oppose teaching modern
sciences to madrasa students.

Even Sayyid Hamid, the most sincere and enthusiastic supporter of 'modernization', has acknowledged that madrasas have
not taken to the idea of introduction of modern subjects enthusiastically.[23] A majority of *ulama* and a relatively large number
of Muslim intellectuals further reject the idea of teaching modern subjects in madrasas because, if implemented, such a system
of dual education would make their students imperfect in both
kinds of knowledge—Islamic and modern.[24]

As to the government's schemes of 'Modernization of Madrasas' (MOM), they are never fully worked out and from the beginning have the potential for failure. Apart from sanctioning huge grants for MOM programmes, the latest Scheme has not paid any attention, just like the previous failed scheme, to several relevant factors: (a) No thought is given to either the process of implementation; or the proper criteria for selection of madrasas for grants (the criteria offered are very generalized and can apply to most madrasas); or to the process through which various madrasas would be contacted and examined for their deserving the proposed grants. (b) No thought is given to the problem of how so many modern subjects could be taught along with an already very heavy madrasa syllabus. (c) There is no clarity regarding which modern subjects are to be included for teaching in madrasas. (While at some places only science is mentioned along with maths and languages, at other places social sciences are mentioned as being included in the MOM Scheme.) (d) There is no proper provision for supervision and assessment of the implementation of the scheme by individual madrasas receiving grants. (e) No effort is made to address the basic grievance of madrasas that the grants reach them at the end of the year, thus causing financial hardship.[25]

The central government's concern for 'modernization of madrasas' is questionable on several counts. (Of course, we are not suggesting here that the government has some secret design of controlling madrasas in its MOM scheme.) First, even though we have not contended so far, madrasas are minority institutions established to preserve Islamic religion and culture; therefore a secular government has got no business to spend the exchequer's money on the modernization of madrasas. Professor Bipan Chandra points out that there is a clear provision in our Constitution (Article 27) that the state cannot levy any taxes on its citizens meant to aid and support any particular religion or religious institution.

Though theoretically right, this argument is not wholly convincing. First, there is a constitutional provision for non-discrimination between different educational institutions while providing monetary aid which obviously includes minority institutions vide Article 30(A2), even though the intention behind this provision is not fully clear. Second, the state has been aiding several Hindu institutions, such as various Sanskrit universities, and now even departments to study *jyotish* (astrology), which was tripled during the NDA rule (1998–2004). Third, there is a certain tension between the concepts of a secular state and that of a welfare state. A welfare state may have to take certain measures which are denied to a secular state. For example, the Indian State takes elaborate measures to ensure the security and comfort of pilgrims, both Hindu and Muslim, even though these pilgrimages are fully religious.

However, there is truth in Bipan Chandra's objection that a secular state has no business to aid and support institutions of religious education. Above all, the efforts and money that are being spent on the modernization of madrasas are better spent on establishing modern schools near Muslim majority areas.

As compared to the government's scheme, Sayyid Hamid's conception of MOM is clearer and much more comprehensive, though we do not know if he has written down his stray suggestions systemically anywhere. According to him, all modern subjects—Hindi, English, mathematics, the three natural sciences and three or four social sciences—should be taught in madrasas till the high school level. Even though S. Hamid's version of 'modernization' is truer to the conception of 'modernity' or modern education, and also very comprehensive, as we have found earlier, it is also not fully worked out. Though he acknowledges that madrasa syllabus would have to be shortened, he has as yet not given any concrete suggestions for the same.[26]

The advocates of madrasa modernization, including S. Hamid, opine that if modern subjects are included in madrasas, their degrees should be recognized by universities and indirectly by the employment agencies.[27] It does not seem to be a reasonable proposition, as almost all madrasas are autonomous, and there is hardly any standardization of their curriculum and internal examinations. Even if modern subjects are taught in madrasas, there is no supervising agency to assess their success in teaching and learning modern subjects.

Of course, madrasa students can give the Open School examinations and if successful the certificates of Open Schools would be recognized by universities and employment agencies, and not madrasa certificates. However, there are many related difficulties in this suggestion of Open School examinations. The textbooks prescribed and even the subjects needed in Open School examinations are very different from those of other regular Boards, while all MOM schemes as well as most Madrasa Boards assume or state clearly that the textbooks prescribed should be those of regular Central or State Boards (though Open Schools are also mentioned). The main difficulty remains that two such heavy syllabuses cannot be combined, that is, no student can successfully master them as even the Open School syllabus is quite heavy (due to poorly written books).

Sometimes, the idea of a Common Madrasa Board is mooted by the government. But so far there has been no effort at clarifying the envisaged role of this Madrasa Board, whether it would determine the syllabus, or would be merely an examining authority, or would also supervise the functioning of various madrasas. In the face of these uncertainties, naturally the *maulanas* are opposed to any such suggestion.

In this context, we have to repeat very briefly the discussion in chapters 6 and 7. First, the two courses—madrasa curriculum and the modern curriculum—in themselves are very heavy, so much so that students doing any one of them alone find them difficult. Therefore, to expect that madrasa students would be able to master both is to expect the impossible. Second, the mindsets and emphases in the two syllabuses are so very different that to combine them into one, or to teach them simultaneously to the same group of students would be quite stressful for both teachers and the students. This does not mean that madrasa students can never be taught modern subjects, only that they cannot be taught advanced modern subjects along with their extremely heavy madrasa syllabus.

Third, if we must teach madrasa students modern subjects, along with their traditional syllabus, then the latter would have to be drastically shortened. As observed earlier, the *ulama*, and other traditionalists are against the proposal to introduce modern subjects in madrasas.[28] A drastic shortening of the traditional syllabus, without which all modern subjects cannot be included in the madrasa curriculum, would not be acceptable to the *ulama*, and perhaps others who perceive madrasas as the preserves of Islamic religion and culture. Moreover, such a shortening would be undesirable as it would defeat the very purpose of madrasas being there.

Alternatively, we can shorten the modern syllabus by making it introductory or simple. Significantly, Hamdard's Evaluation Report on 'Modernization of Madrasa Education Scheme' suggests a drastic reduction in the content and volume of modern subjects:

1. A special curriculum should be devised for madrasas. This is necessary as the time available with the madrasas for teaching these subjects is not likely to exceed two periods daily of 45 minutes each.

2. Curriculum of science subjects should be prepared in the specific context of madrasas, as the curriculum of mainstream education cannot be accommodated in the Madrasa timetable.[29]

The just quoted suggestion is the most sensible one that we have found anywhere in all the writings and talks on madrasa education. It seems from this short passage in the Report that the members of the evaluation team, and possibly its chairman, were not contemplating any revolutionary reduction in the madrasa curriculum. In spite of all claims to the contrary, the madrasa *maulavis* and management have mostly not accepted the idea of 'modernization of madrasas'. The traditionalist *ulama* and *maulanas* would not accept the inclusion of advanced modern subjects in the madrasa syllabus as that would undermine the basic thrust thereof, but they may well agree to the introduction of elementary-level modern subjects. Aligarh Muslim University is already engaged in developing an abridged course in modern subjects, though we have not been able to find out the present status of its efforts.

Here let us ask a question which we have so far refrained from asking—what is the purpose or goal of 'Modernization of Madrasas' scheme? Is it to improve the employability of madrasa students? Then their knowledge of medieval *fiqh* and Arabic may not help much, while they cannot master the full course of modern education. Even if they are able to manage modern subjects along with the full syllabus of madrasas, it is not the certificates of autonomous madrasas but only those of Open School or State Board examination that would be counted by the employing agency. But as we have been arguing, no student anywhere can successfully carry the load of two such heavy syllabuses and not many would agree to the drastic shortening of madrasa syllabus. The only sensible option left them is a drastic shortening of modern syllabus. However, if this is done, the madrasa certificates may not improve the employability of madrasa students.

If the goal of MOM is to widen the outlook and approach of madrasa students, so that they do not remain as traditionalist and backward looking as they are now, then the goal is right; and it can best be served by teaching them modern subjects in an introductory but comprehensive manner. It is a very desirable option, as having learnt some modern knowledge and modern languages, the madrasa pass-outs would not be cut-off from the larger society, and there would be better communication between them and others.

However, if the goal of MOM is to give Muslim children modern education, a goal based on the presumption that *most* Muslim children *naturally* study in madrasas, then both the goal and the presumption are wrong. As we have seen, Qamar Uddin has expressed the hope that most Muslim children, including those of English-educated parents, would come to madrasas once their teaching methodology is changed, and minimum modernization is carried out.[30] The same presumption that if we want to uplift Muslims and give them modern education, we must 'modernize' madrasas is implicit in all the government schemes dealing with 'modernization of madrasas'.

We disagree with any such presumption that most Muslim children study in madrasas, or should do so, or that the best Muslim minds should go to madrasas, and its derivative that if we want to educate Muslim children we must 'modernize' madrasas. It is time that not only *ulama* but also those writers who praise the madrasas for their contribution to the national goal of universal education and those relatively lesser number of academics who seriously want 'modernization of madrasas' to realize that madrasas as they now exist ever since the beginning of British rule, are meant for *dini* education, i.e. they are institutions for providing instructions in traditional Islamic subjects. As such they are not meant for the education of the majority of Muslim children and youth.

A second point to remember is that Muslim society does not

need an ever increasing number of *ulama, muftis* and *maulanas*. Moreover, as everybody knows, those passing out from existing madrasas have very few and unenviable career options. The larger the number of children going to these traditionalist institutions, the greater would be the economic deprivation of the community. In fact, the lesser the number of such specialists the better it would be, as it would give the common Muslims some space to develop on their own and live their own lives—an opportunity currently denied to them due to the overwhelming influence of *ulama* and *maulanas*. As observed by Mushir-Ul-Haq and quoted earlier, the Muslim community is very concerned about its religious identity, as is attested by its 'unquestioning reliance on the madrasah-educated *ulama* for religious guidance in almost every matter through the institution of *fatwa* (authoritative religious decrees)'. Haq further points out that, since the '*ulama* approach even the most complex contemporary problems through a procedure established in earlier days, the religious advice available to the community is often hopelessly incongruous'.[31]

If so, a minimum liberalizing of the attitude and approach of these *ulama* is essential for the sake of the Muslim masses. Therefore, instructing them in modern subjects and modern outlook would be a good idea. If madrasa students are given some modern education in order to soften their harsh traditionalism and widen their outlook, it will do plenty of good, especially since their traditional, highly conservative outlook and approach influence Muslim masses. But this goal does not require that the madrasa students should be loaded with the burden of the entire course of modern schools. Instead of forcing the madrasas to 'modernize' by imposing the full load of modern subjects on them, it would be far better if most Muslim children are persuaded to study in modern schools.

4. RELIGIOUS EDUCATION WITHOUT DEPRIVING MUSLIM CHILDREN OF MODERN EDUCATION: THE KERALA MODEL

The problem of madrasa education and its possible reforms is not limited to the students of existing madrasas, as it is not only the specialists of Islam, but also common Muslim children who are said to need religious education. In fact, the greatest problem before anyone arguing for modern education for all or most Muslim children is the problem of how to satisfy the said need of Muslim children for religious education.

Maktabs are generally regarded as sufficient for imparting religious education for common Muslim children both by the masses and *maulavis*. The *ulama* are happy because they remain the only experts in Islam with the right to explain the Quranic text as well as the *sunna* or the traditions of the Prophet. This makes them very powerful indeed.

We have discussed earlier the limitations of maktab education, where we observed that maktabs, as they mostly exist in northern and eastern India, hardly provide education in our sense of the term. (This does not apply to the few primary sections of bigger madrasas.) Wherever the maktabs have tried to include modern subjects in their syllabus, the result has been somewhat disastrous. First, lack of resources and absence of teachers of modern subjects result in very poor imparting of modern subjects to maktab children. Second, gullible parents are misled to believe that their children have had both religious and modern education in the maktabs, and therefore, do not need to go to modern schools. But this is depriving a large section of the young population from availing its right to get good quality modern education.

In fact, even the religious education imparted in maktabs largely consists of rituals and Arabic alphabets. This is very insufficient. Islam is not exhausted by the Holy Quran alone—it is another matter that even the Quran is not taught in the maktabs. A proper understanding of Islam, even of the Quran itself, requires the knowledge of the *sunna* or the *hadiths*.[32] Such a detailed knowledge can only be had in madrasas and not in maktabs as they exist in the North, Bengal and North-East.

On the other hand, madrasas do not have short-term courses to familiarize Muslim children with the fundamentals of Islam, its creed and the duties demanded from a Muslim. Some larger madrasas do have such courses but they are meant for students who have studied in modern schools and last 3–4 years. Some writers have vociferously argued that instead of madrasa students being taught modern subjects, it should be the other way round, that is, short-term courses must be developed for those (misguided) children and youth who study in modern schools.[33] Such courses, which are as yet not very common, are not meant as a substitute for elementary maktab type of education for the masses of Muslim children.

Meanwhile what is the sloution for providing religious education to Muslim children, while at the same time not depriving them of modern education? The most commonly cited solution to this impasse is the so-called Kerala model, wherein maktabs, called madrasas, function in the morning or evening for two hours, according to the school timings. Children are encouraged to study in mainstream schools in the day and later attend maktabs, thus receiving both kinds of knowledge. The greatest positive thing in Kerala system is that unlike the North, no conflict is seen between religious education and modern education. The two—the religious and the modern or secular educations—are kept apart, which may go against the Islamic ideal that Islam is the guide for entire life of the individual and *umma* or Islamic society. However, there is a big difference between the approaches of *ulama* in the North and those in the South. Those in the North see English language or modern education as contradictory or even harmful to Islamic religion and culture, and affirm that if modern sciences have to be taught in madrasas, they have to be first Islamized. In sharp contrast to this approach, the Muslim teachers and students in Kerala have an open mind towards modern subjects, and there is a smooth transition from one to the other. Thus the Muslim children in Kerala are able to receive both kinds of education in parallel successfully. This system is also being tried in Andhra Pradesh and Karnataka.

Another good thing about the Kerala madrasas is that they do not attempt to teach modern subjects, thus keeping madrasa time exclusively for religious education. It also means that there is no attempt to either 'Islamize' modern subjects or teach them in a slipshod manner, as is done in most 'modernized' madrasas in the North. Since children are going to modern schools any way, there is no unnecessary repetition of modern subjects.

The maktabs/madrasas have the time to teach religious subjects in detail since they do not waste their time in teaching other subjects. Also children attend the madrasas for one or two years more than the children in the North. This gives them more time to learn the Quran, the *hadiths* in brief, as well as Arabic.

Kerala's maktabs/madrasas are run in an organized manner unlike in the North where all or most maktabs/madrasas are run by private groups and are fully autonomous, excepting a few run by the Jamaat-e-Islami Hind. Sectarian differences are prominent in Kerala, so there are several Islamic organizations with their own education boards and madrasas. Almost every madrasa in Kerala is affiliated to one or the other religious organization. The latter decides its own syllabus, even prescribes its own textbooks and holds regular examinations. Thus the students are able to learn much more in these madrasas than in the maktabs of the rest of India. Of course, sectarian maktabs/madrasas are not good in the larger perspective of Islam but the overall arrangement of children receiving both kinds of education simultaneously, as well as comprehensively, is a very good one.

Another significant point is that most madrasas in Kerala are co-educational. Since their course is longer and continues for several years, girls continue the education even after puberty, another break from the North. Most colleges in Kerala are also co-educational. This could be one of the main reasons for the high female literacy rate among Muslims in Kerala.

Adopting the 'Kerala model' for religious education seems to be the best option for ensuring that Muslim children get modern education, along with religious education in improved maktabs. Importantly, a large number of *ulama* agree to this suggestion as a better option than the 'modernization of madrasas'.

The first condition for ensuring that all or at least most Muslim children get both religious and modern education is the adjustment of maktab timings. Most maktabs and madrasas function in the morning for a few hours. Since normal schools also function in the forenoon, children cannot attend both. In bigger cities schools sometimes run in two shifts, but not so in villages and towns. Now, if Muslim children are to get both kinds of education, the maktab timings should be such that children can go to schools after attending the maktab, or alternatively, they can go to the maktabs in the evening after attending regular school. (In Delhi most maktabs run morning and evening shifts.)

The second requirement is a discontinuation of the new trend of city maktabs teaching modern subjects. Often the minimum of modern subjects that the children learn in maktabs are thought by Muslim parents to be sufficient for their children, so that they feel no need to send them to modern schools. Actually the very idea behind the organizers' introducing modern subjects in maktabs was that children are not expected to go to modern schools. Therefore, it is better that maktabs do not try to teach modern subjects at all and confine themselves to their main purpose of providing religious education.

The third requirement is to somehow standardize the syllabus of maktabs, or rather make it more advanced so that it covers at least the reading and understanding of the Quran and some knowledge of the fundamentals of Islam. The Urdu book *Talim ul Islam* is used in many maktabs and some madrasas in the early classes. Perhaps it would be good to adopt it universally. If the course content is increased, then maktab studies may take one or two more years, as in Kerala. Since maktab timings would not clash with the timings of regular schools, children can learn about Islam without foregoing modern education.

But this is a tall order. Almost all maktabs are fully autonomous and are often attached to some mosque, the *Imam* acting as the teacher. When it is near impossible to trace and count, far less try to improve, the madrasas which are about thirty to forty thousand in number, it is all the more impossible to trace and count the maktabs, and then ask them to adopt a new, uniform syllabus. Perhaps it would be best if general awareness as to the need to change the timings of maktabs, as well as the need to teach more about Islam in them is spread. Muslim clerics spend enough energies in their Tablighi movement and in their efforts to 'reform' Islam; if the same energy is directed to improving the level of education in maktabs, as well as acknowledging that all modern education is not against Islam and is a requirement of the times, then things would change. Big organizations like Dini Talimi Council of Uttar Pradesh and Milli Council in Delhi can take the task in their charge. Also local Islamic organizations can take the lead in improving the conditions of maktabs.

So far Dini Talimi Council has tried to establish maktabs/ madrasas as self-sufficient institutions which try to give both kinds of education to Muslim children. This is an entirely misguided policy. The new maktabs should confine themselves to giving religious education in a well organized manner and to a somewhat higher level, while ancouraging their students to go to regular schools for modern education. The same pattern must be followed by other such organizations. It is important that the idea of separate educational institutions combining the two systems of education for Muslim boys and girls is discarded once for all. The same purpose can be easily served by maktab-modern school combination being suggested here.

5. SCHOOLS AS INSTITUTIONS FOR THE EDUCATION OF *ALL* INDIAN CHILDREN AND THE NEED TO OVERHAUL GOVERNMENT AND AIDED SCHOOLS

Throughout this study we have insisted that *all* or at least most Indian children must study in the same educational institutions. This is because first, if they study in separate institutes, their identities as Hindus, Muslims, Christians and so on are hardened and they will never perceive themselves as Indians. Second, if modern education is thought to be desirable for the rest of Indian children, it is equally desirable for Muslim children and there is no reason why we should treat the latter as 'untouchables'. Often enough Muslim leaders assert that the government should not interfere with the affairs of 'minorities', and Muslims themselves must take care of the education of their children.[34] Often the government too, for fear of hurting their sensitivities, hesitates in bringing about changes in the personal laws of the 'minorities' or legislate on issues relating to their backwardness, even if they are required by humanitarian considerations.

However, the government must have equal responsibility towards all its citizens, especially the weaker sections among them. It must not shun its responsibility towards them just because they are supposedly 'minorities'. Members of minorities have the same socio-economic and educational needs as others, and just because some of their ultra-conservative or aggressive leaders assert that the government must not interfere, does not mean that it should surrender its right and responsibility towards the masses, whatever their religious affiliation. We personally do not believe in any vertical division of the populace into communities called 'majority' and 'minorities', exclusively based on the criterion of religious affiliation.[35]

We also disapprove the idea of minority educational institutions to teach modern subjects, as we cannot understand why Muslim children need separate schools for learning modern subjects which are well taught in common schools. It will again create walls between Indian children. The very idea that Muslims themselves should take up the education of their children suggests an alienation with the rest of society and State, and children-youth who study in such schools would bring this sense of alienation with them when they start their adult life in the larger society.

Perhaps, here the larger society is to blame. If there are no good schools in the vicinity of Muslim majority areas, then it is the duty of all concerned citizens, and not of Muslims alone, to bring the pressure of public demand on the concerned department of the government to establish such schools, as well as for the government to take care that schools are available in the vicinity of Muslim majority areas. But all this talk of 'taking the education of our children in our own hands', is undesirable.

We have discussed earlier the poor condition of both the infrastructure and standard of education in government and aided schools. Granted that we want all or at least most Indian children to study in modern schools, the very conditions of government schools, especially in villages and near city slums, put off parents from sending their children to government schools. Since very few parents can send their children to expensive English-medium schools, and since other private schools are generally no better, Muslims opt for madrasas for the education of their children. In order to encourage them to send their children to government schools we have to drastically improve the overall condition of those schools. It is a stupendous task, especially in view of the geographical spread of our population in very remote regions of India.

To put it very briefly, our efforts to educate Indian children are confronted by several practical problems, such as parents' poverty, their annual migration, and unwillingness to spare children for education after a certain age. But the greatest challenges come from chronic teacher absenteeism which spoils any chance of children attending school regularly, absence of regular supervision, and the total lack of accountability on the part of teachers and other state officials towards the society for the learning of children. There have been efforts, on the part of Sarva Shiksha Abhiyan of the central government in coordination with state governments, to recruit local teachers, as also involve parents and local people in the functioning of schools. If successful, these efforts would go a long way both in the better functioning of the government and aided schools, as also in the acceptance of modern education by the Muslim masses. But these efforts are still in their initial stages, and knowing the limitations in functioning of the government, we cannot just hope that everything would be set right soon.

Active involvement of the local community in the functioning of the government and aided schools is required for bringing about substantial improvement in school education. The government must try its best to improve the conditions and standard of education in primary and upper primary schools, not only for the sake of the education of Muslim children, but also equally for the sake of the majority of Indian children whose parents cannot afford the high fee of private schools. The *society as a whole* has to wake up to the need of educating *all children* belonging to any religious community.

In most studies and statistics about literacy the only criterion employed is the number of enrolment in schools, or at most their drop-out percentage. Whether the enrolled children attend school and whether they have learnt anything in their school years is hardly given any attention. The result is that the quality of education imparted, as well as the number of children that are able to benefit from school education, remain dismal. So far majority of children are enrolled in schools but their learning achievements are quite poor. It is a matter of common experience that most children who have studied in government or aided schools and poorly run private schools are only nominally literate, that is, they have no knowledge except being able to haltingly read their textbooks, which they often do not understand.

After neglecting elementary and middle level education for

more than 60 years of Independence, we are now concerned about
the relatively poor quality of our higher education when we find
that the majority of young people are incapable of qualifying
for any job, as they know next to nothing about the fundamentals of modern education. Therefore the greatest need is to do
our utmost to provide the best possible modern education to
every Indian child up to the high school level, and if that is not
possible, at least up to the secondary level.

Madrasas should be meant only for those Muslim children
who want to specialize in religious studies. The rest of the Muslim children must study in common modern schools like the rest
of Indian children. For those youth who are studying in madrasas,
we can try some kind of 'modernization' but with the full awareness that madrasas are meant only for the few who really want
to be *imams, muftis* or *maulavis.*

Finally, all this is possible only if the government and private
organizations put in all their efforts to make good quality modern education available to *every* Indian child. Let us quote the
views of Sachar Committee Report on Minorities:

Muslim parents are not averse to modern or mainstream education
and to sending their children to affordable Government schools. They
do not necessarily prefer to send their children to Madrasas. Regular
school education that is available to any other child in India is preferred by Muslims also.[38]

The Committee gives the following advice:

When modernization of Madrasas is planned, policy makers should
be careful to distinguish between these two types of institutions. The
Maktabs and residential Madrasas are necessarily traditional and
meant mainly for religious education, because their social function is
to carry on the Islamic tradition. On the other hand, it is the constitutional obligation (under Article 21A) of the Government to provide
education to the masses. Aided Madrasas are often the last recourse
of Muslims, especially those who lack the economic resources to
bear the costs of schooling, or households where mainstream educational institutions are inaccessible. *The solution in such cases is not
to modernize Madrasas, but also to provide good quality subsidized
'mainsream' education and create an adequate infrastructure for education. Therefore the state must also fulfill its obligation to provide*

affordable high quality education to the masses through the formal education system.[39] (italics added)

In this context, it is often argued that the pitiful state of Muslims is due to the deliberate neglect of the government of their plight. Let us stop blaming the government for everything that goes wrong in our lives. This attitude is a legacy of our days of slavery under the British rule when we blamed the government for whatever happened to us. The government today is made up of ordinary people like us; both the politicians and the government *babus* reflect the national character and our own values and attitudes.

Perhaps, if instead of exclusively concentrating on the plight of Muslims, we look at the problems of the masses on regional, professional, educational and economic bases, we would be able to tackle the challenge of Muslims' backwardness better. Here let us note that even the Sachar Committee has failed to take a comprehensive view of the problems of Muslims. Another urgent need is to free the problem of Muslims' backwardness from the usual framework of 'poor, neglected minorities', and see it in the perspective of approximately 40 per cent of Indian population being in the same state of backwardness, both economic and educational. According to an all India Survey conducted in 2005, about 7 per cent of children in the age group of 6 to 13 years were out of school. This percentage was higher in rural areas than in urban areas, higher among female children than male children; in older children than in younger ones, and higher among Muslims and ST groups than among other groups.[40] Granted that the Muslim children are more educationally disadvantaged, but the differences between them and those of other religious groups in the same economic category are minimal. Therefore, blame game would not help us in tackling this problem. The need is to take into consideration the common problems, such as educational and economic backwardness of large sections of the entire society or region and then try to tackle them holistically. To quote Ali Ashraf:

Muslims are as much the part of the problem as other communities. Literacy and employment programmes are of as much significance to Muslims as to others. Thus the problem of Muslim education cannot be isolated from the national problem of augmenting national resources and facilities and making them useful to the society at large without distinction of any kind. Muslims in all educational systems or institutions must also learn the virtues of citizenship to perform their duties as Indian citizens and enjoy their rights as free equal citizens of India.[41]

Muhammad Miyan also says:

By and large children of minority community who partake only in religious education through denominational institutions remain on the periphery and therefore their personality may not develop fully and their potential is not fully utilized by the society. Efforts are required to bring such children into the mainstream of society so as to enable them to become more effective members of their own community and the society at large.[42]

Another liberal secular writer, Mohammad Akhlaq Ahmad, having presented the traditional system of Islamic education objectively, comes to the same conclusion. He advises the Muslim thinkers and leaders to face the issue of modern education honestly, and 'to take courage in both hands and restrict admission to institutions like Deoband to only those who have chosen theology deliberately as their vocation'. He adds that 'The remaining institutions [madrasas] should be linked to modern institutions'. He further opines that the large number of madrasas throughout India is a drain on the meagre resources of the community; and it is high time that their place is determined in the context of the needs of present society in 'the socialist free India'.[43]

Of course, it is a general suggestion, and we can presume that the management and *maulanas* of no madrasa would agree to convert their madrasa from an institution of Islamic education to that of a modern one. *It is the right time to emphasize that madrasas are not meant for the education of all Muslim children, but only for those who want to become maulavis, muftis, etc., in their adult life.* Providing the madrasa students with some introductory modern education and familiarizing them with modern thinking and languages would be desirable both for their own sake and for the sake of Muslim masses who are under the constant influence of the *ulama* and *maulanas*. *The rest of Muslim children must study in common modern schools, as all other children and youth do*; while the need for religious education of those whose parents want their children to receive it can be taken care of by some improved and better organized maktabs.

NOTES

1. See chapter 2, section 3, notes 29–30 supra.
2. See chapter 2, section 4, notes 31–3. supra.
3. See chapter 2, section 2, notes 25–7; section 4, notes 35–9; supra.
4. See chapter 2, section 4, notes 36–40.
5. Imtiaz Ahmad, 'Muslim Educational Backwardness' (*Economic and Political Weekly*, 5 September 1981). Reprint in *Higher Education in India: The Social Context*, ed. Amrik Singh and G.D. Sharma, New Delhi: Konark, 1988, p. 176.
6. Ibid., p. 177.
7. 'Ninety per cent of the Muslims in India are beyond the pale of education. For them the main source of education, if any, is the madrasas and maktabs, both of which have fulfilled the community's educational needs since medieval times. They spread literacy, impart knowledge and instil values.' Riaz Shakir Khan, 'Madrasa Teachers' Perception of a Successful Teacher', in A.W.B. Qadri, Riaz Shakir Khan and Mohammad Siddiqui (eds.), *Education and Muslims in India Since Independence*, New Delhi: Institute of Objective Studies, 1998, p. 109.
8. Syed Abul Hashim Rizvi, 'The Introduction of Natural Sciences in Madrasa Education in India', in Jan-Peter Hartung and Helmut Reifeld (eds.), *Islamic Education, Diversity and National Identity: Dini Madaris: Post 9/ 11*, New Delhi: Sage, 2006, p. 289.
9. 'Introduction' to Jamal Malik, ed., *Madrasas in South Asia: Teaching Terror?*, London: Routledge, 2008, pp. 6–9. Note: The book contains several edited articles presented in the International Workshop on Islamic Learning in South Asia, Erfurt, Germany, May 2005, while some others are left out. However, we resent the 'Teaching Terror?' part of the title. This conception of madrasas as 'Terror workshops' is an entirely Western conception, as a result of which most modern writers on madrasas waste their ink and energies on apologetically defending madrasas, instead of devoting themselves to other more relevant issues, which we have tried to highlight in our study.
10. See chapter 1, section 3, notes 53–5, 58 supra.

11. This fact of 'conditioning' the minds of the students in madrasas has been clearly brought out by Arshad Alam in 'Understanding Deoband Locally: Interrogating Madrasat Diya' al 'Ulum', in *Islamic Education, Diversity and National Identity*, pp. 182 ff. Also see Mushir-Ul-Haq, quoted in chapter 6, notes 17–18.

12. Mahmud Shaltout explains how 'the message of the Apostle Muhammad includes the foundations of all the previous messages'; and how, therefore for Islam, 'Muhammad is the last messenger; and the Holy Quran is the final "revealed" scripture'. See Mahmud Shaltout, 'Islamic Beliefs and Code of Laws', in Kenneth W. Morgan (ed.), *Islam: The Straight Path*, Delhi: Motilal Banarsidass, rpt., 1987, pp. 87 ff. Almost all traditional writers on Islam have emphasized the ideas of finality of Islamic 'revelation', one universal *umma* as well as the need to blindly follow (*taqlid*) the *shari'a*.

See also Manzoor Ahmad, *Islamic Education: Redefinition of Aims and Methodology*, New Delhi: Qazi Publishers, 1990, pp. 16 ff., 24 ff. for extremely homogenizing concepts of Islam and *umma*.

13. For information on Saiyyid Maududi see M. Mujeeb, *The Indian Muslims*, New Delhi: Munshiram Manoharlal, 1967, pp. 401–3 and the website of Wikipedia: http://en.wikipedia.org/wiki/Abul_Ala_Maududi; also the website of Jamaat-e-Islami: *http//www.jamaat.org/overview/founder.html*.

14. 'If education was devoid of this element, there would be no appreciation of moral values, of moulding of character on human lines'. Maulana Azad quoted in Muktishree Ghosh, *Concept of Secular Education in India*, Delhi: B.R. Publishing Corporation, 1991, p. 124. Various Muslim writers have asserted the need for religious education; and the goal of Islamic education being unique in the sense that it aims at building the intellect, body and mind together. Their views are quoted in Mohd. Sharif Khan, *Education, Religion and Modern Age*, New Delhi: Ashish, 1990, pp. 32–5.

15. 'Education should aim at the balanced growth of the total personality of man through training. [. . .] The training imparted to a Muslim must be such that faith is infused in the whole of his personality and enables him to follow the Quran and Sunnah and be governed by the Islamic system of values willingly and joyfully.' Resolution passed in the First World Conference on Muslim Education, 1977, given in Mohammad Akhlaq Ahmad, *Traditional Education among Muslims (A Study of Some Aspects*

in Modern India), Delhi: B.R. Publishing Corporation, 1985, pp. 187 and following. The Resolutions of three separate Committees in the above Conference are resonant with extreme orthodox perceptions and refusal to face changed circumstances.

For al Ghazali see Saiyid Naqi Hussain Jafri, 'A Modernist View of Madrasa Education in Late Mughal India', in *Islamic Education, Diversity and National Identity*, pp. 44–5.

16. Based on recorded personal interviews with the two *maulanas* of a well-known Madrasa in Old Delhi, Madrasa Alia Arabia, Fatehpuri.

17. 'The problem is that religion for most Indian Muslims is not "philosophy", an "attitude", or a "value", it is something that governs human life in this world and the Hereafter. Religion in this sense is to many Muslims incompatible with the kind of secularism which strips the former of its authoritative character.' Mushir-Ul-Haq, *Islam in Secular India*, Simla: Indian Institute of Advanced Study, 1972, p. 11; also see ibid., pp 3 ff.; 14 ff.

18. Syed Ameer Ali, *The Spirit of Islam: A History of the Evolution and Ideals of Islam with a Life of the Prophet*, Delhi: Low Price Publication, rpt. 1990, p. 182.

19. Ibid., p. 184.

20. See chapter 3, section 1.2, notes 6–10; chapter 3, section 2.3, note 17; also chapter 6, section 2.1, notes 37–8 supra.

21. See chapter 6, section 3.2, notes 79, 80, 94, etc. supra.

22. See chapter 6, section 1.1, 1.2, notes 3–11 supra.

23. See the short 'Foreword' by S. Hamid to Qamar Uddin, *Hindustan ki Dini Darsagahein: Kul Hind Survey,* New Delhi: Hamdard Education Society, 1996.

24. See chapter 6, section 2.1, notes 37–45; and chapter 7, section 3.1, notes 17–25 supra.

25. See chapter 7, sections 2.1 and 2.2, notes 9–13 supra.

26. See chapter 7, sections 1.1 and 1.2, notes 2–7 supra.

27. See S. Hamid, 'Foreword', to *Hindustan ki Dini Darsagahein*.

28. Muhammadullah Khalili Qasmi quotes several writers with approval from Mufti Taqi Usmani to one Muzzaffar Alam as declaring that the purpose of the existence of madrasas is different from that of schools and colleges; and changes in their syllabus, etc. are brought out by madrasas themselves for the preservation of the institution (and not to adjust to the demands of modern times). See *Madrasa Education: Its Strength and Weakness,* Mumbai: Markazul Ma'arf Education and Research Centre, 2005, pp. 146 ff.

The opening lecture by the Rector of Darul Uloom, Deoband at the Conference on Madrasa Reforms held at Deoband in 1994 rejects fully and unconditionally any proposal for introduction of modern subjects in madrasas, with his famous statement that such a curriculum would be like trying to travel in two boats simultaneously. See *Hindustan ki Dini Darsagahein*, pp. 120 ff. Also see the articles of Maulana Mohd. Inayatullah Asad Subhani, Maulana Abul Hasan Azmi, Maulana Abdullah Madani, Maulana Habib Rehan Nadwi et al. presented in the Seminar at Jamiat-ul-Falah, published under the title, *Mulk wa Millat ki Tameer aur Dini Madaris*, Azamgarh: Idara Ilmia, Balariaganj, 1994. All of them say four things (i) Western culture and Indian philosophy weaken Islam; and therefore no such subjects must be introduced. (ii) If at all modern subjects are to be taught, they should be such as to enable the students for propagating Islam. (iii) If any modern subject is taught at all, it should be Islamized first. (iv) And it is better to give Islamic education to Muslim children who are studying in modern schools than to give modern education to madrasa students. See ibid., pp. 22 ff., 175 ff., 186 ff., 278 ff.

29. See *Evaluation Report on Modernisation of Madrasas Scheme* (Uttar Pradesh), New Delhi: Hamdard Education Society, 2003, p. 41.

30. *Hindustan ki Dini Darsagahein*, p. 302.

31. Mushir-Ul-Haq, *Islam in Secular India*, pp. 3–4.

32. Not only *sunna* or *hadiths* but also *shari'a* is integral to Islamic religion, and is so affirmed by all traditional writers and spokesmen on Islam. See note 14 supra. In chapter 5, sections 2.1 and 2.2, we have discussed how *shari'a* is regarded by most *ulama* and *maulanas* as divine and hence inviolable. See notes 16 to 21 of the same chapter supra.

33. 'The students of common schools, whether government or public, are denied opportunities for religious and cultural education. Madrasas can and should introduce short term courses to enable students of common schools to learn their own culture and religion'. Maulana Muhammad Yusuf Baneri, quoted with approval by Khalili Qasmi, op. cit., p. 119.

In the Seminar at Jamiat-ul-Falah, speaker after speaker asserted that madrasas do not need to teach modern subjects, rather students of common schools need religious education, which should be arranged for them. See papers by Maulana Mohd. Inayatullah Asad Subhani, Maulana Abdullah Madni et al., in *Mulk wa*

Millat ki Tameer aur Dini Madaris, pp. 22 ff., 186 ff., etc. Maulana Gilani has emphatically asserted that instead of madrasas becoming modern or secular, schools and colleges must become religious, or rather Muslim. See chapter 6, section 2.1, notes 58–61.

34. B. Sheikh Ali charters out a whole programme of Muslim children's education including Mohalla committees to promote education among Muslim children and youth with the purpose of preserving 'our' culture. He gives the impression that Muslims, and nobody else, can take care of Muslim children's education. See 'Issues and Problems of Muslim Education', in *Education and Muslims in India Since Independence*, pp. 49 ff. There are other contributors in the same collection of essays, like Muhammad Akhtar Siddiqui, who abuses the 'rigorous campaign for free and compulsory education', which has created a challenge for *maulanas* who, in turn, have worked relentlessly to establish more and more madrasas, and so on, thus presenting the obscurantist side of Islamic ideology. See ibid., pp. 72 ff.

    Such views are even more strongly expressed in the Urdu papers presented at the Seminar in Jamiat-ul-Falah, mentioned earlier. Just to give an example, Maulana Abdullah Madni declares, 'Ummat's unity is necessary. Now being a minority it is more important. . . . Modern subjects should not be added. It would make the *nisab* more difficult. Above all, we should find solutions for our own problems, not by borrowing light from others. If the *Ummat* needs engineers, etc. then we should have separate colleges for this; and they should teach according to the *Quran*. . . .' *Mulk wa Millat ki Tameer aur Dini Madaris*, pp. 175 ff. Several other papers are of this view, asserting the complete separateness of Muslims *umma* from the rest of society; though there are one or two exceptions also.

35. See author, *Secularism in India: A Reappraisal*, New Delhi: Har Anand, 1995, pp. 208 ff. Cf. 'Hindus or Muslims or Sikhs or Christian [. . .] did not form a distinct and homogeneous "community" except for religious purposes. [. . .] The religious coordinates did not coincide with the class, ethnic, linguistic, or cultural coordinates.' Bipan Chandra, *Communalism in Modern India*, New Delhi: Vikas, 1989, p. 13.

36. *Social, Economic and Educational Status of the Muslim Community in India: A Report*, Prime Minister's High Level Committee, headed by Rajinder Sachar, published by GOI, November 2006, p. 85.

39. Ibid., p. 78.
40. *All India Survey of Out of School Children in the 6–13 Age
    Group*, conducted by Social & Rural Research Institute, Depart-
    ment of Elementary Education & Literacy, MHRD, GOI, New
    Delhi: Educational Consultant India Ltd., 2006, pp. 1–3. Note:
    We, however, could not understand this limitation to 6–13 age
    group. The Constitutional guarantee is up to 14 years. Even that
    is less. There are a lot of other related issues which we cannot
    attend to here due to lack of space.
41. Quoted in Muhammad Miyan, 'Teachers' Education and Mi-
    nority Educational Institutions', in *Education and Muslims in
    India Since Independence*, p. 117.
42 Ibid., p. 119.
43. See Muhammad Akhlaq Ahmad, *Traditional Education Among
    Muslims*, p. 183.

Bibliography

BOOKS

Ahmad, Aijazuddin, *Muslims in India: Their Educational, Demographic and Socio-economic Status*, vol. 1: *Bihar*, New Delhi: Inter-India Publications, 1993.

——, *Muslims in India*, vol. 2: *Rajasthan*, New Delhi: Inter-India Publications, 1994.

——, *Muslims in India*, vol. 4: *Uttar Pradesh, Urban*, New Delhi: Inter-India Publications, 1996.

Ahmad, Aziz, *Studies in Islamic Culture in the Indian Environment*, Oxford: Clarendon Press, 1964.

Ahmad, Imtiaz, ed., *Caste and Social Stratification among Muslims in India*, New Delhi: Manohar, 1978.

——, ed., *Modernization and Social Change among Muslims in India*, New Delhi: Manohar, 1983.

Ahmad, Manzoor, *Islamic Education: Redefinition of Aims and Methodology*, New Delhi: Qazi Publishers, 1990.

Ahmad, Mohammad Akhalaq, *Traditional Education among Muslims*, New Delhi: B.R. Publishing, 1985.

Ahmed, Leila, *Women and Gender in Islam: Historical Roots of a Modern Debate*, London: Yale University Press, 1992.

Alam, Md. Mukhtar, *Madrasa and Terrorism: Myth and Reality*, New Delhi: Indian Social Institute, 2004.

Ali, Syed Ameer, *The Spirit of Islam: A History of the Evolution and Ideals of Islam, With a Life of the Prophet*, Delhi: Low Price Publications, 1990.

Allana, Mariam, *Muslim Women and Islamic Tradition: Studies in Modernization*, New Delhi: Kanishka, 2000.

Ansari, Shoyeb M., *Education in Dini Madaris: An Opinion Survey of Curriculum, Method of Teaching and Evaluation*, New Delhi: Institute of Objective Studies, 1997.

Aslan, Reza, *No god but God : The Origins, Evolution and Future of Islam*, London: Arrow Books, 2006.

Azad, Maulana Abul Kalam, *India Wins Freedom*, New Delhi: Orient Longman, 1988.

Banerjee, A.C., *Two Nations: The Philosophy of Muslim Nationalism*, New Delhi: Concept, 1981.

Barrow, Robin and Ronald Woods, *An Introduction to Philosophy of Education*, London: Routledge, 1998.

Bell, Daniel, *Communitarianism and its Critics*, Oxford: Clarendon Press, 1996.

Bipan Chandra, *Communalism in Modern India*, New Delhi: Vikas, rpt. 1989.

————, *Essays on Indian Nationalism*, rev. edn., New Delhi: Har-Anand, 2002.

————, *Essays on Contemporary India*, rev. edn., New Delhi: Har-Anand, 2002.

Bipan Chandra, Mridula Mukherjee, Aditya Mukherjee, K.N. Panikkar and Sucheta Mahajan, *India's Struggle for Independence*, New Delhi: Penguin, rpt., 1990.

Chakrabarty, Bidyut, ed., *Secularism and Indian Polity*, New Delhi: Segment, 1990.

Chatterjee, Margaret, *The Religious Spectrum: Studies in an Indian Context*, New Delhi: Allied, 1984.

Deutsch, Eliot, ed., *Culture and Modernity: East-West Philosophical Perspectives*, rpt., Delhi: Motilal Banarsidass, 1994.

Engineer, Asghar Ali, *Indian Muslims: A Study of Minority Problem*, New Delhi: Ajanta, 1984.

———— ed., *Status of Women in Islam*, New Delhi: Ajanta, 1987.

————, *Justice, Women and Communal Harmony in Islam*, New Delhi: ICSSR, 1989.

————, *The Quran, Women and Modern Society*, New Delhi: Sterling, 1999.

————, *Contemporary Politics of Identity, Religion and Secularism*, New Delhi: Ajanta, 1999.

————, ed., *Islam, Women and Gender Justice*, New Delhi: Gyan, 2001.

Engineer, Asghar Ali and Moin Shakir (eds.), *Communalism in India*, New Delhi: Ajanta, 1985.

Frankena, William K., *Philosophy of Education*, New York: Macmillan, 1965.

Gandhi, M.K., *Gandhi Reader for 1988*, ed. M.V. Desai, New Delhi: Namedia Foundation, 1988.

Gandhi, Rajmohan, *Understanding the Muslim Mind*, New Delhi: Penguin Books, rpt., 1990.

Ghosh, Muktishree, *Concept of Secular Education in India*, New Delhi: B.R. Publishing, 1991.

Gilani, Maulana Saiyyid Manazir Ahsan, *Hindustan Main Musalmanon ka Nizam-e-Taleem wa Tarbiyat* (Urdu), Delhi: Nadwatul-Musannifeen, vol. 1, 1976; vol. 2, 1984.

Gilmartin, David, and Bruce B. Lawrence, *Beyond Turk and Hindu: Rethinking Religious Identities in Islamicate South Asia*, Florida: University Press of Florida, 2000.

Haq, Mushir-Ul, *Muslim Politics in Modern India*, Meerut: Meenakshi Prakashan, 1970.

———, *Islam in Secular India*, Simla: Indian Institute of Advanced Study, 1972.

Hartung, Jan-Peter and Helmut Reifeld, eds., *Islamic Education, Diversity, and National Identity: Dini Madaris in India Post 9/11*, New Delhi: Sage, 2006.

Hasan, Mushirul, *Muslim Education in India: Problems and Prospects*, New Delhi: Jamia Millia Islamia (published for limited circulation).

——— ed., *Islam and Indian Nationalism: Reflections on Abul Kalam Azad*, New Delhi: Manohar, 1992.

——— ed., *Islam, Communities and the Nation: Muslim Identities in South Asia*, New Delhi: Manohar, 1998.

———, *Islam in the Subcontinent: Muslims in a Plural Society*, New Delhi: Manohar, 2002.

Hasan, Zoya and Ritu Menon, eds., *In a Minority: Essays on Muslim Women in India*, New Delhi: Oxford University Press, 2005.

———, *Educating Muslim Girls*, New Delhi: Women Unlimited, 2005.

Hasnain, N., ed., *Social Psychological Dimensions of Muslims: The Post Independence Scenario*, New Delhi: Institute of Objective Studies, 1998.

Hiro, Dilip, *Islamic Fundamentalism*, London: Paladin, 1989.

Husain, S. Abid, *Indian Culture*, Bombay: Asia Publishing House, 1963.

———, *Destiny of Indian Muslims*, London: Asia Publishing House, 1966.

Husain, S.M. Azizuddin, ed., *Madrasa Education in India: Eleventh to Twenty First Century*, New Delhi: Kanishka, 2005.

Jha, Jyotsna and Dhir Jhingran, *Elementary Education for the Poorest and Other Deprived Groups: The Real Challenge of Universalisation*, New Delhi: Manohar, 2002.

Jhingran, Saral, *The Roots of World Religions*, New Delhi: Books & Books, 1982.

———, *Secularism in India: A Reappraisal*, New Delhi: Har-Anand, 1995.

———, *Ethical Relativism and Universalism*, Delhi: Motilal Banarsidass, 2001.

Kabir, Humayun, *Education in New India*, London: George Allen & Unwin, 1959.

———, *The Indian Heritage*, London: Asia Publishing House, 1962.

———, *Education for Tomorrow*, Calcutta: Firma K.L. Mukhopadhyaya, 1969.

Kant, Immanuel, *The Doctrine of Virtue: Part II of Groundwork of the Metaphysics of Morals, The Moral Law*, tr. H.J. Paton, London: Hutchinson University Library, 1947.

———, *Fundamental Principles of the Metaphysics of Morals*, tr. Thomas K. Abbot, Indianapolis: Bobbs-Merrill/Library of Liberal Arts, rpt., 1984.

Kaur, Kuldeep, *Madrasa Education in India: A Study of its Past and Present*, Chandigarh: Centre for Research & Rural Development, 1990.

Khan, J.M., *Education among Muslims*, Jaipur: Classic Publishing House, 1993.

Khan, Mohd Sharif, *Islamic Education*, New Delhi: Ashish, 1986.

———, *Eduation, Religion and Modern Age*, New Delhi: Ashish, 1990.

Khwaja, Jamal, *Authenticity and Islamic Liberalism*, New Delhi: Allied, 1987.

Kumar, Krishna, *What is Worth Teaching?* New Delhi: Orient Longman, 1997.

Lateef, Shahida, *Muslim Women in India: Political and Private Realities—1890s–1980s*, New Delhi: Kali for Women, 1990.

MacIver, R.M. and Charles H. Page, *Society: An Introductory Analysis*, London: Macmillan, 1961.

Madni, Maulana Hussain Ahmad, *Composite Nationalism and Islam (Muttahida Qaumiyat aur Islam)*, tr. Muhammad Anwar Hussain and Hasan Imam, New Delhi: Manohar, 2005.

Malik, Jamal, ed., *Madrasas in South Asia: Teaching Terror?*, London: Routledge, 2008.

Mehrotra, Santosh, ed., *The Economics of Elementary Education in India: The Challenge of Public Finance, Private Provision and Household Costs*, New Delhi: Sage, 2006.

Mill, John Stuart, *On Liberty and other writings*, ed. Stefan Collini, Cambridge: Cambridge University Press, 1989.

Minai, Naila, *Women in Islam: Tradition and Transition in the Middle East*, London: John Murray, 1981.

Minault, Gail, *Secluded Scholars: Women's Education and Muslim Social Reform in Colonial India*, New Delhi: Oxford University Press, 1998.

Mondal, Sekh Rahim, *Educational Status of Muslims: Problems, Prospects and Priorities*, New Delhi: Inter-India, 1983.

Morgan, Kenneth W., ed., *Islam: The Straight Path*, rpt., Delhi: Motilal Banarsidass, 1987.

Mujeeb, M., *The Indian Muslims*, Delhi: Munshiram Manoharlal, 1995.

Mulk wa Millat ki Tameer aur Dini Madaris, papers presented in the Seminar at Jamiatul Falah, Azamgarh: Idara Ilmia, Jamiatul Falah, 1994.

Nanda, B.R., *Gandhi, Pan-Islamism and Nationalism*, Bombay: Oxford University Press, 1989.

Naqvi, Saeed, *Reflections of an Indian Muslim*, New Delhi: Har-Anand, 1993.

Nehru, Jawaharlal, *The Discovery of India*, New Delhi: Oxford University Press, rpt., 1989.

Nicholson, R.A., *Studies in Islamic Mysticism*, Cambridge: Cambridge University Press, rpt., 1989.

Palmer, Joy A., ed., *Fifty Major Thinkers on Education: From Confucius to Dewey*, London: Routledge, 2001.

Park, Joe, ed., *Selected Readings in the Philosophy of Education*, New York: Macmillan, 1974.

Qadri, A.W.B., Riaz Shakir Khan and Mohammad Akhtar Siddiqui, eds., *Education and Muslims in India Since Independence*, New Delhi: Institute of Objective Studies, 1998.

Qamar Uddin, *Hindustan ki Dini Darsagahein: Kul Hind Survey* (Urdu), New Delhi: Hamdard Education Society, 1996.

Qasmi, Muhammadullah Khalili, *Madrasa Education: Its Strength and Weakness*, Mumbai: Markazul Ma'arif Education and Research Centre, 2005.

Rizvi, S.A.A., *A History of Sufism in India*, 2 vols., New Delhi: Munshiram Manoharlal, vol. 1, 1978; vol. 2, 1982.

———, *The Wonder That Was India*, vol. II (1200–1700), London: Sidgwick & Jackson, 1987.

Saiyidain, K.G., *Problems of Educational Reconstruction*, Bombay: Asia Publishing House, 1962.

———, *Facets of Indian Education*, New Delhi: NCERT, 1970.

Seminar Papers, presented at the International Workshop on Islamic Learning in South Asia, 19–21 May 2005, Erfurt, Germany, unpublished. Note: Most but not all of the papers are published in Jamal Malik, ed., *Madrasas in South Asia: Teaching Terror*, Routledge, 2008, in an edited form. We have referred only to the papers in their unpublished form, procured from Imtiaz Ahmad.

Shakir, Moin, *Islam in Indian Politics*, New Delhi: Ajanta, 1980.

————, *Politics of Minorities: Some Perspectives*, New Delhi: Ajanta, 1980.

Sharma, Kamlesh, *Role of Muslims in Indian Politics (1857–1947)*, New Delhi: Inter-India, 1995.

Sikand, Yoginder, *Bastions of Believers: Madrasas and Islamic Education in India*, New Delhi: Penguin, 2005.

Sikri, Rehana, *Women in Islamic Culture and Society: A Study of Family, Feminism and Franchise*, New Delhi: Kanishka, 1990.

Singh, Attar, ed., *Socio-cultural Impact of Islam on India*, Chandigarh: Punjab University Publication Bureau, 1976.

Singh, K.S., *People of India*, New York: Oxford University Press, 1994.

Singh, Yogendra, *Modernization of Indian Traditions*, New Delhi: Thomson Press, 1973.

Smart, Ninian, *The Religious Experience of Mankind*, London: Collins, 1974.

Smith, Donald Eugene, *India as a Secular State*, Princeton: Princeton University Press, 1963.

Smith, Wilfred Cantwell, *Islam in Modern History*, Princeton: Princeton University Press, 1977.

Tahsen, Rana, *Education and Modernization of Muslims in India*, New Delhi: Deep & Deep, 1993.

The Meaning of the Glorious Koran, tr. Marmaduke Pickthall, Delhi: World Islamic Publications, 1975.

Tilak, B.G. Jandhyala, *Determinants of Expenditure on Education in Rural India*, New Delhi: National Council for Applied Economic Research, 2002.

Toynbee, Arnold, *An Historian's Approach to Religion*, London: Oxford, 1956.

Wasey, Akhtarul, ed., *Madrasas in India: Trying to be Relevant*, New Delhi: Global Media, 2005.

Winkelmann, Mareike Jule, *From Behind the Curtain: A Study of Girls' Madrasa in India*, Amsterdam: Amsterdam University Press, 2005.

Zakaria, Rafiq, *Is Islam Secular?*, Aligarh: Sir Syed Academy, 1989.

——, *Communal Rage in Secular India*, Mumbai: Popular Prakashan, 2002.

ARTICLES

Afsaruddin, Asma, 'Muslim Views on Education: Parameters, Purview, and Possibilities', *Journal of Catholic Legal Studies*, 2005, vol. 44: 143.

——, 'The Philosophy of Islamic Education: Classical Views and M. Fethullah Gulen's Perspective', see http://fetullahgulen conference.org/Houston/proceedings/AAfsaru-ddin.Pdf./Adobe Acrobat.

Ahmad, Imtiaz, 'Endogamy and Social Change among the Siddiqi Sheikhs of Allahabad, Uttar Pradesh', in Imtiaz Ahmad (ed.), *Caste and Social Stratification among Muslims in India*, New Delhi: Manohar, 1978.

Ahmad, Irfan, 'Familiar Discourse in an Unfamiliar World: Conflict, Protest and Democratization in a Tahriki Madrasa of North India', in the Proceedings of *International Workshop on Islamic Learning in South Asia*, May 2005, Erfurt, Germany (unpublished).

Akhtar, Nasim, 'Islam, Women Education and Indian Madrasas', in S.M. Azizuddin (ed.), *Madrasa Education in India: Eleventh to Twenty Firsty Century*, New Delhi: Kanishka, 2005.

Alam, Arshad, 'Understanding Deoband Locally: Interrogating Madrasat diya' al-Ulum', in Jan-Peter Hartung and Helmut Reifeld (eds.), *Islamic Education, Diversity, and National Identity: Dini Madaris in India Post 9/11*, New Delhi: Sage, 2006.

——, 'Making Maslaks: Constructing Identity in a Barelwi Madrasa', in Proceedings of *International Workshop on Islamic Learning in South Asia*, May 2005 (unpublished). Also in Jamal Malik (ed.), *Madrasas in South Asia: Teaching Terror?*, Routledge, 2008.

Ali, Hasan, 'Elements of Caste among the Muslims in a District in Bihar', in Imtiaz Ahmad (ed.), *Caste and Social Stratification among Muslims in India*, New Delhi: Manohar, 1978.

Alvi, Hamza, 'Ironies of History: Contradictions of the Khilafat Movement', in Mushirul Hasan (ed.), *Islam, Communities and the Nation: Muslim Identitites in South Asia*, New Delhi: Manohar, 1998.

Ansari, Mohammad Shoyeb, 'Students' Perception of Teaching Learning Process', in A.W.B. Qadri, Riaz Sakir Khan and Mohammad

Akhtar Siddiqi (eds.), *Education and Muslims in India Since Independence*, New Delhi: Institute of Objective Studies, 1998.

Azmi, Maulana Abul Hasan, 'Daure Jadid ke Takaze aur Dini Madaris ka Nisab', in *Mulk wa Millat ki Tamir aur Dini Madaris* (Urdu).

Eade, John, 'Modernization and Islamization among Members of Calcutta's Educated Bengali Muslim Middle Class', in Imtiaz Ahmad (ed.), *Modernization and Social Change among Muslims in India*, New Delhi: Manohar, 1983.

Engineer, Asghar Ali, 'Islam, Women, and Gender Justice', in Engineer (ed.), *Islam, Women and Gender Justice*, New Delhi: Gyan, 2001.

————, 'Sharia'h, Women and Traditional Society', Islam and Modern Age Series, August 2005.

Fatima, Talmeez and N. Hasnain, 'Adjustment, Alienation and Defeatism in Muslim and Hindu Adolescents', in N. Hasnain (ed.), *Social, Psychological Dimension of Muslims: The Post-Independence Scenario*, New Delhi: Institute of Objective Studies, 1998.

Goodfriend, Douglas E., 'Changing Concepts of Caste and Status among Old Delhi Muslims', in Imtiaz Ahmad (ed.), *Caste and Social Stratification among Muslims in India*, New Delhi: Manohar, 1978.

Hasan, Farhat, '*Madaris* and the Challenges of Modernity in Colonial India', in Hartung and Reifeld (eds.), *Islamic Education, Diversity, and National Identity: Dini Madaris in India Post 9/11*, New Delhi: Sage, 2006.

Hasnain, N., 'Prejudice Across Communities', in N. Hasnain (ed.), *Social, Psychological Dimensions of Muslims*, New Delhi: Institute of Objective Studies, 1998.

Husain, S.M. Azizuddin, 'Introduction', in S.M.A. Husain (ed.), *Madrasa Education in India: Eleventh to Twenty First Century*, New Delhi: Kanishka, 2005.

————, 'Mir Fathullah Shirazi's Contribution for the Revision of the Syllabi of Indian Madrasas During Akbar's Reign', in *Madrasa Education in India: Eleventh to Twenty Firsty Century*.

Hartung, Jan-Peter, 'The Nadwat al-'ulama: Chief Paron of Madrasa Education in India and a Turntable to the Arab World', in *Islamic Education, Diversity and National Identity: Dini Madaris in India Post 9/11*, New Delhi: Sage, 2006.

Islahi, M. Sultan Ahmad, 'Hindustan ki Maujuda Talimee Tahrikat, ek Jayja', in *Mulk wa Millat ki Tamir aur Dini Madaris*, papers presented at a Seminar in Jamiatul Falah (Urdu), Balariaganj, Azamgarh: Idara Ilmia, 1994.

Jafri, Saiyid Naqi Husain, 'A Modernist view of Madrasa Education in Late Mughal India', in Jan-Peter Hartung, Helmut Reifeld (eds.), *Islamic Education, Diversity and National Identity: Dini Madaris in India Post 9/11*, New Delhi: Sage, 2006.

Jakson, Paul, S.J., 'Madrasa Education in Bihar', in *Islamic Education, Diversity, and National Identity: Dini Madaris in India Post 9/11*.

Jeffry, Patricia, Roger Jeffry, and Craig Jeffrey, 'The First Madrasa: Learned Mawlwis and the Educated Mother', in *Islamic Education, Diversity, and National Identity: Dini Madaris in India Post 9/11*.

Madni, Maulana Abdullah, '*Daure Jadid ke Takaze aur Dini Madaris ka Nisab*', in *Mulk wa Millat ki Tamir aur Dini Madaris* (Urdu).

Mayaram, Shail, 'The Indian National Congress and the Ulama: Some Implications for Indian Muslims', in Iqbal Narain (ed.), *Secularism in India*, Jaipur: Classic, 1995.

———,'Rethinking Meo Identity: Cultural Faultline, Syncretism, Hybridity or Luminality?', in Mushirul Hasan (ed.), *Islam, Com-munities and the Nation: Muslim Identities in South Asia*, New Delhi: Manoher, 1998.

Mayer, Peter B., 'Tombs and Dark Houses: Ideology, Intellectuals and Proletarians in the Study of Contemporary Indian Islam', in Imtiaz Ahmad (ed.), *Modernization and Social Change among Muslims in India*.

Mazhari, Waris, 'Reforming Madrasa Curriculum', in Akhtarul Wasey (ed.), *Madrasas in India: Trying to be Relevant*, New Delhi: Global Media, 2005.

Mohammad Talib, 'The *Tablighi* in the Making of Muslim Identity', in Mushirul Hasan (ed.), *Islam, Communities and the Nation: Muslim Identities in South Asia*.

Mohd. Arshad, 'Tradition of Madrasa Education', in Akhtarul Wasey (ed.), *Madrasas in India: Trying to be Relevant*.

Nadwi, Mohd. Habib Rehan, '*Dini aur Asri Idaron ke Mabain aur Bahmi Tallukat wa Masail*', in *Mulk wa Millat ki Tamir aur Dini Madaris* (Urdu).

Qamar Uddin, 'Re-orientation of *Madrasa* Education', in S.M. Azizuddin Husain (ed.), *Madrasa Education in India: Eleventh to Twenty First Century*.

Rahman, Tariq, 'Madrasas: Religion, Poverty and the Potential for Violence in Pakistan', in Proceedings of *International Workshop on Islamic Learning in South Asia*, Erfurt, May 2005, (unpublished).

Rizvi, Sayed Abul Hashmi, 'The Introduction of Natural Sciences in Madrasa Education in India', in Jan-Peter Hartung and Helmut Reifeld (eds.), *Islamic Education, Diversity, and National Identity: Dini Madaris in India Post 9/11*.

Rizvi, Syed Najmul Raza, 'Shi'a Madaris of Awadh: Historical Development and Present Situation', in *Islamic Education, Diversity, and National Identity: Dini Madaris in India Post 9/11*.

Sanyal, Usha, 'Ahle Sunnat Madrasas: the Madrasa Manjar-e-Islam, Bareilly, and Jamia Ashrafiyya, Mubarakpur', in the Proceedings of *International Workshop on Islamic Learning in South Asia*, May 2005, Erfurt, Germany (unpublished).

Sheikh Ali, B., 'Issues and Problems of Muslims Education', in *Education and Muslims in India since Independence*, in A.W.B. Qadri, Riaz Shakir Khan and Mohammad Akhtar Siddique (eds.), New Delhi: Institute of Objective Studies, 1998.

Siddiqui, Iqtidar Husain, 'Madrasa Education in Medieval India', in S.M. Azizuddin Husain (ed.), *Madrasa Education in India: Eleventh to Twenty First Century.*

Siddiqui, Muhammad Akhtar, 'Development and Trends in Madrasa Education', in *Education and Muslims in India Since Independence.*

Sikand, Yoginder, 'The Indian Madaris and the Agenda of Reform', in *Islamic Education, Diversity, and National Identity: Dini Madaris in India Post 9/11.*

Subhani, Maulana Mohd. Inaytullah, '*Dini Madaris apna Mutawaqqa Kirdar kyun na ada kar sake*', in *Mulk wa Millat ki Tamir aur Dini Madaris* (Urdu).

ENCYCLOPAEDIAS

The Encyclopedia of Religion, ed. Mircea Eliade, New York: Macmillan.

The Encyclopaedia of Islam, New Edition, ed. H.A.R. Gibb, J.H. Kramers et al., Leiden: E.J. Brill, 1960, 1978.

The Encyclopaedia of Islam, New Edition, ed. C.E. Bosworth, E. von Donzel et al., Leiden: E.J. Brill, 1997.

STUDIES, REPORTS, CIRCULARS PUBLISHED FOR
ACADEMIC OR INTERNAL CIRCULATION BY
THE GOVERNMENT OR SOME NGO,
BUT NOT FOR SALE

Anjum, Ghulam Yahya, *Nisab-e-Taleem (Bra-e-darjat-e-'aliya): Imtahanat Arabi wa Farsi, Uttar Pradesh Board,* New Delhi: Jamia Hamdard (Urdu), 2000.

All India Survey of Out of School Children in the 6–13 Years Age Group, conducted by Social and Rural Research Institute, for Sarva Shiksha Abhiyan, Department of Elementary Education and Literacy, MHRD & Educational Consultant India, May 2006 (unpublished).

Brochure of Madhya Pradesh Madrasa Board, Circular signed by Professor Muhammad Haleem Khan, Chairman, Madrasa Board (unpublished).

Draft: *National Curriculum Framework,* 2005, chaired by Yashpal, New Delhi: National Council of Educational Research and Training (unpublished).

Evaluation of Alternative Schooling through Maktabs in Assam: Darrang, Dhubri and Morigaon Districts, Mussoorie: National Society for Promotion of Development Administration, Research and Training 1999 (unpublished).

Evaluation Report on Modernisation of Madrasa Scheme (Uttar Pradesh), New Delhi: Hamdard Education Society, 2006 (unpublished).

Julka, Anita, Neerja Shukla and Md. T.A. Rahi, *Existing Curriculum in Madrasas: A Study,* New Delhi: NCERT (unpublished).

Nisab e-darjat-e-'Ali'a wa Uli'ya, Madrasa Ahl-e Bait, New Delhi, their publication in Arabic.

Nisab-e-Taleem: Darjat-e-Arabia wa Urdu, Diniyat wa Farsi, Deoband: Darul Uloom, Nisab Committee (Urdu).

Nisab-e-Taleem: Darul Uloom Nadwatul-Ulama, Lucknow: Nadwatul Ulama (Urdu).

Present Madrasa Education: Curriculum and Need for Reforms, A Report of two day National Seminar on Education of Muslim Children in Assam: Problems and Prospects, Guwahati: Markazul Ma'arif, 2003 (unpublished).

Razzack, Azra and Anil Gumber, *Differentials in Human Development: A Case for Empowerment of Muslims in India,* prepared for National Council of Applied Research, New Delhi; sponsored by United Nations Development Programme, New Delhi (unpublished).

Reorganized Senior and Title Madrasa Curriculum, Courses and Syllabi, 1992, Guwahati: State Madrasa Education Board, Department of Education, Government of Assam (unpublished).

Social, Economic and Educational Status of the Muslim Community of India: A Report by the Prime Minister's High Level Committee, headed by Justice Rajinder Sachar, New Delhi: Government of India, November 2006 (unpublished).

Strengthening the Government School System: Lessons from Promising Practices, Report commissioned by Department of Elementary Education, GOI, and International Labour Organization, by Kameshwari Jandhyala and Vimla Ramchandran. Case Study VI, 'Combining Deeni Taleem and Duniyavi Taleem: Madrasa Education in Madhya Pradesh', done by Shobhita Rajgopal, Educational Resource Unit, 2006 (unpublished).

The Social Context of Elementary Education in Rural India, a Report by Sujata Reddy, prepared for Azim Premji Foundation, October 2004 (unpublished).

Index

Ahle-Hadith (Hadees) 160–1, 177,
    196–201, 311; madrasas 199,
    201, 212, 313; madrasas and
    syllabus 201; as Partisans 196;
    tenets of 198–9; society 268;
    version of Islam 202
Ahle-Sunnat 142, 160–1, 194–6, 197,
    212, 214; 338; madrasa 195,
    311
Ahmad, Imtiaz 72, 87, 103, 114,
    374–5, 376, 378
Ahmad, Manzoor, on Muslim
    community 31–2, 283, 292, 294
Ahmad, Mohammad Akhlaq 398
Ahmed, Leila 244–8, 251, 257, 273
Akbar 128, 178, 378; army of 100
al Ghazali 379
Alam, Arshad 291–2
Al Shafai'i 175
Alam, Muzaffar 378
Alavi, Hamza 147
Ali, Ameer 227, 253, 273, 275, 289–
    91, 379
anganwadi workers 80
Anjum, Ghulam Yahya 69, 118, 207,
    352
Anjuman-i-Islam 143
Ansari, Shoyeb 201, 213, 282, 285,
    308
anti-Muslim bias 70, 100
aqeeda' 140
Arabi Farsi Madrasa Board of Uttar
    Pradesh 207–9, 335, 352
Arabi-Farsi script 103
Arabi or sale auwal 182–3
Arabic, classes 156, 183, 189, 193,
    201, 269, 338; education 260,
    309, 338; language 129, 158–9,

170, 173, 192, 204, 209–10,
    234, 284, 289, 293, 297, 304,
    307, 345, 353; kitabat 126
Arya Samaj 28
Ashraf, Ali 397–8
Ashraf, S.S. 43
Aurangzeb 130–1
Azad, Maulana Abul Kalam 30, 40,
    42–3, 142, 147, 148, 316

Barani, Ziauddin 129
below poverty line, category 73, 74,
    77–8, 81, 90; families 74, 77–8,
    90
beradari 101, 116–17; Muslims 116;
    panchayats 117
bhakti poetry 101
Bipan Chandra 101, 384
British 131–5; revolt against 131;
    madrasas in period of 137–44
Buddhism 41
burqa 85

caste 76, 88, 90, 114–17, 180, 294, 336
Central Sponsored Scheme for
    Providing Quality Education
    in Madrasas (SPQEM) 336
Chatterjee, Margaret 36–7
children, education of 71, 75, 77–80,
    101, 105, 280; out-of-school
    376; role of family in education
    of 77–81; in schools and non-
    attendance 75–6
Christ, Jesus 37, 38
Christianity 40, 136–7, 202, 250;
    Gospels in 41; sermons in 41
Christians 76, 202, 310, 393
Common Madrasa Board 385

common schools 85, 87, 107, 144,
      149, 155, 201, 206, 209, 211,
      265; female teachers in 85;
      for girls and female teachers
      85–7
communalism 32, 63, 64, 111, 115,
      295
communities 28–9, 31–3, 36, 72–3,
      101–2, 115, 216, 227, 292,
      397; Mushirul Hasan on
      Muslim 34; religious 33
Coulson, Noel J. 251–2; and Doreen
      Hinchcliffe 252
culture 99–100, 131–2, 134, 137–8,
      230, 242–6, 249, 292, 294–5,
      297; common 191, 263;
      differences in 34; religion-based
      135
curriculum 128–30, 142–3, 149–50,
      153, 161, 172, 204, 284–5,
      352–3
customs 105, 109–10, 113, 116, 135,
      145, 214, 218, 233–4, 237,
      263–4, 294

Da'wa 180–1, 201
Dars 343, 345
Dars-i-Nizami 131, 157, 159, 179,
      181, 188, 194, 196, 206–8,
      269, 286, 288, 302–3, 305,
      318, 332, 342
Dar-ul Musannifin 142
Darul Quran or *Hifz madrasas* 155–6
Darul Uloom 138, 141, 143, 156, 173,
      176, 178; Deoband 178–83;
      Manzar-i-Islam 142;
      Nadwatul-Ulama 186–9
Deoband 138, 141, 150, 157, 176,
      178–81, 183, 186–7, 189–90,
      193, 195, 199, 201, 255,
      curriculum 180; Islam 177,
      180; *maulanas* 147, 176, 181,
      183, 186, 267, 312; movement
      139; *nisab* 176; syllabus of 138,
      140, 142, 158–9, 162, 179–80
      196, 268; *ulama* 146

dini (religious) 127, 130, 134;
      education 318, 387; *madaris*
      127, 135, 139, 179, 380–1;
      subjects 139, 142, 182, 188,
      192, 210, 215, 303–5
Dini Anjuman Council 101
Dini Talimi Council 106, 152, 392
Districts Information System on
      Education 82

education 43–5, 55–6; access to
      women 44; cost of modern 88–
      91; essence of 61; Indian views
      on 50–5; Islamic conception of
      60–1; madrasa system of 43;
      Muslim views on 45–9; and
      religious education 55–7;
      Western views on 49–50; basic
      89, 365; cost-effectiveness of
      80, 90; free 88, 158, 280, 375;
      higher 79, 129, 396; *maktab*
      97, 173, 363, 367, 389; *maktab-*
      level 94; modern system of 72,
      292, 297, 377; moral 210, 381;
      of Muslim children 98, 288,
      395; non-formal 364–5; secular
      138, 170–1, 256, 332, 364,
      390; system of 78, 141–2, 169,
      186–7, 283, 305, 308, 362,
      377, 380, 393; traditional 127,
      144, 204, 266, unified system
      of 283, 293
educational institutions 83, 144, 171,
      204, 278, 286, 348, 373, 375,
      383, 393–4, 396; non-
      governmental 283; systems
      of 141, 349, 366, 376, 398
English education 103, 134, 136, 140,
      151, 179, 293, 298, *see also*
      English medium schools ; and
      middle-class Muslims 265;
      Muslims and 294, 382
English language 103, 133, 140–1,
      193, 305, 390
English medium schools 93, 96, 104,
      279; private 71

Fatwa-i-Alamgiri 130
fatwas 113, 118, 147, 150, 183–4,
    196, 215, 236–7, 255–7, 287,
    353, 379; against founders of
    Deoband madrasa 142;
    institution of 255–7
Fiqh (Islamic jurisprudence) 127, 129–
    30; Firangi Mahal of Lucknow
    and 130, 138; schools of 160–1,
    176–7, 198, 240

Gandhi, Mahatma 146, 249, 315, 375
Gandhi, Rajmohan 140
Gangohi, Maulana Rasheed Ahmad
    138, 178
Gilani, Sayyid Manazir Ahasan and
    development of madrasa
    system of education 128, 295,
    303–5, 307, 308, 314, 315, 329
girls, education for 262–9; madrasa
    for 268–72, *see also* madrasa,
    for women; maktabs
government schools 70, 76, 81, 83–5,
    87–9, 91–4, 96, 98, 101, 150,
    152, 285, 337–8, 372–4, 394;
    Hindu ambience in 373–4; and
    Muslims 81–5, 98–9; poor
    quality of education in 91–4
government-aided schools 82, 84, 86,
    88–9, 100, 373
grants 82, 335–41, 351–2, 357–9,
    361–2, 383
groups, religion-based 74, 85; religious
    74, 83, 110, 115, 397; social
    72–6
Gumber, Anil 74, 76, 91

hadiths 60, 158–61, 175, 177–82,
    189, 197–9, 214–15, 229–36,
    239–42, 247, 249–51, 253–4,
    262, 269–70, 303–4; literature
    185, 243
Hamdard Education Society 154,
    335–6, 338, 339, 358, 359, 360
Hamid, Sayyid 319, 332–4, 382
Hasan, Mushirul 72, 118, 149, 296,
    310, 378

Hasan, Syed Hamid 43
Hastings, Warren, madrasa in
    Calcutta (Madrasa-i-Aliya) by
    132
Hifz 85, 155–6, 187–8, 190, 320;
    madrasa 155–6, 190
Hindu Bhakti tradition 39;
    philosophy 39–40; reform
    movements 136
Hinduism 40; *ashrams* 41; and
    definition 39
Hinduization of Hindi textbooks 101
Hindus 136
Hindutva or Hindu *rashtra* 35, 114
Hobbes, Thomas 59
Holy Quran and *Sunna* 97
human rights 59
Hume, David 57
Hussain, S.S. 43

identity 35, 110, 113–15, 146, 181,
    203, 205, 216, 281, 374; *see
    also* religious identity
Ilm in Islam 125–7
Imams 117, 155, 177–8, 195, 198,
    237, 242–3, 255, 287, 305,
    363, 392
Imrana case 183–4, 235, 237, 255–6
Indian Muslims 104, 113, 147, 149,
    153, 185, 191, 292–4;
    descendency of 34
intra-community differences, Mushirul
    Hasan and Imtiaz Ahmad on
    34–5
Islam 40, 215, 227–8, 321; history of
    185, 210; meaning of 227–8;
    Quran and *Sunna* as sources of
    228–32; reforms and 135, 310,
    392; teaching of 142, 301
Islami tarikh 188
Islamic, beliefs 145, 182, 189, 200;
    culture 144–5, 294; education
    102, 127–8, 130, 137, 144,
    151, 159, 169–70, 180, 213–
    14, 379–80, 398; *fiqh* 189, 231,
    240, 317, 321; law 129–31,
    178, 230–2, 234–5, 246–7,

252–5, 259; madrasas 362; religion 97, 138, 151, 171, 284, 383, 385, 390; *sharia* 97–8, 137, 174–5, 177, 184, 189, 202, 234, 247, 254, 258–9, 262; society 249, 390; system of education 129; teachings 141, 152, 199; values 151, 283, 299
Islamization 116, 205, 331

Jahangir 131
Jamaat-i-Islami Hind 149, 177, 202–4; curriculum of 142; Mushirul Hasan on 149; Sayyid Ahmad Khan 149–50; madrasas of 161; and Muslims 204
Jamea-tul-Hidaya 362–3
Jamia 156
Jamia Ahle Bait in Okhla 206
Jamia Ashrafiyya 196
Jamia Salafiyya 177
Jamiat-al-Falah 158, 202, 204; at Azamgarh 173
Jamiat-e-Ulama-e Hind 149, 293–4
Jayasi, Malik Mohammad 101
Jha, Jyotsna 74–5
Jhingran, Dhir 74–5

Kabir 101
Kant, Immanuel 57
kaum 28–30
khalifa 136; institution of 147
Khan, J.M. on 115–16
Khan, Sir Sayyid Ahmad 86, 135, 140, 146, 158; Aligarh movement of 140, 186
Khankhana, Abdul Rahim 101
Khilafat, movement 146–9, 151, 256, 293, 297; in Turkey 147–8

liberal Muslims 70, 159, 334
literacy rate of Muslims 71, 84
Locke, John 57, 59

Madni, Maulana Hussain Ahmad 30–1, 149, 295–6

Madrasa Al Azhar 126
Madrasa Ashrafia 312
Madrasa Boards 162, 207, 210, 344, 351, 354–7, 359, 361–2, 385
madrasa, *see also* modernization of madrasas; of Ahle-Hadith *maslak* 177; certificates 361, 384, 387; children 304, 349, 354, 358, 361; curriculum 127–35, 169–74, 179, 212, 304, 308, 311, 316, 344–5, 349, 385–6; education, levels of 154–7; emotional closeness with 96–7; function of 171; of Khairabad and Iranian philosophy 138; *maulavis* 351; and modern schools 375–82; modernization and 314–19, 336, 343–4, 367, 387, 396; *nisab* 190, 200, 214, 286, 288, 291, 297–8, 300, 302–3, 314, 316, 331–2, 343–4, 350; reforms 278, 296–314, 319–22; rural Muslims and education of 80, 263; students 162, 183–4, 186, 191–2, 211, 289, 308–9, 318, 333, 344–5, 349–50, 360, 381–2, 384–5, 387–8; syllabus 134–5, 138, 162, 170–1, 172, 174, 179, 181, 185, 214–15, 288, 314–15, 332–3, 342, 345–6, 348–50, 386–7; system of education 69, 125, 128, 130, 153, 155, 157, 170–1, 203, 282, 297, 300–1, 377, 380; system 96, 141, 153, 170, 187, 201, 278, 288, 296–7, 300, 311, 379, 381; teachers 211, 214, 271, 289, 307, 310–11, 313, 315, 318, 331, 333, 342–4, 347–8, 357; teaching 138, 290; traditional 162, 347, 357; for women 142, 266, *see also* madrasa-educated mothers
madrasa-educated mothers 80
madrasa affiliation 207, 211; State Madrasa Education Board of

Assam 209–10; Madhya
Pradesh Madrasa Board 210–
11
madrasas for girls 156
Madrasat-al-Islah 142
maktabs (or *makatib*) 69–70, 75,
95–6, 126, 128, 144, 152, 154–
8, 172–4, 192–3, 264, 362–7,
389–93; and madrasas 96;
modernization of 363–6;
timings 391–2
Malik, Jamal 376, 377–9
Manto, Saadat Hasan 103
Maududi, Saiyyid Abu Ala Hasan
149, 382, 378; scheme of 378
maulanas 117, 178, 179, 184, 186,
187, 191, 194, 195, 197, 203,
215, 216, 217; dictates of 97
maulavis or teachers 81, 96, 113
Mazahar-e-Uloom 178
Mazhari, Waris 311, 316–18
midday meal 85, 356
Mill, J.S. 44–5, 59
millat 30, 31, 145, 147, 180, 181, 283,
295
missionaries 131–2
Miyan, Muhammad 398
modern education 381–2; cost of 87,
94, 373; desirability of and
MOM 382–8
modernity 57–60, 376–7; conception
of 61
modernization 57–60
modernization of madrasas 279, 284,
288, 296–7, 302, 305, 307,
309, 314–16, 318–19, 334,
355, 367, 383–4, 387; concept
of 331–3; government's
concern for 334–41, 383;
programme 357–8, 366–7, 383;
problems in 342–51; Sayyid
Hamid on 332–3, 344, 350;
schemes, 359, 361, 366–7,
383, 385
mohalla (locality) committees 116, 117
morality 315

Moslems *see* Muslims
mosques 96, 109, 116, 118, 126,
144–5, 154–5, 236–7, 263,
365, 392
muftis 113, 117–18, 127–8, 139, 150,
183, 195, 214–15, 235, 237,
255–7, 268, 286, 375, 388
Muhammad, Prophet 37, 42, 125–7,
135, 143, 160, 174–8, 189,
194, 197–8, 202, 229–31, 239–
40, 244, 246, 248–50, 253;
sunna of 228–9, 234
Muhammaden Anglo Oriental (MAO)
College of Sayyid Ahmad Khan
140–1, 158, 378
Mujeeb, M. 140, 213
Mujtahid, or *Usuliyun* 178
mullas and fear of modern education
151
Mungeri, Maulana Muhammad Ali
141
Mushir-Ul-Haq 215, 217–18, 298,
348, 388
Muslim children 69–72, 75–6, 83–5,
93–5, 98–9, 105–8, 169–72,
279–80, 282, 285–8, 387–98;
discrimination against 93–4;
dropout rate of 75; education
of 105, education in mother
tongue 105; to modern schools,
reason against 91–4
Muslims 253, 290, 380; as alienated
people 109–14; backwardness
and madrasa education 278–
82; *bastis* of 116; community
96, 114, 139, 146, 170, 204,
213, 290, 300, 380, 388;
culture 102, 115, 211;
education 141, 264, 332, 397;
families 70, 74, 90, 203, 216;
girls 86–7, 98, 156, 265–6;
identity 115; in India 71, 105,
112, 161, 202, influence of
ghetto living 115–18; for
Islamic education 97–8; and
jobs 73; language of 103–4,

108, 365; literate women in villages 174; for madrasas 69, 96–7, middle class 72, 150, 281, *millat* 181; personal law board 258; poets 101; as poor 71; population 71–2, 74, 78, 81–3, 86–7, 113, 267, 352; poverty among 73–6; reform movements and 136; separate identity of 216, 334; and their system of education 282–5; traditional 262; women 77, 115, 237–8, Leila Ahmed on *shari'a* and women 245–8, Naila Minai on Islam and women 248–9

Nadwat-al-Ulama 141–2, 176, 186–90; *Nisab-e-Taleem* 187
Nadwi, Maulana Habib Rehan 141, 318
Nadwi, Maulana Sayyid Hasan Ali 141
namaz, 118, 126, 155, 195, 204, 215, 228–9, 233, 251, 254–5, 263–4, 305, 313, 363
Nanautawi, Maulana Qasim Muhammad 138, 142, 178, 298
National Council for Promotion of Urdu Language (NCPUL) 337
National Policy on Education 336
nationalism 191
nation-society 29
NCERT books 100, 101; objections on contents of textbooks 100–2
Nehru, Jawaharlal 29–30; and communalism 32–3
Nizamuddin, Mulla 131
Noumani, Allama Shibli 141–2

Open Schools 384–6; examinations 384–5

pan-Islamism 30, 148–9, 151, 186, 292–3, 297
pan-Islamist 148
Parvaiz, Muhammad Aslam 316–17

Persian 102, 129, 131–4, 139, 156, 161, 178, 182, 184, 188, 193, 200–1, 206, 304, 319, 352–4
post-Partition feeling of alienation 151
primary, education 88–9, 93, 105–6, 173, 183, 269–70, 272, 355, 363
private schools 71, 76, 88–9, 91–3, 101, 109, 282, 394–5
purdah (veil) 77, 85, 115, 116, 118, 158, 260, 266–9, 281
pure Islam, conception of 377–8

Qamar Uddin's *Kul Hind Survey* 301–3, 339
Qasmi, Muhammadullah Khalili 170–1, 284
qazis 139
Quran 228–32, 236; *hadiths* in 39, 41, 42; 'revelation' in 39; and *shari'a* 39; and *sunna* 42

Rahman, Tariq 288
Rasool, Muhammad 160
rationalists 58
Raza, Ahmad 143
Razzack, Azra 74, 76, 91
reform movements among Muslims 144–50; and religious communities 135–7; madrasa reforms 297–8
reformers 234
religion 32–6; differences within 39–40; ethics and 37; for religious instruction 41–3; meaning of 36–9; nature 38; Ninian Smart on 38; reforms 140, 145; and religious instruction 41–3; rituality and 37; social dimension 37–8; Swami Vivekananda on 75
religious education, Kerala model of 388–93; modern education and 55–6
religious, communities 72, 74, 76–7, 79, 83, 93, 101–2, 109, 111,

135–6, 282; education, 118,
139–40, 152, 170, 287, 297–8,
304–5, 315–16, 378–9, 388–
93, 398; identity 78, 97, 115,
133, 215–16, 278, 287, 293,
296, 388; instructions 152, 315;
knowledge 118, 170, 179;
toleration 110, 112, 235
Rida, Rashid 200
Right of Children to Free and
Compulsory Education Bill,
2008 45
Rousseau, Jaques 44, 57, 59
Roy, Rammohun 135
Roza 233

Sachar Committee Report 70–3, 91,
154, 279, 343, 372, 396
Salafiyya madrasas 160
samaj 28–30, 82, *see also* society
Sarva Shiksha Abhiyan 45, 85, 395
schools, aided 84–5, 92, 94, 393–5;
education 80, 89, 105, 280,
395; for girls 85, 87; of Islam
142–3, 159, 194, 347; regular
270, 364–5, 367, 391–3; rural
92; of Sunni Islam 142, 194;
textbooks 100–1; *versus*
madrasas 94–5; village 87, 91,
338
Shari'a (religious law) 97–8, 116, 118;
as Islamic way of life 41–2;
two concepts of *shari'a* 232–4;
orthodox version of 234–6;
Asghar Ali Engineer on 240–4;
and cultural relativity 238–40;
and Fiqh 161, 250–4; Leila
Ahmed on 244–8; Mujeeb on
332–3; *shari'a* and women
238–48, 252, 257–61
Shi'as 161, 174, 177–8, 185, 205,
207–8, 214, 242, 251, 352;
madrasas 156, 161, 177,
205–7; sect of 177–8; and
understanding of Islam 161

Shiism 177
Shikwa to God 148
Shiraji, Mir Fathullah 128
Singh, K.S. 35
Smart, Ninian 36–7
society, concept of 27–32; multi-
religious 217–18, 309; Western
44
Socio-Religious Categories 71, 91
State Madrasa Board of Madhya
Pradesh 355–7, 359–60, 362
State Madrasa Education Board,
Assam 352–5, 359–61
Sufi *khanqah* 196
sunna 60, 175, 228–32
Sunnat-al-Nabi 174
Sunnis 160–1, 174, 176–7, 194–5,
205, 207–8, 251, 311, 352;
Islam 142, 160, 174, 194–5,
214; Islam sub-sects of 174–7;
madrasas 161; schools 160,
198, 200
syllabus: modern 171, 345, 349, 386–
7; traditional 385

Tablighi Jamaat, founded by Maulana
Muhammad Ilyas 145–6;
movement of 105, 146, 180,
233–4
tafsirs 190
talaq 241, 256, 258
Tarikh-e-Islam 182
Tayyabji, Badruddin 143
teachers, female 85–7, 271
teaching, of Arabic language 289,
345; methodology 302, 314,
358, 387; religious 126, 186
Thanwi, Maulana Ashraf Ali 298
tolerance, religious 191, 217, 236,
295, 310
Tusi, Abu Jafar 177
Two Nation theory 29–30, 147

ulama 132, 141, 153, 186, 191, 199,
334; affirming maktab

education 97–8; madrasa-
educated 287, 382
umma 30–2, 153, 292
universal education 44–5, 88, 183,
375; national goal of 169, 172,
285, 382, 387
Urdu, medium schools 104, 106–7,
200; and *bambaiya* Hindi
combination 106; Bihar
government for 106; Imtiaz
Ahmad on 103–4; language
102–3, 290; as lingua franca
of north India 102–4; in
modern schools 104–9;
rejection of 70–2; textbooks
107–8, 336
Usmani, Mufti Taqi 284, 298, 299–
300

Vedas 41

Wahhabi movement of Shah
Walliullah 179
Walliullah, Shah 135, 136, 138, 180,
290
women 77, 80, 115, 174, 248, 259,
263–5, 281, *see also* Muslim,
women; educational level 80,
262–72; of higher classes 127;
Naila Minai on Muslim women
248–50; position of 237–8,
246; *shari'a* and 257–62; slave
245, 247; teachers 87

Zaehner, R.C. 36–7
Zafar, Bahadur Shah 131